W. H. Auden

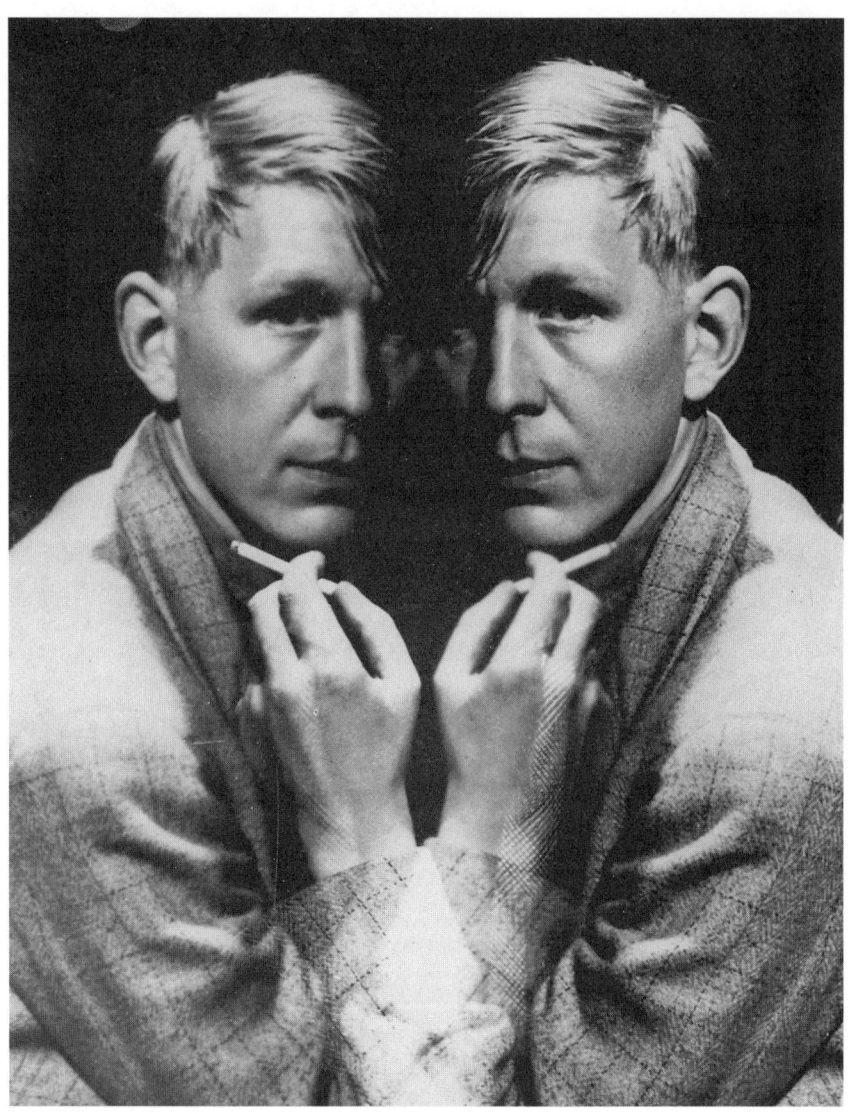

"Mirror Image." Portrait of W. H. Auden, 1930, by Cecil Beaton. Courtesy of Sotheby's Picture Library, London.

W. H. Auden

Contexts for Poetry

Peter Edgerly Firchow

Newark: University of Delaware Press
London: Associated University Presses

© 2002 by Rosemont Publishing & Printing Corp.

All rights reserved. Authorization to photocopy items for internal or personal use, or the internal or personal use of specific clients, is granted by the copyright owner, provided that a base fee of $10.00, plus eight cents per page, per copy is paid directly to the Copyright Clearance Center, 222 Rosewood Drive, Danvers, Massachusetts 01923. [0-87413-766-7/02 $10.00 + 8¢ pp, pc.]

Other than as indicated in the foregoing, this book may not be reproduced, in whose or in part, in any form (except as permitted by Sections 107 and 108 of the U.S. Copyright Law, and except for brief quotes appearing in reviews in public press).

Associated University Presses
440 Forsgate Drive
Cranbury, NJ 08512

Associated University Presses
16 Barter Street
London WC1A 2AH, England

Associated University Presses
P.O. Box 338, Port Credit
Mississauga, Ontario
Canada L5G 4L8

The paper used in this publication meets the requirements of the American National Standard for Permanence of Paper for Printed Library Materials Z39.48-1984.

Library of Congress Cataloging-in-Publication Data

Firchow, Peter Edgerly, 1937–
    W. H. Auden : contexts for poetry / Peter Edgerly Firchow.
      p.   cm.
    Includes bibliographical references (p.) and index.
    ISBN 0-87413-766-7 (alk. paper)
    1. Auden, W. H. (Wystan Hugh), 1907–1973—Criticism and interpretation.
2. Great Britain—Intellectual life—20th century. I. Title.

PR6001.U4 Z687   2002
811'.52—dc21   2001041521

PRINTED IN THE UNITED STATES OF AMERICA

For David Haley
Scholar, Colleague, Friend

"A serious scholar has great merits. But a serious scholar who is also a good man knows not only his subject but the proper place of his subject in the whole of his life."

—Iris Murdoch (1970)

Contents

Preface	9
Acknowledgments	15
Introduction: Early Auden: Poet, Teacher, Healer	19
1. Crossing Frontiers: Poetic Espionage in Late 1920s Berlin	37
2. The Group, the Leader, and *The Orators*	70
3. Poetry and Politics in a Low, Dishonest Decade	120
4. The American Auden: A Poet Reborn?	168
5. The Sage of Kirchstetten: Thinking and Thanking	203
Appendix: Auden in Austria: Two Interviews	231
Notes	238
Bibliography	250
Index	267

Preface

THIS IS A BOOK I HAVE WORKED ON (AND OFF), IN ONE WAY OR ANOTHER, FOR nearly twenty-five years. Whatever else this lengthy period of time may signify, it surely testifies to the enduring power of Auden's poetry to intrigue and fascinate, though naturally I hope that it has also helped to season my critical judgments and to situate them in a wider and deeper context. The book first began as an essay intended to debunk Auden's early poetry for what I thought was its parlor Marxism. In the process of reading my way through the poetry and criticism, I changed my mind. Still, though I had come to mock, I did not quite stay to worship. While my admiration for the poet as poet grew as my knowledge of his work deepened, my conviction that the poet as person was often fallible remained unchanged, as did my awareness that he was deeply conscious of that fallibility. Although he usually saw the better, he often followed the worse, or, at any rate, he followed the not-so-good and sometimes even the silly. This is especially true of his early uncritical endorsement of the peculiar psychological theories of D. H. Lawrence, Georg Groddeck, and Homer Lane; of his hero worship of those great public posturers, T. E. Lawrence and Wyndham Lewis; as well as, a little later, his naive support of Marxism and Leninism. Auden's intellectual life shows a distinct pattern of needing leaders to admire as well as, paradoxically, a pattern of needing to reject them. This holds as true of Freud, Marx, and Rilke as it does of John Layard and D. H. Lawrence. The only hero who consistently remained heroic for him through later life was Charles Williams, though it is doubtful that he ever thought of Williams as "heroic" in the same way that he did the others.

To be sure, Auden's shifting intellectual, literary and political loyalties, especially during the thirties and early forties, may have been due, as Auden later sometimes claimed and possibly believed himself, to the absence of a real identity of his own. Was the young Auden perhaps only a kind of echo chamber, an intricate machine for making poetry, a person who had no real beliefs or convictions of his own? Is that why, when at last he did settle, more or less permanently, on a position halfway between the Church of England and existentialist despair, he became so adamant about denouncing the young poet he had once been for endorsing ideas he had supposedly never believed in himself? Certainly, whatever the answers to these questions, unlike the Old Masters of whom he maintained in one of his best known poems that "they were never wrong" about suffering, Auden came to believe that he had been often wrong, not only about suffering but about a number of other important aspects of his own experience and that of humanity in general. Still, he never gave up trying to understand the meaning of that experience, both in his own case and in that of the rest of us—by means of psychology, sociology, art, religion, as well as poetry and criticism. That is why the memorable lines that he wrote about the "childish creature," mankind, at the close of the opening sonnet of *In Time of War* (1938) might well serve as the motto for his early and very varied intellectual career:

> Who by the lightest wind was changed and shaken,
> And looked for truth and was continually mistaken . . .

Auden also, if you will forgive the pun, not only sometimes followed the worse, he also and always followed the verse. At the beginning of his career especially, he followed his verse wherever it took him, reading omnivorously in a variety of languages, mostly literature, but also in the social and natural sciences, at first primarily in order make his verse more powerful but then, in early middle age, to make it more truthful. He also made a point of traveling, both in his native England and abroad, not just as a tourist but more in the guise of a "quester," looking, as it were, for an elixir that would quench the doubts he kept feeling about himself and his society, rather like his naive protagonist (and alter ego?) Alan in *The Dog Beneath the Skin*. But he did not journey to the usual places that writers of his generation were "supposed" to visit, like Paris and Rome; indeed, such places are dismissed in *The Dog Beneath the Skin* as versions of a "Paradise Park" where writers succeed in avoiding rather than facing reality. He was among the first poets of the post-Great War generation to take up residence in Berlin and he was certainly the first major English poet after William Morris to visit Iceland for any length of time. With Isherwood, he went to China and to the United States, and in the latter part of his life he spent long periods in Italy and Austria—though, significantly, not in Rome or in Vienna. Aside from writing poetry, drama, and criticism, he had an active and abiding interest in music, and collaborated on operas and musical drama with several composers, including Benjamin Britten, Igor Stravinsky, and Hans Werner Henze. He is probably the most versatile and international poet of his generation—at least in the English-speaking world—international in the way he lived his life but also in the ways he thought and wrote about it.

He was a poet of a bewildering number of identities: amateur psychologist; teacher; "group" leader; "healer;" dramatist; "Uncle Wiz;" homosexual; "explorer" of Berlin; practical joker; comic versifier; fellow traveler; poetical journalist; musician; conversationalist; propagandist; anthologist; critic; literary tourist; book-club adviser; "Norseman;" Yorkshireman; Englishman; American; and, in the end, "Austrian." In Cecil Beaton's famous photograph, he is shown in a mirror-like double exposure, as a kind of "Double Man" (also the title of one of his books). But Auden is more than a double man, he is multiple man, attempting to compress a whole world of identities into a single person and lifetime. His life represents an almost emblematic search for wholeness, for integrity, for a way of fusing the contradictions of private and public existence, just as in his work he sought to reconcile the often conflicting claims of individual and society.

Inevitably, given the variety and complexity of Auden's experience of life and letters, his own work tends to be variously complex. That is why it requires, as the title of this study suggests, "contextualization." While the virtuosity of Auden's craftsmanship must by now be immediately apparent to all, his meaning, especially in the early poetry, is often obscure, sometimes, as in *The Orators*, deliberately so. The by-now traditional means of coping with such poetic obscurity, namely close reading of a "new critical" sort, has not shown itself particularly helpful in Auden's case, though of course it remains a necessary starting point. Other kinds of criticism have been more illuminating: psychological, philosophical, intellectual-historical, and biographical criticism, so that much of Auden's poetry is now better and more widely understood than ever before. A large body of accumulated critical work of the most variegated sort, together with the continuing new editions of Auden's poetry, drama, libretti, and prose issuing from Princeton, have made reading and thinking about Auden a great deal easier than it was for critics like Hoggart and Spears a generation or two ago. In this connection, I want also to acknowledge the special debt I owe to the tradition of teaching and writing about Auden begun at the University of Minnesota in the forties and fifties by Joseph Warren Beach and continued here through the seventies and eighties by George ("Ted") Wright.

W. H. Auden: Contexts for Poetry is an attempt to consolidate the critical findings of the last quarter century, and to then take them a step further in the direction of seeing how some of Auden's most important poems can be better understood against the background of his own intellectual development and the often troubled history of his time. This book is at least as much an attempt to show how a certain type of critical methodology, which combines intellectual and social history, biography, and textual analysis, and that I call "contextualization," helps to illuminate poems (or parts of poems) that have hitherto remained imperfectly understood. It also "contextualizes" Auden's poetry—or, at any rate, the specific poems that I deal with—within the main parameters of existing Auden criticism, taking into account and evaluating the critical insights of the last two generations of Auden critics. Not that I presume for this reason (or any other) to provide anything like a full understanding of even the limited number of poems I deal with, for despite Yeats's rather grandiose claim—as Auden knew full well and himself maintained—neither perfection of the life nor of the work is possible. I also want to stress that, whatever else it is, this book is not a "survey" or a guide to all, or even to all the most important of Auden's poems, though it does follow the general outlines of Auden's development as a poet and thinker.

The introductory chapter of *W. H. Auden: Contexts for Poetry* places Auden's poetry in the context of his lifelong career as a teacher, showing how it is best understood—even at its most obscure—as an attempt (admittedly among other things) to "teach" his readers about how to best live their lives in the modern world. The following chapter focuses on Auden's experience of Berlin—the first truly adult experience of his life—and on how that experience helped to shape the poetry that he wrote there, as well as in the immediately following years. For the first time, his verse play, *Paid on Both Sides*, along with some of his shorter early poems, is placed in the context of Auden's German experience, with the result that this important early work is now seen as freighted with considerable social, and not only psychological, import. The first chapter also shows how the young Auden's preoccupation (obsession is not too strong a word) with real and symbolic frontiers and spies reflects his profound uncertainties about his homosexual identity, both in Berlin and subsequently. The second chapter correlates Auden's self-conception of himself as the leader of a "gang" of writers (later known as the Auden Group) with his treatment of leaders/groups in his first major work, *The Orators*. In addition, it juxtaposes Auden's conception of groups and leaders with contemporaneous events and leaders in Britain and elsewhere. Finally, it shows how John Layard's anthropological work in the New Hebrides provides an essential key for understanding some of the more obscure parts of *The Orators*. The third chapter deals with the changes in Auden's conception of the social/political function of his poetry in the 1930s, beginning with the overtly propagandistic "A Communist to Others" and moving on to a much greater and more ambiguous political poem, "Spain." After comparing the young Auden's ideas on the subject of political poetry with those of another eminent political poet, the late Yeats, the chapter concludes with a discussion of his change of mind (and heart) in the great elegy on

Yeats and in one of the most memorable and popular poems in the Auden canon, "Musée des Beaux Arts." The fourth chapter examines the impact of the American experience on his poetry, especially *The Age of Anxiety*. Using his Criterion anthology of American poetry as a basis, it argues that Auden may reasonably be thought of (and in some ways thought of himself) as an American poet. The chapter also considers the influence of American poetry on Auden's work, and vice versa. The final chapter treats Auden's last creative years in Austria, together with the poems that he wrote about his life there, especially the cycle *Thanksgiving for a Habitat*. It evaluates his role as a "healer" and bridge builder between Anglosaxondom and the German-speaking countries after the Second World War, seeing Auden's life and work as coming full circle—from metropolitan Berlin to rural Kirchstetten, from the world of a very private poet who made his most intimate privacies public to that of a very public poet who vainly hoped to find refuge in privacy.

In conclusion, I want to express my thanks to Dr. Brigitte Reiffenstein, Librarian of the English Institute of the University of Vienna for helping me get in touch with some of Auden's old friends and acquaintances in Austria; to the National Endowment for the Humanities for awarding me a travel grant in 1992 to examine the Auden holdings of the Berg Collection in the New York Public Library; to the University of Minnesota Department of English and to the Graduate School for prompt help at a crucial moment in this book's life; to the University of Minnesota Library and its Rare Book division for help in researching this and other books over the course of the years; to Professor Edward Mendelson of Columbia University for allowing me generous access to various Auden manuscripts and for permission to quote from Auden's writings, both published and unpublished; and to the University of Minnesota for granting me sabbatical leave in order to complete this book. I also want to thank my friend, former student and very independent scholar, Dr. Janice Rossen, for helping me to avoid various blunders, stylistic and otherwise. For all those blunders that may still remain I, however, assume sole responsibility. Finally, I want to thank my wife, Evelyn Scherabon Firchow, whose conviction that this book would one day actually appear kept me believing it myself.

Acknowledgments

To FABER & FABER LTD FOR PERMISSION TO QUOTE FROM AUDEN'S POEMS, AS published in *The English Auden* and in *Collected Poems;* and to Random House, Inc., as follows: "Under Which Lyre", copyright © 1976 by Edward Mendelson, William Meredith and Monroe K. Spears, Executors of the Estate of W. H. Auden; "Good-Bye to the Mezzogiorno", copyright © 1958 by W. H. Auden; "The Cave of Making", copyright © 1964 by W. H. Auden; "A Walk after Dark", copyright © 1966 by W. H. Auden; "New Year Letter", copyright © 1947 by W. H. Auden & renewed 1975 by the Estate of W. H. Auden; "Shorts," copyright © 1974 by the Estate of W. H. Auden; "Their Lonely Betters", copyright © 1951 by W. H. Auden; "Sonnet XIX", copyright © 1976 by Edward Mendelson, William Meredith and Monroe K. Spears, Executors of the Estate of W. H. Auden; "Whitsunday in Kirchstetten", copyright © 1962 by W. H. Auden; "Thanksgiving for a Habitat," copyright © 1963 by W. H. Auden; "Bridges," copyright © 1976 by Edward Mendelson, William Meredith and Monroe K. Spears, Executors of the Estate of W. H. Auden, from *W. H. Auden: Collected Poems* by W. H. Auden. Used by permission of Random House, Inc.

Chapters 2 and 4 have appeared before in somewhat different form and under different titles. I want to thank the editors of *PMLA* and *American Literary History*, respectively, for granting permission to reprint my work. Chapters 2 and 3 incorporate, in very much altered form, fragments of essays that have appeared before in the *CEA Critic* and in *American Notes and Queries* (published by Heldref Publications), whose agreement to use this material in my book is herewith acknowledged. I especially want to thank Professor Ulrich Broich of the University of Munich for his hospitality in giving my essay on Auden's Kirchstetten years a home in his *Festschrift;* and for granting me permission to reprint it in revised form here.

Permission to quote from Auden's unpublished correspondence has been generously granted by Edward Mendelson, Executor of Auden's literary estate, and by the following libraries: the Berg Collection of English and American Literature, The New York Public Library, Astor, Lenox and Tilden Foundations; the Bodleian Library, The University of Oxford (UK); and the

Harry Ransom Humanities Research Center, The University of Texas at Austin.

Permission to reproduce "Landscape with the Fall of Icarus" by Pieter Brueghel (Inv. 4030) has been granted by the Royal Museum of Fine Arts of Belgium; and Auden's photograph by Cecil Beaton is reproduced by permission of the Cecil Beaton Archive at Sotheby's, London.

W. H. Auden

Introduction: Early Auden: Poet, Teacher, Healer

"They must teach; they must preach."
—Virginia Woolf (1940)

"Lawrence, Blake and Homer Lane, once healers in our English land;
These are dead as iron for ever; these can never hold our hand."
—W. H. Auden (1930)

MAKING A LIVING AS A PROFESSIONAL POET IN THE TWENTIETH CENTURY WAS A relatively rare accomplishment. Even at the height of his career, W. H. Auden could only manage it by supplementing the advances and royalties he received for his books of poetry, along with the fees he got for individual poems, by reviewing books, by going regularly "on the circuit," and by winning the occasional well-endowed literary prize or fellowship. During the early part of his career, when opportunities for making money in these ways were either fewer or less remunerative, he depended almost entirely on teaching to pay the bills. At first, since he had only barely scraped through the Oxford University English program with an undistinguished pass, the only kind of teaching he could get was in remote, unprestigious, and poorly paid preparatory schools like Larchfield Academy in Helensburgh, Scotland, where his immediate predecessor had been his old friend, Cecil Day-Lewis.[1] Later on, after he became famous and moved to the United States, he taught at much better known schools and universities for more money, notably at Swarthmore and the University of Michigan. Like many other poets of his generation who got jobs at universities and colleges, however, Auden rarely taught what later came to be called creative writing. He taught the regular literature curriculum, and, by all reports, he taught it very well. How knowledgeable he was in virtually all periods and genres of English and even world literature is amply apparent from the great number of influential critical essays he published, only some of which he later collected in *The Dyer's Hand*. It is also evident in the various poetry anthologies he edited or co-edited.

Though Auden was a teacher primarily because he had to be, he was not only good at his job but liked it and devoted a great deal of thought to it. Most of his early published prose is on the subject of education. Not surprisingly, there is in Auden—everywhere in his poetry and, by all reports, in his conversation—a strong didactic streak. This was probably more or less congenital, since, as a boy in preparatory school, he would enthusiastically instruct his fellow students, many of whom were older than he was, in the mysteries of sex. It was a topic about which he had informed himself by consulting physiological textbooks in his father's library. His father, a tolerant, bookish man who never ceased to be amazed at the extraordinary son he had produced, was a medical doctor and professor of public health at the University of Birmingham. But Auden was not only the offspring of teachers and healers, he was also descended, on both his father's and his mother's side, from a long line of Church of England clergymen, and both of his parents were genuinely religious in a conventional way.

Teaching and preaching, then—as well as healing, for that matter—were practices that came naturally to Auden. They were, so to speak, part of the family tradition. Teaching, in particular, was also something that he saw as fundamental to the culture he had been born into—the essentially protestant, work-oriented culture of Northern Europe. Certainly, his sense of having to live a "useful" and examined life, of needing to continue "learning" long after having left school, was one of the chief reasons why he eventually concluded that he could not keep spending his summers in the supposedly happy-go-lucky culture of Southern Italy. In "Good-Bye to the Mezzogiorno," the poem that he wrote on leaving his summer residence on the island of Ischia in 1956 for the last time, he expresses his awareness that

> between those who mean by a life a
> *Bildungsroman* and those to whom living
> Means to be visible now, there yawns a gulf
> Embraces cannot bridge.
>
> (CP, 488)

Quite deliberately, then, he spent a large portion of the remaining fifteen years of his life in the small, unpretentious country house in Kirchstetten, Austria, that he had bought in 1957 with the proceeds of the generous Italian Feltrinelli Prize, no doubt amused by the irony of it all. In Kirchstetten, he was pleased to be greeted by the locals as "Herr Professor," as, after being elected Oxford Professor of Poetry in 1956, he had every right to be. There, in provincial Austria, well off the beaten tourist track, Auden was able to indulge his passion for writing and learning largely unimpeded by unwelcome visitors or disturbances.

Auden's varied and sometimes even contradictory intellectual and poetical life is perhaps best understood as a series of attempts to remake himself to fit a new and, presumably, truer conception of who he thought he *really* was. So, to begin with, he conceived of himself as the bringer of glad, if often somewhat incomprehensible, psychotherapeutic tidings to an England where "nobody was well." (EA, 62) After discovering to his dismay that, despite his efforts to cure them, his English patients stubbornly insisted on remaining unwell, and, indeed, from the standpoint of economic health, were even becoming worse, he shifted from advocating primarily psychological remedies to proposing socioeconomic ones. But here, too, the patient was unresponsive, so that by end of the thirties, Auden tentatively reached the conclusion that a cure was not really possible in this world. Getting truly well was something that only God's grace could manage successfully. By this time, however, Auden had already decided to abandon the England where nobody was well as pretty much a hopeless case, in favor of a United States where at least he himself would feel better. Understandably, however, this was an act that met with scant favor at home, so that in England, his reputation for the remainder of his life was tainted with a stigma of opportunism if not downright cowardice. It was, oddly enough, an outcome that he himself had already foreseen near the beginning of his career as a poet when, in the Prologue to *The Orators*, he had his young teaching and preaching protagonist carry "the good news to a world in danger," only to return home and receive "odd welcome from the country he so defended: / The band roars 'Coward, Coward', in his human fever, / The giantess [bourgeois Mother England?] shuffles nearer, cried 'Deceiver' " (EA, 61).

Put another way, Auden's own life bears eloquent—and sometimes also ironic—witness to what John Fuller calls Auden's "central theory of social and psychological death and rebirth," namely, the notion that the inner and outer (or spiritual and economic) evolution of humanity requires a successive and also progressive shedding of former, outdated selves (Fuller, *Commentary*, 59). For this view of the human condition, Auden first found ample support in the psychological writings of especially Freud and D. H. Lawrence, which so influenced his early poetry, and, later, in the Marxism—both orthodox and "vulgar"—which he sometimes espoused in his prose, and to a lesser extent in his poetry, during much of the mid-thirties. To achieve a better world, it was therefore necessary first to realize that the present world needed to be annihilated so as to provide room for new growth. "Since you are going to begin today / Let us consider what it is you do," begins one of Auden's hortatory poems on this subject, written in late 1929, concluding that "your" fate is to "suffer the loss they were afraid of, yes, / Holders of one position, wrong for years" (EA, 44–45). A few months later, he was telling himself, and his fellow English sufferers from the disease of modern life, that if they really wanted to live, "we'd better start at once to try; / If we don't it doesn't matter, but we'd better start to die" (EA, 49).

Just why was it that it did not matter? Because, as an inexorable Nature and an almost equally inexorable History "taught" anyone who cared to learn, it made no difference whether "we" cooperated with the process of [r]evolution. What was destined to happen would happen anyway, for

> It's no use turning nasty
> It's no use turning good
> You're what you are and nothing you do
> Will get you out of the wood
> Out of a world that has had its day.
>
> (EA, 125)

Auden's poetry, both early and late, unmistakably bears the marks of his having lived life as if it was a *Bildungsroman*, or "a novel of education." It bristles with odd and foreign words (like *Bildungsroman*, for example) which require the reader to turn to "dictionaries (the very / best money can buy)" (CP, 521) if she wishes to understand their meaning. And more than the work of any other leading twentieth-century poet writing in English, it is cast in a sometimes bewildering variety of more or less complex forms, alluding in this way alone to a multitude of other poets, both living and dead. Reading a poem by Auden is invariably, to begin with, at least, hard work—even on a purely formal level. It is work, to be sure, that is usually rewarded, sometimes richly rewarded. This is true even when the poetry is not particularly "serious," for despite his penchant for serious didacticism and, especially after the onset of early middle age, serious preaching, Auden was one of the great comic poets of his age. Still, even when Auden's poetry is fun, it needs work to be enjoyed; and even at its lightest, his poetry poses challenges to be overcome. And at its most serious, as in the great elegy on Yeats, it is not only profoundly moving but deeply instructive. There, in the memorable closing stanza, which also serves as the motto for his memorial in Westminster Abbey, Auden invokes what he saw as the two great functions of poetry—to heal and to teach—at a moment in history when the world around him seemed to be collapsing into chaos and tyranny:

> In the deserts of the heart
> Let the healing fountain start,
> In the prison of his days
> Teach the free man how to praise.
>
> (EA, 243)

Thus, as befits his Protestant background, Auden is never a facile poet, though he tends to be more difficult in the early, rather than in the middle and later, stages of his career. In this respect, Auden, of course, resembles his immediate predecessors—notably T. S. Eliot and Ezra Pound—as well as a few of his contemporaries, such as Dylan Thomas. That is no doubt why some of Auden's first critics saw him primarily as treading somewhat irreverently in the footsteps of the first modernist generation of poetical greats. This is essentially the position of Edwin Muir when, in 1940, he argued paradoxically that, while on the one hand, "W. H. Auden is the most original poet since Eliot," he is also, on the other hand, "the most derivative. His work shows more influences even than Pound's: the influence of Eliot, of Hopkins, of Yeats, of Anglo-Saxon poetry, of the Icelandic saga, of Marx, Freud, the newspaper, the music hall, the detective story, the public-school magazine, the Boy Scout's handbook, the popular broadsheet, the adventure story, the private joke and the private cliché. He is indiscriminately derivative, that is to say, not by choice, like Pound" (Muir, 119). According to Yeats, it was Pound even more than Eliot who was "probably the source of that lack of form and consequent obscurity which is the main defect of Auden, Day Lewis, and their school . . ." (Yeats, *Oxford*, xxv). But then, obscurity, as Baudelaire observed long ago, is one of the most effective weapons in the battle waged by the modern poet against a tasteless but powerful bourgeosie (Hugo Friedrich, 10).

However, Auden also differs—at times, a great deal—from his predecessors and contemporaries in the ways in which he is difficult. In the case of the early Eliot, for example, the reader is usually faced with the task, as it were, of putting a puzzle together of which various important pieces appear to be missing. If only the right intertextual links can be found, so one is led to believe, then the original whole can somehow be reconstructed, and the puzzle "solved." As with most puzzles, success depends partly on the reader's memory and ingenuity, as well as on the availability of a good reference library. For the solution to the puzzle posed by Eliot's poetry almost always lies in finding the missing pieces in "public" places like dictionaries, encyclopedias or other works of literary, historical, or mythological reference. Aside from the usual critical skills, finding one's way through *The Waste Land* involves looking up names and quotations, tracking down literary and other allusions, and checking words in German, Latin, Italian, and Sanskrit dictionaries. Or so at least it did for Eliot's first readers. Now, of course, we can rely gratefully on industrious editors and scholars who have done most of the necessary verbal digging for us.

In his precocious autobiography, *Lions and Shadows* (1937), Christopher Isherwood describes how, after Eliot became "the master," Auden would habitually mix "quotations and misquotations . . . together with bits of foreign languages, proper names and private jokes. Weston [Auden] was peculiarly well-equipped for playing the *Waste Land* game. For Eliot's Dante-quotations and classical learning, he substituted oddments of scientific, medical and psycho-analytical jargon: his magpie brain was a hoard of curious and suggestive phrases from Jung, Rivers, Kretschmer, and Freud" (Isherwood, *Lions*, 191). Still, despite his precocious mastery of the Waste Land Game, Auden was, according to Cyril Connolly, "the only young poet to survive" the potent influence of Eliot (Connolly, *Enemies*, 51). What differentiated the young Auden most strikingly, perhaps, was the fact that, while for him, too, the dictionaries and reference works were undoubtedly important, the body of public knowledge that Auden presupposed in his readers was not primarily literary or historical but psychological, scientific, and, increasingly in the 1930s, social. In addition, there was also a private aspect to the young Auden's poetry that can only be approached through the letters, criticism and autobiographies of his close friends and collaborators, as well as through the journals that he himself kept (and hid) and the letters he wrote (and later ordered destroyed).

The inaccessibility of this body of private information—in some cases not made public until many years after Auden's death—constituted a formidable obstacle to a satisfactory understanding of Auden's poetry for most of his contemporaneous readers, as it still does, to some degree, for us. Edith Sitwell, whose own verse was not always pellucid, and who prided herself on being able to understand, and deliver authoritative judgments upon, just about all contemporary poetry, concluded summarily in 1934 that "[t]he meaning of Mr. Auden's poems is frequently so obscure that it defies detection, and it is this obscurity, I imagine, which has frightened certain critics into this excessive admiration" (Sitwell, 239). Or, as Laurence Whistler remarked sourly when looking back in 1937 at this early phase of Auden's work (and that of his friends): "There were excellent reasons for disliking the earlier work of Auden. It was very obscure, uncouth, full of private associations and private jokes. There were patches of unassimilated influence—Hopkins, Old English. Poets of this clique seemed to have shrugged their shoulders at the public and written only for themselves" (Whistler, 7). Even a sympathetic critic like David Daiches found Auden's mixing of private with public life an obstacle to proper appreciation and even plain understanding: "[S]ometimes he is addressing a group of his personal friends and using symbols intelligible to them alone, and at other times he is addressing an indeterminate audience, using symbols some of which are broadly enough based to have a fairly wide appeal but others of which are carried over from the first group and are therefore only confusing" (Daiches,

215). In the opinion of a less sympathetic critic like W. W. Robson, Auden's annoying penchant for such supposedly indiscriminate mixing of public with private references was something that was not restricted to his early period alone but remained a permanent feature of his poetry: "But even in the most successful 'public' poetry of his early period Auden had a tendency to vacillate between a tone of facile knowledgeableness—the fashionable jargon of an eclectic culture—and an unabashed use of private reference, a self-consciously esoteric game. Some would judge that this tendency has remained in his later work, though expressing itself in somewhat different forms" (quoted in Spender, *Concise*, 51).

Auden, so it seemed to many of his first frustrated readers, was writing in a dialect of English where the meaning of only some of the words was known and for which the unknown words had no entries in any available dictionary. Even that formidable guru of obscurity, T. S. Eliot, after poring over the typescript of *The Orators* that Auden had sent him for editing and publication, told him, with only a hint of annoyance, that its "second part ['Journal of an Airman'] seems quite brilliant though I do not quite get its connexion with the first" (Smith, "Loyalty," 62). Not that the young Auden was by any means unaware of the potentially irritating effect of his obscurantism on readers, including readers as sophisticated as Eliot. His conscious strategy of *épatering* his non–in-group readers is apparent even as early as the Preface to *Oxford Poetry 1927*, written by Auden along with his friend and co-editor Cecil Day-Lewis, in which they unabashedly proclaimed that "[a]ll genuine poetry is in a sense the formation of private spheres out of a public chaos . . ." (Auden, *Prose*, 4). Later on, to be sure, Auden felt regrets—or at least expressed regrets—at having puzzled his readers unduly, reacting to his friend and admirer Naomi Mitchison's criticisms to this effect with apparent surprise and contrition: "Am I really so obscure? . . . Obscurity is a bad fault" (quoted in Mendelson, *Early*, 36).

Even here, however, in the often murky regions of Auden's early verse—sometimes deep and darker than any sea dingle, one may be tempted to add—he is very much of a teacher. If this is something that only a very few readers noticed or remarked on at the time, it is easy to understand why. The reason is simply that, at this early stage of his career, his teaching methods were so unorthodox that it was (and often still is) hard to tell what he was up to. Still, it is certainly not accidental that many of the early plays and poems, including *The Orators*, are partly or entirely set in institutional environments, or that they frequently launch into energetic, pedagogically-oriented exhortations and/or secular sermons. Significantly, as with other distinguished teachers and preachers before him, including Socrates and Christ, Auden loved to use parables to intrigue his audience and make them, as it were, "learn" for themselves rather than provide them with instruction from on high. According to his old friend and sometime collaborator, Louis MacNeice, Auden was an *"anima naturaliter parabolica,"* (a congenitally parabolical soul) whose "poems are full of 'sacred objects'; but more often than not they are sacred to him as a private individual and for reasons which may be mainly accidental (e.g. the landscapes—Midland slag heaps, Cornish tin mines and so on—which he happened to meet as a child)" (MacNeice, *Varieties*, 106).[2] Auden, in other words, was introducing his readers into an admittedly private realm of sacred experience, doing so in his capacity as an essentially "religious" teacher. It was an idea that MacNeice was later to state more directly when he observed that "[p]oetry is related to the sermon and you have your penchant for preaching . . ." (quoted in Carter, 59).

That the young Auden knew that he was being obscure, and that he nevertheless persisted in that obscurity to the point of delighting in it and even playing games based on it—sometimes with different games going on simultaneously among different types or groups of readers—is evident from the opening line of the "Epilogue" to what is, by far, the most obscure production of his early period, *The Orators* (1932):

"O where are you going?" said reader to rider.

(EA, 110)

This line represents a direct challenge to the meek and the weakhearted, to all those who have yielded too easily, as Edith Sitwell evidently did, to despair in their quest for meaning, for the "rider," of course, is also the *writer*, who in this ironically obscure way shows his bemused contempt for all those readers who are too fearful to accompany him on his bewildering adventures down the dark but mysteriously exciting lanes of the Unknown.

It is in this restricted sense that Monroe K. Spears is right in arguing that Auden's obscurity is not merely something accidental, an unplanned by-product of youthful exuberance or undigested influence. On the contrary, the obscurity is, as he says, "also meaningful in itself, as a way of saying that the present state of things doesn't make sense, that jokes and false beards are the only proper reaction" (Spears, *Auden*, 45). Edward Mendelson makes the same point somewhat more emphatically and systematically when he proposes that Auden's obscurity is, in fact, what Auden's early poetry is all about: "The absence of a clue is the clue itself. The poems' central subject is their own failure to be part of any larger interpretive frame. Their metaphors refer to their own state of division and estrangement. As soon as one stops looking for the key to a set of symbols, and recognizes that the poems focus on the self-enclosing patterns that bar their way to a subject in the world outside, their notorious obscurity begins to vanish" (Mendelson, *Early*, 10). While this argument is reassuring and even comforting, unfortunately if one takes it to its logical conclusion, it turns out that the only way of satisfactorily reading the early Auden is to read each poem as if it made no sense and as if it had no meaningful relation to any other Auden poem preceding or following it. Accepting this view, in other words, means accepting that there is no "meaning" at all *in* these poems, because Auden has deliberately left all the doors of his poetry locked and ridden off into the sunset after having cocked a snook at his readers and thrown away the key.

What is more, Mendelson's hypothesis actually leads to an inescapable contradiction, for, inevitably, the utter lack of any "interpretive frame" becomes, as Mendelson is of course fully aware, that very frame itself. Knowing in advance that each Auden poem will be unrelated to any other Auden poem or, for that matter, to anything outside itself, the reader must approach each poem armed with the vision (or, more accurately, the blindness) that its meaning will invariably be equatable to the lack of any meaning outside its self-referential, "self-enclosing" patterns and metaphors. Paradoxically, then, the young Auden's poetry is transformed in this way into a predictable, tedious and rather nebulous exercise. But that is precisely what it was and is not, either when it was first published or now. Philip Toynbee grasped this aesthetic fact at once when he encountered the work of Auden and Company for the first time in the early thirties: "It is hard for younger generations to realize just how utterly new and strange these poets appeared to us then . . . to a reader as young as myself their whole conception of what poetry is and could be was utterly bewildering. . . . But in spite of all these obstacles I was impelled to go on reading these strange, difficult verses. However little I understood them, they gave me a sense of genuine elation. I had never been so strangely affected by any of the poetry I had read before" (Toynbee, "Five," 17). Like Toynbee, the novelist and playwright John Mortimer was immensely impressed by Auden's verse, seeing it as preoccupied with the specific concerns of his class and generation: ". . . it would be hard to overestimate the effect Auden had on me and my generation of middle-class schoolboys. He wrote about *what we understood*: juvenile jokes about housemasters, homosexual longings, the Clever Boy, the Form Entertainer and the Show Off" (Mortimer, 37; my italics).

The main difficulty with Auden's early poetry, I think, as with most modernist poetry—and Auden's early poetry undoubtedly *is* modernist, that is, it belongs to the second generation of modernist poetry—is that it simultaneously requires two kinds of readings, the first one of which might usefully be called a passive reading and the second, an active one. Writing in 1934, Geoffrey Bullough noted that Auden was really a poet who spoke with two voices, the first of which was "cerebral and elliptic" and the second "spontaneous, overflowing with humour to the verge of doggerel" (Bullough, 160). Both of these voices, in his view, were in different ways indebted to the example of T. S. Eliot, who, on the one hand, was the epitome of modernist cerebrality but, at the same time, was also the innovator in English poetry of the burlesque, cabaret style: "The loose manner to which Mr Auden," so Bullough concluded, "tends more and more in *The Orators* and *The Dance of Death* is a deliberate departure from the constipated technique of the 'cerebral school'; yet it is an expansion of Mr. Eliot's adaptation of popular song/rhythms and idiom to serious poetry." (Bullough, 161–62) Unlike Eliot, however, Auden did not keep his cerebrum and his emotions in separate aesthetic compartments; he fused, and sometimes, admittedly, also confused them, with the result that he left his readers either delighted or benighted, or both. Eventually, he came to conclude that this had been a mistake. Writing in early November 1937, he told a correspondent that he "used to try and concentrate the poem so much that there wasn't a word that wasn't essential. This leads to becoming boring and constipated" (HRC, Letters).

Though by the end of the thirties Auden would become a much more accessible and lucid poet, he never became—or wanted to become—an easy or facile poet. Speaking generally about obscurity in poetry in 1960, but clearly having in mind his own particular case, he accused critics and readers of being obtuse: "Sometimes I think that what they regard as obscurity shows that they take poetry a little too seriously; one of the elements in poetry is the riddle, that you do not call a spade a spade. It is evident that people enjoy solving riddles, because otherwise crossword puzzles would not have the popularity they have. It is odd that some of the people who spend hours doing crossword puzzles, and love doing them [as Auden himself loved doing them], are the first to raise objections because they do not understand a line of poetry" (Quoted in Burton, 787).[3] Of course, what Auden neglects to add here is that most crossword puzzle addicts are never in doubt that at the end of the book (or in tomorrow's paper) they will be able to find a correct answer (and usually only one correct answer) to their puzzle, whereas the same is not true (or only sometimes true and even then only partly) of puzzling poetry. Still, the point that Auden makes is worth remembering with respect to his own practice, namely that for him at least there *is* a correct answer to the poetical riddles he sets for his readers. What is more, he could sometimes become very irritated when readers got the answer wrong, as in the case of Stephen Spender's supposed misreading of the poem, "A Change of Air." "You're a *naughty* girl," he wrote Spender on 12 July 1963, "and in her reply your Mother, sweet old lady we all know her to be, has had to give you a little spank-spank" (Berg).[4] Addressing in a rather more serious way the shade of his dead friend Louis MacNeice, Auden put the case for difficult poetry more persuasively if no less assertively:

> After all it's rather a privilege
> amid the affluent traffic
> to serve this unpopular art which cannot be turned into
> background noise for study
> or hung as a status trophy by rising executives,
> cannot be 'done' like Venice
> or abridged like Tolstoy, but stubbornly still insists upon
> being read or ignored; our handful
> of clients at least can rune.
>
> (CP, 522)

Though not referring specifically to Auden's early poetry, T. S. Eliot made a distinction analogous to Bullough's when, in "The Use of Poetry and the Use of Criticism," he observed that "[t]he more seasoned reader . . . does not bother about understanding; not at least at first. I know that poetry to which I am most devoted is poetry which I did not understand at first reading; some is poetry which I am not sure I understand yet: for instance, Shakespeare's" (*Selected*, 93). In the preface to his 1930 translation of St.-Jean Perse's *Anabasis*, Eliot goes on in greater detail to describe how this kind of reading works: "There is a logic of the imagination as well as a logic of concepts. People who do not appreciate poetry always find it difficult to distinguish between order and chaos in the arrangement of images; and even those who are capable of appreciating poetry cannot depend on first impressions. I was not convinced of Mr. Perse's imaginative order until I had read the poem five or six times. And if, as I suggest, such an arrangement of imagery requires just as much 'fundamental brain-work' as the arrangement of an argument, it is to be expected that the reader of the poem should take at least as much trouble as a barrister reading an important decision on a complicated case" (Eliot, Preface, 8).

How fully the young Auden appreciated this characteristically modernist or Eliotesque way of reading and understanding poetry is apparent from a conversation he had with Neville Coghill, his tutor at Oxford, probably sometime in 1927. In words that anticipate Eliot's—and also echo I. A. Richards's—, "Auden explained with clarity and pity that to 'understand' a poem was not a logical process, but a receiving, as a unity, a pattern of co-ordinated images that had sprung from a free association of subconscious ideas private to himself." Not surprisingly, Auden concluded this little lecture on how to read modern poetry by recommending to Coghill "the works of T. S.

Eliot" (Press, 173). (In this connection it is also worth noting that "Eliot pointed out to Auden the debt of 'Argument and Statement' [sections of *The Orators*] to the *Anabase* of St. John Perse" [E. Smith, 106].) It is with something like this idea in mind that Auden in 1935 came to the conclusion that "[o]f the many definitions of poetry, the simplest is still the best: 'memorable speech.' " Poetic speech is *memorable* because, as he goes on to say, we as readers "must surrender" to the stimulus of the "audible spoken word and cadence . . . in all its power of suggestion and incantation . . . ." (Auden, *Prose*, 105). Poetry, in other words, is something that works its potent effects deep within the reader's psyche, and that is also why it is so memorable. *Un*memorable speech, or prose, is of the surface. Memorable speech, or poetry, is of the depths. Though Auden would later radically change his mind with respect to what poetry was and did (or should do), at this relatively early stage of his career, Auden was still convinced that, as he put it, "poetry is a struggle to reconcile the unwilling subject and object," that is, its principal function is to harmonize the inner or private world with the outer, public one. It was for this reason that poetry, in fact, was uniquely qualified to provide psychological healing, a process precisely definable as the *reconciliation* of the private world of the individual with the public world of his society. Or, to cite Auden's own extraordinary words, "since psychological truth depends so largely on context, poetry, the parabolic approach, is the only adequate medium for psychology." (Auden, *Prose*, 105, 108) In other words, poetry—or at least poetry of the right parabolic, Audenesque sort—is quite literally psychotherapy; it not only appeals, it also heals.[5]

Here lies the most important key to unlocking the obscurities of the young Auden's poetry, as well as to understanding how and why he conceived of that poetry as performing an important didactic function. Poetry for the young Auden was essentially a kind of cure for the psychologically ill, if only because it could and did reach levels of the psyche not accessible to prosaic, logical expression. That is also why his early poetry is filled with "sacred objects," as Louis MacNeice put it, or with recurrent, even "obsessive" images, to use Joseph Warren Beach's memorable phrase for them. It is by means of these sacred objects that the poet both probes and restores to health his own damaged unconscious, and thereby goes on to provide an instructive example of what he has done for his readers. In this sense, Auden's early poetry depicts not so much a *paysage moralisée* as a *paysage psychologisée*; a landscape of the mind, especially of the dark, "obscure" portions of the mind. The poet's task is to cast a healing illumination over this mental landscape, to make the reader "see" with the inner eye of the imagination where and what has made her ill. The poet is, in fact, a kind of shaman, a healer, teacher, and preacher rolled into one, providing help for all those who are prepared to open themselves up to receive that help, and excluding only those whose will is negatively inverted. Where a confused and ill-attended *Id* was, there the poethealer has made room for a healthy *Ego*—or, at any rate, he has attempted to do so.

Despite its "deep" psychological nature and impact, it would, however, be wrong to maintain that Auden's early poetry has no—or only a relatively small—surface or "rational" dimension. Though his early poetry is admittedly directed primarily at those private regions of the mind that are not theoretically accessible to the public or rational mind, much of it also makes sense in more ordinary ways. If it didn't, the young Auden would be classifiable as a surrealist rather than as a modernist poet, and there would be little point in attempting to show how the "private" parts relate to the "public" ones, because there would be no public dimension to relate to. For Auden, as for D. H. Lawrence—whose poetry (and "philosophy") he admired greatly in the early stages of his career—the "deep passional soul" had to be complemented (and completed) by a passionate body and an intelligent, sensitive mind. This is something that his close friends understood perfectly. As Isherwood was to say many years later, "[e]ven now I regret that I didn't write a great deal more about Auden's work. There was a time when I could have gone through all of his early poems and told you the genesis of almost every line, with endless reminiscences" (Wickes, 51). In other words, in Isherwood's memory, Auden's poetry didn't spring full-blown out of his fertile subconscious mind, but was instead a carefully considered (and in fact, much reconsidered) product of conscious deliberation. Or, as Stephen Spender put it, "[e]very line of his poetry—which has been called obscure—*means* something in the sense that it has an immediate relation to some real event which he interprets as a psychological or spiritual or sociological symptom. His poetry is, as I say, a brilliant commentary on our contemporary history, and to understand it one has to see what it is about, as well as enjoying the poetry" (Spender, "Auden and His Poetry," 77). In short, there is little room here for the idea that Auden's poetry consists entirely of an invariable pattern of self-referential, self-enclosed metaphors.

Even the shape of Auden's poetic career changes. During the momentous period from the late 1920s to the end of the 1930s, it reveals a progressive movement towards the public or conscious mind and away from the private, unconscious one. The earliest Auden was intent on teaching the individual, always including himself, how to be "cured" of psychosomatic illness, but by the middle of the decade, he began with equal conviction to be increasingly concerned with teaching the group how to remake society in order to foster a healthy community. Now he came to think, as he put it, that "education succeeds social revolution, not precedes. You cannot train children to be good citizens of a state which you despise" (*Prose*, 30). By the end of the decade, he had changed his mind again, teaching and preaching that salvation lay neither in the individual psyche nor in the collective state, but in God. It is during the half-decade lasting from about 1936 to 1941 which—if it had not turned out in retrospect to have been the period of Auden's greatest and most moving poems, one might be tempted to call transitional—that Auden experienced the greatest difficulty in making up his mind about what the social role of the poet was supposed to be or what form of social organization he really preferred. Symptomatic of his lack of clarity and consistency is the epigraph from Montaigne that Auden chose for his collection of poems, *The Double Man* (1941), expressing a sentiment he evidently expected readers to apply more to him than to themselves: "We are, I know not how, double in ourselves, so that what we believe we disbelieve, and cannot rid ourselves of what we condemn." Not surprisingly, therefore, G. S. Fraser was to conclude, with scarcely concealed sarcasm, that Auden had been consistent only in his doom-saying, first "threatening his readers with a variety of calamities—disease, madness, death in war or revolution, and now eternal damnation." (Fraser, *Essays*, 136–37). While Auden's "threats" were, in fact, usually more in the nature of exhortations or, at worst, warnings, it is true that in the thirties Auden did shift, often with astonishing rapidity, from enthusiastically advocating one kind of salvation to another. Not that Auden's frequent changes of mind were ever arbitrary or whimsical, though he himself later claimed that he had actively espoused during the 1930s doctrines that he had never really believed in himself. Still, viewed from the outside, it undoubtedly seemed as if, as François Duchêne observed, "[h]is career has been a bewildering succession of apparently absolute 'truths.' " (Duchêne, 18)

In any case, when Auden shifted his primary attention away from the individual psyche to the public mind, he also made a corresponding shift in the kind of poetry he wrote. Though he never became an easy or superficial poet, he no longer tried deliberately to obfuscate the bourgeoisie or to use his poetry as a substitute for psychological treatment. The poetry he wrote after his "conversion" to socialism in late 1932 or thereabouts became increasingly less "cerebral" (and less modernist) and more emotional and "popular." Not that Auden ever stopped being intellectually challenging—even, as we shall see, in his most unmitigatedly propagandistic poems, such as "A Communist to Others," there is still an appeal to the mind—and one of the greatest poems from his "socialist" period, "Spain" (1937), is in its fragmentation and abstraction still very much a modernist poem. By and large, however, Auden now deliberately began to reach out to an audience that he believed, quite rightly, was not much given to reading poetry except when written by the likes of Kipling. (Significantly, Orwell was later to call the Auden of this period a "gutless Kipling.") While the audience he now addressed, or at least hoped to address, was still not primarily working class, it was far larger and more influential than the relatively small group of fellow poets, friends and hangers-on who had been the principal readers of his poetry up to this time. Auden now realized that as his views on the relation between society and the individual changed, he would have to change the kind of poetry that he wrote as well. Despite his continuing admiration for Eliot, he knew that modernist poetry was simply not an adequate vehicle for affecting society or group behavior. As R. D. Charques phrased it in 1933, using the Marxist idiom of the age, modernist poetry "is 'class' poetry in the sense that it is addressed to a privileged and particularly cultivated section of society—a section specially engaged in literary pursuits or interests. In the sense that it seeks to express in a language peculiarly his own the personal fantasies of the poet, modernist poetry is perhaps a final stage in the growth of the individualist tradition in art" (Charques, 76–77). From about the end of 1932 until at least sometime in late 1937, Auden wanted to have as little as possible to do with such bourgeois, liberal, individualistic traditions, at any rate in his poetic practice.

Despite the radical change in the form and direction of his poetry, the didactic strain remained for him a stable, though not particularly still, center throughout the thirties. Indeed, it is precisely in order to more fully satisfy his didactic impulses that Auden transformed himself from a private to a public poet. As he wrote Neville Coghill on 24 April 1933, ". . . thought and action do not exist separately. (I know this is a commonplace but how many people behave as if it were.) Applied to poetry this means that 1) you cannot have doctrines in a poem without action (in action I include sensory images of all kinds) and 2) that in any poem except a short lyric you must have doctrine. Dante is the supreme example of the combination of both worlds." Lest he leave Coghill in any doubt about how to relate the religious elements of his poetry to this idea of poetry as action, Auden stressed that he explicitly included "in doctrine, not only specific dogma but all pious ejaculations," an injunction that presumably also pertained to piously Marxist ejaculations (Berg). To be sure, the task of teaching poetic sociology, as it were, to an impersonal and often indifferent world rather than poetic psychology to a few familiar, friendly individual pupils brought with it new challenges and risks. For one thing, it left Auden open to a charge of insincerity and even opportunism. For, despite changing some of the externals and many of the internals of his poetry, he could not (or would not) change the way he lived. Though he might put on worker's caps or take pleasure in occasionally referring to members of the working class as "comrades," or receive letters addressed to him (as he did from Brecht) as "Comrade Auden," still in his personal habits and way of life he remained very much what he had always been: a comfort and freedom loving/seeking intellectual of the middle class. Nor, at some deep, psychological level, did he really want to be anything else, for, given to authoritarian attitudes in his own private life and conversation, he naturally tended to dislike any organization or doctrine that told him what to do and how to do it. In one of the illuminating autobiographical asides in "Letter to Lord Byron" (1936), he admits as much himself, though he puts the actual words in the mouths of some unnamed left-wing friends:

> I hate pompositas and all authority;
>   Its air of injured rightness also sends
> Me shuddering from the cultured smug minority.
>   'Perpetual revolution,' left wing friends
>   Tell me, 'in counter-revolution ends.
> Your fate will be to linger an outcast
> A selfish pink old Liberal to the last.'

(EA, 190)

A selfish, pink old *anarchist* would actually have been a more precise description of his aesthetics and politics at this time, but, humor and irony aside, Auden knew that because of his class origins, education, accent and "handsome profile," he would never be able to successfully bridge the gap separating him, along with his more orthodox and rather less honest left-wing friends, from actual members of the working class. How right he was is something George Orwell gleefully and a little maliciously pointed out in 1940. To be sure, unlike bourgeois Auden, bourgeois Orwell was entitled to publicly wagging his index finger in this way, for he had actually taken the working-class road to Wigan Pier and paid homage to Catalonia by risking his life there. "[I]t is a fact," Orwell writes, "that in Auden's work, especially his earlier work, an atmosphere of uplift . . . never seems to be very far away. Take, for instance, a poem like 'You're leaving now, and it's up to you boys.' [Significantly, there is no such Auden poem. Orwell is actually quoting a line from Day-Lewis's "Magnetic Mountain."] It is pure scoutmaster, the exact note of ten minutes' straight talk on the dangers of self-abuse. No doubt there is an element of parody that he intends, but there is also a deeper resemblance that he does not intend. And of course the rather priggish note that is common to most of these writers is a symptom of release. By throwing 'pure art' overboard they have freed themselves from the fear of being laughed at and vastly enlarged their scope. The prophetic side of Marxism, for example, is new material for poetry and has great possibilities.

... *But at the same time, by being Marxised literature has moved no nearer to the masses.* Even allowing for the time-lag, Auden and Spender are somewhat farther from being popular writers than Joyce and Eliot, let alone Lawrence" (Orwell, "Inside," 238, my italics).

Essentially, Auden's problem was the very common and human one of wanting to have his cake and eat it too. He wanted the privileges and comforts of bourgeois fame, accepting, for example, with only minimal qualms, the King's Gold Medal for Poetry in 1937; but at the same time, he also wanted to be perceived as, and admired for, being on the side of the working class, actively participating in the "struggle" to make a more socially equitable world. To be sure, in his poetical pursuit of the latter, Auden never sank to such naively propagandistic depths as did his friend Cecil Day-Lewis, who produced effusions like the one on "On the Twentieth Anniversary of Soviet Power," written at the very moment when the notorious show trials were in full swing:

> Twenty years have passed
> Since a cry, All Power to the Soviets! shook the world.
> We have seen new cities, arts and sciences,
> A real freedom, a justice that flouts not nature,
> Springing like corn exuberant from the rich heart
> Of a happier people.
>
> (Quoted in Osborne, 154–55)

By the end of the thirties, of course, Auden had "seen the light," repudiated his sometime Marxist sympathies, and departed for the United States. But before the low and dishonest decade came to an end in the violent conflagration of the Second World War, Auden was quite content for several momentous years to inhabit what Virginia Woolf referred to as his "leaning [ivory] tower." Nor did Auden himself altogether escape, as he later acknowledged, being affected (and infected) by doses of lowness and dishonesty, though, to be sure, he was certainly not the only occupant of the fashionably left-leaning tower. It had, in fact, been inherited by him and his fellow artistic friends more or less intact, and in a more or less vertical position, from the previous generation, a situation almost unparalleled in Europe, as Virginia Woolf and the rest of Bloomsbury knew only too well. Elsewhere, the ivory towers had, not long before, been pretty well leveled to the ground, either by war or by revolution (or both). To be sure, though in England the tower was still left standing, what made it so unstable in the thirties was the great pressure of the world war that everyone knew was coming. Indeed, it was the threat of impending war that caused Auden and his friends, in Woolf's view, to come together "more than their predecessors into a group." The very fact that the tower was leaning also made them aware that they were living precariously at the edge of collapse as no previous generation had done. Therefore, the Auden generation was, as Woolf put it in a memorable phrase, acutely "tower conscious." This awareness caused them first to feel guilt, then discomfort, and finally anger. But it was a curiously insincere and ineffective kind of anger, for how, Woolf asked, "can you altogether abuse a society that is giving you, after all, a very fine view and some sort of security?" It was this peculiar combination of hypocrisy and frustration that produced in Auden and his friends, so she thought, the "bleat of the scapegoat [that] sounds loud in their work, and the whimper of the schoolboy crying 'Please, Sir, it was the other fellow, not me.'"

Living in their splendid but fragile tower, Auden and Company looked down upon the world below and pretended to themselves that they were part of it and could influence its workings. It was a state of mind that, as far as Woolf was concerned, explained much that was otherwise incomprehensible in their work: "If you think of them, that is, as people trapped in a leaning tower from which they cannot descend, much that is puzzling in their work is easier to understand. It explains the destructiveness of their work; and also its emptiness. . . . How can a writer who has no first-hand experience of a towerless, of a classless society create that society? . . . It explains the pedagogic, the didactic, the loud speaker strain that dominates their poetry. They must teach; they must preach" (Woolf, "Leaning," 114). In the end, of course, with the failure of the Republican armies in Spain and the apparent inability of European parliamentary democracies to stem the onrush of fascism in Czechoslovakia and elsewhere, the political and moral foundations of the tower gave way. (The final push was given by the Molotov-Ribbentrop Pact.) Before that happened, however, some of its inhabitants, including Auden, had parachuted to safety and made a rush for the last of the still standing ivory towers of the West. From now on, there would be no more talk of towerless societies. The new tower, when it wasn't using its "full height to proclaim / The strength of Collective Man" (EA, 245), could be seen leaning a little to the right, but with no real danger of collapse. For it was safely removed from troubled Europe and all those other "darkened lands of the earth," located, as it was, just off the brightly illuminated coast of New York and looking very much like the Statue of Liberty.

1
Crossing Frontiers: Poetic Espionage in Late 1920s Berlin

"And I gave them lessons in deciphering codes,
I warned them of spies in acrostic odes."
—W. H. Auden, "A Happy New Year," (1932)

"And so unconsciously the liberal becomes the secret service of the ruling class, their most powerful weapon against social revolution."
—W. H. Auden, *Scrutiny* (1932)

I

Two men are seated in a train compartment approaching the German frontier. One is about twenty-five, the other a little more than twice that age. They are strangers. Bored, and in order to break the awkward silence, the younger man asks the older if he knows " 'what time we arrive at the frontier?' " It is an innocuous question to all appearances, but the response he receives is anything but innocuous. "Its effect on the stranger," he notes with surprise, "was remarkable. I had certainly succeeded in arousing his interest. He gave me a long, odd glance, and his features seemed to stiffen a little. It was the glance of a poker-player who guesses suddenly that his opponent holds a straight flush and that he had better be careful. At length he answered, speaking slowly and with caution: 'I'm afraid I couldn't tell you exactly. In about an hour's time, I believe.' "

This scene occurs at the beginning of Christopher Isherwood's *Mr. Norris Changes Trains* (1935), the first of his two celebrated novels about the last traumatic years in Berlin before the Nazis took over (Isherwood, *Berlin*, 2). It also sets the tone for the rest of the novel. A seemingly ordinary situation involving seemingly ordinary people is suddenly shown to be deeply implicated in mystery. An everyday railway journey from one European capital to another acquires symbolic significance. " 'All these frontiers . . . ,' " the older man (Mr. Norris, of course), ventures petulantly, " 'such a horrible nuisance.' " The journey that had seemed boring a moment earlier to the young traveler is now full of interest and even amusement. Attempting to determine the source of Norris's evident uneasiness, Isherwood's narrator and alter ego, William Bradshaw, speculates whimsically that he may be an eccentric advocate of international understanding, possibly some enthusiastic supporter of the League of Nations. " 'They [the frontiers] ought to be done away with,' " he suggests. " 'I quite agree with you,' " Norris replies. " 'They ought indeed' " (Isherwood, *Norris*, 3).

As it turns out—though Bradshaw discovers the truth only much later—Norris is rather more of an advocate of international misunderstanding than he is of international understanding. While he definitely possesses redeeming qualities, along with a great deal of incidental charm, Norris neither is, nor isn't (as his name implies), what he appears to be. This is an impression that is reinforced when Bradshaw becomes aware of the fact that Norris is wearing a wig. On the one hand, his hairpiece testifies to Norris's vanity but, on the other, it also shows to what absurd (and quite ineffectual) lengths he has gone to hide who he really is. Norris is, in fact, a spy in the pay of the French government, specializing at this particular historical moment in selling information about the activities of the German Communist Party in Berlin. He is not at all worried about the League of Nations—nor about being caught smuggling perfume, another idea that crosses Bradshaw's busy mind—but he is very much worried about whether the German border police are aware of his dealings and have him blacklisted.

Paradoxically, despite the evident sincerity of his desire to abolish national frontiers, Norris's profession requires their continued existence. Without frontiers, there would be no need for spies. Without frontiers, there would be no nations, perhaps no organized (and certainly no organizing) officialdom at nonexistent border crossings or elsewhere. Without frontiers, there might even be some hope for the state to wither away, a utopian condition that some of Bradshaw's best friends, along with Norris's primary victims, the members of the German Communist Party, are presumably striving to bring about. It is, so Isherwood's narrative implies, frontiers that not only separate nations but, even more important, also separate individuals; it is frontiers that breed distrust and spying, and, along with them, spies like Arthur Norris. Paradoxically, however, it is also frontiers that make life interesting and amusing for people like William Bradshaw, and make it worthwhile to write novels about people who, like Arthur Norris, cross them.

Mr. Norris Changes Trains is dedicated to W. H. Auden, Isherwood's close friend and frequent collaborator. It was Auden who first introduced Isherwood to the quite genuine but also very troubling pleasures of Berlin at the end of the 1920s. Not surprisingly, therefore, the young Auden's poetry is often concerned with many of the same themes and marked by many of the same images as is Isherwood's fiction. How important this was for them both in the late twenties is evident from the birthday poem Auden wrote for Isherwood in August 1935 ("August for the People"). There, he remembered how nine years earlier

> Our hopes were set still on the spies' career,
> Prizing the glasses and the old felt hat . . .
>
> (EA, 156)

To be sure, unlike Isherwood's prose, Auden's early poetry is never ordinary or even seemingly ordinary. On the surface, its powerful concentration makes it appear radically different from Isherwood's deceptively casual and prosaic manner.[1] Also, the young Auden's poetry is even more densely populated with spies and shadowy figures who resemble spies or who engage in spy-like activities than are Isherwood's novels. Not surprisingly, Auden's first major literary interpreter, Richard Hoggart, was struck—and puzzled—by it. Why, he asked, was this "whole group" of writers "so interested in the apparatus of the spy story?" (Hoggart, 1951, 20).

Auden's first extended literary work, the verse charade, *Paid on Both Sides*, which I will discuss in more detail later, combines elements drawn from Old Norse epics, traditional mummery plays, farce, public school experience, secret in-group lore, oddments of psychological theory, and surrealistic fragments of spy stories. In one of the central scenes of the play, a spy is caught, tried, and executed. Auden's first successfully staged play, *The Dog Beneath the Skin* (1935), written together with Christopher Isherwood, includes among its main characters a young man who disguises himself as a dog (wearing, as it were, a less expensive but more extensive hairpiece than Arthur Norris) and spies on friend and foe alike. Another, somewhat earlier, collaboration with Isherwood that has never been staged, "The Enemies of the Bishop" (1929), contains a misguided police spy who fails to detect a gang of disguised white slavers, as well as a conspiratoral Spectre who is invisible to everyone except his double. A short poem dating from the same period, to which Auden later gave the title "Secret Agent" (1928), describes the impending doom of another spy who, because his reports have gone unheeded, is about to be captured and shot.

The Orators (1932), Auden's most ambitious early work, features as its central character an airman who is also a spy. Other spies or spy-like figures, sometimes with revolutionary overtones, also lurk at the margins. The opening scene of this long, profoundly puzzling and disturbing work (see chapter

2 for a fuller discussion), shows a pompous but apparently innocuous Old Boy or former student addressing his school on Prize Day. He is an amusing windbag who, not altogether unlike Arthur Norris, unexpectedly reveals himself to be the agent of revolution and imprisonment of unsympathetic teachers and administrators. The point, it would seem, is that "we" have successfully infiltrated the enemy's defenses and are ready to undertake the overthrow of the old order. Only a few pages later, the aid of a variety of spies and detectives is urgently invoked as if they were the saints of a new religion. After first praying to the Four Just Men to "spare us," Dixon Hawke, Sexton Blake, Bulldog Drummond, Ferrers Locke, Panther Grayle, Poirot, and Holmes are solemnly asked to "deliver us" (EA 66–67). Of all these names, probably only the last two are still familiar to most literate people, but among readers of thriller fiction during the late twenties and early thirties, all of the rest were household names. The Four Just Men refer to the celebrated group of secret avengers in Edgar Wallace's much reprinted novel of the same name (1905); Sexton Blake, Dixon Hawke, Ferrers Locke, and Panther Grayle were all popular counterspies in the adolescent fiction of the early decades of the century; and Bulldog Drummond is the hero of numerous thriller novels by "Sapper" (the pseudonym of H. C. McNeile and his successor, G. T. Fairlie). The point of all this seems to be to establish a kind of espionage/detection framework for the reader in which to place the mysterious people, events, and messages that she will continue to encounter in her reading of *The Orators*.

John Fuller sees these prayers as a parody of the Anglican liturgical responses and goes on to point out the humor of Auden's contrasting "private" detectives with the "public" houses that are invoked in the rest of the poem (Fuller, *Guide*, 58). While Fuller is probably right, his remark about detectives is, I think, misleading, since, with the qualified exception of Holmes and Poirot, the other figures in the catalog belong more to what we would today call the category of secret agents rather than detectives. None of them, to be sure, is actually in the direct employ of the government, but they usually act in its behalf and most of their adventures involve frustrating the malicious activities of foreign spies. Hence, the stories in which they feature really fall into the genre of the "thriller" rather than that of the "mystery." This seems important because of its clear links to the central section of *The Orators*, where the Airman is much more like a spy than a detective. As Richard Rowan noted in 1929, the use of airmen as spies, or as conveyers of spies across frontiers, was one of the great innovations in the techniques of spying during the new century (Rowan, 98).

Auden draws the distinction between detectives and spies quite clearly in "The Guilty Vicarage" (1948) by placing the focus of the thriller on "the ethical and eristic conflict between good and evil, between Us and Them," whereas the "interest in the detective story is the dialectic of innocence and guilt." This distinction also neatly describes the difference in outlook between the early, pre-conversion Auden and the later, religious one. Not surprisingly therefore the later Auden goes on to observe that, although addicted to reading detective fiction, he "rarely" enjoyed thrillers. Here, the older poet presumes to speak authoritatively for the younger, making it appear as if both had always had the same preferences and prejudices.[2]

In the middle section of *The Orators*, the principal character, the neurotic airman/spy, depicts in his journal (a document that, as we shall see in the following chapter, sometimes literally requires decoding) a series of graphs that are to be used to distinguish the "enemy" from his friends. The "enemy," one should recall here, quite simply meant "Germans" for most British readers during the late twenties, just as "spies" were almost always German spies. Not coincidentally, the idea of the "enemy" was to become prominent in Auden's poetry during and after his stay in Berlin. Unlike the stiff, unimaginative German enemy of most spy stories, however, Auden's enemy is able to assume a variety of shapes (and is in fact something of a shape-shifter) but beneath his many masks the enemy is usually recognizable as British bourgeois conformity in its inner and outer manifestations. Auden is especially given to representing this enemy in female form, presumably with the emblematic figure of "Britannia" in mind. In the "Prologue" to *The Orators* the enemy becomes an allegorical "giantess," and in the prefatory verses to *The Dog Beneath the Skin* he describes her as a "genteel dragon" about whose power the young must be warned:

> Boy with lancet, speech or gun
>   Among the dangerous ruins, learn
> From each devastated organ
>   The power of the genteel dragon.
>
> (*Plays*, [189])

In *The Orators*, the Airman notes that "THE ENEMY IS A NAIVE NOT A LEARNED OBSERVER," with "naive observation" equalling "insight," and "introspection," "spying" (EA, 74). The alert reader (and observer) immediately perceives the irony of identifying spies with introspection in the self-conscious context of a private journal, as well as the further irony that insight is attributed to the "enemy," spying, to the self. When the enemy finally attacks, however, s/he uses fifth-column tactics such as having "the widow bent into a hoop by arthritis" giving "the signal for attack by unbending on the steps of St. Philip's" (EA 92), or by introducing secret catalysts "into the city reservoirs [to] convert the entire drinking supply into tepid urine" (EA 93). The enemy, we are made to realize, makes use of spies just as much as "we" do, and perhaps even more imaginatively and with more panache. The enemy, we also gradually begin to realize, is not someone living beyond the frontier. The enemy, as Auden noted in another poem he wrote while living in Germany, is also and especially ourselves:

> "We take that hill" the colonel cried.
> And so they did, though most of them died,
> And the enemy were their own side.
>
> (EA, 50)

II

Auden's first poetic achievement of any lasting significance is his verse play, *Paid on Both Sides*, a draft of which he had brought with him to Berlin and that, in the course of the following year, he subjected to extensive revision. As he told Stephen Spender, he wasn't sure at first about what direction his revisions would take, but he did know that the end result would be a new play. "The old play," he wrote, not long after arriving in Berlin, "is joining a new one probably and turning into something else, I am not quite sure what yet" (Berg, Late autumn, 1928). But by Christmas 1928, he knew. While retaining the original setting of the play in the remote hill country of the Pennines, as well as the rudimentary saga-like (or even cowboy-like) episodic plot dealing with a seemingly irreconcilable feud between two families and their hangers-on, Auden now introduced new materials and emphases that suggest that he meant the play to be read as a parable for the conflict between England and Germany during and after the Great War. To begin with, he introduced new characters, with a couple of them bearing distinctively German names (Kurt and Zeppel). In one instance, a character named Culley uses the customary German term "Prosit" when drinking to Kurt's health, while the latter replies with a typically English "Cheerio" (EA, 4). Another character refers to a baby bearing the German name Ingo (EA, 5). In the revised version, Auden also marks the difference between members of the two opposing families by providing them with distinctively colored armbands, whereas, in the original version, only the Nower group wears handkerchiefs on their left arms. Displaying emblematic armbands to indicate political allegiance was common among adherents both of the Nazis and the Communists in Germany during the 1920s and early 1930s.[3]

More important, however, than these externals is the theme of festering suspicion, spying, violence and vengeance passing from one generation to the next. The revised play begins with the report of the killing of John Nower's father, George, in an ambush while on the way to consult with Auden's friend and mentor in Berlin, John Layard, presumably about peaceful ways of resolving the feud. In the succeeding generation, George's son avenges his death by ambushing the killer Red Shaw and executing one of his sons for spying; then, like his own father, but using different means, he attempts to bring about an end to the feud by getting married to Anne, Red Shaw's daughter. Though John and Anne truly love each other, their private love, as it turns out, is not (and perhaps cannot be) sufficient, even when formalized in marriage, to alter the course of past public hatred. At the urging of Anne's mother, her brother Seth reluctantly kills John, and the apparently unstoppable cycle of vengeance takes another bloody turn.

Just what started the feud between the Nowers and the Shaws in the first place or what it is all about is never made entirely clear; it is as if its causes and nature do not matter. It is a conflict, so it would appear on the surface, with virtually no overt political dimension. But the surnames of the two families hint at a generational and even political significance, with "Nowers" referring to "now" or the present, and "Shaws" functioning as an anagram for "was" or the past—a contrast that is borne out by the fact that it is primarily the Nowers who attempt to make peace in both generations, who want, as it were, to insist on the here and *now* and throw off the dead hand of the past, whereas it is the Shaws chiefly who seem intent on preserving the *feu*dal "tradition" of war.[4] The addition of the distinctively Old Testament names in the revised version of the play on the Shaw side (Aaron and Seth) may be intended to signal their adherence to the past, as well as, according to John Fuller, to suggest differences between Germans and Jews. However, though the differences between the two feuding groups are meaningful and important, Nowers and Shaws are portrayed as essentially the same (Fuller, *Guide*, 14). As one of the Nower party remarks just before the killing of Red Shaw, echoing some famous lines from *The Merchant of Venice*, "What do we want to go on killing each other for? We are all the same. He's trash, yet if I cut my finger it bleeds like his" (EA, 5). The idea of a fundamental identity of both sides, transcending mutual hatred, is evident also in the note following the list of *dramatis personae* in the play, which specifies how the characters are to be doubled. One character is explicitly assigned a role among both the Nowers and Shaws. As it happens, this is also the very same character, Trudy, who speaks the lines just quoted. Significantly and ironically, the part she plays among the Shaws is that of Seth's mother, the person who is most immediately responsible for compelling the continuation of the feud.

How irresistible the weight of the past is on the present becomes apparent early on in the play, when Joan Nower recites a combined elegy (for her recently deceased husband, George) and lullaby (for her newly born son, John). "New ghost," she says, "learns from many / Learns from old termers what death is, where" (EA, 2). "Ghost" here refers not only to George's recently departed soul, but also (and with even greater force) to John's newly minted one, which will now be indoctrinated in the school of life, receiving a warped education that invariably leads to early death. "Unforgetting is not to-day's forgetting," Joan continues:

> For yesterday, not bedrid scorning,
> But a new begetting
> An unforgiving morning.
>
> (EA, 2)

The begetting of John, she realizes, is also the begetting of another generation of hatred, which will lead to a further unforgetting—the play on words here is on "not forgetting" and "not begetting" (i. e., un*for*getting)—and to an "unforgiving morning" (with the pun on *mourning* clearly intended) rather than a new dawn.[5]

Ironically, it is also this grieving Joan—a Joan now grown old and vengeful herself—who, in the extraordinary dream sequence added by Auden to the play in Berlin, threateningly brandishes her gigantic baby bottle like a huge gun at Red Shaw's condemned son. And it is her own son who becomes the most articulate spokesman for the values of hatred and the past. "I know we have and are making terrific sacrifices," he declaims in a painful parody of the patriotic rhetoric that Auden must have heard regularly at his preparatory school during the Great War, "but we cannot give in. We cannot betray the dead. As we pass their graves can we be deaf to the simple eloquence of their inscriptions, those who in the glory of their early manhood gave up their lives for us? No, we must fight to the finish" (EA, 8). It is in the name of this rhetoric of remembering and enshrining the past, and specifically the past of the Great War, with its lying war aims, unconditional surrender, and memorials to the dead, that John then shoots Shaw's son, the *spy* who has crossed the frontier and been caught. Significantly, the shooting occurs immediately following the appearance of a mysterious (Every) Man-Woman figure in the guise of a prisoner of war who speaks to John (and us) from behind a barbed wire enclosure. Like a latter-day Anglo-German Tiresias/Sybil, this cryptic figure warns us that his/her appearance is not to be interpreted as heralding "an anniversary" (presumably of the 1918 Armistice), nor should we fall into a mistaken belief that our "illness [is] healed" (EA, 9). Our illness is hereditary and incurable. It will continue to fester, for neither Father Christmas (a partly comic figure perhaps representing conventional Christianity) nor the farcically incompetent medical doctor (i.e., the plethora of so-called experts, scientific and political)—both important characters in the dream sequence—are able to provide a cure.

There is, it is clear, no escaping the doom that awaits John and, along with John, the rest of "our" generation. John shows his complete awareness of this fact when he rejects Anne's suggestion that they should escape together in a car that she has secretly kept waiting for them. As in Greek tragedy, fate must be allowed to work its inevitable way out to the very end. In that end, as the Chorus observes, "his mother and her mother won," while all the rest of us lost (EA, 17). However, the ultimate responsibility for this loss is perhaps not so much to be laid at the barricaded door of the Mothers—of Mother England and Mother Germany, as it were—, as it is on the *illness* that has infected all of our psyches, an illness that manifests itself in violence and hatred rather than in love and peace, in exclusion rather than inclusion. Ultimately, it is in the lack of true forgiveness on all our individual and collective parts and hearts, as urged by those marginalized and unheeded healers John Layard and Homer Lane, of whose doctrine Auden had first become aware in Berlin, that the root of the tragedy of twentieth-century history lies.

Layard, who was sixteen years older than Auden, had been living in Berlin since 1926, mostly in order to get treatment for a psychosomatic condition that had paralyzed him since his return from the New Hebrides in 1915. It was this mysterious illness that had originally led Layard to Homer Lane and that Lane had partly succeeded in treating before being deported from Britain in 1925 and dying in Southern France later that same year. The heart of Lane's doctrine—or his "key," as Layard called it—was *forgiveness*, that is, Christian charity, but without any moral preconditions or moralistic rigamarole. This sort of open-ended charity definitely began at home; it was necessary to start forgiving oneself as—and even before—one forgave others, by expressing (and also acting out) fully and freely whatever emotions one felt. It followed from this apparently familiar but essentially radical doctrine—Christianity, as it were, taken quite literally—that all illness ultimately derived from incomplete spiritual and emotional self-expression, or, to use the odd terminology Auden picked up from Layard and inserted cryptically into his own poetry, it came from being insufficiently "pure in heart" (Carpenter, 85–87; Bucknell, 178–80). In various psycho-sociological transformations, this ethic was to remain central to Auden's work throughout his career. One of its most unambiguous statements occurs in Auden's play *The Chase* (an early version of *The Dog Beneath the Skin*) where the Chorus urges us to

> explore every avenue of enlightenment
> For there is nothing that is not unimportant: but the final issue is always
> Between the loving and the unloving; the unforgiving and the forgiving:
> the trust and the fear.
>
> *(Plays*, 180)

Layard's exposition of these ideas was to exert a profound influence not only on Auden's work (as we shall have particular occasion to note in the next chapter), but also on his life in Berlin, allowing him especially to begin working through and resolving the guilt feelings he had experienced ever since becoming aware of his own homosexuality some years earlier at his public school. In Berlin, Auden seems to have thought for a time that he would "outgrow" his homosexuality, though the fact that not long after his return to England he broke off his engagement with Sheilah Richardson suggests that he must have changed his mind, perhaps even before he left Germany. He was throwing away the key to conventional, bourgeois life and setting forth on an uncertain, but unquestionably more exciting quest for a new sexual and artistic identity (Carpenter, 90–91). However, in a purely pragmatic sense (and thus bourgeois after all?), Auden may also have thought that homosexuality was more likely than heterosexuality to lead to significant artistic achievement. This is an argument advanced by Katherine Bucknell, who buttresses it with a long quotation from Auden's 1929 journal, part of which states that "it is not always realized by oneself that the attraction of buggery is partly its difficulty and torments. Heterosexual love seems so tame and easy after it. I feel this with Sheilah. There is something in reciprocity that is despair. How one likes to suffer. Anyway writers [? do], it is their income" (Quoted in Bucknell, 232). Notice the curious shifting in and out of active and passive constructions in this passage, suggestive of Auden's reluctance to see his own identity as being defined by the issue. In this connection, Richard Davenport-Hines points out that according to Freud the only true expression of sexuality was between men and women, a belief shared by the British social psychiatrist Trigant Burrow, whom Auden read at this time and who had argued that homosexuality was a result of "intercepted growth" (Davenport-Hines, 100). Even as late as 1947, Auden told Alan Ansen that he had "come to the conclusion that it is wrong to be queer," though he followed up this remark almost immediately with the wishful thought that "what I would really like would be a brothel where you simply go in, pay your money, and go home at a reasonable hour without any misunderstandings on either side. In Berlin I lived next door to a brothel, and I didn't have to wait until late at night" (Ansen, 17–18).

At the urging (and expense) of his parents, Auden had at an earlier date sought unsuccessfully to be "cured" of his homosexuality in Belgium, and one reason why he had chosen to come to Berlin rather than to any other European city was undoubtedly connected with his awareness that it was a place where he might meet with better success.[6] Clear evidence of a process of self-treatment is visible in the running Layardian critique of Freud conducted by Auden in the journal he intermittently kept in Berlin during the early Spring of 1929 (Bucknell, 166ff). Without, however, in any way belittling the importance of Auden's sense of guilt about his homosexuality, it does need to be stressed that he also vastly enjoyed his sexual exploits in Berlin. If nothing else, the long, Leporello-like list entitled "Boys had. Germany 1928–29" that he kept in his journal bears witness to that fact.[7]

III

The expansion and revision of *Paid on Both Sides* is certainly Auden's principal poetic achievement during his first stay in Berlin. Its focus on mental illness and on past (and future) conflicts between England and Germany is unmistakably the result of Auden's direct experience of Berlin. Compared with the poetry that Auden had been writing before he came to Berlin, the final version of *Paid on Both Sides* represents a major poetic advance in terms of its ambitious themes and complex technique. This is something that T. S. Eliot seems to have recognized at once when he agreed to publish it in *The Criterion* not long after he had rejected the manuscript of Auden's first collection of poems for Faber, a collection consisting entirely of work written before Auden had gone to Berlin. That is also why Basil Bunting, reviewing *Poems* (1930) in early 1932, immediately recognized the striking originality of *Paid on Both Sides*, arguing that it contained no "resemblance, accidental or other to any contemporary," and that in terms of its quality it was also "very much beyond" the other poems in the collection (Bunting, 270–71).

But *Paid on Both Sides* is not the only poetic consequence of Auden's Berlin stay. As Richard Davenport-Hines points out, "the great creative sequel to these months [in Berlin] is *The Orators*, which he did not begin until the spring of 1931" (Davenport-Hines, 88). In point of fact, however, some parts of what was eventually to become *The Orators* were actually written in Germany, during the 1931 holiday that Auden spent with Isherwood and Spender on the island of Rügen (David, 130). This may also be why François Duchêne sees "something of the hysteria of the death throes of the Weimar Republic in *The Orators*" (Duchêne, 73). To this statement, one might add that not just *The Orators*, but also much of the poetry that Auden wrote in the period during and immediately following his stay in Germany, is profoundly influenced by his experiences there. This applies not merely to the psychological, or Lane/Layard, dimension of his poetry, but also to the powerful, new influx of imagery and themes having to do with spies, frontiers, "enemies," and obscure conflicts. There is a nervous tension in the Berlin and post-Berlin poetry that is absent from Auden's earlier work, a tension that reveals his increasing concern with the often discordant links between the private, individual psyche and the public, social world.[8]

Eventually this tension would find its fullest and perhaps most satisfactory expression in two seriocomic plays written—partly during brief visits to Germany—in the early thirties, *The Dance of Death* and *The Dog Beneath the Skin*. But it is also at the heart of the poem he later called "1929," in which Auden attempts to gauge, as he already had in a more impersonal way in *Paid on Both Sides*, the distance between self and other, between psychology and politics, between public and private. This long, complex, partly autobiographical poem contains some unusually explicit references to Berlin and Germany that show more clearly than other work from this period how great a difference crossing the frontier from England to Germany made in Auden's life and work during this period. As Auden was to recall a year before he died, one of the two "really significant experiences" he had when he first went to Berlin in 1928 "was that I realized the world was no longer a safe place, that the foundations were shaking," and secondly that, in Germany, he had "no class status, and so could make friends with members of the working class in a way I could never have done at home" (Auden, "Saint-Simon," 5).

The first two (of four) sections of the poem were written in Germany during the spring of 1929, and have recognizably German settings; the last two date, respectively, from late summer and autumn of the same year, shortly after Auden's return home, and, while their settings are less immediately identifiable than those of the first two sections, they seem to be located, first, in a cottage in rural England (like the one owned by Auden's parents) and, later, in a mixed landscape of coastline and sanatoria, mining country and alkali-tips, culminating in a kind of fantasy countryside of "sullen valley" and "clear lake." The poem opens at Easter, with the speaker walking in the "public gardens,"—almost certainly the Berlin Tiergarten, as the following references to the speaker's German friends, Kurt Groote and Gerhart Meyer, suggest. These names belong to actual people whom Auden knew in Berlin, boys whom he had met in his favorite "male brothel," a working-class homosexual bar called the "Cosy Corner." The speaker contrasts Kurt's happiness and Gerhart's courage (he is the "truly strong man") with the evident unhappiness of an unidentified solitary man, weeping while seated on a park bench, as well as with the

> ... death by cancer of a once hated master,
> A friend's analysis of his own failure,
> Listened at intervals throughout the winter
> At different hours and in different rooms.
>
> (EA, 37)

The failed friend referred to here is evidently Auden's friend John Layard, who, like the speaker, is good at "analysis," or abstract, theoretical thought, but evidently not so good at actual living, whereas Kurt and Gerhart, though (or perhaps because) they lack analytic capacity, clearly are.[9] That is also why the latter are "truly strong": they live their lives simply and directly, rather than wasting them in useless rationalizations and self-defeating attempts to "prove" their worth to themselves and to others, as the "truly weak" do. This contrast between the "truly strong" and the "truly weak" is explained by Isherwood in *Lions and Shadows* as deriving from a case analyzed by the Swiss psychiatrist, Eugen Bleuler. In Isherwood's description, the truly weak man is always trying to measure himself according to arbitraily established "tests," whereas the truly strong man is oblivious of such matters (Isherwood, *Lions*, 207ff). Auden depicts the "truly weak man" succinctly in a short poem dating from his year in Berlin:

> Pick a quarrel, go to war,
> Leave the hero in the bar.
> Hunt the lion, climb the peak,
> No one guesses you are weak.
>
> (EA, 50)

This theme of thought versus life is also the principal focus of the second section of the poem. Like spying, thought is essentially spectatorial, a matter of watching rather than doing. The initial setting shows the speaker in the city (Berlin, though it is not named), "leaning on harbour parapet" (the River Spree, with its urban docks), observing a "colony of duck" carelessly preening and dozing below, utterly unconcerned with the speaker's existential problem that "coming out of me living is always thinking."[10] They know nothing of the "shadow" of this "homesick foreigner / Nor restlessness of intercepted growth"—the latter, a likely reference to Auden's (as well as Freud and Trigant Burrow's) idea that homosexuality is to be "analyzed" as a process of interrupted emotional maturization. There, then, follows a short verse paragraph that, for the first time anywhere in Auden's poetry, explicitly describes a contemporaneous political event:

> All this time was anxiety at night,
> Shooting and barricade in street.
> Walking home late I listened to a friend
> Talking excitedly of final war
> Of proletariat against police—
> That one shot girl of nineteen through the knees,
> They threw that one down concrete stair—
> Till I was angry, said I was pleased.
>
> (EA, 38)

In early May 1929, rioting and fighting broke out in the streets of Berlin, and public order was only restored after a number of people had been killed. In terms of the poem, the description of this scene of urban, revolutionary unrest seems to function along the same lines as did the emblematic figures of Kurt (unthinking happiness) and Gerhart (unthinking courage) in the first section. The instinctive uprising of the workers and their willingness to risk their lives are implicitly contrasted with the repressive, conscious behavior of the police, acting in behalf of a conformist bourgeoisie. Significantly, these events and the excitement communicated by the (working-class?) friend's account, bring about a sympathetic emotional response on the part of the speaker. He is no longer the completely uninvolved observer of some solitary, weeping man or indifferent ducks, or a mere listener to an analytic friend's complaints, but he is now both angry and pleased at what he has seen and heard. Thought and feeling are no longer kept in entirely separate compartments.

The latter part of the second section is set in the small town of Gutensberg in the German province of Hessia, an actual place where Auden and Isherwood, along with some of their Berlin boy friends, enjoyed a rural holiday not long before Auden returned to England in the summer of 1929. In a situation that would become almost archetypal for Auden's poetry of the 1930s, the speaker is described as looking down on the idyllic town from a lofty hilltop observation point, while reflecting on his own inadequate place in nature and society. He regrets his inability to translate theory into practice. In lines that seem to echo Joan's lullaby/lament in *Paid on Both Sides*, he is able to utter the right Layard/Lanean mantras, but he cannot experience them emotionally:

> He say [sic] "We must forgive and forget",
> Forgetting saying but is unforgiving
> And unforgiving is in his living;[11]
>
> (EA, 38)

Still, even for the thought-ridden intellectual, there can be moments of respite. A sudden flow of quasi-Wordsworthian joy invades him, despite the recognition of his inability to permanently fuse thought and emotion:

> In me so absolute unity of evening
> And field and distance was in me for peace,
> Was over me in feeling without forgetting
> Those ducks' indifference, that friend's hysteria,
> Without wishing and with forgiving . . .
>
> (EA, 38–39)

But the moment quickly passes, and a final realization occurs that such glimpses of unity cannot represent an enduring solution to his existential problem: " 'Cannot', I said, 'being no child now nor bird'." (The curious syntactical and grammatical aspects of the language of this section of the poem may be intended to reflect Auden's sense of alienation while living in a non–English-language environment, or, conversely, they may represent, as in *The Dance of Death*, Auden's version of what speaking and thinking in German "feels like" to a native English speaker.)

The third section postulates, among other things, a possible future for the speaker's "frightened soul," vainly seeking refuge in a return "home." Realizing, as in the previous section, that there is no simple solution to his problematic dissociation of sensibility, he hopes for a cure for this characteristically modern and metropolitan illness through a gradual semi-evolutionary process, an idea already broached in *Paid on Both Sides* in the memorable chorus, "To throw away the key and walk away" (EA, 12). Interestingly, in this instance, the process is described in a way that evokes the experience of strangers entering a new country, that is, of something analogous to Auden's own experience when he first went to Berlin:

> And as foreign settlers to strange country come,
> By mispronunciation of native words
> And by intermarriage create a new race
> And a new language, so may the soul
> Be weaned at last to independent delight.
>
> (EA, 39)

One is reminded in this connection of Auden's grammatically and idiomatically flawed efforts, described by Isherwood in "Some Notes on Auden's Early Poetry," (1937) to write poetry in German not long after his arrival in Berlin. When Isherwood showed these poems to a knowledgeable German critic (unnamed, but perhaps Ernst Curtius), the latter remarked that it was apparent that they had been composed by "a poet of the first rank" (Isherwood, *Exhumations,* 21).[12]

The evolutionary process described by the speaker requires, however—as does Darwinian evolution, for that matter—the extinction of former selves in order to allow for the (re)birth of new ones. The speaker's account leaves it ambiguous as to whether this process is meant to be read as wholly metaphorical or if it involves an element of real death and rebirth. (Here Auden anticipates a major theme of *The Orators.*) There can be no doubt about its relevance to the central meaning of the poem, however, for the process is structurally embedded in the pattern of seasonal imagery represented in each of the four sections of the poem; and it is also unmistakable in the reference to Easter in the first line of the poem. Just as spring brings the world to new life, so winter brings death; and the Easter season commemorates not only Christ's crucifixion but, also, His resurrection.

The fourth and final section of the poem recapitulates a number of themes broached in the preceding three parts, with the opening line ("It is time for the destruction of error") promising a kind of revolutionary harrowing of a psychic (and perhaps also social) hell anticipated by the rising of the proletariat against the police. An apocalyptic "dragon's day" is now dawning and the worried bourgeois "enemy" will respond by seeking

> to enforce
> Conformity with the orthodox bone,
> With organized fear, the articulated skeleton.
>
> (EA, 40)

The enemy, however, cannot be vanquished simply by confronting him with the combined forces of life and love. As in *Paid on Both Sides*, individual love is not powerful enough to combat the powers of collective hatred. Addressing an unnamed beloved (possibly Christopher Isherwood), the speaker reminds him that

> we know that love
> Needs more than the admiring excitement of union[. . .]
> Needs death, death of the grain, our death,
> Death of the old gang[. . .]
>
> (EA, 40)

Paradoxically, as the Bible tells us, the grain must first die if it is to be reborn and live; and the enemy, we are made to realize once again, is also ourselves. The enemy is not merely external, but also within—a psychological enemy as well as a social one, compelling psychological uniformity along with social conformity. Still, there is now a hope of victory over this foe, whereas in *Paid on Both Sides*, there was none. The old gang (and the old ganglia) will be "forgotten in the spring," to be replaced by the Christlike "lolling bridegroom, beautiful," whose resurrection awaits us (or, at any rate, our future selves) "deep in clear lake," bringing with him the promise of rebirth and salvation.[13]

IV

A generation ago, Joseph Warren Beach sought to characterize the development of English poetry between the wars by noting the persistent recurrence of certain *topoi*, a feature for which he coined the phrase—also, the title of his book—"obsessive images" (1960). Although Beach was among the first thoroughgoing, (but by no means entirely sympathetic), academic critics of Auden's work, he does not include Auden's spies among those obsessions, nor does he deal with them in his slightly earlier critical study of Auden's poetry, *The Making of the Auden Canon* (1957).[14] This omission was, however, remedied not long afterwards by Monroe K. Spears, who observed that, among "the dominant images (one could say 'myths') and ideas" of *Poems* (1933)—that is, Beach's "obsessive images" by another name—there is "the Spy, the Secret Agent." At this stage in Auden's development, Spears maintains, the Spy is still primarily a symbolic representation of a war within the psyche, but there are already hints that he is also participating in an actual external, social conflict (Spears, 34).

Though Beach fails to see the significance of Auden's spies, he does clearly recognize how prominent the frontier motif is in Auden's early poetry as well as, less persuasively, in the poetry of other modern writers, arguing that it is chiefly "ideological and ethical," but he throws up his hands at trying to make anything more specific of it (Beach, 194). To be sure, Beach is aware that Auden's "riddling style" with its "dark hints of danger and disguise familiar to the departments of 'intelligence' and counterespionage—as well as the presumably serious undercurrent of 'ideological' thinking—must have been a main point of appeal to the reading world in all the early poetry of Auden" (Beach, 221). From this, it seems clear that, for Beach, Auden's spies were part of the playful surface of his poetry, whereas his ideology was part of its depths. Similarly, according to Stephen Spender, Auden's preoccupation with frontiers was primarily the result of deep, personal concerns: "His early poems contain images of barriers, impassable frontiers, broken bridges, which seem to express his feelings of personal isolation, but in impersonal guise." (Spender, DNB, 24). Still, even if Spender sees Auden's frontiers as exclusively psychic phenomena, and Beach hardly touches on Auden's obsession with spies and discusses his preoccupation with frontiers only rudimentarily, the latter's general notion of obsessive images remains useful in helping to isolate an important aspect of the early Auden's poetry, which clearly has links, as Beach's phrase implies, with the individual and, more tentatively, with the social psyche. For, of course, Auden's spies are not "just spies." Though they undoubtedly originate primarily in the formula spy stories published in the once vastly popular Boys' Weeklies, usually featuring villainous German spies, they tend to have more in common with conflicts inside than outside the self. Introspection, as Auden's Airman noted, really *is* spying.[15]

Part of this "inner" dimension of espionage in Auden's early work is broadly hinted at in the circumstance that, generally speaking, the spying goes on within the same country. Unlike the formula spy stories and, no doubt, contrary even to the expectations of his younger and more sophisticated audience, enemy and friend alike are almost invariably British. This fact makes telling enemy and friend apart difficult and confusing both for Auden's characters and for his readers, though there is never much doubt that, in a general way, the "enemy" is identical with the established institutions of bourgeois society, such as the public schools and the nuclear family, especially when centered on a dominant mother.[16] That is why much of *The Orators* is devoted to attempts at defining these differences in a variety of ways, and at different levels of meaning. In order to escape the machinations of the enemy, we first need to be able to recognize the characteristics of that enemy but, at the same time, without alerting her to the fact that this is what we are doing. Reading *The Orators*, therefore, is rather like trying to cope with a complex message written in a cypher that is at once familiar and impenetrable.

The "frontier" in this sense is the line separating "us" from "them." This line can be drawn nationally and generationally, as is it in *Paid on Both Sides*; or socially, but more in terms of bourgeois vs. antibourgeois rather than of bourgeois vs. working class, as it is in Auden's post-Berlin poetry; or sexually, but in terms of straight vs. gay, rather than of men vs. women, as in *The Orators*. As we will see in greater detail in the following chapter, an essential part of the message hidden in the code of *The Orators* is the central role of homosexuality. Read in this way, crossing the frontier means (and, for Auden quite specifically meant) recognizing who one was in a sexual sense. Thus, it was only after his stay in Berlin that he finally decided to break off his engagement with Sheilah Richardson and become reconciled to his homosexual identity. Almost inevitably, therefore, being homosexual meant being a spy, for, like a spy, the homosexual had to continually pretend to be someone he was not. Or like Francis in *The Dog Beneath the Skin*, he had to don the disguise of the despised dog if he was to pass unnoticed and unmolested in normal society. But, like Francis again, once he dropped that disguise and revealed his true self, it became possible for him to work openly, as Francis puts it, to bring about the destruction of "a social system in which love is controlled by money," meaning, that is, heterosexual bourgeois society and morality (Auden and Isherwood, *Plays*, 287).

The spy is not merely divided in his relation to the world outside himself, the public world; he is also divided in his relation to his inner, private world, a division that, for the early Auden, is often deeper and more important than outward or public differences. As the epigraph to *The Orators* memorably puts it: "Private faces in public places / Are wiser and nicer / Than public faces in private places" (EA, [59]). Since the primary frontier at this point in Auden's poetic thinking tends to be psychic rather than social, the central irony of Alan Norman's lengthy quest in *The Dog Beneath the Skin* consists in the fact that the answer has been staring him in the face all along. The final frontier, as it were, is the frontier running down the middle of the divided self. Crossing that frontier means destroying the old, fragmented self, and reconstituting it into a newly integrated one. It means being psychologically reborn. That doing so is not easy (and sometimes even impossible) is suggested by a poem written in November, 1929—not long after Auden's return from Germany—where the reader is told that she should not "imagine you can abdicate / Before you reach the frontier you are caught" (EA, 45). To have any hope at all of crossing the frontier involves recognizing first that the enemy is not primarily an external force, but an internal one. Or, as the Airman puts it, "the only efficient way" to destroy the power of the enemy is "self-destruction, the sacrifice of all resistance, reducing him to the state of a man trying to walk on a frictionless surface"(EA 93). That this advice also contains unmistakable Christian overtones is surely not accidental. The cross in "crossing" is simply too obvious to miss.

What is the point of such apparent orthodoxy? Not, I think, to propagandize for institutional Christianity, but rather to show the striking proximity of unconventional psychological theory, especially that of Homer Lane, to conventional religious doctrine. (The original meaning of the word *psyche*, as Auden knew very well, is "soul.") For, although the young Auden's public commitment to conventional Christianity was minimal, the Airman's "conversion" is profoundly suggestive of those continuing, if perhaps only partly conscious, religious concerns that eventually led Auden to return to the faith of his childhood. That some of his friends overtly identified Auden with his Airman and anticipated a "change" in him is clear from Day-Lewis's famous exhortation to "Look west, Wystan, lone flyer, birdman, my bully boy! . . .

Gain altitude, Auden.... Migrate, chaste my kestrel, you need a change of air" (Day-Lewis, *Collected*, 128). As in "Petition," one of the best-known of Auden's early poems, the Christian practices of prayer and confession are implicitly seen as closely resembling the kind of practical help provided by psychiatric healers living, as did John Layard and Homer Lane, not in heaven or in vicarages, but in cities or "country houses at the end of drives" (EA, 36).

The Airman's climactic epiphany is poetically summarized in the enigmatic and justly celebrated "Epilogue" to *The Orators* (later called "The Three Companions"), in which a succession of three stanzas featuring three passive, fearful questioners is answered consecutively and concisely in the final stanza by three active, courageous questers:

> "O where are you going?" said reader to rider.
> "That valley is fatal where furnaces burn,
> Yonder's the midden whose odours will madden,
> That gap is the grave where the tall return."
>
> "O do you imagine," said fearer to farer,
> "That dusk will delay on your path to the pass,
> Your diligent looking discover the lacking
> Your footsteps feel from granite to grass?"
>
> "O what is that bird," said horror to hearer,
> "Did you see that shape in the twisted trees?
> Behind you swiftly the figure comes softly,
> The spot on your skin is a shocking disease?"
>
> "Out of this house"—said rider to reader
> "Yours never will"—said farer to fearer
> "They're looking for you"—said hearer to horror
> As he left them there, as he left them there.
>
> (EA, 110)

That the multiple passive voices here are, in fact, identical with the active ones—while at the same time, remaining radically distinct—becomes clear through their nearly complete homophony (reader/rider; fearer/farer; hearer/horror). The difference is only slight, but it is precisely this apparently insignificant—though in fact, crucial—difference that must be bridged. The frontier dividing the opposing selves is very small, yet immensely difficult to cross. Still, it can and must be crossed, as the insistent repetition of the final half-line makes clear: "As he left them there, as he left them there." Plural number is now magically transformed into singular number, as the kinetic will overcomes the static conscience, and the unknown enemy is recognized as being nothing more than the familiar divided self. It is evident, too, that a successful integration of the total personality, symbolized here by the process of a multiple "they" turning into a unique "he," is only possible if the courageous quester resolutely suppresses his fears and self-doubts—his opposing selves, in other words. In the end, then, while the result may not be grammatically right, from a psychological point of view, it is the only possible resolution. Indeed, the capacity for superseding the conventional approaches to communication embodied in fixed grammatical structures may be a necessary condition for achieving wholeness.

V

What dire consequences may follow the failure to integrate the self is the subject of another of Auden's best-known early poems, "O What Is That Sound Which So Thrills the Ear" (October 1932), to which he later gave the title "The Quarry." Here, a single fearful questioner describes his reactions to the answers he receives from a single interlocutor as he listens to the threatening sound of marching feet drawing ever nearer, ever more quickly. In the concluding stanza, the soldiers break down the door and turn, with "burning" eyes, to attack the now helpless and abandoned speaker—abandoned because, just before the soldiers arrive, his respondent departs:

> O where are you going? stay with me here!
>   Were the vows you swore me deceiving, deceiving?
> No, I promised to love you, dear,
>   But I must be leaving.
>
> (EA, 126)

The opening words of this stanza echo precisely, and no doubt deliberately, the opening question of the epilogue to *The Orators*. Here, too, the respondent acknowledges his intimate links to the questioner; that is, in psychological terms, he affirms his identity with him (an identity also suggested by failing to distinguish between the two speakers by not using quotation marks); and again the "hearer" shows no compunction whatsoever about leaving the "horror" behind. That Auden probably meant this poem, like the "Epilogue" to *The Orators*, to be read, at least in part, as a kind of psychological case study is evident from his use of the poem in his Freud lecture of 12 March 1971 (Fuller, *Commentary*, 154–55). Unlike "Epilogue," however, now the questioner's fate seems rather grimmer than that of the three questioners in the earlier poem. Here they (or is it merely "he"?) are not merely left behind to stew in the vague juices of their fear and reluctance to act, but now that fear assumes concrete shape and threatens to annihilate the passive questioner:

> O it's broken the lock and splintered the door,
> O it's the gate where they're turning, turning;
> Their feet are heavy on the floor
> And their eyes are burning.

(EA, 126)

This added difference is, I think, due primarily to the fact that in this poem, unlike the "Epilogue," the enemy within is not sought out actively but is simply denied under cover of the false security provided by conventional (heterosexual?) love. Such mistaken faith in the power of a merely external love, we again seem meant to conclude, is not only no adequate protection, but actually works in collusion with the enemy, turning him into a kind of spy who knowingly sees and even foresees what is about to happen and who does nothing to stop it. Integration of personality, in other words, requires confrontation of the spy/enemy within the self. That is the lesson. Hence, the striking frequency of exhortations at the close of poems from Auden's early period to undergo a "change of heart" (EA 36), to realize that "it is time for the destruction of error" (EA 40), to "Shut up talking, charming in the best suits to be had in town, / Lecturing on navigation while the ship is going down" (EA 49).

"The Quarry" was written exactly a year after Auden had finished *The Orators*. In the intervening period, the deepening economic crisis at home and abroad—along with the increasing threat of Hitlerism—had led Auden, along with many of his friends, to become convinced that the enemy was not only a psychological but also a social enemy, not just an enemy within, but a very real and threatening external force. No longer were the soldiers with their burning eyes only sinister agents of the immense Army of the Super Ego, led by a malignant general looking remarkably like one's mother. Now these same soldiers were also seen to be waging a war in behalf of a monstrously inequitable economic and social system. That is not to say that psychological considerations suddenly ceased to matter for Auden, or that social considerations had been utterly irrelevant before. It was merely that a new, perhaps even more urgent and demanding truth had now been added to the old. The problem for this new, Marxisizing Auden—though he rarely mentioned Marx by name in his poetry or plays—was that psychology unaided by sociology was not enough, that an integration of the divided inner self had come to seem increasingly earned at the expense of preserving a diseased society. In the words of Auden's most extended prose analysis of this subject at the time, "Psychology and Art Today" (1935), the problem was that psychology sought to "adapt the neurotic to the system, thus depriving the [socialist] of a potential revolutionary" (*Prose*, 103). That is to say, by adjusting the neurotic individual to a neurotic group, psychology was obstructing, or at least delaying, a necessary social upheaval that might lead to a restoration of social health. Therefore, only once such an upheaval had taken place would it be possible for psychology to help bring about a genuine change of heart. Curing society would now take precedence over curing individuals.

How closely Auden's early verse plays already adhered to aspects of Marxist aesthetic doctrine is evident even in some of the formal choices he made. This is especially true of his striking use of the chorus, a dramatic device that is prominent both in *Paid on Both Sides* and in *The Dance of Death*. The latter play (or *masque*, as Auden called it) was written in 1932/33 for his friends Robert Medley and Rupert Doone of the Group Theatre; it was also dedicated to them. Admittedly, to some degree, the young Auden's use of the chorus is related to his general enthusiasm for putting his poetry into premodern contexts and forms, for example, the plethora of Anglo-Saxon influences and usages, which are intended apparently to suggest the deep sociopsychological origins of contemporary Britain's problems. In part, however, his use of the chorus harks back not to Greek models but forward to Marxist ones. For, as Arthur Koestler points out, in the Berlin that Auden encountered in 1928, "the highest form of music was the choral song because it represented a collective, as opposed to the individualistic approach. The same argument led to a sudden and unexpected revival of the Greek chorus in the Communist *avant-garde* plays of the 'twenties. Since individual characters could not be banished altogether from the stage, they had to be stylised, typified, depersonalised" (Koestler, *Invisible*, 34).

The Dance of Death is actually one of the rare instances in Auden's creative work where Marxism is explicitly proposed as an answer to society's problems. Not only does Karl Marx himself put in a cameo appearance at the close of the play, proclaiming that "the instruments of production have been too much for him [i.e., the Dancer, emblematic of the middle class]. He is liquidated," but the message is made unmistakably clear when the Announcer opens the play with the observation that "We present to you this evening a picture of the decline of a class." While vainly dreaming of a "new life," this moribund middle class, in fact, as the Announcer puts it, "secretly desire[s] the old [life], for there is death inside them. We show you that death as a dancer" (*Plays*, 107). Once again, the old gang—namely ourselves and our *selves*—has to be destroyed first if we are to be reborn and "saved."

And once again, as in *Paid on Both Sides*, Auden's message seems almost more of a *mess*age, that is, it is apparently mixed up with an assortment of extraneous material, such as the first long Chorus repeatedly urging people to "come out into the sun" (*Plays*, 83). In fact, however, the masque presents a coherent allegory of the projected demise of the bourgeoisie.[17] So, the middle class (Dancer and Chorus) are initially represented as dressed only in bathing suits. Their nakedness is to be understood not merely in terms of the fashionable sun-worship of the period (a fashion mostly practiced in or imported from Germany), but it is also symbolic of their vulnerable and unprotected condition. Lest we miss the point, the Announcer explicitly makes the connection after the Dancer hides their clothes in a basket, thereby depriving them of "their social defences." Once the theft is discovered and the basket returned, it turns out that the clothes inside have been replaced by uniforms (*Plays*, 86, 88). The middle class, in other words, is being manipulated into a new war. Both the Audience (i.e., the masses) and the Chorus immediately grasp what is going on and call for revolutionary action, repeatedly shouting "Red Front," the traditional call for solidarity among German Communists. A member of the Audience urges the "workers [to] unite before it's too late," and the entire Audience as a group responds with a chant that is prophetic of the Vietnam War protests a generation later:

> One, two, three, four
> The last war was a bosses' war.
> Five, six, seven, eight
> Rise and make a workers' state.
> Nine, ten, eleven, twelve
> Seize the factories and run them yourself.
>
> (*Plays*, 90)

Their laudable revolutionary zeal is, however, quickly diverted into different channels when the Announcer, making himself out to be one of them and addressing them as "Comrades," tells them that they must not imitate the Soviet Russian revolutionary model, but work instead for a natively "English revolution suited to English conditions, a revolution not to put one class on top but to abolish class." That this diversion is actually a fascist ploy becomes apparent (if it hasn't already) when the Announcer persuades both Audience and Chorus that "the Anglo-Saxon race is in danger" and provokes them to assault the Manager for being "a dirty Jew" (*Plays*, 90–91). The Announcer then assumes command of the English Ship of State (represented on stage by actors in "ship formation"), with the Chorus serving as willing and gullible crew:

> We are all of one blood, we are thoroughbred,
> We'll not lose our courage, we'd sooner be dead.
> Like one big family we're all united
> In our hearts burns a fire that has long been lighted.
>
> (*Plays*, 92)

Instead of reaching the "Promised Land," however, the Ship of State is battered in a storm and founders. Simultaneously, the whirling Dancer collapses in an epileptic fit. His death is only postponed when a representative of the upper class, Sir Edward, insists that he be revived with an injection, that is—to make the allegory unmistakably explicit—by "pump[ing] in fresh capital" (*Plays*, 95). He is then allowed to die, but only after Auden provides us with a versified review of world history in Marxist dialectical terms and after various possible alternatives (specifically, futile escapes into the countryside or into sexuality, as in *Paid on Both Sides*) are rejected.

How closely *The Dance of Death* approximates Auden's experience in Germany is apparent not only in the obviously Brechtian (and political cabaret) devices of Announcer/Commentator, audience participation, dance revues, and jazz music. It is evident also in the language itself. For example, the Manager shifts in and out of heavily accented English, saying things like "Vy make so a trobble in my theatre" and "Gut [German for 'good'], then everything ends" (*Plays*, 88–89). Even more unusual and striking are the exchanges among actors on stage and Audience that consist of literal translations from the German. (These are no doubt the "German addictions" that Auden later complained about.) Take, for instance, the following dialogue:

> B. Day, my sir.
> C. Day, my sir. How goes it thee?
> D. Thou seest dreadful out—
>   Thou hast thyself too well amused, not true?
>   No, swindle not.
> B. Hast a cigarette for me?
> A [*distributing cigarettes for DANCER by throwing them from a box.*] Catch.
> B. I thank.
> A. Thee also.
> C. I thank.
> D. Forget me not, my sire, I thank.
>   (*Plays*, 103–4)

The curious phrasing of this dialogue only makes sense if one knows German:

B. Tag, mein Herr.
   C. Tag, mein Herr. Wie geht es Dir?
   D. Du schaust schrecklich aus—
       Du hast Dich zu gut amüsiert, nicht wahr?
       Nein, schwindle nicht.
   B. Hast eine Zigarette für mich?
   A [*distributing cigarettes for DANCER by throwing them from a box.*] Fang.
   B. Ich danke.
   A. Dir auch.
   C. Vergiß mich nicht, mein Herr. Ich danke.
       [my translation]

A subsequent scene depicting a New Year celebration is also unmistakably influenced by German usage, with the waiter being asked to "send round the boot," that is, to pass around the traditional glass champagne receptacle made in the shape of a boot.[18]

The point of all this (aside from sounding and even being funny) seems to be that the Germans and the English are to be viewed as being indistinguishable from a social(ist) point of view. They face the same problems— economic collapse; a helpless middle class; the threat of fascism—and they are offered the same solution, namely Communist Revolution. And both are warned of the danger of substituting an "inner" or psychological revolution for a "real" or external one, as in the following ironic passage:

> Revolutionary worker
> I get what you mean.
> But what you're needing
> 'S a revolution within
> So let's begin.

(*Plays*, 97–98)

It is Karl Marx, after all, who appears as the *deus ex machina* at the end of *The Dance of Death*, not Sigmund Freud—or John Layard or Homer Lane, for that matter.[19]

Still, as Auden concluded in "Psychology and Art Today," "both are right" (*Prose*, 103). And, despite the egregious example of *The Dance of Death*, that is, generally speaking, how most of his poems and plays dating from approximately 1932 until 1938 or 1939 deal with the relation between individual psychological and collective social problems. But the choice is never clear-cut. The existence of two, quite distinct, endings for *The Dog Beneath the Skin* is symptomatic of Auden's (and Isherwood's) uncertainty. In the first version, Francis's last long speech to the village leaders suggests that his years of spying on them in the disguise of a dog (while keeping a meticulous journal, apparently much like that of the Airman) may have been primarily due, as he now recognizes, to a psychological problem of his own. "Hadn't it all been just a romantic escape . . ." he asks rhetorically. "Wasn't it life itself I was afraid of, hiding in my dog-skin?" The real problem, he discovers, does not lie in his psyche but in his society, not in the private world but in the public. "You are significant," he tells the villagers in conclusion, "but not in the way I used to imagine. You are units in an immense army: most of you will die without ever knowing what your leaders are really fighting for or even that you are fighting at all. Well, I am going to be a unit in the army of the other side. . ." (*Plays*, 582). Francis's peroration inspires five of the younger villagers to join him and his friend Alan in their quest to become units in the opposing army. The enemies have been clearly distinguished, though not as yet extinguished, and the play closes as the little band of heroes—anything but "units" really—winds its solitary way towards the (by now almost inevitably symbolic) frontier.[20]

In the other version—essentially identical with the one that was actually performed by the Group Theatre—Francis's last speech has a quite different emphasis. Here, Francis, after shedding his dog-skin, repeats his charge that the upper crust of villagers are "just units in an immense army," but now he omits all mention of the existence of an opposing army. Instead, he disclaims any intention of imposing action on them, desiring only to "show you what you are doing and so force you to choose" (*Plays*, 286). Choice is what is most important here, "choice is what you are all afraid of." It is this fear of choosing a new life that makes the villagers "unpleasant" and that leads to even more unpleasant social consequences, such as the desire for dictators. The root cause of this behavior seems, therefore, to be psychological rather than social, though the primary enemy is still their own selves. "You are fighting your own nature," Francis says in conclusion, sounding very much like a younger version of Homer Lane, "which is to learn and to choose. Fear of growth is making you ill."

A striking individual instance of this pathogenetic fear is Mildred Luce, who suffers from the delusion that the Germans killed her two sons during the First World War. Francis, who had spied on her during his dog days, knows that she never had any sons and proceeds to make this knowledge public. Oddly enough, however, he specifically repudiates any straightforward psychoanalytic explanation of her behavior. "A doctor would say you hate the Germans because you dare not hate your mother," he tells her, "and he would be mistaken. It is foolish and neurotic to hate anybody. What you really hate is a social system in which love is controlled by money. Won't you help us to destroy it?" (*Plays*, 287). Mildred answers this essentially

Christian request by killing Francis, much as official, bourgeois England had killed Homer Lane a decade earlier.[21]

As these two quite different endings illustrate, Auden and Isherwood had difficulty making up their minds as to what, in the memorable words of *The Orators*, was wrong with England, "this country where nobody is well" (EA 62). The first version clearly leans towards a primarily social/socialistic diagnosis in which the individual psyche plays almost no role and only vast, impersonal and perhaps even ignorant armies of revolutionaries or counter-revolutionaries clash by night. In the second version, on the other hand, the individual psyche matters a great deal, and individuals like Francis or Mildred can alter social life for better or worse. Even in terms of large social issues affecting the development of entire countries, it is ultimately the collective psyche rather than collective class consciousness (or interest) that produces a social order that is not so much unjust as it is diseased. The primary aim, therefore, is not to change the economic relations of society by means of group action, but to bring about a prior change in the collective psyche, which will then lead to a change in social behavior. Like the earlier, more psychological Auden, the socialist Auden of this period still retains a residual belief in the efficacy of a change of heart. The chief difference now is that such change must take place in the group rather than in the individual. The agent for change in either case, however, remains the secret agent; but now, instead of being an airman, he is a dog, and, instead of providing the psychological overview of the hawk or the helmeted airman, he provides an underdog's perspective on the unsightly, overfed belly of the ruling class.

VI

Auden's use of spies to illustrate psychological and social problems is virtually unique in the poetry of the 1930s.[22] A few other examples do exist, but these tend to be more or less direct imitations of Auden, written by close friends like Cecil Day-Lewis or Stephen Spender. So, the conclusion of Spender's long poem, *Vienna* (1934), gives greeting to, among others, "Those burrowing beneath frontier, shot as spies because / Sensitive to new contours . . ." (Spender, *Vienna*, 42); and in "Looking Within" (1934) John Lehmann has "sentries take their aim / Lynx-eyed along the frontier, at the stations, / Before they post you *Traitor* on the walls / Plant spies in ports . . ." (Lehmann, *Noise*, 21). The image of the spy, then, does seem to be obsessive, but—pace Joseph Warren Beach—mostly for Auden rather than for anyone else. The case is a little different when it comes to prose. Certainly Isherwood's novel, *All the Conspirators* (1928), makes use of a framework that shows family life consisting of two camps of enemies (the older and the younger generations) who interact chiefly by carrying out raids across generational frontiers, replete with family equivalents of imprisonment, interrogation, treason, and spying. The same is true of at least the first of Isherwood's two novels about Berlin during the Weimar period, *Mr. Norris Changes Trains* (1935), where Norris, as we have seen, turns out to be a spy, and Isherwood's fictional alter-ego even engages in some embarrassed spying of his own. That none of this shocked Auden any more than it did Isherwood is evident from the little poem he wrote in "honor" of Gerald Hamilton (a.k.a. Mr. Norris) in Brussels in 1936:

> So it's you I now raise my glass to,
> Though I haven't the faintest idea
> Of what in hell you are up to
> Or why in God's name you are here.
>
> (Quoted in Cockburn, 188)

In the first and most celebrated installment of his autobiography, *Lions and Shadows* (1938), Isherwood also acknowledges that what he hoped to achieve in his fictional work was "to learn how to spy . . . unnoticed" on his fellow countrymen, and that therefore, rather like Francis in *Dog Beneath the Skin*, "my problem is how to perfect a disguise" (Isherwood, *Lions*, 248). In a broader figurative sense, the task of the novelist has often been compared to that of the spy, as for instance, by Jacques Barzun: "The novel is dedicated to subversion; the novelist is a spy in enemy country" (Barzun, 169–70). This is true of all sorts of fiction, as Barzun points out, from *Gil Blas* to the novels of Henry James, but it is perhaps not too much to say that it is even more true than usual of the fiction of the thirties. So, for example, the narrator of Orwell's *Down and Out in Paris and London* (1933) is clearly a bourgeois spy crossing the class frontier in disguise and sending back detailed accounts of his experiences. Flory in *Burmese Days* (1934) becomes a kind of double-agent for the colonized against the colonials, reporting secretly from the heart of the enemy's camp at the Club. Elizabeth Bowen's Portia in *Death of the Heart* (1938) similarly feels herself to be—and is perceived by most of the other characters as being—a spy in their midst, keeping track of the enemy's activities in her journal.

The decade of the 1930s is, of course, a period during which spy or thriller fiction flourished as never before. There are obvious historical reasons for this. As the decade wore down, there was an increasing sense of impending doom, as war, revolution, and/or economic disaster seemed to be drawing ever closer in direct relation to the speed with which Hitler and the depression gained ground. Significantly, however, a small but qualitatively high proportion of the mass production of espionage fiction during this period represented a radical departure from the previous norm. Most notably, and for the first time, the spy-protagonist was no longer invariably and predictably the agent of patriotic and upper-class interests. Both Graham Greene and, a little later, Eric Ambler, began to introduce into their novels sympathetic, if not always successful, spies working in behalf of progressive, left-wing forces. It is interesting to note, however, that both of these prose writers were anticipated by Auden's unconventional, poetical, underdog spies.

The decade was also notoriously a period when real spies flourished as never before. Some of these spies included well-known writers: Graham Greene, for example, briefly worked as a spy for the German Secret Service during the early 1920s and was later to spend part of the Second World War in Africa working for British Military Intelligence. (He is also rumored to have offered his services at various times to other, more or less respectable, left-wing governments.) Christopher Isherwood probably did a little amateur spying for his sometime friend, Gerald Hamilton, and Auden himself is said to have remarked that "if he had been more clever, he would have been a criminal or a spy" (Sinclair, 42).

The thirties' penchant for literary spying may seem more shocking now than it did then, for there were illustrious precedents. Only a few years earlier W. Somerset Maugham and Compton Mackenzie had both revealed in print their extensive wartime intelligence work for the British Government. And there were to be illustrious successors, too, including Malcolm Muggeridge, Ian Fleming, John LeCarré and Len Deighton (Masters, 38). Some of Auden's best friends were spies. Aside from Isherwood, there was Tom Driberg, with whom Auden had been intimate since 1926. Driberg spied intermittently for (and possibly also against) both British Military Intelligence and the Communist Party of Great Britain (P. Wright, 361). According to Isherwood, Stephen Spender's "adventures as an amateur intelligence agent, snooping around Gibraltar and Tangiers [during the Spanish Civil War], would make a great satirical novel, and I often beg him to write it" (Isherwood, *Exhumations*, 59). Though not a close friend like Driberg or Spender, Auden knew Malcolm Muggeridge well enough to be on first name terms with him, and he was probably aware that the latter was employed by the British Secret Service. Most ominously, Auden was close to at least two of the four (or was it really five?) notorious Cambridge Spies. Not long after meeting Anthony Blunt through his friend and literary collaborator, Louis MacNeice, he stayed in Blunt's apartment in November 1936. (This was at roughly the same time that Bertolt Brecht wrote Auden a letter in which he addressed him as "Comrade Auden.") According to Andrew Boyle, another one of the

Cambridge spies, Donald Maclean, attended Gresham's, Auden's public school, and Auden's name "often cropped up conversationally in the hearing of Maclean and [James] Klugman" (Boyle, 52–53). Guy Burgess, probably the most notorious of the Cambridge spies, had visited Isherwood and Auden in Berlin during the early thirties, and perhaps the last thing Burgess did before departing clandestinely for the Soviet Union at the end of May 1951 was to try several several times, without success, to reach Auden by telephone. He was planning to visit Auden at the latter's summer home in Ischia, where he apparently hoped to escape the attentions of his pursuers (Hamilton, *Way*, 40–41; Carpenter, 368–69; Mitgang, 173–76).

Auden was even married to a spy. In 1936, Auden had agreed to marry Erika Mann, the gifted daughter of Thomas Mann, in order to provide her with a British passport and thereby assure her immunity from Nazi harrassment. He liked getting married so much that he urged his homosexual friends to do the same for other German women. (" 'What are buggers for?' " he inquired humorously and a little ironically.) Auden and Erika Mann, of course, never lived together as man and wife, but he did develop an affection and friendship for her, something that probably came easily because he was already acquainted with her homosexual older brother, Klaus, and would later become friendly with a younger brother, Golo. In 1936, Auden dedicated *Look, Stranger!* to Erika Mann, with the following prefatory lines: "Since the external disorder, and extravagant lies, / The baroque frontiers, the surrealist police; / What can truth treasure, or heart bless, / But a narrow strictness?" (EA, [111]) The apparently odd conjunction of Erika Mann, truth, heart, and a narrow strictness (as opposed to a heartless and truthless Nazi frontier and their mad police) suggests that Auden is here announcing for the first time that preference for truth over art that would characterize virtually all of his aesthetic pronouncements during the late thirties and early forties. During the Second World War, Auden saw Erika occasionally in New York and in Princeton, where his father-in-law, Thomas Mann, resided for a time. As for Erika, though she was lesbian and as little interested in a sexual relationship with Auden as he was with her, she referred to him repeatedly in her correspondence as "my husband" (Erika Mann, 92). In the early summer of 1940, Erika voluntarily contacted the FBI, offering to provide them with information about other German exiles living in the United States. This she continued to do until well after the end of the war, though probably without knowing that the FBI was also keeping tabs on her brother Klaus. They were convinced that he had been, as his file put it, an "active agent for Stalin in Paris for many years" (Stephan, 174; 156 n).

In the immediate postwar period, Auden continued to associate with spies, or, at any rate, with one very notable ex-spy. This was Norman Holmes Pearson, Professor of English at Yale, with whom Auden coedited the multivolume *Poets of the English Language* (1950). Pearson had been the wartime head of American counterintelligence in Britain, and had recruited at least three promising young Yale graduate students for the Office of Strategic Services: Reed Whittemore, Richard Ellmann and J. J. Angleton. The last named eventually became one of the most influential heads of the C.I.A. Pearson was widely known as "the father of American counterintelligence." (Weinberger, 51–52).[23] It may also very well be Pearson whom Auden had in mind when in his 1946 Harvard Phi Beta Kappa poem, "Under Which Lyre," he recounts how

> Professors back from secret missions
> Resume their proper eruditions,
>   Though some regret it;
> They liked their dictaphones a lot,
> They met some big wheels, and do not
>   Let you forget it.

(CP, 260)

On the other hand, Auden may actually be thinking of himself. For in March 1945, Auden had left his teaching position at Swarthmore in order to take up duty with the Morale Division of the U.S. Strategic Bombing Survey. His job was to interview German civilians in order to discover what impact the intensive bombing of German cities had had on their morale. In effect, he was doing a kind of low-level spying. Auden was fully aware of the peculiar situation he found himself in. Objecting to the very name of his unit, he told a friend, "This *Morale* title is illiterate and absurd. How can one learn anything about morals, when one's actions are beyond any kind of morality?" (Carpenter, 334). Judging from his hostile reaction against the official objectives of his mission, it seems likely that the reports Auden sent back to his superiors must have included acid observations about the damage that the sometimes indiscriminate bombing of German cities did to the morals of the victors, as well as more sober evaluations of their effect on the morale of the vanquished. If so—and perhaps one day, if these Army records are ever recovered and released, we will know for certain—here, too, Auden would have been true to his characteristic support of the underdog hidden beneath whatever skin he found him in; and here, too, the spy was morally balanced by the counterspy.

Certainly, Auden was very fond of finding out secrets and perhaps even of keeping them. Despite his well-known antipathy for biographical criticism, he claimed that one of his favorite questions when reading others' poems was: "What kind of guy inhabits this poem? . . . What does he conceal from the reader? What does he conceal even from himself?" (Auden, *Dyer's Hand*, 50–51). Judging from his penchant for nosing out other people's secrets, one can appreciate why, no matter what his actual involvement in spying during or before the war may have been—no doubt minimal even at worst (or best)—Auden not only obviated most attempts to pry into the details of his own private life, but also feared a posterity that he knew was determined to investigate the most intimate corners of his own past. Hence, the notorious request to friends to destroy all his surviving letters, as well as his refusal to authorize a biography. What was the point of all this secrecy? What did Auden himself have to conceal? Probably nothing. Certainly not the fact of his homosexuality, for towards the end of his life, mainstream society was beginning to accept homosexuality, especially when it involved gifted people in the arts; and besides, by the late 1950s, Auden had pretty well emerged, or had been made to emerge, from any closet he may have been hiding in when he acknowledged authorship of "The Platonic Blow." But if not homosexuality, what then? Nothing secret, I think, nothing that could, or would, or will be ferreted out by some assiduous scholarly spy or publicity-hungry biographer. Rather, I suspect, it was primarily an image of himself that Auden wished to hide, as well as, secondarily, another, quite different image that he hoped to perpetuate. The first was an image of a youthful quester/jester who had ventured/adventured across a variety of psychological, social and intellectual frontiers with an abandon that his contemporaries found both exhilarating and a little unreal, a spy delving into the unconscious and sending back reports that were sometimes absurd, sometimes hilarious, sometimes moving, always compelling. The second image, on the other hand, was one of a staid, somewhat eccentric but utterly responsible poet *en pantoufles* who preferred the sober, if sometimes boring, truth to any seductive aesthetic illusion. This latter image was one Auden carefully cultivated in his middle to later years by a selective process of revision and excision of his earlier poetry. It is in this sense that the late Auden turned himself into a poetic ex-spy who finally succeeded in covering his tracks so effectively that, to many of his readers, it seemed as if he had never been out in the cold at all.[24]

2

The Group, the Leader, and *The Orators*

"Before a man wants to understand, he wants to command or obey instinctively, to live with others in a relation of power..."
—W. H. Auden, *Scrutiny* (1932)

"Much more research needed into the crucial problem—group organisation (the real parts)."
—W. H. Auden, *The Orators* (1932)

I

IN THE PUBLIC MIND, INSOFAR AS IT HAS BEEN SHAPED BY UNIVERSITY CURRICULA and literary histories, the thirties have by now become ineradicably identified with the poetry, plays, and political proclamations of the so-called Auden group. Looking back from the vantage point of the fifties, at about the moment when this new literary-historical truth was solidifying into permanence, Rayner Heppenstall recalled that this was not at all how it looked to him at the time. To contemporary eyes, the great range of peaks—Auden, Spender, and C. Day-Lewis—which have since come to dominate the leftist poetic landscape of the period seemed little more than hills (Wood, 72). Here, as so often, the real impact of innovation became discernible only years later.

As with most other significant literary groupings in this century—the Georgians, Bloomsbury, the Angries—much ink has been spilled and innumerable typewriters and word processors pounded in an effort to determine if an Auden group ever existed and, if so, what it might have stood for. The confusion regarding its existence and essence is, however, not due to obfuscations of journalists and critics, at least not principally. It derives, rather, from the subsequent disillusion and, in some instances, outright rejection by many alleged members of the group of the poetry they wrote and the politics they preached and sometimes practiced in the thirties. As Beret Strong puts it bluntly, "The poets themselves, who stood to gain from the united front, encouraged it when it served their needs and rejected it when it did not" (Strong, 133). Auden's reconversion around 1940 to Anglo-Catholicism, Stephen Spender's and Day-Lewis' desertion of the Marxist god that failed, and Christopher Isherwood's departure for Vedantic pastures new at approximately the same time, threw their earlier joint activities into a new and problematic perspective.

By 1960, it seemed to Julian Symons—sometime editor of *Twentieth Century Verse*, and a personal acquaintance of most of the supposed principals—that an "Auden group" had never really existed. At most, Symons was willing to grant that the poetry and powerful personality of Auden had shaped a "climate of feeling," but a group, no, that was a figment of the critical imagination. And in the same year, Day-Lewis gave the quietus to anyone who might have doubted Symons by confessing, in his autobiography *The Buried Day*, that he, Auden, and Spender had met together in one room for the first time in 1947. Confronted with this item of news, it was thereafter preposterous to think of these poets as belonging to an identifiable grouping. Not surprisingly, therefore, Justin Replogle, in his 1964 article on the "Auden Group," treats the notion of a group as a myth, fostered primarily by Auden himself, that bore little relation to reality. The group from then on could only be thought of as existing between quotation marks (Symons, *Thirties*, 16; Day-Lewis, *Buried Day*, 216–17; Replogle, "Group," 135).

But despite the apparently overwhelming evidence, the impression that there had once been a real Auden group stubbornly survives. Even Julian Symons observes some forty pages after denying its existence that "the primary function of [John Lehmann's] *New Writing* was to provide a bigger audience for the writers of the Auden group" (Symons, *Thirties*, 59). F. R. Leavis felt that the kind of bad poetry Auden was supposedly writing by the mid-thirties was due to "the uncritical support of a group" (Leavis, 327). To George Orwell, it was axiomatic that Auden and his friends hung together as a group. "When one compares these writers," he writes contemptuously in "Inside the Whale" (1940), "with the Joyce-Eliot generation, the immediately striking thing is how much easier it is to form them into a group. Technically they are closer together, politically they are almost indistinguishable, and their criticisms of one another's work have always been (to put it mildly) good natured" (Orwell, *Essays*, 237). Of course, Orwell, by 1940, had an ax to grind against those whom he considered to be scoutmasters of the Left, but his conclusion is nonetheless hard to refute. From a literary-historical point of view, Auden and the writers associated with him do fall into a definable grouping.

By the time he came to write his autobiography, Day-Lewis had also apparently forgotten that when, as a young and relatively unknown poet, he had written *A Hope for Poetry* (1934), he had by no means inveighed against the habitual yoking of his own name with those of Auden and Spender, despite disclaiming, in the first person plural, the "honour" of initiating a new boom in poetry. The poetry for which there was hope, according to Day-Lewis, was characterized by a "perpetual interplay of private and public meaning" in which "the inner circle of communication—-the poet's conversation with his own arbitrarily isolated social group—-is perpetually widening into and becoming identified with the outer circles of his environment" (Day-Lewis, *Hope*, 25, 37). This most recent poetry, though not named more specifically, is, to judge from the citations and analyses provided in the body of Day-Lewis's book, almost exclusively that of the *New Signatures* poets, especially of Auden, Spender, and, with some prefatory apologies, Day-Lewis himself. And it is to this "arbitrarily isolated social group" that Auden and the poets associated with him customarily address themselves; this audience forms the preliminary barrier between the poet and the wider public—the barrier that makes the Auden group's poetry peculiarly obscure and, yet, relatively homogeneous. In *Letters from Iceland* (1937), Auden admitted as much himself:

> Art, if it doesn't start there, at least ends,
> Whether aesthetics like the thought or not,
> In an attempt to entertain our friends;
> And our first problem is to realize what
> Peculiar friends the modern artist's got.

(EA, 185)

There is some evidence, in fact, to suggest that Day-Lewis's story of his meeting Auden and Spender together for the first time in 1947 is a canard. Significantly, when Auden repeats the story in his introductory letter to the Handley-Smith bibliography of Day-Lewis' works, he gets the date wrong, claiming that the first meeting of the three poets took place in 1949 in Venice. The immediate source of this confusion is a photograph included in the bibliography that shows Auden, Spender, and Day-Lewis seated in the Piazza San Marco in 1949. But surely this is not the "room" that Day-Lewis refers to, and certainly it is not the date (Handley-Taylor, v). The contradiction, though minor, is enough to rouse one's suspicions, suspicions that are confirmed when one turns to Constantine FitzGibbon's biography of Dylan Thomas and discovers that Auden, Spender, Day-Lewis, and MacNeice joined with Thomas to broadcast a reading of their poems in the fall of 1938. This broadcast, FitzGibbon affirms explicitly, was not recorded, but live (Fitzgibbon, 225).

While it seems difficult to reconcile this fact with Day-Lewis's claims, or with Auden's for that matter, there is no real reason to suspect Auden of disingenuousness in this strange affair. To be sure, he may have jumped a little too eagerly at a chance to revise not merely his poems but also his past. But then, Auden's memory regarding his own person was often less than perfect, as I shall have occasion to note again later. In any case, it seems probable that the three poets met together long before 1938, as much as a decade earlier, in fact. Gabriel Carritt—to whom one of the Odes in *The Orators* is dedicated, and who knew Auden at Oxford in the late twenties—recalls meeting Auden "in various circles, sometimes with the friends who were senior to me, Rex [Warner], Cecil Day-Lewis, Louis MacNeice, and, from Cambridge, Christopher Isherwood and Edward Upward. . . . More often I met him with my own contemporaries, Stephen Spender, Sidney Newman . . . and Dick Crossman." Even if—as seems unlikely—these "various circles" were always mutually exclusive, Carritt's recollection confirms what the brouhaha about the three poets only meeting after the Second World War tended to obfuscate, namely, that the Auden group was not confined to Auden, Spender, and Day-Lewis, but included at least Isherwood and Upward as well (Carritt, 45–46). According to Martin Green, it was Auden himself who, along with the other founding members of his group, actively enlarged the membership: "Auden brought in Gabriel Carritt, the son of an Oxford don, Derek Kahn, A. J. P. Taylor, and Hugh Gaitskell; Spender brought in Isaiah Berlin, an intellectual historian, and Richard Goodman, a poet; Day-Lewis brought in Rex Warner; and so on. Several dons were associated with the group, like Maurice Bowra, Neville Coghill, and R. H. Crossman. Various members edited the magazines, *Oxford Outlook* and *Oxford Poetry*, and made the group's power felt" (Green, *Children*, 282). In any case, whatever the truth behind Green's claims, it is clear from an epistolary poem that Auden sent Day-Lewis from Berlin in late February 1929 that a closely-knit group, consisting at least of Auden himself, Day-Lewis, Rex Warner and Isherwood had already existed at Oxford:

> I spoke of friends and now there come to mind
> Associations of a different kind.
> I see the features and the voices hear
> Of Margaret [Marshall], doctor, Christopher severe,
> Of Rex who looked at much and much saw through . . .
>
> (S. Day-Lewis, 310)[1]

Finally, in his 1994 introduction to a new printing of his autobiography, *World Within World* (1951), Stephen Spender (to whom *The Orators* is dedicated) recalled that the thirties were "a time when Auden and Isherwood, Day-Lewis and MacNeice and I *often* met one another at anti-Fascist committees we attended . . ." (Spender, *World*, 1994, xx, my italics). Even earlier, in 1953, Spender had noted that as an undergraduate, Auden's "relationships with his fellow human beings had fallen into a pattern. They were really of two kinds—teacher-to-pupil and The Colleagues. Those of us who automatically fell into the role of pupil went to him for information about poetry, our psychological ailments, the art of living, and so on. The Colleagues—consisting preeminently of Christopher Isherwood (at Cambridge), Day-Lewis, and Rex Warner—were a little group (sometimes called 'The Gang') who were rather like a shadow cabinet, the successors to the literary heritage of tomorrow" (Spender, "Auden and His Poetry," 74). Not that the line between "pupils" and "Colleagues" was ever impermeable, for as Spender's own case shows, he was eventually elevated into the status of Colleague, despite occasional relapses into pupilhood.

Regardless, however, of whether the poetical trio of Auden, Day-Lewis and Spender ever set foot in the same room together in the thirties, or of whether the two who did meet face-to-face studiously avoided mentioning their conversations to the absent third, it is undeniable that they and their "peculiar friends" shared similar social and educational backgrounds, usually public school followed by ancient university. Moreover, they regularly appeared together under hard and soft covers, notably in *New Signatures* and *New Country*, but also in Geoffrey Grigson's polemical journal, *New Verse*. By 1937, Auden, at thirty, was enough of an established cult figure to rate a special "Auden Double Number" of *New Verse*, with salutes from (among others) Spender, Day-Lewis, Christopher Isherwood, and Louis MacNeice.

The impression that Auden and his friends formed a poetical clique was also reinforced by Auden's habit of dedicating books and individual poems to friends, along with frequently and sometimes cryptically dropping those friends' names in public places. Even more striking, perhaps, was Auden's collaboration with Isherwood on a series of plays that received considerable publicity, and later on with Louis MacNeice in *Letters from Iceland*. When Isherwood's precocious autobiography *Lions and Shadows* (1938) appeared, full of thinly disguised references to Auden, Upward, and other members of the group, Grigson hailed it as the "key book of the Auden Age and the Auden Circle"(Grigson, "Education," 19). It seems then that if Auden and his friends were not part of an actual group, they were part of something that was, practically speaking, indistinguishable from a group.

Moreover, Auden's friendship left marked literary as well as personal traces. Why, Stephen Spender asked himself in *World Within World*, were he and Auden and Day-Lewis so often linked together? "Partly, I think," came the reply, "on account of the influence of Auden, which was responsible for much of the subject matter of the early poems of Day-Lewis. My own work showed his influence in certain imagery, the tone of certain lines. What we had, then, in common was in part Auden's influence, in part also not so much our relationship to one another, as to what had gone immediately before us" (Spender, *World*, 139) And it was, almost inevitably, whether at Oxford, Berlin, or later on in the United States, Auden, who, assuming the mantle of leadership strode confidently "before us," laying down the psychosocial law to his often puzzled but admiring followers.

II

Was Auden the leader of a "group"? Or was he merely the figurehead of a generation? According to Samuel Hynes, who baptized and chronicled the so-called Auden Generation some twenty-odd years ago, perhaps in order to avoid having to deal with the more troublesome notion of a group, that generation officially began in 1914–28, transitioned in 1929–30, flourished and decayed from 1931 to 1940. At the end of this period, the generational leader himself, W. H. Auden, had just turned thirty-three. When he died in 1973, he had survived the presumed death of his own generation by another thirty-three years, a number traditionally considered to be the equivalent of a generation. On the other hand, Humphrey Carpenter has proposed an alternative but simultaneous generation, one that he calls the "Brideshead Generation" (also the title of his 1989 book), with Evelyn Waugh at its head. Waugh, who turned thirty-seven in 1940, had been busily denouncing the low, dishonest decade for much of the decade itself in a series of devastating satirical novels. He was soon to denounce Auden and Isherwood in person as the low Parsnip and the dishonest Pimpernel who had abandoned Britain in the hour of her greatest need.

Two distinct generations, then, both nearly contemporaneous, both born into much the same class, some even related to each other—Graham Greene, for example, was Christopher Isherwood's cousin—often educated in the same preparatory and public schools, almost all Oxbridge graduates, with the two supposed generational protagonists separated chronologically by four years. It all seems very odd. What sorts of "generations" are these? Surely the word is not being used here in the conventional sense that refers, quoting the *Oxford English Dictionary*, to "a whole body of individuals born about the same period." As Hynes and Carpenter use it, "generation" pertains neither entirely to time, nor to class, nor to profession, for the representatives of both "generations" are almost all writers, with an occasional exception like Cecil Beaton. Nor does the word refer logically even to any sort of consistent self-conception, despite Hynes's effort to persuade us that "generations" arise the moment they grow aware of their existence. Nothing is, so it would appear, until writing makes it so. "Evelyn Waugh's contemporaries didn't know that they were Bright Young People," Hynes informs us at the outset of *The Auden Generation*, "until Waugh told them they were; then they looked back to Oxford and the Hypocrites' Club and saw they were significant. So it was with the 'thirties: the generation grew into consciousness as its artists devised the forms in which they could express contemporary history, and the new consciousness evolved and changed as events, and the expressions of events, occurred" (Hynes, 11). But if that was the case, then how is it that Waugh and his "generation," who chronologically belonged to and wrote much of their best work during the thirties as much as Auden and his "generation" did, failed to take a left political turn as the new decade opened and the new "consciousness" began to be expressed? Isn't the *real* difference here simply to be found in the rather mundane fact that Auden and most of his friends wrote poetry, whereas Waugh and most of his friends wrote prose fiction?

To be sure, what Hynes says about Waugh and his so-called generation is clear enough: they were people who shared a common nostalgia for the exclusive male-dominated Oxford world of the twenties, with its clubs, parties, sets (or "groups"), and coteries, a kind of brief but glorious last burst of Edwardian sunshine. They expressed an old consciousness, as it were, rather than a new one. The Auden generation, on the other hand, was something altogether different, reacting to current events and taking the temperature of a continually evolving consciousness—the here-and-now, in other words, as opposed to the there-and-then. The fact that the presumed members of both "generations" were all born at about the same time has apparently nothing to do with the "generation" they are assigned to. This is a view which, implicitly at least, Carpenter seems also to endorse: the Brideshead that provides the name for his chosen generation is, after all, the Brideshead of Charles Ryder's and Sebastian Marchmain's exuberant Oxford youth, a kind of living aesthetic ideal by which all subsequent experience is measured and found wanting. It is a view that even Auden himself came to share in middle age, when like Waugh, he sought solace in organized religion and looked back with regret to the prelapsarian pre-1914 days of supposedly perpetual Edwardian sunlight and seeming stability. Viewed from this perspective, then, the main difference between Waugh and Auden is not so much that they belong to two different literary groups as that it took Auden a great deal longer to achieve the essential conservatism, religious and social, that constitutes the underlying link between the two groups. Already in 1932

Auden, however, was deeply concerned with diagnosing the psychosocial ills that had made of England, as he puts it in *The Orators*, "this country of ours where nobody is well." Waugh's concern was, in the final analysis, really no different.

The word "generation," it turns out, confuses a good deal more than it clarifies, and it is to Humphrey Carpenter's credit that he is not always entirely comfortable with it, as is evident from the subtitle of his book ("Evelyn Waugh and his Friends"), which refers to a linking by friendship rather than chronology. So too the author's note prefacing his book makes no mention of a "generation," but instead speaks of "several writers and their circle, whose work has certain ideas and beliefs in common, and who, I believe, are better understood when they are considered in relation to each other." (Could Carpenter perhaps be thinking of a *group*?) Even this description is, however, not altogether accurate because it suggests a kind of literary movement with an agreed-upon program and suggests, too, its survival over a rather long period. This is surely not the case with the two hypothesized prime movers of the Brideshead generation, Brian Howard and Harold Acton, both of whom vanish from the circular scene of Waugh's acquaintance after the late twenties, though the former is featured prominently—and in an unfriendly way—in Waugh's fiction many years later. Besides, it would be an exaggeration to argue that Howard was a friend of Waugh's at any stage, or that they ever shared similar views on society, art, literature, morals, or much of anything else, especially in view of Howard's subsequent identification with left-wing causes. They happened to overlap briefly at Oxford, where Howard cut a faded Wildean figure; that is all. In fact Waugh, as Carpenter makes only too clear, had very few friends, and quarrelled with almost all those he did have, so that by the end of his life he was almost completely isolated. It is, ironically, in this last respect that he most resembles Auden.

Samuel Hynes, too, grows increasingly uncomfortable with his concept of an "Auden Generation" as he delves into it more deeply and as its inherent contradictions become more apparent. Eventually, Hynes is compelled to admit that he is really writing about a group rather than a generation. "As the generation, in the larger sense, became definite," he postulates, "so the literary generation—the Auden Gang, the *New Signatures* poets, whatever one called that group of writers who became identified with the decade—also began to become established and noticeable, at least among their contemporaries" (Hynes, 85). How a generation can at one and the same time "become definite," or more limited, "in the larger sense" is something Hynes does not explain. Nor does he clarify the process by which "that group of writers" that is supposedly identical with the decade (thus making it more limited; or is it larger?) can be conceived of as "generational" if their "contemporaries" (i.e., those belonging to their generation) recognize them as a distinct entity. It is to escape such difficulties as these that, taking his cue from Orwell, Hynes proposes to use as a criterion for group membership their habit, or least the habit of "the narrowest circle of the group," of dedicating their books to each other. In this way, he suggests, one can tell "without any guidance except the books themselves . . . quite precisely who was in the inner circle and who was not." That is, we can know who was a member of the group and who wasn't. Even so, several chapters later, Hynes apparently forgets about this supposedly infallible method of identifying members of the group, and proceeds to deny the existence of a group altogether. "By 1936 the *New Signatures* poets," he declares categorically, "had come to be widely regarded as a group or a school, but in fact they were no such thing. They did not resemble each other in their work (except Day-Lewis, who resembled all the rest at one time or another), and they did not have a common theory of literature" (Hynes, 205–6).

Martin Green's attempt to discern a pattern of coherence among the writers reaching maturity during the late twenties and early thirties is not a great deal more helpful. In *Children of the Sun: A Narrative of 'Decadence' in England After 1918* (1976), which was published in the same year as Hynes's *Auden Generation*, Green argues that the Auden and Waugh generations constitute a single generation, namely the between-the-wars generation that grew up into the war but was too young to fight in it. It was a generation that, after enjoying a brief fling of irresponsible high life in the twenties, was then forced, in the following decade, to confront the political/social/economic mess that resulted partly from their own folly along with that of their parents' generation. (John Maynard Keynes had foretold it all in *The Economic Consequences of the Peace*.) Green is, of course, fully aware that there were two apparently quite different "subsets" of this generation, who "thought of themselves, in the early 1930s, as mutually opposed, because the first were frankly aesthetes, the second frankly not so." Here, once again, the diachronic model seems to break down and a synchronic one is silently substituted, for what could this "subset" be if not a group? Nevertheless, Green tries to have the best of both worlds by claiming that his subsets represent "varieties of the same imaginative temperament." Both were the literary progeny of T. S. Eliot, both tried to make high-brow literature accessible to lowbrows, and both nevertheless despised the bourgeoisie. Not that Green, therefore, includes everyone as a sun-child who was born just after the turn of the century. Orwell, for example, is for him a notable exception, one of the necessary generational antitheses to the solar thesis, a kind of child of the moon as it were. Julian Symons and, less convincingly, F. R. Leavis are others.

Sometimes Green loses himself in a mania for curious classification, as when he divides his so-called sun children up into dandies (Waugh and presumably Auden), rogues (Randolph Churchill, Guy Burgess), and naifs (Spender, Betjeman). Sometimes his search for cultural analogues leads him to make vast and untenable claims, as, for example, his assertion that the *commedia dell'arte* and the ballet exercised a great influence on this generation. (It did excercise a great influence, but on the preceding generation). It is easy, therefore, to see why Carpenter relegates his lone mention of Green's book to a footnote and faults him for treating "Waugh and his circle exclusively as dandies, scarcely considering other aspects of their character and work." Still, Green's concept of a generationally shared "imaginative temperament" manages to provide a loose, but certainly more comprehensive, as well as marginally more convincing account of what happened in British literature during the two decades following the First World War than either Carpenter or Hynes does.

Despite Carpenter, it is hard to believe that a Waugh group—and much less a Waugh generation—ever existed, at least in the sense that an Auden group did. The paucity of intellectual links between Waugh and his so-called friends strongly suggests a conclusion that Carpenter struggles hundreds of pages to avoid, namely that Waugh and his "friends" were actually an assemblage of quite distinct individuals who belonged to the same social class, shared certain typical educational experiences, reacted negatively to the rapid postwar industrialization and "Americanization" of England, and saw each other occasionally but otherwise had little in common. If they shared anything, it was a kind of defiant provincialism and pseudo-aristocratic contempt for mere scribblers. Their travel books, especially, are revealing in this respect, designed to show how travel should narrow one's horizons rather than broaden them. Even in Waugh's fiction, class and ethnic prejudice tend to be confirmed and even affirmed rather than denied. In this respect, the Auden group (or subset) was quite different, for, as Samuel Hynes has shown convincingly, they at least were real intellectuals who shared important cultural, political, and literary assumptions. They were open (perhaps too open) to new ideas from abroad, even from America; and they also, for a time, oriented themselves towards their leader, Auden, in a way that no important writer in Waugh's circle ever did.[2]

It seems, therefore, right for Beret Strong to be impatient with critics who doubt or even deny the existence of an Auden group. Just because the various individual members of this group did not always move or write in lockstep does not mean, as she points out in *The Poetic Avant-Garde: The Groups of Borges, Auden, and Breton* (1997) that they were not a group. And it certainly does not mean that they could not justifiably think of themselves and even call themselves a group—as they (or at least some of them) did. After all, unless organized by some official organ of the state or by a political party, groups of writers tend to remain individuals, as well as individualistic, even as and when they become members of loosely associated collectives. This is true of literary and cultural groups as different as the Bloomsbury Group in England before the First World War and the Group 47 in Germany after the Second World War. Still, as Strong says, "groups of poets differ from individual poets; their work is part of a discursive body bound by a group ideology and a collective project. Creating the group involves a process of minimizing differences and focussing on common ground" (Strong, 7).

How deeply Auden was concerned with the question of how individuals (especially homosexual individuals) relate to groups at about the time he was writing *The Orators* emerges clearly from a letter he wrote to John Pudney in late July, 1932. Here, he contends that there is a fundamental confusion among homosexuals between two basic human desires, the need for sex and the need for belonging to a group. The problem with homosexuals, in Auden's view, is that, being unable to express their sexuality by entering "a particular woman and having a child by her," they compensate by substituting promiscuity and, in this way, seriously inhibit their ability to form significant groups. This is especially problematic in large urban areas like London where people with similar sexual inclinations tend to seek refuge in likeness rather than difference. "This is disastrous," Auden argues. "You end up by eating each other. The whole value of a group is that its constituents are as diverse as possible, with little consciously in common. Plurality in unity." Even poets, Auden concludes, require the emotional security provided by a group, despite their professional need for individuality, for without the support of the group "they have no material, must split their emotions into ever finer and finer hairs" (quoted in Mendelson, *Early*, 23).

Part of the problem, Auden believed, was the increasing isolation and, to use the term popularized by Marx, "alienation" of the individual, regardless of whether he was homosexual or heterosexual, for the pressures on both groups were the same in a modern society characterized by divorce and advanced technology. It was, after all, during the Victorian Age that, as Auden put it in an essay published in late 1938, that "the atomisation of society into solitary individuals, which is one of the effects of laissez-faire capitalism, first began to be felt actively" (*Prose*, 467). Since the old Victorian family structure could no longer be relied on for security, young people had to turn elsewhere for a sense of community. Not that this was all bad, for, as Auden had shown in *Paid on Both Sides* and Isherwood in *All the Conspirators*, the family was by no means an unproblematic way of resolving the problem of alienation. Besides, even if the family had ever been an attractive solution, the modern family was decreasing not only in importance, but also, in size. In other words, the problem was actually growing more severe, for as the family faded into the background and as travel became easier, "the family is rapidly ceasing to be the natural social unit." Nevertheless, the need for a feeling of group solidarity was not disappearing. On the contrary, the modern alienated intellectual was "still looking for a group of some kind." Ominously, in the absence of the family, the only seemingly viable alternative was the totalitarian state, for it, so Auden insisted, is "a family image" (Auden, "Groups," 92–93). Raised in a social framework where the only stable group structure was either the family or "the school-team," modern youth could only conceive of two possible choices, liberalism or "irrationalism." But since the former "involves faith in reason and he has never had that," the only really viable choice was some kind of irrational dictatorship. In practical terms, this meant either communism or fascism. Both were fundamentally irrational and both used the same sorts of appeal and techniques (especially "the cell or small group"). For Auden, the fact that, regardless of ideology, political movements of the extreme right and left were using the same structures suggested to him that "the importance of the small group is beginning to be realized. Only in a group of very moderate size, probably not larger than twelve, is it possible for the individual under normal circumstances to lose himself, for his death instincts to be neutralized in the same way as those of the separate cells of the metazoa neutralize each other in the body" (Auden, "Groups," 98). Groups of politically likeminded contemporaries—and fanatics—were clearly going to be dominating the intellectual and artistic landscape of the future.

The ideology of the Auden Group is something that was never clearly formulated, officially or uniformly. The closest the Group ever came to a "manifesto" was Michael Roberts's polemical preface to the *New Country* anthology.[3] Nevertheless, by the early 1930s, the Auden group struck perceptive contemporaneous observers like Malcolm Cowley as being identified with a coherent left-wing ideology. In his view, Auden and Spender were nothing more than "the vanguard of a group that includes Charles Madge, John Lehmann, Cecil Day-Lewis (in some ways the most promising of all), Richard Goodman, Julian Bell and others. All of these poets are young, gifted in their various fashions, and seem to know what they are doing. All of them are able to write about political issues, not drily or abstractly, but in terms of human beings. Most of them are radical without being proletarian" (Cowley, 189). Or as James Burnham put it at about the same time, Auden and his friends "should be approached as a group, for in this way we can see them to be part of a definite movement that is somewhat more than literary . . . All of them, in spite of sound Public School training, are or claim to be communists, at least to the extent of accepting, and wishing to work in their own way toward, a classless society" (Burnham, 164).

By the mid-thirties, it was clear to virtually everyone interested in contemporary poetry and poetic drama that there existed a vocal left-wing group with Auden at its center. When Stephen Spender published *The Destructive Element* in 1935, Geoffrey Grigson proclaimed that it was Auden's mind that had engendered the book "as it has engendered something of a poetry revival, half of Mr. Spender and nine-tenths of Mr. Cecil Day-Lewis" (Grigson, 1935, 17). It was at this juncture, too, that Christopher Caudwell became convinced that contemporary English poets had moved from a position resembling that of the Surrealists to "its opposite—a communist revolutionary position, such as that adopted by Auden, Lewis, Spender and Lehmann" (Caudwell, 116). Though Caudwell, who died in 1937 fighting against the Franco forces in Spain, was more than skeptical about the depth of these poets' commitment to the party, as well as about the quality of their political verse, he recognized clearly what they wanted to be and also what prevented them from fulfilling their hopes. Their principal fault, he thought, was their bourgeois origin. (Caudwell was bourgeois himself.) Without naming Auden specifically, Caudwell concluded that, as a bourgeois poet, he was incapable of accepting the primacy of proletarian solidarity in the arts, so that, inevitably, "his living as a proletarian" diverged "increasingly from his art as bourgeois." Since, however, such a glaring disparity could not simply be suppressed, the former erupted into the latter "in the form of crude and grotesque scraps of Marxist phraseology and the mechanical application of living proletarian theory." In the end this led to "an unconscious dishonesty in his art"—a conclusion, interestingly enough, that Auden himself arrived at while in Spain, though, as we shall see, for quite different reasons (Caudwell, 285).[4] By the late thirties, just before the time Auden felt compelled to turn away from overt political commitment, another left-leaning, bourgeois poet, William Empson, publicly lampooned him and his "boys" for their naively Marxist expectations of an end to capitalism:

> What was said by Marx, boys, what did he perpend?
> No good being sparks, boys, waiting for the end.
> Treason of the clerks, boys, curtains that descend.
> Lights becoming darks, boys, waiting for the end.
> (Empson, *Poems*, 63)

Even a decade earlier, however, at Oxford, the inner circle of the group (Auden, Day-Lewis, Spender, Isherwood) acted and wrote according to a set of more or less unformulated ideological premises that can be roughly summarized as follows: 1) psychology helps to resolve personal and cultural problems; 2) psychology can be usefully incorporated into poetry and fiction, usually by means of parable; 3) sexuality, especially homosexuality, is intimately connected to the individual and social psyche; 4) class and national prejudice get in the way of useful experience; 5) the enemy is not Germany but conventional bourgeois belief, especially when found in oneself; and, finally, 6) Germany and the Soviet Union provide better aesthetic and social models for the English than France or even Britain do. Looking back from the relatively recent perspective of 1946, Stephen Spender was to recall that in "the thirties there was a group of poets who achieved a very wide reputation as a 'school' of modern poetry. They were not in a deliberate sense a literary movement; they were rather a group of friends, contemporaries at the Universities of Oxford and Cambridge, influenced by each other in a personal way." Aside from subordinating themselves to "the powerful intelligence and personality of W. H. Auden," the members of the group in general shared the following tendencies: a common subject matter, focusing on "machinery, slums and the social conditions which surrounded them;" an emphasis on community; and a powerful awareness of "communal disease," for which the group sought "a communal cure in psychology and leftist politics." They also lacked "sensuality, and their approach to all problems was very intellectual" (Spender, *Poetry*, 28).

As the Auden group became more established, and as the economic crisis in Britain and the rest of the world deepened, they added a strong socioeconomic component to this list. Their work began to show a powerful sense of social urgency, especially the work of those members of the group who had lived in Germany or were still living there. Something needed to be done quickly, preferably along the lines of the Soviet Five Year Plans. During this period (roughly from 1932 to 1939), the Auden group may be seen as shaping itself in reaction to a moment of great national crisis. In this respect they were not unusual, for such a reaction often holds true of literary groupings, and it helps to explain why a "group" is suddenly perceived to exist where none was visible before. Nothing, it would appear, concentrates the mind—especially the group mind—like a great crisis. Overnight, the Auden group became the "depression" writers and poets, in much the same way as the group of writers known as the Generation of '98 in Spain was born of reaction against the sudden loss by that country of international prestige and power at the close of the nineteenth century.

In terms of *The Orators*, it is important to realize that Auden and his friends considered themselves to be members of a group (even of a "gang") because in *The Orators*, Auden attempted to raise and resolve important problems implicit in group ideology, and, at the same time, to evaluate the usefulness of the group structure for doing so. Groups, after all, as Auden must already have become aware in Germany, were from the socialist point of view a definite step forward from the antiquated bourgeois preference for individualism. *The Orators* is, in other words, simultaneously a poetic manifesto about groups and leadership, and a poetic critique of that manifesto. That is why it is so difficult to understand or even to know how to react to it. As the Airman notes in his journal, "Much more research needed into the crucial problem—group organisation (the real parts)" (EA, 91). The group *is* the crucial problem because it is perceived as providing the only way to salvation in an age when the interests of the "collective" were seen as superseding those of the individual. Something had to be done. But, while it is evident from the very outset of *The Orators*, that immediate action is being called for against an unnamed Enemy, it is less clear what that action is supposed to be.

III

After 1932 especially, there was a quite genuine ideological and political bond uniting Auden and Company. None of the contributors to the *New Country* anthology is known to have objected to Michael Roberts' prefatory call for an English Lenin or to his remark that "I think, and the writers in this book obviously agree that there is the way of life for us: to renounce that system [of capitalism] and to live by fighting against it" (Roberts, 12). The earlier and exclusively poetical *New Signatures* had been less overtly political, but even there, John Lehmann was later to remember, "we were trying to make a new intellectual and imaginative synthesis that would be positive, not negative and pessimistic in its attitude to the problem of living in the twentieth century" (Lehmann, *Own*, 115). This "we," by the way, was meant to be understood as synonymous with "our group." Even Louis MacNeice who, despite inclusion in Roy Campbell's "MacSpaunday" monster, is generally thought of as an outsider, explicitly published his *Modern Poetry* (according to his preface) as a "plea for impure poetry, that is, for poetry conditioned by the poet's life and the world around him" (MacNeice, *Modern*, n.p.). Even as far back as 1926, Auden (together with Charles Plumb) had argued in the preface to *Oxford Poetry* that "poetry which does not at least attempt to face the circumstances of its time may supply charming holiday-reading, but vital interest, anything strictly *poetic*, it will certainly not" (*Prose*, 3).

Political commitment, it is evident, did not come overnight to the Auden group. Still, when Spender and Isherwood, living in Berlin in 1932, received word from Upward that he had joined the Communist Party, they apparently were shocked. "Communism to us," Spender recalls in his autobiography, "was an extremist, almost unnatural cause, and we found it hard to believe that any of our friends could be Communists" (Spender, *World*, 132). But, in his book on the student revolts of 1968, *The Year of the Young Rebels*, Spender offers quite a different picture of his reactions to Communism in the thirties. "So if in 1930 one was twenty-one," Spender (who was) writes, "Communism did not mean the Stalinism of the mid-thirties at the time of the trials. It meant, in Berlin, where I was much of my time, the revolution as projected by Eisenstein and the other great directors of that time, and as written up by travelers to the Russian Revolution still in ferment" (142). As Arthur Koestler, who was himself a member of the German Communist Party at the time, points out, "in 1930, the progressive intellectuals of Germany were only too familiar with the sad record of the Socialist Party, but as yet few unfavourable facts about Soviet Communism had become public knowledge. Trotsky, leader of the Opposition, had been exiled; but as revolutions go, exile is a relatively mild punishment. No prominent Soviet politician had been tried in public, no member of the Opposition had been executed. Those were comparatively idyllic days; the purges, the show trials and the Terror only started four years later, after the assassination of Kirov, in December 1934" (Koestler, 257). Looking back ruefully some thirty years later at his sometime enthusiasm for the Soviet Union, Auden tried to excuse himself by arguing, rather more crudely than Koestler, that he and his contemporaries "had felt that the Russians "weren't 'white folks' and therefore should not be judged too harshly" (Hope, 87).

Going to Soviet films seems to have been the extent of Spender and Isherwood's Communist (though not Socialist) sympathies at this time. For Isherwood, who was fond of assuming a pose of anti-intellectual ordinariness, joining the party would have been too melodramatic an action in any case, though the very positive portrait of the head of the Communist Party in Berlin that he provides in *The Berlin Stories* leaves no doubt as to where his sympathies lay. In the late 1920s at Oxford, according to Louis MacNeice, the main preoccupation of serious undergraduates was poetry. "The conception of mechanized collective man" seemed to him and his friend John Hilton "as crude as the White Man's Burden" (MacNeice, *Strings*,113–14). And Julian Bell, who was later to die in the Spanish Civil War, testifies that the same aesthetic, apolitical attitude prevailed in Cambridge at this period (Wood, 104). Auden himself agreed thirty years later that at Oxford "we were politically ignorant and indifferent" (Auden, "As," 182).[5]

Though Auden, unlike Spender and Day-Lewis, never joined the Communist Party (neither did Brecht for that matter), the most thorough investigation—Justin Replogle's 1965 article on "Auden's Marxism"—suggests that Auden's fellow-traveling phase (at least in literary terms) lasted primarily from 1933 to 1938 (Replogle, "Marxism," 593). Auden greatly admired the Soviet films that he first saw in Berlin and he may also have fallen under the spell of the Communist propagandist, Willi Münzenberg, as did his friends Christopher Isherwood and Richard Crossman. It was Münzenberg who first recognized the use to which bourgeois intellectuals with guilty consciences could be put in furthering the cause of the party (Gross, 216).[6] That Auden was aware of and admired the Soviet Union as early as the summer of 1928 is apparent from his enthusiastic quotation of an Ilya Ehrenburg poem about the 1917 revolution:

> Read about us and marvel!
> You did not live in our time—be sorry!
> (Quoted in Isherwood, *Christopher*, 10)

In any case, there is no doubt that Auden was writing political poetry with a definite Leftist (if not specifically Marxist) bias, from at least 1930 onward, and so were many of his friends. In fact, according to Stephen Spender, Auden discussed the subject of social revolution with him in late 1927 or early 1928 while both were still at Oxford. "In a revolution," Auden told him, "the poet lies on his belly on the top of a roof and shoots across the lines at his best friend who is on a roof-top on the other side." And further: "Of course, at heart, secretly, the poet's sympathies are always with the Enemy." (Spender, "W. H. Auden," 14) Here again, the conflict is ultimately more within than outside the self. According to Spender, there are also recognizably Marxist elements in *The Orators*, particularly in its conception of history, though unfortunately Spender does not make any specific identifications. (Spender, *Destructive*, 296)

The watershed year was probably 1931 when, as H. W. Häusermann observes in his 1939 article on the politically engaged poetry of the thirties, the collapse of the Labour government "increased the number of Communists in England immensely, because it appeared clearly that the character and policy of the Labour Leaders were incapable of any real re-organization of national life" (Häusermann, "Left-Wing," 205). In *The Prolific and the Devourer* (1939; 1981), Auden also indicates that it was round about 1931 that politics began to strike a number of young writers as an exciting new subject, though by the end of the decade he became convinced that they didn't have "the faintest idea what they were letting themselves in for" (Auden, *Prolific*, 20). Until he went to Spain in 1937, Auden's politics remained strictly literary, with virtually no personal, physical participation on his part in furthering the Communist cause, not even to the extent of distributing propaganda leaflets, something Isherwood at least had done in Berlin. As Julian Bell was to remark in 1933: "Communism in England is at present very largely a literary phenomenon, an attempt of a second 'post-war generation' to escape from the Waste Land" (quoted in Sinclair, 34).

That there was a very noticeable and specifically political dimension to *The Orators* must have been understood by many readers who registered the connection between the title of the work and Stephen Spender's name in the dedication. Even if they were unaware of the precise relationship between Stephen Spender and (his uncle) J. A. Spender, they would likely have been alerted that an allusion was being made to the latter's autobiography, *A Public Life* (1925), when they noted the dedication's preference for private over public faces. Stephen Spender's uncle was the best-known and most influential Liberal journalist of his day, a friend or acquaintance of most of the principal political figures ranging from Campbell-Bannerman to Asquith. Readers, therefore, who had bothered to decode the dedication, would have grasped that Auden was preferring the private, unknown Stephen Spender, here appearing in a public place (the dedication), to the public man J. A. Spender, who was parading his private life in the context of a very public autobiography.

Not that this was by any means the whole of Auden's implication. The consistent attack on bourgeois individualism, liberalism and journalism that is mounted in *The Orators* derives at least in part from the link with J. A. Spender as a kind of representative "public man." The ways in which Auden uses the private/public distinction in *The Orators* also receive clarification if one places them in the context of certain passages drawn from *Public Life*. So, for example, at the very beginning of his book, J. A. Spender makes clear that he is using the concept "public life" as being relevant only to politicians, especially such politicians as are also members of Parliament (J. A. Spender, 1:xi, xiii). Parliamentary democracy, in his view, is a sacred trust, without which the "way is cleared for adventurers and revolutionaries who will make short work of traditions and conventions and institute the methods of the soldier or the terrorist"—in other words, the methods of the Airman and his cohorts. (J. A. Spender, 1:xv) The Parliamentary public man is also, above all things, a debater and an orator, as Spender makes clear in the following passage:

Everyone who has watched the House of Commons is aware of a peculiar quality permeating its atmosphere and governing the conduct of its members in debate. It is the quality, if I may attempt to define it, of *speech directed to the practical end of governing the country*, a quality which excludes idle rhetoric, imposes strict verification of fact, and requires words to be subordinate to action. The great parliamentary orators have differed widely in their verbal accomplishments, but they have all worked in this medium and regarded speech as a mode of action. (J. A. Spender, 1:125)

Rhetoric, in Spender's view, is a skill that ought to enjoy greater respect, especially in the educational institutions of Britain, for "a man who has had 'rhetoric' instilled into him in his youth will be in little danger of becoming either a wind-bag or a demagogue in later years." (J. A. Spender, 1:136–37) Furthermore, a real politician makes no distinction between his public and his private life—Gladstone and Campbell-Bannerman are cited as good examples of the fusion of private man and public personality. In a modern democratic state, politicians "can no longer rail off one half of their existence and call it their 'private life' with which the public has no concern," and even if the politician wanted to, "the public man who says that his private life is his own affair no longer has the power of making it so." (J. A. Spender, 1:147–48) Public Uncle Spender, it is clear, turns out to be a very different animal from private nephew Spender, just as the poet differs from the politician, or, as Auden would later put it, taking his cue from Blake, the prolific is the enemy of the devourer.

In this respect, *The Orators* really represents the beginning of Auden's lifelong attack on, and suspicion of, rhetoric, along with all the people who use it and live by it—that is, "orators" or poets who try to achieve in their work the kind of effects orators do in their hearers. Auden is here, of course, following a very old tradition of questioning the ethics of rhetorical persuasion, a tradition that goes back at least as far as Plato. In the "Gorgias," Socrates asks the following questions of the cynical sophist Callicles, questions that anticipate Auden's fear in *The Orators* that those who claim to speak for the welfare of the nation are, in fact, helping to destroy it:

> What, then, is the nature of rhetoric addressed to the people of Athens and of the other cities of free men? Does it seem to you that orators always speak with an eye on what is best and aim at this: that their fellow citizens may receive the maximum improvement through their words? Or do they, like the poets, strive to gratify their fellows and, in seeking their own private interest, do they neglect the common good, dealing with public assemblies as though the constituents were children, trying only to gratify them, and not caring at all whether this procedure makes them better or makes them worse? (Plato, 313)

Along with the overt hostility against "public" policies and politicians, there was also a "private" sexual aspect to the Auden group. Though at least one of the core group (Louis MacNeice) was wholly heterosexual, the sexual preferences of the group as a whole were distinctly homosexual, at least at this point in their lives. As we will see later, this homosexual bond was part of the "secret" message hidden in *The Orators*, but it also had a political significance in that it inclined Auden and his friends to sympathize with other socially oppressed groups, notably with the working class and with Weimar Germany, which for most of the twenties, was perceived by left-wing sympathizers as a liberal/socialist state that was being bullied by the conservative, victorious powers, especially France. With the Auden group, this sense of being connected by a secret link never went as far as it did with the roughly contemporaneous Cambridge Spies, though both groups had intimate relations with each other and were really different manifestations of the same 1930s "Homintern." (This word was coined by Isaiah Berlin, himself loosely associated with the Auden group [Koch, 155]). Though none of Auden's close friends had attended Cambridge—or, as in the case of Isherwood, had attended it so briefly as to make no real difference—something of the same sense of secret superiority underlay their strong feeling of group identity.[7]

The usual notion that the earliest Auden is apolitical, as voiced by Jarrell or Spender (e.g., in the famous remark that Auden "came to politics by way of psychology"), is true only in a very qualified sense: that is, by excluding his political poems from consideration (Spender, "Oxford to Communism," 9). Francis Scarfe, on the other hand, overstates the case by claiming that "already in 1930 Auden shows a remarkably developed political sense. He was fully conscious of the disintegration of values and the forces which were to produce Hitler and the Spanish war," but as "1929" shows, there was a case to be made. (Scarfe, *Auden*, 16) How quickly the political and, specifically, the Marxist nature of Auden's poems was sensed can be seen from Edgar Foxall's 1934 article on "The Politics of W. H. Auden," which praises Auden for being, "apart from the few regular communists, [the] chief propagandist" of the doctrines of Marx. (Foxall, "Politics," 474) The real reason why Auden came to politics by way of psychology is that Auden's pre-1932 psychology contained a very powerful political element. It was a psychology that definitely preferred action to contemplation, as in Poem xxii of *Poems* (1930), where we are told to

> Shut up talking, charming in the best suits to be had in town,
> Lecturing on navigation while the ship is going down.
>
> (EA, 49)

Hence, his heroes—chiefly Lawrence, Blake, and Homer Lane, according to another couplet from the same poem—are active and political psychologists insofar as they are psychologists at all: Blake marrying Heaven to Hell and denouncing the established state and the established church; Lawrence advocating the overthrow of conventional morality and submission to a strong, antidemocratic leader; and Homer Lane creating in his Little Commonwealth a kind of New Jerusalem for disturbed adolescents. What connects these three rather disparate figures is not their commitment to psychology, unless defined so broadly as to have no real meaning, but their utopianism. Homer Lane particularly, with his insistence on the laws of love and freedom, is principally interested in realizing his ideas in "political" rather than literary or abstractly psychological ways; and those ideas derive more immediately from Christ than they do from Georg Groddeck.

To be sure, the psychopolitics of the immediate poetic predecessors to *The Orators*, namely *Poems* (1928 and 1930), tend to be of a rather odd sort. Much of the earlier volume is incorporated into the latter, which, while, generally speaking, is more descriptive and less violent than the former, is still full of birds, unidentified interlocutors, ill-defined frontiers, spies, and quarrels over unnamed issues. The framework, however—the sociopolitical framework—for both volumes is chiefly the school or the "gang." While evident throughout, it rises most closely to the surface, as we have already seen in the previous chapter, in the long opening charade of *Poems* (1930), "Paid on Both Sides." To some not easily definable degree, these literary "gang" fantasies reflect real aspects of the Auden group. This is true not merely on the level of a shared group fantasy, such as the famous Mortmere world that Isherwood describes in *Lions and Shadows*, but also in the more mundane aspects of the day-to-day lives of Auden and his friends. There is, for example, Auden's habit of keeping a gun in his desk while still an undergraduate at Oxford (not a real gun, apparently, but a signaling pistol); or the way he thought about his friends, as a "gang" into which new members were periodically recruited. Especially noteworthy is the way each member of the alleged gang seemed to know instinctively his place in relation to the others, with Isherwood looking up to Upward, Auden to Isherwood, and Spender to Auden. In part, at least, Auden's early poems are a working out in public of the experiences and fantasies of his own and his friends' private lives. One recalls in this connection again the prefatory verses to *The Orators* with their preference of private over public. It was a preference that was to remain a constant for Auden for the remainder of the 1930s. Thus, writing in 1939, he noted that "[i]t is folly to imagine that one can live two lives, a public and a private one. No man can serve two masters" (Auden, *Prolific*, 16). Though he never abandoned the group as an ideal—most notably, the "Just City" of his later years may be said to represent a more public and Christianized version of his private and pagan comitatus—in practice, he thereafter lived his life as a confirmed individualist.

IV

Inevitably, the carrying over of private preoccupations into a public act like writing and publishing poetry brings with it confusion and misunderstanding. Hence, the early Auden is a difficult and obscure poet. Of no work is this more true than *The Orators*, the most extended of the group fantasies of the early Auden. Auden himself had second thoughts about it, and wanted to preface it with a warning that "this book is more obscure than it ought to be. I'm sorry, for obscurity, as a friend once said to me, is mostly swank." But his editor (and in this case also mentor), T. S. Eliot, dissuaded him from inserting such a prefatory warning. Eliot also deleted his attempt to "explain" the main subject and tripartite structure of the book, namely that "the central theme is a revolutionary hero. The first book describes the effect of him and his failure on those whom he meets; the second book is his own account; and the last some personal reflections on the question of leadership in our time" (quoted in Mendelson, *Early*, 96). Eliot apparently realized that such an explanation would lead to more confusion, rather than less. And, as it turns out, he was right, for in the event, Auden's "hero" has struck most readers as anything but revolutionary, and Auden's attempt to make sense of the three very different parts of the poem has been as unpersuasive as just about every other attempt to account for it in rational terms. How confused, not to say swankish, Auden himself was about the meaning and structure of *The Orators* is evident from the very different description he sent to Naomi Mitchison:

> In a sense the work is my memorial to [T. E.] Lawrence; i. e. the theme is the failure of the romantic conception of personality; that what it inevitably leads to is part 4.
> Formally I am trying to write abstract drama—all the action implied. The four parts, corresponding if you like to the four seasons and the four ages of man (Boyhood, Sturm und Drang, Middleage, Oldage), are stages in the development of the influence of the Hero (who never appears at all).
> Thus Part 1. Introduction to Influence.
> Part 2. Personally involved with hero. Crisis.
> Part 3. Intellectual reconstruction of Hero's teaching. The cerebral life.
> Part 4. The effect of Hero's failure on the emotional life.
> The litany is the chorus to the play. (Quoted in Mendelson, *Early*, 98)

Among the several very odd things about this summary of the opening section of *The Orators*—not the whole work, as the quotation seems to imply—is the apparently serious claim in the last sentence that it is supposed to be a "play." Indeed, Auden prefaced his summary with the remark that "[f]ormally I am trying to write abstract drama—all the action implied." In the event, it turned out that all the "drama" was implied also, since there is no dramatic structure at all to this section of *The Orators*, either abstract or otherwise. Hard to accept, too, is Auden's claim that the "Hero" never appears but, nevertheless, somehow manages to keep on being a Hero. He inexplicably becomes a kind of allegorical Everyman who is not revolutionary, but romantic, as well as a failure. If all this adds up to drama, then it is only because it is drama as in the proverbial sense of *Hamlet* without a Hamlet.

Describing in more detail "the second half" of the book (the "Journal of an Airman") to Mitchison, Auden claimed that it represented "the situation seen from within the Hero." The "flying symbolism" he considered "fairly obvious" and therefore did not bother to elucidate it. To another correspondent, however, he expressed his outright dissatisfaction with the book, especially his failure to get across its function as "a critique of the fascist outlook." Instead, he claimed to have realized, to his dismay, that "it can, most of it, be interpreted as a favorable exposition. The whole Journal ought to be completely rewritten," a task, however, that Auden did not undertake then or even when he eventually did decide to republish it some thirty odd years later. (Quoted in Mendelson, *Early*, 103–4)

So obscure is *The Orators* that critics have been at a loss even for what to call it. Is it a "poem," or a fairy tale or a joke or a story or a collage? Or something else? John Sparrow, in desperation, is reduced to calling it a "thing" and Monroe K. Spears is not much more helpful with his "piece" (Sparrow, *Sense*, 153; Spears, *Auden*, 45). For Stuart Hampshire, it is "pop-art" of a hitherto unheard-of kind; for W. W. Robson, a "strange fantasy;" for D. E. S. Maxwell, a literary counterpart of German Expressionist cinema; and for John Fuller, an assemblage of automatic writing (Hampshire, *Modern*, 22; Spender, *Concise*, 50; Maxwell, *Poets*, 158; Fuller, "Early Auden," 90).

This confusion reflects a prior confusion of Auden's, very likely an intentional one. The title of the work suggests that it is intended to be read as an "oration," an intention that seems confirmed by the opening "Address for a Prize Day." But this address, with its direct echoes of Dante's purgatory and indirect ones of Milton's infernal revolutionaries, suggests that Auden's orators are engaged not merely in speechifying, but also in prayer. The root meaning of oratory—and its original English meaning, according to Auden's favorite reference work, the *Oxford English Dictionary*—is, after all, "prayer," and it is unlikely that Auden would not have known this and meant his readers to interpret his title in its dual significance. Indeed, the "Prologue" to *The Orators* becomes comprehensible only if one reads it with this secondary sense of oration in mind, and the final ode of Book III, the last segment of *The Orators* proper, is unquestionably a prayer. This ambiguity is admittedly confusing, but confusing in a way, I submit, that enriches rather than impoverishes the work as a whole. The same is true of Auden's subtitle, "An English Study," which adds an essayistic, perhaps even a "scientific," dimension to a work that is already self-avowedly rhetorical and religious. M. K. Spears has argued that there may be a pun here, which would make of *The Orators* not only a study of the English, but also a study of the English language. The pun certainly reinforces the rhetorical (or, rather, anti-rhetorical) aspects of the work, but the primary meaning surely remains a "study" of England, as carried out in a quasi-essayistic fashion in "Argument" and other sections of the work as well as, as I shall show later, in the anthropological material underlying book 2 of *The Orators*, the "Journal of an Airman." Finally, *The Orators* is also a poem, though this seems to have occurred to Auden only as an afterthought when he included the whole of *The Orators* in his *Poems* (1934). But it is precisely this afterthought that more than any official title provides the reader of *The Orators* with the necessary hint that it is, or is supposed by its author to be, an integrated work of art.

Finding one's way through this poetical-rhetorical-religious-scientific mirkwood is much like venturing past malodorous middens, loathsome birds, and twisted trees, over the pass and into the valley where all will become clear. In fact, it resembles that journey so closely that Auden's reader, like the reader in the "Epilogue," is usually left behind unilluminated in the company of horror and fearer (or furor?), while the mysterious writer rides (and writes) contemptuously away. More than a decade later, Auden seems to have had some second thoughts about playing tricks of this kind on his public (with the connivance of that other public composed of his private friends), for in the preface to his *Collected Poetry* (1945), he calls *The Orators* "a fair notion fatally injured" and places it in "the most painful" category of "good ideas which his incompetence or impatience prevented from coming to much." The phrasing of this piece of self-criticism unmistakably suggests that what Auden regretted in *The Orators* was not what he said, but the way he said it, though even here it is questionable how sincere that regret is, since among the poems that follow these prefatory remarks is more than one lifted from *The Orators*, including the very obscure "Letter to a Wound." In any event, it is undeniable that the obfuscation of *The Orators* is deliberate and that, if Auden's "idea" is hidden behind a verbal smokescreen, it is because Auden wanted it to be. Is such deliberate obfuscation good or is it bad? Most adherents of modernism would argue, at least for its compensatory aesthetic merits, on the grounds that the difficulty one encounters in interpreting a complex work of art mirrors the difficulty of living a complex modern life. While this observation may be true in the abstract, the usual reaction of modern, nonprofessional readers, including most more or less normally industrious and intelligent students in American university classes, has, in practice, been largely negative, even while citing virtually the same reasons: that is, if modern life is difficult and complex, shouldn't modern art at least attempt to make that life easier to understand rather than even more difficult?

"All of you must have found out what a great help it is," the Prize Day orator observes early on in his tirade, "before starting on a job of work, to have some sort of scheme or plan in your mind beforehand" (EA, 62). Auden's plan, I think, is more in the nature of a scheme, one that involves putting something over on his public reader for the delectation of his private one. Dylan Thomas, who was no mean master of obscurity himself, grasps this point perfectly in his Audenesque "Letter to My Aunt Discussing the Correct Approach to Modern Poetry" (1934), in which he observes that "few understand the young Auden's coded chatter / But then it is the few who matter" (Thomas, *Poems*, 84). How few these "few" actually were Thomas does not say, but it becomes sadly apparent from the sales figures during the whole of the 1930s which, for *The Orators*, amounted to less than two thousand copies (Hope, 85). Still, according to Michael Roberts, those miniscule numbers still meant that Auden's audience was larger at this time than Eliot's (Roberts, *Critique*, 223).

It should not be surprising, then, that *The Orators*, taken as a whole, does not lend itself readily to critical analysis of the "close reading" type. The most fruitful attempt to provide an interpretation along such lines is Monroe K. Spears's essay on *The Orators* in his *Poetry of W. H. Auden* (1963), but stimulating as it is, it ultimately fails to persuade because it relies so heavily and, I am afraid, so unavoidably on the very personal responses and speculations of the critic. More helpful, I think, and more rewarding is the thematical approach that draws on "extraneous" information, above all when that information comes from members of the Auden group. The early Auden's language is, to a marked degree, an in-group dialect, intentionally designed to be incomprehensible to outsiders. "Young writers," Christopher Isherwood observes in the 1958 preface to his first novel, *All the Conspirators* (1928), "are apt to employ [obscurity] as a secret language which is intelligible only to members of their group. Outsiders are thereby challenged to admit that they do not understand it or dared to pretend that they do,—to be unmasked in any case, sooner or later, as squares" (Isherwood, *Exhumations*, 91). The same observation might equally well have been made of *The Orators*, which is a very "young" book full of animosity against an "Enemy" who is undoubtedly square.

Isherwood, who later confessed that during the 1930s, he claimed "the right" to interpret Auden to the world, is also one of the best guides through the strange topography of *The Orators*. In his 1937 essay, "Some Notes on Auden's Early Poetry," Isherwood proposes three rules for reading the young Auden: (1) that he is a scientist or, even better, a "schoolboy scientist;" (2) that he is a musician and a ritualist; and (3) that he is a Scandinavian. Isherwood then goes on to point out the relation of the world of the Icelandic sagas to that of the school ("with its feuds, its practical jokes, its dark threats conveyed in puns and riddles and understatements") and recounts how this observation stimulated Auden to write "Paid on Both Sides" (Isherwood, "Notes," 4–5).

The underlying social structure of *The Orators* is also very close to that of the groups or gangs characteristic of the sagas or the school.[8] The main section of book 1 (subtitled "The Initiates") depicts an older leader type urging on a group of schoolboys to "draw up a list of rotters and slackers" who will be shoved down a "Black Hole" and made to die without issue; and the six odes of book 3, in one way or another, all provide variations on the group or gang fantasy. But its most complex expression occurs in the "Journal of an Airman," book 2 of *The Orators*. The Airman is the most fully developed and important symbolic figure in the book, a character whose closest literary analogue is Kipling's Stalky, a kind of authoritarian antiauthoritarian, a paranoic who, together with his group of friends, populates his surroundings with "Enemies," whom he proposes to trick or teach a lesson to or, in extreme cases, eliminate. Though like the other orators in the book he is more of a planner and self-exhorter—and windbag—than he is a doer, this airborne Stalky has proved to be, by far, the most controversial feature of *The Orators*.

While it bears repeating that the "Journal," along with the rest of *The Orators*, is on some level intended to be read as an in-group joke, it has sinister overtones that prevent one from laughing too heartily. "A man doing nothing is not a man," reads one of the aphoristic entries in the Airman's diary, which is immediately followed by a notation of the Enemy's "extraordinary idea that man's only glory is to think." The Airman is greatly impressed by practical jokes, as a species of guerrilla warfare against the establishment, again a cast of mind reminiscent of Stalky & Co. In fact, according to another entry, one of the ways of telling that someone is "one of us" is that he shares a propensity for practical joking.

The Airman's uncritical glorification of action, his denigration of reason, his thinking in terms of abstract enemies and friends rather than individuals, all these are highly suspect to ears that have heard similar sentiments in other, more ominous historical contexts. Even contemporary ears twitched a little. In *The Thirties*, Julian Symons recalls how anxiously his circle of friends debated the question of the Airman's (and, by implication, Auden's) fascism (Symons, *Thirties*, 17). Stephen Spender, as we have seen, speculated uneasily in *The Destructive Element* (1935) about an Airman who is "planning Fascist (?) coups" (Spender, *Destructive*, 268); two years later, Edgell Rickword absolved Auden of disloyalty to the leftist cause, but denounced parts of the fourth ode for being representative of "the essence of Nazi demagogy" (Rickword, "Auden," 21–22); and in 1939, Philip Henderson argued that *The Orators* "reads more like the plans for a Fascist coup than a Communist revolution" (Henderson, *Poet*, 205).[9] Twenty-five years later, it still seemed to G. S. Fraser that "Auden is certainly imaginatively attracted, in many passages of *The Orators*, to a mood that can engender Fascism" (Fraser, "Young," 102). Auden himself, on the occasion of the 1966 reissue of the (revised) book, remarked in a brief prefatory note that the kind of person who had written it must have been "someone talented but near the border of sanity, who might well, in a year or two, become a Nazi"[10] (Auden, *Orators*, 1966, 7).

It is hard to believe that Auden was not originally aware that *The Orators* and especially the "Journal of an Airman" contained Fascist elements. The reference to the march on London and the seizure of power in the fourth ode is unmistakably an allusion to Mussolini's march on Rome in 1922. Moreover, the Airman himself must have struck many readers as modeled on the quasi-Fascist airman-artist-orator Gabriele D'Annunzio, who in 1919 created a worldwide sensation by seizing Fiume in defiance of the established governments of Europe. During the war, he had been Italy's most decorated pilot, losing an eye on one mission. "D'Annunzio delighted in a kind of individual enterprise," writes his biographer, Anthony Rhodes, "in which, together with some chosen Ulyssean companions in a motor-boat, he would glide into an Austrian harbour by night, and fire off torpedos, at shipping or at the shore. Or in an aeroplane, he would fly over enemy cities dropping, instead of high-explosive, hundreds of leaflets couched in his own high-sounding prose." Auden's Airman, one remembers, has ten thousand copies of one of his poetical orations cyclostyled for "aerial distribution." After the seizure of Fiume, the dreams of this Italian super-Stalky seemed to have come true. He proclaimed a new constitution, issued pronunciamentos, delivered orations, and conducted either personally or through his lieutenants a variety of blockade-breaking adventures that were as much practical jokes as serious military exploits. Though ultimately D'Annunzio failed, at the height of his power "he believed, probably sincerely," his biographer observes, "that a new era for humanity was dawning, and he was confident that his example would be followed all over Italy" (Rhodes, *Poet*, 157, 184). Is this not also the dream of the Airman, not to speak of Auden, but with a diseased England in mind?

There is no hard evidence that Auden was actually thinking of D'Annunzio, despite the striking similarities. Though it is hard to believe that Auden was unaware of D'Annunzio's notorious exploits from reading newspapers or just paying attention to contemporaraneous events, there is also the possibility that he may have heard about him more directly from his Berlin friend, Gerald Hamilton, who had met D'Annunzio not long after the end of the Great War (Hamilton, *Way*, 99). Whatever the case, some years later, in his open letter to Hamsun of 1940, Auden mentions D'Annunzio, along with Sorel, as one of the "miserable clerks who, too weak to become civilized themselves, attempted to justify their failure by impudent attacks on every civilized notion" (Auden, "Open," 23). While this does not sound exactly like the failure of the romantic hero in our time, it does remind one distinctly of Benda's failed intellectual, the treasonable clerk who betrays the values of the group to which he belongs.

There is, however, a real possibility that Auden may not only have been thinking of the proto-fascist D'Annunzio but also, and perhaps primarily, of Lauro de Bosis, another Italian airman and promising young poet who had already gained something of an international reputation with a verse drama about Icarus and who, at the time of his death, was finishing work on his edition of *The Golden Book of Italian Poetry* for Oxford University Press (Origo, 38). De Bosis dropped more than 400,000 antifascist leaflets over Rome on 2 October 1931, crashing and dying shortly afterwards when his aircraft ran out of fuel over the Adriatic. It was an event that was reported widely in the English press, including the Manchester *Guardian* and the London *Times*, at a time when Auden was, if Edward Mendelson's dating is correct, working most intensively on "The Journal of an Airman" (EA, 94, 420). De Bosis, who had monarchist sympathies and came from an upper middle-class family, had been an early admirer of D'Annunzio and Mussolini, but eventually became utterly disillusioned with fascism and hoped to attract international attention to the antifascist cause by using characteristically fascist means. Literary heroism in the air, he was convinced, must no longer remain the exclusive province of fascist airmen like D'Annunzio.[11] Furthermore, by consciously following up an earlier flight made by the Italian socialist airman, Bassanesi (who had dropped antifascist leaflets over Milan), he hoped to establish a credible claim in behalf of Italian conservatives to being as antifascist as the socialists and communists were (Origo, 52). Finally, like Auden's Airman, De Bosis was much preoccupied with the question of organizing and maintaining an effective group structure. To this end, he founded and became leader of a conservative resistance group called the *Alleanza Nazionale*, whose membership, however, seems to have been miniscule (Origo, 62). A large part of the reason why he felt compelled to make his ill-fated flight was, in fact, due to his feeling that he had to show solidarity with the two followers who had been arrested by the Fascists and sentenced to long prison terms.

Auden never mentioned DeBosis or D'Annunzio in connection with *The Orators*. Or, for that matter, Hermann Goering, who had been an ace in the First World War and a member of Manfred von Richthofen's Flying Circus. According to David Trotter, Auden at some unspecified time admitted that Goering "was an example of the kind of figure he had in mind," but unfortunately Trotter provides no specifics for this claim (Trotter, 111). The only influences Auden publicly admitted (in his 1966 preface) were Baudelaire's *Intimate Journals*, along with some unnamed "dotty semi-autobiographical book" by General Ludendorff, and the D. H. Lawrence of *Fantasia, Kangaroo*, and *The Plumed Serpent*. However, only two of these writers seem really relevant to *The Orators* and then only in a limited way, so that one wonders how well the Auden of 1966 remembered the Auden of 1931/32. Striking, for example, is the fact that Auden never mentions the name of the most celebrated airman of the between-the-wars period, namely Charles Lindbergh. In 1927, Lindbergh's courageous solo transatlantic flight electrified the entire world and turned his name into a household word. Undoubtedly, somewhere in the background of Auden's Airman lurks the glamorous, youthful figure of Lindbergh, though Lindbergh's notorious sympathy for the Nazis can have no relevance here since it only became public some time after the publication of Auden's poem. In point of historical fact, initially at least, Lindbergh was as attractive symbolically to the left as he was to the right. Bertolt Brecht's radio play "Flug der Lindberghs" (1930), which Auden may have heard while in Germany, presents him as a defiantly angelic Airman who was driving a reactionary god out of the heavens:

> And so I battle against Nature and
> myself.
> Whatever I am and whatever nonsense I believe in
> When I'm flying, I am
> A true atheist . . .
>
> Therefore take part
> In the struggle against everything primitive,
> In the liquidation of the hereafter and in
> The expulsion of every sort of God, wherever
> He may put in an appearance.
>
> Viewed through more powerful microscopes
> He vanishes.
> He is banished

> From the air by improved machines.
> The cleansing of cities,
> The annihilation of misery
> Make him disappear and
> Drive him back to the first millenium.
>
> (Brecht, "Flug," 9; my translation)

To some undefinable extent, Baudelaire's *Intimate Journals*, which Auden had persuaded Isherwood to translate in 1929, also probably contributed to the erratic and obscure form of the Airman's journal, but there are no striking or detailed resemblances of any kind. A more discernible influence flows from the later D. H. Lawrence, who liked strong men and loathed democracy. As George W. Bahlke remarks, "Auden's Airman bears an oblique relation to Lawrence's authority figures" (Bahlke, "Lawrence," 218). Moreover, Lawrence's interest in psychology and his preference for the "deep passional soul" over the rational faculty also appealed to the young Auden. But again, it is difficult to find any detailed influence. Certainly, Francis Scarfe does not demonstrate any such, and neither does George Bahlke, though both see Lawrence as dominating Auden's early writing (*Auden*, p.13). W. H. Sellers, while proclaiming *The Orators*' "primary dependence on the writings of D. H. Lawrence," provides a psychological reading that might equally well derive from Freud or Groddeck (Sellers, "Light," 455). No, if there must be a Lawrence in this book, then T. E. Lawrence is the better candidate, as Monroe K. Spears has suggested, and as Auden himself wanted to point out in the foreword that Eliot left unpublished. T. E. Lawrence at least was an airman ("Airman Shaw," as he styled himself in later life) who, in Isherwood's words, "had a giggling laugh, played practical jokes, and interspersed his conversation with schoolboy slang" (Isherwood, *Exhumations*, 13, 23). Moreover, according to Isherwood, T. E. Lawrence was the myth hero of the 1930s, for whom he and Auden had a fascination and whom they tried to recreate in the character of Michael Ransom in *The Ascent of F6* (1937).[12]

Auden speaks openly and favorably of T. E. Lawrence in "A Happy New Year" (1933) and in *Letters from Iceland*. As for Field Marshall Erich von Ludendorff's "dotty semi-autobiographical book," it does not exist. Edward Mendelson speculates briefly that it might be *Meine Kriegserinnerungen* (1919), but this work is a straightforward and rather dull account of Ludendorff's military activities (Mendelson, "Coherence," 117). So, too, with Ludendorff's other autobiographical book, *Mein militärischer Werdegang* (1933), which is equally straightforward and whose date of publication disqualifies it as a possible influence in any case. If Auden really did mean to cite Ludendorff rather than, say, Hitler or D'Annunzio, then the only works that are at all relevant are his occasional dotty but non-autobiographical pamphlets, such as *Das Geheimnis der Jesuitenmacht und ihr Ende* (1929), an attack on one of Ludendorff's favorite bogeys, the Jesuits, or, perhaps, as D. E. S. Maxwell suspects, *Weltkrieg droht auf deutschem Boden* (1931), which was published in England in the same year under the title, *The Coming War* (Maxwell, 154). Certainly, this latter work contains enough muddled thinking (as well as flashes of astonishing insight and prophecy) to make the Airman seem Cartesian, so that, in a general way, it may very well have acted as an influence on Auden. Even so, it could not have contributed to any latent fascism in Auden, since in this work, Ludendorff attacks the Fascists and the Nazis (and the Bolsheviks) with a fury he otherwise reserves only for his dealings with Jesuits, Jews, and Freemasons.

Aside from T. E. (and perhaps also D. H.) Lawrence, the main source for the undoubted fascist elements in *The Orators* is probably the year that Auden spent in Germany, when he witnessed the effects of fascism every day in the streets of Berlin. A secondary, but unquestionably important, source is his own public schooling. In his brief contribution to Graham Greene's anthology, *The Old School* (1934), Auden states that "the best reason I have for opposing Fascism is that at school I lived in a Fascist state" (Greene, *The Old School,* 17). Here, to be sure, Auden is probably exaggerating and, in any case, he is using "fascism" in an unjustifiably broad sense, but even so, to the extent that he really did believe his schooling had taken place in a fascist environment and to the extent that his attitude toward that schooling was ambivalent (note his obvious fascination with schools and schoolboys in all of his early work), Auden was paradoxically and perhaps unconsciously sympathetic to fascism. Finally, Auden may also have used elements of the melodrama he saw being played out in the pages of the national press at the time he was writing *The Orators*, namely, how a youthful man of action, left-wing Sir Oswald Mosley, broke away from the Labour Party together with a small group (or gang?) of adherents—among them Harold Nicolson and John Strachey—to form the more radical and dynamic New Party. Like many willful strong men, however, Mosley was impatient with established procedure and the quibbling objections and delays of democratic old men. To save society, to prevent England from foundering on the rocks of an antiquated capitalism, he soon perceived, meant changing the New Party into the British Union of Fascists.

According to Francis Scarfe, Auden was an early opponent of Mosley, providing him with a "hot reception" at Oxford (*Auden,* 11). Scarfe provides no date or evidence for this event, but if it did take place, the most logical time would have been while Auden was still living at Oxford as a student, in other words, no later than 1928. But at this time, Mosley was still a respectable and promising left-wing member of the Labour Party and it is unlikely that Auden would have given such a person anything but a polite welcome. In fact, the only explicit references to Mosley in Auden's early work are either ambiguous or neutral. In the fourth ode of *The Orators*, the future fascist dictator John Warner proposes to place various enemies in a zoo or else have them

> ducked in a gletcher, as they ought to be,
> With the Simonites, the Mosleyites and the I.L.P.
>
> (EA, 105)

Here, Mosley's party is classed with other offshoots of existing political parties and is by no means singled out as a special danger. And in "A Happy New Year," Auden very briefly mentions seeing "Mosley, the descendant of Pitt," a remark that can hardly be interpreted as derogatory (EA, 448). Indeed, how little the Auden group objected to the policies of Mosley in 1931 is evident from Isherwood's willingness to write an article on "The Youth Movement in the New Germany" for Mosley's journal, *Action*. And possibly, it is also significant to note that Mosley had been considerably assisted in his political career by an outstanding war record—as an airman. Better than any other contemporary British figure, he fits Auden's notion of the "failure of the romantic conception of personality." As Mosley's sometime friend (and Auden's acquaintance) Harold Nicolson remarked of him in January 1932: "He is a romantic. That is a great failing" (Griffiths, 36). It is an assessment that, if we are to believe David Luke, Auden might also have made of himself (Luke, 110).

How closely *The Orators* approximated the thinking of at least one Mosleyite is dramatically revealed in Nicolson's novel *Public Faces* (1932), which draws its title, and epigraph, from Auden's dedicatory verses to Stephen Spender. Nicolson, to be sure, does not use the distinction of public and private in quite the same way Auden does. For him, "private" seems to mean only personal (in a Forsterian sense), whereas with Auden, it assumes (at least) the additional meaning of "private" in terms of group adherence and linguistic usage; and, on the other hand, "public" for Nicolson refers not only, as in Auden, to the world beyond the individual and his friends, but also and quite specifically to the State, almost as a kind of fascist ideal. Despite these differences, there are some striking resemblances, especially in terms of motifs and what it is perhaps not inappropriate to call obsessions. There is, for instance, the "enemy" who, in Nicolson's novel, grows to massive proportions, with the whole world leagued at one stage of the narrative against Britain.

Britain, of course, as befits the Stalkyish nature of this scientific fiction, is easily a match for them all, especially in view of its possession of secretly developed and spectacularly speedy rocket airplanes, whose sudden appearance throws Paris, Berlin, Moscow, and Baghdad into utter confusion. Her invincibility is also about to be assured by the development of "atomic bombs" as small as inkstands. Ultimate responsibility for Britain's glorious and chiefly diplomatic victory is attributable to the public impulsiveness of a paranoic Air Minister (the Airman?) as well as to the private manipulations of two minor public officials, John and Jane. After the crisis is over, we are granted a brief glimpse of the "Mosley Cabinet of 1942," one of whose "many valuable achievements" is the suppression of the "syndicate of popular newspapers" on whom much of the original crisis is blamed (*Public Faces*, 284). In this connection, one is reminded of the Airman's vigorous denunciation of Beethameer (Beaverbrook plus Rothermore) and Heathcliffe (Northcliffe). *Public Faces* closes with an appendix, composed in a fictional 1978 in a puerile "futurese" by an apparent descendant of the author, a certain "Leonid Nikolson." This is a feature of the book that may have influenced George Orwell to provide a similar, but much more significant, linguistic appendix fifteen years later in *Nineteen Eighty-Four*.

There are other, even more striking connections between Mosley and *The Orators*. Mosley's gifts as an orator, employed both in Parliament and in the streets, were well known, as even relatively unsympathetic accounts of his career attest (e.g., L. C. B. Seaman's *Life in Britain between the Wars*, 194). Some of his oratory even employs language evocative of Auden's own, such as the conclusion to the speech he gave in the House of Commons on 28 May 1930: "What I fear more than a sudden crisis is a long slow crumbling through the years . . . a gradual paralysis, beneath which the vigour and energy of this country will succumb" (Skidelsky, *Interests*, 193). Like the Airman, Mosley was—and was known to be—a great practical joker, and Robert Skidelsky in his biography gives an account of the twenty-year-old Mosley playing a prank with a pseudocorpse that is reminiscent of the Airman's gruesome sense of humor. Suggestively, Skidelsky also sees a "strong link between fascism and aviation with its 'fascist' combination of individual daring and futuristic technology" (*Mosley*, 68, 320).

How closely apparently unrealistic works of art can approach actual life is strikingly—and tragically—illustrated by comparing *The Orators* with the Earl of Lytton's biography of his son Anthony, Viscount Knebworth. Knebworth, roughly Auden's contemporary at Oxford and a conservative member of Parliament, took up flying in the late twenties, making trips especially to

Italy, Austria, and Germany. By the early thirties, his sympathies with fascism and Roman Catholicism were growing and he engaged in a long—and rather fantastic—correspondence with a friend (both using pseudonyms) in which "they imagined themselves as engaged in a crusade against a certain tendency of modern thought exemplified in the works of Noel Coward and others, from the influence of which they desired to rescue their girl friends. They called this 'The War;' they exchanged poems about it, and it was the chief topic of their correspondence during these months." Knebworth crashed his plane and died, at the age of twenty-nine, while practicing formation flying with his reserve squadron (Lytton, *Anthony*, 336, 339).[13]

All this is not to say that Auden was a fascist or even a Mosleyite. After all, the Airman does see the error of his ways and, in the end, repents of his violent fantasies. The "enemy," he comes to realize, is always the enemy within, never merely the external enemy. The real enemy is always some part of oneself. Auden's intention, I suspect, in "Journal of an Airman" is to show the fallacy of fascism as a force that always seeks an external enemy, a scapegoat. Certainly, such a case could be made, all the more so because that is precisely what Auden does in *The Dance of Death*. But granting this intention, the realization is, to say the least, ambiguous, and it is, perhaps, ultimately to this ambiguity that Auden refers when he calls *The Orators* a "fair notion fatally injured." Even so, a number of important questions still remain unanswered, such as why book 3 takes up the Airman's fantasies of destruction all over again and why the "Epilogue," with its clear preference for action over contemplation, confirms them. And why does the preoccupation with groups and strong leaders in *The Orators* dovetail so neatly with a similar preoccupation of Auden and his friends in real life? And why does Auden revert repeatedly to sympathetic portrayals of young, dynamic, charismatic leaders as a major feature of his work, such as Sir Francis Crewe in *The Dog Beneath the Skin* (1935) or Michael Ransom in *The Ascent of F6*?

The answer to these questions involves positing an Auden who, while never a fascist, came at times perilously close to accepting some characteristically fascist ideas, especially those having to do with a mistrust of the intellect, the primacy of the group over the individual, the fascination with a strong leader (who expresses the will of the group), and the worship of youth. Some of these ideas, of course, are shared by Communism, producing something that might conveniently be called "comfascism." Nor was Auden unaware of the close psychological and emotional links between Communism and fascism. "Anyone who has spoken to a young Nazi or Communist convert," he wrote in 1934, "will know that they exhibit the same symptoms. He will tell you likewise that his movement has given him back his soul" (Auden, "Groups," 98). Such views were not merely passing fancies for

Auden. As late as January 1939, he claimed to be "seeing the end of liberal democracy and there are two alternatives to it. One of them is Fascism; and the other is something which I shall call Social Democracy. I am not very optimistic about the future of Social Democracy in this country during the next twenty years at least; yet *I consider the end of liberal democracy a good thing*. . . . Fascism—make no mistake about it—owes its success to the fact that it appeals to the sense of justice of good people. . . . The danger of Fascism arises because Liberal Democracy, by failing to mete out justice in society, has made people feel that freedom is not worth while" (*Prose*, 463–65; my italics).

The Auden group's sympathy for such "comfascism" perhaps also accounts for the otherwise paradoxical praise that various members lavished on Wyndham Lewis. In 1931, Lewis had published a notorious book praising Hitler and presenting him as a "prophet, Mahomet, Mussolini, or Lenin" (Lewis, *Hitler*, 48). Stephen Spender praises Lewis in *The Destructive Element* (208); Grigson praises him in *New Verse* ("Education," 1); Auden praises him in *Letters from Iceland* (233); but most effusively, Cecil Day-Lewis praises him in *A Hope for Poetry*, describing him as a shade "too bitter" but standing nevertheless "head and shoulders above every other contemporary writer in England" (41–42).[14] Day-Lewis writes in the same fulsome vein about D. H. Lawrence, reserving for him his highest admiration and commending him for enunciating the truth that "the cerebral part of civilized man has been forced into unnatural growth at the expense of the soil, the rest of him; that the conscious has outstripped the unconscious and this cutting of communication has rendered impossible a healthy give-and-take between the two." At the same time, and without any apparent sense of contradiction, Day-Lewis complains that too much contemporary English revolutionary verse is marred by muddleheadedness, that its authors are "apt to produce work which makes the neutral reader wonder whether it is aimed at winning him for the communist or the fascist state." He then goes on, oddly enough, to attribute the confusion to Lawrence's influence, discovering in "Auden's preoccupation with the search for the " 'truly strong man,' " Lawrence's evangel of spiritual submission to the great individual (55–56). Hope for poetry, it was clear, there might be; but for reason and common sense, not much. One can understand, therefore, Julian Bell's undertone of annoyance when he inquired of Day-Lewis in "The Proletariat and Poetry:" "And who is Mr. Auden's private war directed against?"(Bell, 326).

Not that Auden and his friends were by any means alone in being certain that something needed to be done, but they were, at the same time, uncertain and confused as to what and by whom. As Prince Mirsky, that very curious (and also rather confused) commentator on the British intellectual scene of the period, observed, the August 1931 economic/political crisis awakened a strong new interest in the Soviet Union among the young. As a result, in "the course of the 1931–1932 academic year a number of the clubs to the left of the reformists were founded. To-day there are in the London School of Economics, *The Marxist Society*, in Oxford, *The October Club*, while in Cambridge the old *Heretics* now has a marxist leadership and a radically inclined membership. In all this fermentation of course there is much snobbery and fashion . . . and much youthful nonsense . . . and much emotion-mongering easily likely to blow yesterday's young 'marxist' into to-day's fascist camp" (Mirsky, 235–36). Even to an old hand and Marxist convert like Mirsky, it was clear that the dividing line between Marxism and fascism was, as far as young British intellectuals were concerned, a very thin and precarious one. As if to confirm Mirsky's theory, A. L. Rowse—Auden's exact contemporary at Oxford—published in *Politics and the Younger Generation* his view that "Russia offers the spectacle of an experiment at once noble and exhilarating, and yet tortured and harassed; at one time it seemed as if Germany might lead the way out of the impasse; we need expect no lead from America." Though it was regrettable, in Rowse's view, that the younger generation (in 1931) as yet showed no great interest in politics, he predicted that they would soon change their minds, as disaster was clearly impending for the capitalist world (Rowse, 16–32).

V

In the brief catalogue of influences on *The Orators*, which Auden compiled in his 1966 preface, there are a couple of other surprising omissions besides D'Annunzio, De Bosis or even Lindbergh. Why, one wonders, is there no mention of Homer Lane and why none of John Layard? According to Isherwood's 1937 *New Verse* essay on Auden, Homer Lane's psychological teachings "provide a key to most of the obscurities in the 'Journal of an Airman.' " As an instance of what this key will unlock, Isherwood goes on to mention parenthetically that John Layard, a disciple of Lane's, has pointed out "the psychological relation between epilepsy and flight" ("Some," 27). Stephen Spender, in *The Destructive Element*, makes no explicit reference to either Lane or Layard, attributing instead the same association of epilepsy with flight to "certain natives," but he also sees it as an important "mythology" for understanding the Airman (268). Auden himself occasionally mentions Lane by name in his early poetry and at other times silently incorporates recognizable elements of Lane's "doctrine" into that poetry, with "Petition" being perhaps the best-known example. As late as 1937, Auden cites Lane and Layard as two of the chief influences in turning him away from the "pure" poetry of his undergraduate years to the "committed" verse that was to make him famous. In the fourth and largely autobiographical part of his "Letter to Lord Byron" in *Letters from Iceland*, Auden writes:

> Three years passed quickly while the Isis went
> Down to the sea for better or for worse;
> Then to Berlin, not Carthage, I was sent
> With money from my parents in my purse,
> And ceased to see the world in terms of verse.
> I met a chap called Layard and he fed
> New doctrines into my receptive head.
>
> Part came from Lane, and part from D. H. Lawrence;
> Gide, though I didn't know it then, gave part.
> They taught me to express my deep abhorrence
> If I caught anyone preferring Art
> To Life and Love and being Pure-in-Heart.
> I lived with crooks but seldom was molested.
> The Pure-in-Heart can never be arrested.

(EA, 195)

Nor, unfortunately, can the Pure-in-Heart be readily understood, especially when they neglect to inform their readers of the literary sources of their self-proclaimed purity.

Without Isherwood's (and, to a much slighter degree, Spender's) guidance, it would have been nearly impossible during the thirties to grasp the connection between *The Orators* and the work of Lane and Layard. Even with that guidance, it was a job of some difficulty, since both Isherwood's comments in his 1937 essay and Spender's in *The Destructive Element* are imprecise. Much more helpful was Isherwood's barely fictionalized autobiography *Lions and Shadows*, where we are told that Auden (thinly disguised as the poet Weston) had met Layard (fictionalized as the anthropologist Barnard) "purely by chance late in 1928 in a café" in Berlin, where the latter had begun to tell him about "the great psychologist" Homer Lane. "Barnard had been a patient and pupil of Lane's," Isherwood confides, "and now, since the master's death he was one of the very few people really qualified to spread Lane's teachings and carry on his work. In Weston, he had found an intelligent listener who became, overnight, an enthusiastic disciple." When Auden returned to England for the Christmas holidays, he was so full of enthusiasm for Lane that he was incapable of talking about anyone else, spouting off about "death-wishes" and analyzing the psychological sources of Isherwood's physical ailments.

The basis of Lane's doctrine, according to Isherwood, consisted in recognizing and resolving the conflict between man's conscious and unconscious selves, or, to use Isherwood's vocabulary, respectively between the Devil and God. The fundamental error of modern education is to deny God and worship the Devil, with the inevitable consequence that the imprisoned divinity breaks out in disease. The liberation of God, therefore, invariably means recovery from illness: "Every disease, Lane had taught, is in itself a cure—if we know how to take it. There is only one sin: disobedience to the inner law of our own nature." These notions, as Isherwood and Auden perceived, bore a close resemblance to D. H. Lawrence's ethos, especially as enunciated in *Fantasia of the Unconscious*. Both Lane and Lawrence abhorred pity and the ideal of self-sacrifice: "Self-sacrifice, Barnard had told Weston, only means, in the last analysis, the sacrifice of others to yourself: it is the subtlest and most deadly form of selfishness." Or as Auden put it in one of the epigrams he wrote shortly after his return from Berlin:

> The friends of the born nurse
> Are always getting worse.
>
> (EA, 51)

The answer, then, would seem to be a (by definition) healthy self-expression, untrammeled by the views or interests of others, but oddly enough, Isherwood does not propose such a solution. Instead, he draws up a list of the various ills that the psyche—selfish or otherwise—is heir to. For example, the denial of one's creative self produces cancer; extreme obstinacy, rheumatism; the desire to return to childhood, consumption; or the "attempt to become an angel and fly," epilepsy. The means of avoiding these diseases is not, as might be expected, freedom and self-expression, but—and even Isherwood seems a little put out by this—being pure in heart. "The pure-in-heart man," he notes, "became our new ideal. He represented, indeed, our picture of Lane himself." So powerful an influence did Lane's doctrine become for Isherwood, that it gave final shape to his decision to abandon a self-sacrificial career in medicine for a full-time "selfish" devotion to literature. In the spring of 1929, he left London and his old life for Berlin and the source of new inspiration, Auden and "perhaps, Barnard himself." On this note of spiritual (not to say, oratorical) conversion and rebirth, Christopher Isherwood brings his autobiography to a close (Isherwood, *Lions*, 299–312).

From Isherwood's account, it is evident that Lane must have had a profound impact on the young Auden's thinking and probably on that of the

Auden group as a whole. In the "education of the twenties," he may be said to have represented a kind of postgraduate course of theoretical instruction. Consequently, critics over the years have dutifully rehearsed his name, in notes and asides, taking more or less on faith what Isherwood had written about him, without bothering to compare his version with Lane's own published writings. But whoever does take the trouble to do so soon finds that there are several curious and major discrepancies. To begin with, the real Homer Lane, while clearly an extraordinary and unconventional human being, was not given, as Isherwood's Lane (and presumably Layard's) is, to socking patients in the eye in order to make them less timid and retiring. He might, and at times did, come close to making them sock him in the eye, but never the other way around. He was, in fact, an utterly nonviolent though by no means timid person, for whom being pure in heart was not synonymous with being pure in genitals—on the contrary. Ironically, it was his compelling urge toward self-sacrifice and perhaps self-destruction rather than toward self-expression that led to the closing of the Little Commonwealth, the reform school he directed from 1913 to 1918. He simply refused to undertake a proper defense of his own conduct. The same is true of the trial that led to his eventual expulsion from Britain. In E. T. Bazeley's and W. D. Wills's studies of his life and work, he emerges as an eminently humble and practical/impractical man, a cross between Christ, Henry Ford, and Casanova who, during his active life had little use for spinning out elaborate theories or even for doing any kind of serious writing at all. His only book-length work, *Talks to Parents and Teachers*, was first published in 1928 (three years after his death) and is, as the title suggests, fundamentally a handbook of useful advice. Its subject is the education of children and its approach is direct and commonsensical, with illustrations drawn largely from Lane's own experience at the Little Commonwealth. Though to some degree indebted to Freud, Lane tends to avoid abstract psychological vocabulary, concentrating instead on such generally accepted notions as freedom, love, and happiness. A term like *death wish*, which Isherwood claims to be characteristic of him, is actually highly atypical of the *Talks* and probably derives from Freud (or Layard) rather than Lane. Even more to the point, Lane, in this work, makes no explicit connection between physical and mental disease, not to mention epilepsy and flight, though he does stress the link between physical environment and mental well-being.

Lane's teachings, insofar as they can be considered original at all (which even such ardent admirers as the Earl of Lytton and the Bishop of Liverpool do not claim), are implicit in the practical success he achieved in the reeducation of asocial adolescents at the Little Commonwealth. His strategy was simply to be entirely permissive and "loving," which, in practice, meant that his pupils were forced to turn to themselves for the "authority figure" Lane refused to provide. For him, as for Rousseau, "human nature is innately good," and all that is required to make it flourish is a free environment. "The freer the child is," so Lane concludes, "the more it will be considerate and social" (Lane, *Talks*, 148). According to W. D. Wills, Lane did endorse Groddeck's theory that physical disease has psychological roots and believed that "no one was ever ill unless he had a psychological need for that illness," but this idea seems to have played hardly any role in the actual, day-to-day running of the school, which is perhaps best described as supervised anarchy (Wills, "Influence," 29). In 1918, the Little Commonwealth closed down after Lane had been accused (but not convicted) of having sexual relations with some of his female pupils, and after several years' private and extremely successful practice (with Layard as one of his patients), he was again brought to trial and deported to France, where he died in 1925. His spiritual legacy survived for a time in A. S. Neill's experiments in antiauthoritarian education at Summerhill.

Between this Lane and Isherwood's Lane there exists only a limited resemblance. It is possible that Isherwood was consciously enlarging and mythologizing the real Lane for the purposes of his admittedly fictionalized autobiography, but it is not probable. The general outlines of Isherwood's conception of Lane's work are identical in *Lions and Shadows* and in the nonfictional *New Verse* essay. The fact of such consistency suggests that the source of the new Lane lies elsewhere. But where? In Auden? Not likely, because Auden in late 1928 would have had neither the knowledge nor the motive for deliberately reshaping the actual Lane into a super-Lane. There remains only one logical possibility: Layard.

Just why Layard should have undertaken to remodel Lane for Auden's delectation is unclear, but one can speculate that Layard, like so many psychological patients, had reacted to his analyst by making him into a larger-than-life father figure, much as Auden's Airman does with his Uncle Henry, who may actually represent Lane or, more likely, Layard. It is also possible, though only barely, that Lane may have introduced Layard to Groddeck's psychosomatic theories without bothering to mention that they were not his own, thereby leading to Layard's and Auden's confusion. Lane had been treating Layard with moderate success for a mysterious paralytic condition he had contracted while doing research in the Pacific. In the biographical note to one of the *Eranos Yearbook* collections, presumably based on material supplied by Layard himself, he describes himself as having done "analytical work with Homer Lane" and others, but since Lane was never legally licensed to practice psychiatry in Britain, all of his patients were, officially speaking, his pupils (*Spiritual*, 454). If Stephen Spender is right in supposing that Edward Blake, in Isherwood's novel *The Memorial* (1932), is a portrait of Layard, and if Isherwood is following here his usual practice of keeping fairly close to the originals of his characters, then it seems likely that Layard was really much more of a patient than a pupil.[15] Blake at one point in the novel receives treatment from a German psychiatrist and, at another, engages in a love affair partially in order to be "cured" of homosexuality, thereby following (unsuccessfully) Lane's principle that love is the best medicine. He is, significantly, depicted as having been an air ace in the war and as attempting, and failing, to commit suicide—as in fact Layard did. The identification with Uncle Henry in *The Orators* is made even more complete by his relationship with the ostensible hero of the novel, the young pure-in-heart Eric, who first considers Blake to be his enemy but later comes to regard him as a friend. Blake had also been almost like a brother to Eric's dead father and therefore qualifies as a kind of spiritual uncle.

What does Lane have to do directly with the development of *The Orators*? Or, to be more precise, what do the real and the mythical Lanes have to do with it? And is it true, as Isherwood claimed, that references to Lane's theories are to be found "generally" in *The Orators*? If by "theories" Isherwood means, as he evidently does, Groddeck's notion of the psychological origins of disease, then this is hardly "generally" true of *The Orators*, unless that "generally" is very general indeed. It is partially true, at best, of the "Journal of an Airman," where the notion may help to explain (in a general way) the curious dichotomy between the Airman and his hand.[16] More useful, however, is the fundamental distinction that Isherwood's Lane draws between the conscious mind (the Devil) and the irrational desires (God). Applying this distinction to the "Journal," it appears that the Airman moves progressively away from "God" and toward the "Devil" until at the very end he repudiates the former in order to embrace the latter. This is, in fact, how M. K. Spears—without making use of the Isherwood-Lane terminology—does read the "Journal," concluding that the Airman's conversion must therefore be seen as ironic. (*Poetry of W. H. Auden*, 53) This supposition, in my view, is incorrect, but the possibility of such an interpretation seems to have worried Auden—as it should have, since it indirectly endorses the Airman's fascism. In a 1934 review of a study of T. E. Lawrence, he makes a clear and unambiguous statement on the subject. After quoting Lawrence's dictum that "happiness comes in absorption," Auden warns that "a misinterpretation of absorption is one of the great heresies of our generation. To interpret it as blind action without consideration of meaning or ends, as an escape from reason and consciousness; that is indeed to become the Truly Weak Man, to enlist in the great Fascist retreat which will land us finally in the ditch of despair" (Auden, "Lawrence," 22). T. E. Lawrence, as we have seen (and as Spears suggests), is one of Auden's probable models for the Airman, which implies that Auden meant his readers to apply his warning to *The Orators*.[17]

Isherwood's Lane, then, does not play an especially prominent role in shaping *The Orators*. But what about the real Lane? Unfortunately, there is no explicit evidence that Auden had actually read *Talks to Parents and Teachers*, but it is at least arguable, with his great enthusiasm for Lane, that he did. In a review published late in 1934 in *The Listener*, he wondered out loud if the author "is acquainted with the work of Homer Lane but everything she says is a striking confirmation of his teaching" (Auden, *Prose*, 78). The confidence with which Auden speaks here of the "work of Homer Lane" suggests that it was based on an actual reading of that "work," and specifically of *Talks to Parents and Teachers* since that was the only readily available specimen of Homer Lane's writing. Certainly the link between *The Orators* and the real Lane is at least as strong as that between *The Orators* and the mythologized Lane. For, like the former in his Little Commonwealth, Auden is concerned in this "English Study" with a group of asocial and unhappy human beings whom he hopes to be able to help. Like Lane, his advice seems to be to realize the self to the fullest possible degree in a condition of freedom that at the same time involves respect for the group. Second, like Auden, Lane is impatient with a static happiness of possession (for which he uses the symbol of the rabbit); instead, he urges a dynamic, romantic happiness of doing and becoming (symbolized by the dog). "Of the two capacities for happiness," he writes, "the creative involves an element of danger, surprise or uncertainty, as shown, for example, at a later age in athletic contests and games, or in mountaineering, exploration or hunting" (Lane, *Talks*, 141). Auden's heroes are never happy except in action; with them, the Lanean dog is always just beneath the skin.

On a more specific level, Lane's work provides a clue to interpreting the Airman's mysterious preoccupation with his hands. In Lane's view, the infant's recognition of his hands is one of humanity's most meaningful experiences. "The first dawn of consciousness," he writes, "is when the child does something with definite purpose, and recognizes his power over his own hand." On the basis of this perception, Lane then goes on to develop his important distinction between doing and having, which later culminates in the double notion of possessive and creative happiness. The hand is the symbol of doing but it is also the symbol of having (Lane, *Talks*, 14, 29). For the Airman, of course, the problem is that he does not always have control over his hand. In Lane's terms, this means either that the Airman reverts temporarily and intermittently to a pre-infantile state of unconsciousness (perhaps, to anticipate for a moment, epileptically induced); or else, which seems more likely, that his hand's desire for possessions (kleptomania) overpowers his mind's desire for action. In other words, the Airman's urge for creative happiness, which by definition involves risk and danger, is occasionally overwhelmed by his urge for possessive happiness, which places security above all other considerations.

How does this all fit in with epilepsy and flight? Isherwood's Lane, as we have seen, specifically makes the association, explaining epilepsy, rather mysteriously, as caused by a desire to be like an angel and fly. Isherwood's Lane may have got this from Groddeck, but Groddeck's "Book of the It" or *Buch vom Es* (1923), which Auden is known to have read carefully, does not make any such connection. Elsewhere, to be sure, Groddeck associates flying with the motion of the fetus when the mother is walking, but this essay, "Über das Es," though written in 1920, was not published until 1966 (Groddeck, 59). The usual Freudian symbolic interpretation links flight with sexual intercourse; and the same is true of the Freudian interpretation of epilepsy. One is almost tempted to pass the whole thing off as a red herring, thrown out by the Auden group as bait to gullible readers.

However, this would be a bad mistake, for in Auden's next work of any scope, *The Dance of Death*, the principal character, the Dancer, expresses a wish to be known as the "Pilot" not long after having suffered an epileptic fit. It therefore seems possible, and even likely, that a similar connection exists in the "Journal" as well. The intention behind linking epilepsy with flight in the later work is clearly symbolic: the Dancer, as the representative of a doomed bourgeoisie, seeks to escape his fate by "flight" (in both senses); and his epileptic fit is, to take a cue from Groddeck, the physical expression of his psycho-social malady. The same sort of reading, however, does not work with the Airman. His loss of control is restricted to his hands and leads to kleptomania and/or masturbation, with the latter, in any case, according to Groddeck, constituting the basis of civilization. These symptoms do not fit any class of epilepsy known to medicine. Moreover, the Airman's flight, unlike the Dancer's, is not an escape, since even after his conversion and repentance he continues to fly, though, admittedly, perhaps to death. His flight seems more closely related to the urge to reach high places that motivates so many of Auden's protagonists in the 1930s, an urge that has utopian political overtones rather than epileptic ones.

What really lies behind the Airman's supposed epilepsy and symptoms of neurosis is not the psychosomatic speculations of Groddeck, but the anthropological researches of John Layard. As both Isherwood and (somewhat less explicitly) Spender sought vainly to persuade readers of *The Orators* during the thirties, Layard provides an essential key to understanding the otherwise rather puzzling "Journal." Layard, in fact, bears something of the same relation to *The Orators* that Sir James Frazer and Jessie Weston do to *The Waste Land*, and it seems at least possible that this was the sort of relation that Auden originally had in mind and wished to evoke in the minds of his readers. It certainly bears a marked resemblance to what Isherwood calls "the Waste Land game" in *Lions and Shadows*, a game that Auden came to be adept at playing by the late twenties: "Quotations and misquotations were allowed, together with bits of foreign languages, proper names and private jokes. Weston was peculiarly well equipped for playing the Waste Land game. For Eliot's Dante quotations and classical learning he substituted oddments of scientific, medical and psychoanalytical jargon" (Isherwood, *Lions*, 191).

By the time Auden met Layard in Berlin, the latter had already been involved for over a decade with the study of primitive societies in the South Sea islands. As a young man of twenty-five, he had coedited a report (1916) on the collections made by A. F. R. Wollaston's 1912–13 expedition to Dutch New Guinea, and he had gone to Malekula in the New Hebrides himself for about six months in 1914–15 to gather material on the Stone Age natives. Like Malinowski and Mead, he was a careful, not to say compulsive, compiler of data—especially on sexual matters—but unlike them, he frequently went well beyond the perimeter of his research in order to draw psycho-anthropological conclusions of an unorthodox sort. So overpowering was his experience in the South Seas and so extensive the data he collected that Layard needed decades to order and write them up in *The Stone Men of Malekula* (1942), a vast compendium running to over eight hundred pages, including maps, illustrations, and photographs. Layard's odd mix of field work and Jungian psychology also led him at approximately the same time to produce *The Lady of the Hare* (1944), in which, with singular industry and lack of humor, he analyzes the "hare-raising" dreams of a simple country woman, comparing them with mythological hares drawn from all times and places. Neither of these books has a direct bearing on *The Orators*, though their curious contents and methodology may suggest a spiritual kinship between Layard and the young Auden (and his Airman). A demonstrable connection does exist, however, between *The Orators* and two of Layard's essays published in the *Journal of the Royal Anthropological Institute*, entitled "Malekula: Flying Tricksters, Ghosts, Gods, and Epileptics" and "Shamanism: An Analysis Based on Comparison with the Flying Tricksters of Malekula." From a reading of these two essays, it becomes obvious that Auden must either have known and made use of them or else have got at essentially the same information through Layard himself.[18] Given their dates of publication (both 1930), it is likely that Layard was working on them in 1928/29 in Berlin, at the time when he and Auden were most closely linked.

The first of the two articles is by far the more important, both as an original contribution in its own right and for its relevance to *The Orators*. The flying tricksters, or "Bwili," who are the subjects of the study, are a secret society or group of sorcerers who, according to Layard's native informants, can "all fly, in the form of fowls, and have in addition the power of assuming the form of other men or women, of animals, reptiles, birds, trees, or fruit. In these forms they indulge their spite by killing their enemies, though at other times their activities take the form of playing practical jokes on their friends" ("Flying," 504). Though not distinguishable physically from the rest of the native population, the Bwili constitute a separate, but not necessarily ruling, group or class. Other natives usually either know or suspect their true identities as Bwili and fear them or are amused by them, depending on whether they are victims or spectators. Generally speaking, the Bwili content themselves with playing harmless practical jokes, but sometimes their perverse and unpredictable nature compels them to kill. In such cases, the unhappy victim's urine invariably turns white and he dies seven days later. Very rarely will one Bwili attack and kill another; otherwise they are (while metamorphosed) immortal.

Most interesting, in the light of the "Journal of an Airman," is Layard's account of the Bwili initiation rites, derived largely from a native story about a Bwili who initiates his sister's son. The choice of the nephew over the son—who merely serves as a helper at the rite—is emphasized by Layard and is especially significant. The ceremony itself, which is preceded by a period of sexual abstinence, involves the gradual but complete dismemberment of the candidate, who must laugh or at least smile as each extremity is lopped off in succession, culminating with the head. If he successfully passes this grotesque test, his severed limbs reassemble and the candidate at once assumes the powers and status of a Bwili.

So much for the native myth. What follows is Layard's analysis of the sources and meaning of that myth which, significantly, he refuses to regard as wholly unreal. The original source, in his view, is ghosts and gods, both of whom the Bwili resembles by virtue of his survival after dismemberment; in other words, on one level the Bwili is a kind South Sea Fisher King who has the power of healing his own wounds (and here too, perhaps, is to be found the origin of Auden's "Letter to a Wound"). A secondary and rather more surprising source is epilepsy. This malady, Layard proposes, is essentially psychological and is frequently produced at will. The epileptic state and the subsequent recovery therefrom, he argues, constitute, in fact, the archetype of the idea of death and rebirth. It is for this reason that epilepsy is called the sacred disease.

From this point onward, Layard's imagination takes flight, almost, one is tempted to say, like a Bwili. "The purpose [*sic*] of epilepsy being to drown out one side—and that the adult side—of a conflict," he writes, "the epileptic retains an infantile mentality, with the result that he is apt to be childlike in his tastes, irresponsible, roguish, and playful, while the misunderstanding he invariably meets with tends at times to render him spiteful and malicious" ("Flying," 520). Moreover, on the rather slender basis of the "well-known epileptic aura" of feeling a cold wind blow across one's face, which "in one case known to me" was associated with the sensation of flight, Layard proceeds to establish the (by now) notorious connection between epilepsy and flight ("Flying," 521). But epileptics do not merely fly, they also have a predisposition toward homosexuality. Why? Because homosexuality is essentially caused by the same reluctance to face up to sexual maturity and adult responsibility as epilepsy. (This was also the established view, as Auden was fully aware, of Freud and Trigant Burrow.) To be sure, Layard himself admits that he possesses no evidence that the Bwili are homosexual, except for the fact that during the initiation rites candidates are penetrated anally by the "Malekulan ghost" ("Flying," 523).

Layard's other essay, dealing with Siberian shamanism and not based on any field work of his own, seeks to apply and consolidate some of his Malekulan findings. Like the Bwili, Layard argues, the shamans have the power of flight, a power that seems ultimately derived from semimystical states that can only be termed epileptoid. The states of possession, which characterize the true shaman, can also be viewed as a kind of temporary suicide, similar to the ritual dismemberment of the Bwili, which brings Layard again to the death-rebirth archetype. Moreover, shamans, while by no means exclusively homosexual, do often practice homosexual acts at the command of their spirits, and they are, in any event, so Layard speculates, probably descended from homosexual epileptics.

Without going any further, it is clear that Auden's Airman is flesh and blood of Layard's Bwili and shamans. He flies, he plays practical jokes, he tries to kill enemies, he worries about sexual abstinence, he is probably homosexual, he dies (figuratively at least) and is reborn, and he is initiated into airmanhood and oratory by his uncle. After all this, it seems safe to assume that he is also epileptic, though the text itself lends very little detailed support for such a conclusion. Moreover, the Airman's uncle is unquestionably a Bwili, since he, in fact, does die and is reborn. But, granting all this, what is the point of it all? Why has Auden gone to the considerable trouble of incorporating wholesale Layard's at best extremely obscure and rather dubious conjectures into the main segment of his poem? And why, after having gone to that trouble, did he not provide any clue to his readers of what he had done?

The answer, I suspect, rests with the fact of the existence of an Auden group. Like the Bwili, the members of this group were all initiates who possessed power and knowledge not given to lesser mortals. They knew about Layard and the Bwili and the Airman and epilepsy, and they could enjoy the elaborate in-group joke. Only years later did they try, a little forgetfully and halfheartedly, to pass that knowledge on to a by then, perhaps understandably, not specially interested public. The preference for private faces in public places might, in a Forsterian way, produce authentic art, but driven to this kind of extreme, it could not make that authentic art great. Eliot a decade earlier had deigned to add explanatory notes to *The Waste Land,* even if he later grew unsure about their significance and value. The Waste Land Game, it seems, has its losers as well as its winners.

VI

The Auden group is probably the main reason for Auden's complex game of intellectual hide-and-seek in *The Orators.* But there are also other reasons. One of them, surely, is the fun of the game itself, the pure pleasure of not being found out—and of providing his reader with the creative happiness of trying to solve the riddle. This was perhaps especially true of a game where one of the answers was homosexuality. As we have seen, Auden nowhere makes either the Airman's or his own homosexuality explicit. But it is obvious that if the connection between Layard's Malekulan essays and *The Orators* had been public knowledge, so too would have been Auden's homosexuality. It is doubtful that the young Auden would have wanted that, though, to be sure, by the early thirties homosexuality no longer was as publicly shocking as it had been in the late nineties. That is why J. G. Southworth is wrong, I think, in saying that the obscurity of Auden's early poetry is attributable exclusively to its homosexual content, though I am also convinced that he is by no means altogether wrong (Southworth, 189).[19]

Aside from using Layard as a joke or as a disguise, Auden may also, paradoxically, have seen in him a marvelous opportunity for serious symbolic statement. The angels whom the Prize Day orator in the opening section of *The Orators* uses as a model for his public school audience probably derive as much from Layard as they do from Milton and Buchman. Like flying anthropologists or Oxford Groupers, they gather their materials in all parts of Britain and then assemble to collaborate on a report, which may very well be identical with *The Orators.* And the resemblance of the Airman, who is an orator and a poet, to the dismembered Bwili and, by extension, to the dismembered Orpheus must also have struck Auden as it would have any other reader of Layard, or D. H. Lawrence, for that matter. The Airman, like the Bwili, the shamans, and Orpheus, inhabits a magical and imaginary world of such tremendous power that it assumes control over the real world itself, in much the same way as Isherwood and Upward's Mortmere did. It is only by going back to the original sources of vatic poetry—even or especially if these sources are epileptic or homosexual—that the modern poet can regain a portion of that pristine strength for himself and, defying the laws of physical and spiritual gravity, begin to fly. In this way the oratorical poet, the poet as priest, might be restored to a position of central importance and power, for which he would nevertheless (as a kind of perennial practical joker) not have to assume a boring day-to-day responsibility.

Knowing Layard's theories obviously helps one to understand something of what is going on in the "Journal of an Airman" and it illuminates other segments of *The Orators* as well as it does, for instance, the series of sudden metamorphoses in the "Prologue." Layard is certainly a key, though he probably is not the master or skeleton key that, as M. K. Spears once felt, would unlock all the trapdoors of *The Orators* (*Poetry*, 45). Whatever Isherwood may have thought, there is much besides Layard and Lane in the "Journal," and even much beyond epilepsy, flight, and homosexuality. The root, I think, of the Airman's difficulty lies not so much in epilepsy as it does in his ambiguous relationship to his Uncle Henry, who committed suicide fourteen years earlier, when the Airman seems to have been about seventeen. His earliest memories are of disliking Henry and of sensing in him a rival, but at the same time, paradoxically, of being elated whenever he secured Henry's approval. When the Airman was sixteen and a half, he was invited for the first time to Henry's flat for dinner and champagne, and there he discovered "who and what he [Henry] was—my real ancestor." Just what this means is not clear, though there may be a hint here, as Spender suggests, that they discover a homosexual bond. This is perhaps also the cause of the Airman's self-recriminations for not having avenged "the boy's faked evidence at the inquest," presumably following Henry's suicide. On the other hand, it is well to remember Isherwood's third rule about Auden's Scandinavian heritage and to note that the Airman makes it quite clear that Henry is his maternal uncle. Not only in the New Hebrides, but also in the Norse sagas, the closest relationship of man to boy is that of maternal uncle to nephew, a fact that could also account for the Airman's need for revenge. Moreover, the Airman has another uncle who is still alive, to whom he also feels in some sense spiritually related. Uncle Sam is a less prominent character than Henry, but at the same time, his relationship to the Airman is much more explicit: he is also a kleptomaniac. "Only once here, quite at the beginning, and I put it back," reads one of the Airman's two entries dealing with Sam. "Uncle Sam, is he one too? He has the same backward-bending thumb that I have. I wonder." Here it seems clear that, unless we assume by some Groddeckian leap that kleptomania is equatable with homosexuality, the Airman suspects Sam of being a thief and nothing else; and suspects, too, that his own kleptomania is therefore hereditary or "ancestral." What the kleptomania really points to is a symbolic "family" or class guilt, something that is also at the root of his violence. The Airman and his uncle are bourgeois and as such, in Auden's view, social kleptomaniacs and parasites, regardless of their good intentions. How close to the bourgeois family of Auden and company Uncle Henry and his flying thief of a nephew actually were can be appreciated by comparing the "Journal of an Airman" with the following passage from the second installment of Christopher Isherwood's "autobiography" *Kathleen and Frank* (1971): "Soon after Christopher came of age, Henry [Isherwood's wealthy uncle who died, apparently, of natural causes] had started giving him an allowance; a very small one, but enough to make him independent when it was added to his own savings and what he got from Kathleen. Henry referred to Christopher as 'my favorite nephew' and recommended his books to his friends. Their bond wasn't literature, however, but the discovery that they had similar sexual tastes. When they dined together at Henry's flat, they giggled like age-mates over Henry's adventures with guardsmen and Christopher's encounters in the boy-bars of Berlin." Henry also seems to be the model for Lancaster, the well-to-do "uncle" (actually a cousin) of the protagonist in Isherwood's novel *Down There on a Visit* (1962).

The next stage in Henry and the Airman's relationship is reached through a dream in which the Airman sees himself at a ferry crossing, with a football match in progress on one side and an execution for sabotage on the other (again the doubling of the school and gang motifs, as well as an echo of Malekulan dismemberment). He is handed a newspaper photograph of Henry, bearing the inscription, "I have crossed it." This message eventually leads to the Airman's renunciation of violence and hatred. "To my Uncle, perpetual gratitude and love for his crowning mercy. For myself, absolute humility," he writes toward the close of his journal. And he passes a final verdict on the journal itself: "Thoughts suitable to a sanatorium"—not very far from Auden's own verdict a generation later. Having found humility, having "crossed it" himself, having killed his old identity, the Airman's "hands are in perfect order." There is peace at ten thousand feet.[20]

One does not need to be clairvoyant to recognize that what Auden is describing here is a Christian conversion, using quite traditional imagery, away from the old gods of revenge and war and toward the new God of love and peace. Auden may, in fact, be invoking here, for the private delectation of his little group of friends, the intensely religious dream-vision he had experienced during a severe illness not long after leaving Oxford in 1928. In Stephen Spender's fictional account, published for the first time nearly seventy years later, an Airman-like Auden seems to "fly through many hundreds of miles of darkness studded" with stars that are really angels. In this visionary dream he moves through and past the angels towards a "centre whose position he felt rather than perceived. As he approached this centre the angels grew always more beautiful and tall. At last he came to a place where there was only a dazzling light. He knew that this brightness was like a thick veil, behind which there was the figure, too bright to see, of divine love" (Spender, "Instead," 27–28). Regardless of whether we are meant to view the sources of the Airman's conversion as originating in Layard's Malekula or in Auden's soul, the experience is unquestionably one of death and rebirth. Monroe K. Spears is surely wrong to read it as ironic and as proof that "the death-wish has conquered" a possibly insane Airman. On the contrary, (inner) death and rebirth lead to immortality and salvation. Instead of flying off to Valhalla or Malekula, Henry has crossed into heaven, to become the Airman's tutelary saint. "Uncle, save them all," the repentant Airman prays, "make me worthy."

How seriously should we take this conversion? Very seriously indeed, on one level; very lightly, on another. "A clean shirt, collar and handkerchief each morning till the end" is one of the last resolutions of the Airman who has turned square. And Uncle Henry loses much of his sainted grandeur after we learn that he appears to have committed suicide with an air gun. But then, perhaps, it is appropriate that an orator who is, on at least one level, a windbag, should use an air gun to kill himself.

In the final analysis, then, what are we to make of the Airman and his friends? Are they simply intellectual Peter Pans, permanent adolescents flying off to a semifascist, quasi-socialist Neverland? Or are they airmen-artists, descendants of Daedalus (and Stephen Dedalus) flying off into new realms of conscience and consciousness, exploring new modes of being? Or are they just lame ducks waddling down the corridors of English literature as an in-group joke of Auden and company? The answer to all of these questions, I suggest, is *yes*. For that is precisely what makes the young Auden's poetry so baffling, so annoying, so pretentious, so brilliant, and so irrepressibly alive.

3

Poetry and Politics in a Low, Dishonest Decade

"All I have is a voice
To undo the folded lie."

—W. H. Auden (1939)

"To pore over the literary shortcomings of twenty years ago, to attempt to patch a faulty work into the perfection it missed at its first execution, to spend one's middle age in trying to mend the artistic sins committed and bequeathed by that very different person who was oneself in youth— all that is surely vain and futile."

—Aldous Huxley (1946)

I

Comrades, who when the sirens roar
From office, shop and factory pour
    'Neath evening sky;
By cops directed to the fug
Of talkie-houses for a drug,
Or down canals to find a hug
    Until you die.

(EA, 120)

So BEGINS THE POEM THAT AUDEN ORIGINALLY PUBLISHED UNDER THE TITLE OF "A Communist to Others" in September 1932 in *Twentieth Century,* and a year later reprinted in the second Hogarth anthology of thirties verse, *New Country*. It is probably the best known of the handful of overtly left-wing propaganda pieces that he wrote during the early thirties, and it undoubtedly contributed powerfully to Auden's reputation at the time as one of the most outspoken supporters of left-wing politics. Though when he republished it a few years later in *Look Stranger!* (1936), Auden toned down the most obviously Communist aspects of the poem by dropping both the title and several stanzas, along with substituting *brothers* for *comrades* in the opening line, he eventually realized that patching the piece up (or down) in this way only made it worse. In the end, he abandoned it altogether and regretfully consigned it, as he told Robin Skelton, to the category of "trash which he is ashamed to have written" (Skelton, 41).[1]

Trash, of course, it wasn't and isn't, if only because at this stage of his career Auden was already incapable of writing trash. For one thing, the poem is, even in its original version, wonderfully and deliberately comic. That comedy and Communism were, in Auden's view, compatible was already amply evident from the conclusion of *The Dance of Death*, but in a letter to his old friend John Pudney he made explicit his belief that, for conscientious fellow travelers, the writing of non-comic poetry would have to await the withering away of the state: "In our line it is only possible to write comic poetry: not the Punch variety, but real slapstick. After the Revolution it may be different" (Berg, April 1931). Nevertheless, that fanatical advocate of the "serious" in poetry, F. R. Leavis, was not amused, concluding that in "A Communist to Others" Auden's "irony is not the irony of the mature mind—it is self-defensive, self-indulgent or merely irresponsible" (Leavis, 323). To less censorious minds, however, the rant that this poem dumps so enthusiastically on the middle- and upper-class enemies of the proletariat is unforgettably and delightfully exaggerated, "real slapstick," as it were:

> Let fever sweat them till they tremble
> Cramp rack them till they resemble
>   Cartoons by Goya:
> Their daughters sterile be in rut,
> May cancer rot their herring gut,
> The circular madness on them shut,
>   Or paranoia.[2]

(EA, 123)

What, one wonders amidst this barrage of malediction, is a herring gut in a human being? Or the circular madness? Not that the answers matter much, since not even the intended victims of this harangue could have been expected to take its wildly imaginative threats seriously, much less the comrades themselves—who, of course, were for the most part utterly ignorant of the poem's existence.

It is, in fact, the absent comrades who are the real problem here. From Auden's personal perpective, they are probably absent because, aside from German working-class boy-lovers like Kurt Groote, he actually knew no proletarians "to speak of." This was something that did not escape the wrathful eye (and pen) of Julian Bell, who censured Auden and his friends for naively idealizing the manual worker:

> The worst of the cant, after the glorious revolution live happily ever after world without end without tears amen, is the proletarian savior. . . . Yet saviours are what you [Cecil Day-Lewis] and Auden and Spender and your minor followers are trying to make of them. The idealised hero, the Proletarian, the Worker, of the cartoons and posters, ruggedly Grecian, stripped to the waist, muscular, with hammer or axe in hand; lean and brawny, smashing, kicking, humiliating the round fat capitalist in top-hat and striped trousers. Quite apart from the mischief this romantic fiction causes, does it not strike you as a little absurd? And so very like its dialectically interpenetrated opposite, the fascist youth, just as muscular and arrogant and full of kicks and clouts. (J. Bell, 314)

These strictures are all the more hurtful because Bell was "one of us," that is, he was a strong supporter of left-wing political causes in the thirties, even to the point of eventually going to Spain and dying there.[3]

Even so, despite the accuracy of Bell's overall analysis, it applies more to Day-Lewis and Spender's proletarians than it does to Auden's. For there are relatively few "muscular" proletarians in Auden's work. Auden's workers are mostly, as they are in this poem, a rather shadowy, physically vague ideal according to which the capitalists and their cohorts are judged and found wanting. If anything, they tend to be victims rather than youthful heroes wreaking vengeance. Auden's actual "heroes," such as the Airman, Francis, or Ransom, may seek to enlist the help of proletarians, but there is never any doubt regarding their status as established members of the middle class. As Louis MacNeice told him in 1937, "I think you have shown great sense in not writing 'proletarian' stuff. . . . You realize that one must write about what one knows. One may not hold the bourgeois creed, but if one knows only bourgeois one must write about them" (quoted in Carter, 59). Whatever else may be said against Auden as a left-wing propagandist poet, he never perpetrated the kind of poetical drivel to which fellow fellow-travelers like Pablo Neruda sometimes descended, as in *Canto: General* where, like saints in a pious canticle, "Molotov and Voroshilov are there, / I see them with the others, the high generals, / the indomitable ones" (Neruda, 39).

The speaker of Auden's poem is apparently a middle-class "comrade" or perhaps only a would-be comrade. Though he is shown in the process of addressing those "Others" who are also comrades, he belongs to a different class. In the third stanza, the speaker reveals his awareness of the gulf separating himself and the comrades by distinguishing between "us" and "you":

> We cannot put on airs with you
> The fears that hurt you hurt us too
> > Only we say
> That like all nightmares these are fake
> If you would help us we could make
> Our eyes to open, and awake
> > Shall find night day.
>
> (EA, 121)

Here "we" appear to be sincerely concerned with "your" (that is, the proletariat's) fears, even to the point of sharing them. Yet, at the same time, "we" possess some unspecified, superior knowledge that allows us to determine that those fears are unreal ("fake"), though, paradoxically, despite this knowledge "we" nevertheless remain blinded to reality and require "your" assistance to be able to open *our* eyes fully to it. The final "our" here may refer to both "us" and "you," but the fact that we-the-readers can't tell one way or the other is characteristic of the overall fuzziness of the poem.

The speaker, then, simultaneously belongs to and yet remains distinct from the proletariat. His "interests" (whatever these may be) are specifically said to be "set" on them, his "comrades," in part because he is able to foresee a future when the oppressors of the proletariat will be overthrown:

> On you our interests are set
> Your sorrow we shall not forget
> > While we consider
> Those who in every county town
> For centuries have done you brown,
> But you shall see them tumble down
> > Both horse and rider.
>
> (EA, 121)

The speaker's certain knowledge of the future, his secure status (unlike the workers, he is not afraid of being fired), his sense of being at once superior and inferior to the proletariat, his greater awareness of the larger social context of their joint struggle, all these circumstances suggest that he must be a middle-class Communist intellectual, possibly a party member or even a party official, certainly someone who presumes to be able to speak authoritatively with "the voice of the people."[4]

Despite, or rather because, of his non-proletarian origins, the speaker is familiar with the futile oppressive strategies of the various enemies of the working class, all of whom are nevertheless "fake" and are therefore doomed (presumably by the unmentioned but inexorable laws of dialectical materialism) to the trash heap of history. The first of these is the upper-class "splendid person" (also the subject of another poem written at about the same time, "I Have a Handsome Profile"), representing the sporting or semi-feudal upper class. Turning now to address this allegorical personage as "you"—for the moment the titular "Others" have ceased to be his comrades and have become merely "others" of another, inimical sort—the speaker acknowledges the physical skill and self-conscious beauty of this antique survivor of the middle ages but pronounces him "completed" or done for:

> Your beauty's a completed thing.
> The future kissed you, called you king,
>   Did she? Deceiver!
> She's not in love with you at all
> No feat of yours can make her fall,
> She will not answer to your call
>   Like your retriever.
>
> (EA, 121)

Having thus eliminated the obsolete ruling or upper class, whom a Marxist-sympathizing Lady Future has contemptuously cast aside, the speaker next turns to religion in the person of a "dare-devil mystic." This figure, vaguely reminiscent of the Airman in *The Orators*, turns out to be as much of a deceiver (and as much deceived) as his "splendid" predecessor. His recipe for "personal regeneration / By fasting, prayer and contemplation" is of no use to the starving working class, and even those, presumably non-proletarian, "others" who have tried it, realize that it leads only to individual despair and a "dry-as-bone / Night of the soul." The "goodness game," in other words, is just as much of a leisure sport (and racket) as the splendid person's cricket, and its real objective is much the same as his, namely self-aggrandizement at the expense of the working class:

> You hope to corner as reward
> All that the rich can here afford:
> Love and music and bed and board
>   While the world flounders.
>
> (EA, 122)

Religion, so it would appear, is not merely the opiate of the working class, it is also one of the greediest parasites feeding on it.

Worst, however, "among the foes which [sic] we enumer," is the bourgeois, liberal intellectual, who treats the suffering of the working class as a kind of contemptible joke behind which he conceals "the boss's simple stuma"—that is, the Capitalist's counterfeit check or false promises with which he exploits the working class (the word is more commonly spelled "stumer"). Clearly, the liberal intellectual is another "fake," but one who is even more despicable than the others because he is aware of his moral opprobrium but nevertheless persists in it, helping all the while those in power to oppress the proletariat. He is a completely conscious hypocrite, whereas the splendid person and the daredevil mystic are merely unconscious ones:

> Because you saw but were not indignant
> The invasion of the great malignant
> Cambridge ulcer
> The army intellectual
> Of every kind of liberal
> Smarmy with friendship but of all
> There are none falser.
>
> (EA, 122)

In the five stanzas devoted to this liberal fraud—including two subsequently omitted ones—the speaker gives his reasons why this enemy is more dangerous than his predecessors. (His significance is further emphasized by the fact that he gets two more stanzas worth of attention than either of his companions.) He is more dangerous because he is more insidious, pretending as he does to friendship, while doing his best (or worst) to undermine the genuine claims of the working class. He does this by practicing a species of theoretical legerdemain proving

> That wealth and poverty are merely
> Mental pictures, so that clearly
> Every tramp's a landlord really
> In mind-events.
>
> (EA, 123)

While Auden, along with other members of his generation, such as Julian Bell, is probably aiming his attack here primarily at the aloofness of the Bloomsbury Group as a whole from political involvement (the exception, of course, is Leonard Woolf), he no doubt also means his readers to bear in mind the apolitical tradition of Cambridge linguistic philosophy identified with G. E. Moore, the young Bertrand Russell, and Wittgenstein. The phrase "mind-events" in particular refers almost certainly to the Cambridge critic and linguistic philsopher I. A. Richards' celebrated notion of "pseudo-statements."[5]

The liberal fraud is a magician who can make reality disappear by means of a barrage of philosophical mumbo-jumbo. But even that is not the greatest threat emanating from this liberal hypocrite. The real problem with him is that his position can be so easily confused with that of the speaker, who also, of course, claims to be on the side of the workers. Suggestively, both argue that the working class has been deceived by a false reality. In the speaker's case, the workers are said to be suffering from a social nightmare that produces "fake" fears that will vanish utterly as soon as they awaken to the truth, as furnished primarily by himself. So too, according to the liberal bourgeois, the workers are supposedly deluded by a sham reality into believing that their real enemy is the capitalist entrepreneur and his associates, whereas the "truth" is purportedly quite different. The structural similarity between these two views and their expression is the reason why the speaker insists on identifying the liberal as a worse enemy than those whose malevolence is more readily recognizable:

> The worst employer's double-dealing
> Is better than their mental healing
> That would assist us.

(EA, 422)

The devious strategy of the liberal class enemy is (as in *The Dance of Death*) to deny the relevance of class, either by disputing its actual existence or by substituting some other farfetched and fraudulent cause, such as attributing "our" discontent to being "jealous of our sisters." (This represents an ironic rejection, presumably, of the Freudian notion of sibling rivalry as an explanation for social revolution.) The liberal's ultimate purpose in doing so is to blunt the workers' anger by persuading them that their bosses have ceased to be rapacious capitalists and have, instead, become "jolly decent." In this way, the liberal deceiver

> Would dissipate all irritation
> Making a weakened generation
> Completely neuter.

(EA, 422)

No need to worry, however, as the speaker assures his comrades, for the liberal enemy will not succeed in duping either him or them, nor will the splendid person or the daredevil mystic, nor, for that matter, any of their various associates, including

> Professors, agents, magic-makers,
> Their poets and apostles,
> Their bankers and their brokers too,

(EA, 123)

for, after having done the working class "brown" for centuries past, it is now their turn to "turn blue" and "fade away like morning dew / With club-room fossils." This is a remarkable prediction, for, though the speaker does not appear to notice it, from a strictly Marxist point of view what he says is not altogether orthodox. Marx, after all, has nothing whatever to say about any future color changes on the part of the bourgeosie, but he does very clearly presage its demise in a violent and bloody revolution. In his view, Lady Future is anything but demure, and the only thing that will "fade away" is the illusion that radical social change can be brought about by rhetorical or literary means, no matter how violent their expression. In this respect the speaker, then, shows himself to be a Communist of very special type, one who believes that evolutionary psychological change can and will assist (i.e., speed up) an inevitable process of historical social change. For him, the answer is to raise real social consciousness rather than shed blood. Such, in his view, is Nature's way, after all, for just as Nature inevitably dries up the dew every morning, so the process of natural social selection inevitably turns certain outmoded social classes into "fossils."

It is because of this unconventional theory of social change (unconventional for a Communist, that is) that the final four stanzas of the poem are addressed to an "unhappy poet" who, unlike "their" poets, occupies an uncommitted, asocial position rather like that of the poet in *Dog Beneath the Skin*. This poet is another one of the "Others" for whom the speaker ventures to predict the future, though here his future is, unlike that of the other "Others" and for reasons not explained, contingent on the poet's own free choice. Urging the poet to escape his self-indulgent escapist world, the speaker tells him that he can "help us if you chose," since he possesses a kind of (imaginative and emotional) wealth that "we" lack. The speaker gently exhorts the poet to "return, be tender; or are we more / Than you could face?" (EA, 422) Here again, as with the comrades earlier, the speaker distinguishes between himself and a "you" with whom he feels at once linked and disconnected. He is, so it would appear, not a poet himself, though when he speaks, his words turn out to be verse. And he seems to place, for a supposedly practicing, hard-nosed Communist, an inordinately high value on poetry's potential contribution to furthering the cause of the party.

Given this curious combination of attributes—party member, orator, prophet, bourgeois intellectual, evolutionary communist, literary critic—one is perhaps justified in concluding that he, along with all the "others," is a fraud, all the more so because it must be obvious that the "comrades" who are ostensibly his primary audience cannot be listening. Nor, for that matter, are the "splendid" people or the "dare-devil-mystic[s]," since neither of these anti-intellectual, conservative political groups is likely to be in the habit of attending to versified Communist harangues. It would seem, then, that of the enumerated possible recipients of the speaker's message—that is, of the "Others" mentioned by the speaker—the only likely audiences are the bourgeois liberal and the "unhappy poet." The response of the former would almost certainly be to brush the whole thing off as a joke, and that of the latter, given his predilection for private over public life, to pay it no heed. But if this is so, then what is the real point of this versified exercise? No point, perhaps? Or the psychological point of a middle-class poet venting his frustrations (hence the violent curses) at being so powerless to effect social change? Or the equally psychological point of pretending to oneself that one can make a difference? Or, just possibly, the point of proving to all those readers of *The Orators* who had suspected its author of concealed fascist leanings that they were dead wrong?

Despite such manifold ambiguities, Valentine Cunningham is, I think, only partly right when he remarks that this poem "is characterized by deep confusion. Its pronouns prove, strictly, unreadable, and so both its addresser and its addressee remain undecidable" (Symons, "Communist," 185). Actually, as we have seen, the confusion is occasioned not so much by our failure to discover *who* is speaking (it's evidently not Auden himself, though the speaker undoubtedly reflects some of Auden's political views) or to *whom* he is speaking (on the whole, the sequence can be made out quite clearly)—but it is a confusion arising primarily out of the reader's inability to determine *why* the speaker should feel as he does about the workers, given the obvious fact that he is almost exclusively motivated by hatred of his own class. How much more real that hatred is can be seen from its vastly greater specificity. The expression of his "love," on the other hand, is by comparison merely vague and pious, as is evident from the speaker's (and behind him, of course, Auden's) tone in the final stanza of the poem, subsequently omitted:

> Comrades to whom our thoughts return,
> Brothers for whom our bowels yearn
>   When words are over;
> Remember that in each direction
> Love outside our own election
> Holds us in unseen connection:
>   O trust that ever.

(EA, 422)

Here, at the end of the poem, the speaker has turned into something of a "dare-devil mystic" himself, mysteriously transforming, as he does, his Communist "comrades" into Christian "brothers" with whom he shares not merely some unspecified "interests," but for whom his "bowels yearn" in a way that evokes the New Testament more than it does *The Communist Manifesto*. Now, too, it is an invisible, nonverbal (mystical?) "love" that bonds "us" with "you" rather than a knowledge of the laws of dialectical materialism, though this love is in its peculiarly Calvinistic way quite as predetermined, or as much "outside our own election," as any of Marx's laws of history. "We" can't help loving "you," in other words, just as we can't help hating all those other folks. That's just how the universe happens to be arranged. "O trust that ever!"

That is why, while Günter Jarfe's assertion that Auden is directing his chief criticism at the speaker himself is not completely persuasive, his argument nevertheless has merit, as one can see from the ending of the poem (Jarfe, 41). Still, what may strike readers some seventy years later as satire was almost certainly intended originally to be read with a straight face, as, for example, Day-Lewis's reaction in similar circumstances: "Yes, why do we all, seeing a red, feel small?" (Day-Lewis, *Time*, 55). That is also why D. E. S. Maxwell says of "A Communist to Others" that "the poem's readers would certainly have taken it as sincerely professed"—a judgment confimed by Julian Symons when he recalls that he and his friends "never doubted that the poet [i.e., Auden, not just the speaker] was himself a Party member . . ." (Maxwell, 132; Symons, "Communist," 178). Symons and his friends, to be sure, were wrong: Auden never joined the party, though some of his best friends were members. But that the belief that Auden *was* a card-carrying Communist was widely shared at the time and, even decades later, is evident from the fact that, as late as 1965, the supposedly authoritative *Concise Cambridge History of English Literature* told its readers that Auden "joined the Communist Party about 1932" but "left it in disgust in 1939 after the signing of the Nazi-Soviet Pact . . ." (Churchill, 969).

II

Given the confusion on the part of the speaker of "A Communist to Others" about his role (and its motivation) in the class struggle, it seems impossible to equate him straightforwardly with Auden, though it is evident from other poems and essays dating from this period that Auden was not entirely clear in his own mind about what the future would be like in political terms. Action might be urgent but its nature was not yet altogether discernible or clear. It is for this reason that Stephen Spender could argue reasonably that readers of "A Communist to Others" should not confuse the speaker's attitude with Auden's. According to Spender, Auden "had a firmer grip of Marxist ideology, and more capacity to put this into good verse than many writers who were closer to Communism. This led to the legend that he went through a Communist phase. But his poem, 'A Communist to Others,' is an exercise in entering a point of view not his own" (Spender, *World*, 225). This is an observation that John Fuller echoes and amplifies when he calls the poem "an exercise in ventriloquised vitriolics" (Fuller, *Commentary*, 163). Humphrey Carpenter, on the other hand, is skeptical and even expresses doubts that Auden had any firsthand knowledge of Marx's writings at all (Carpenter, "Making," 88).

Of course, Auden never went through a "Communist phase" in the sense of actually joining the Communist Party of Great Britain, as Spender did, but the frequency of his calls for left-wing political action of some (or even any) sort in his poems and plays from 1932 to about 1938 certainly indicates that he went through an extended Communist-sympathizing phase. This was quite obvious to Auden's publisher and mentor, T. S. Eliot, who, as Valentine Cunningham has noted, arranged for a group of young poets to appear in his verse drama *The Rock* (1934), proclaiming that "Our verse / is free / as the wind on the steppes [presumably of the USSR] / as the love in the heart of the factory worker" (Cunningham, 27). And a friend, Louis MacNeice, told Auden admiringly in 1937 that "it is a blessing to our generation, though one in the eye for Bloomsbury, that you discharged into poetry the subject-matters of psychoanalysis, politics and economics. Mr. Eliot brought back ideas into poetry but he uses ideas, say, of anthropology more academically and less humanly than you use Marx or Groddeck. *This is because you are always taking sides*" (Carter, 58; my italics). Despite "discharging" these political and other subject-matters into his poetry, Auden, however, never turned into a party organizer like the speaker of "A Communist to Others," but remained a poet, so that his work does not conform narrowly to official party doctrine, though it sometimes endorses it. (Lenin, let us recall, had famously urged writers to be "party-minded," an exhortation that was frequently cited after the first Five Year Plan was instituted in 1927 and Soviet literary policy came to be formulated entirely by RAPP bigots.)

Despite Spender's rationalizations, "A Communist to Others" is more than a mere "exercise;" it is more than a mere putting on of a hat to see what it might look like. If nothing else, the fact that the poem is one of a series of such "exercises" (though undoubtedly the most extreme one) proves otherwise. And even if Auden later disclaimed most of these "exercises" and refused to have them reprinted, that change of heart does not absolve him from all responsibility at having published them in the first place. Given the fact that "A Communist to Others" was printed in an anthology in which the preface called for an "English Lenin," there can be little doubt as to what the first readers of the poem thought about its author's likely political views. Along with Symons, that is certainly what Cecil Day Lewis thought about the "definitely Communist forms" contained in *New Country* and authored by W. H. Auden, and presumably himself, among others (Day-Lewis, *Hope*, 53). Reviewing *New Country* and *The Orators*, Goronwy Rees found the actions recommended in Auden's and Day-Lewis's poems "repellent," along with their "method of personal attack, the bullying, with which they are recommended. They have, I think, two purposes: the first to shake the self-confidence of the reader and the second to impress upon him their own confident personalities. In so far as they are concerned with life and not poetry they may be justified, except that I find they fail in both purposes" (Rees, 245).

Auden's moral position, and that of his speaker, were of course awkward and even doctrinally untenable because of their bourgeois origins. This is a problem that he and his friends were fully conscious of but could find no effective way of resolving, since none of them was actually prepared to give up writing and become an industrial worker. (Had they done so, their accents and education would in any event have proved virtually insurmountable obstacles to working-class solidarity.) Spender addresses this dilemma explicitly in the essay that he wrote for Auden's thirtieth birthday: "From the point of view of the working-class movement the ultimate criticism of Auden and the poets associated with him is that we haven't deliberately and consciously transferred ourselves to the working class. The subject of his poetry is the struggle, but the struggle seen, as it were, by someone who whilst living in one camp, sympathizes with the other; a struggle in fact which while existing externally is also taking place within the mind of the poet himself, who remains a bourgeois" (Spender, "Oxford," 10).

To be sure, Auden's commitment to Communist ideology was never quite so unequivocal, or so enthusiastic, as it must have seemed to many of his readers at the time, including Spender. Or at any rate, to some *few* of his readers, since Auden did not as yet possess anything like a wide audience, though, as H[arriet] M[onroe] put it in *Poetry*, by 1936, Auden and Spender's "communist uplift," enjoyed "comparatively large (and well deserved) sales in England . . ." (H. M., 219). Not only was it still evident, even in an extreme case like "A Communist to Others," that—as Spender noted in his birthday piece—Auden had come to politics by way of psychology, but even after he officially got to politics he continued to see social reality partly through psychological eyes. Though after the autumn of 1932, Auden never again wrote quite so blatantly propagandistic a poem as "A Communist to Others," he did produce several poems whose "messages" were both socially significant and, on the surface at least, remarkable for their lack of ambiguity. This is especially true of the series of grimly comic ballads, "Miss Gee," "Victor," and "James Honeyman," all dating from 1937, to which one might add the rather more complex and interesting "As I Walked Out One Evening," written towards the end of the same year. All of these—even the last—reveal, as Cyril Connolly was to observe a year later, a new Auden who has "attempted to reduce poetry to a record of simple and universal experience expressed in colloquial language." (Connolly, 91).

Aside from their black humor and relative accessibility, all of these poems share a tendency to fuse social and psychological elements. So, while Miss Gee's cancer is primarily "caused," as her doctor diagnoses it—though unnamed, he could easily be Doctor Groddeck—by her "foiled creative fire," that is, by her failure to find an adequate outlet for her sexual drive, the secondary causes of that failure are undoubtedly social. A better, juster society would have understood that clergymen's daughters have bodies as well as souls, and such a society would have made adequate provision for the former as well as the latter. Significantly, at the close of the poem, the two Oxford Groupers who are dissecting her knee pay no heed whatever to her soul. They too, like most of the rest of their society, are suffering from an incurably dualistic outlook, one that has both collective social and individual somatic consequences. Instead of being truly strong, they are truly weak. Similarly, Victor is impelled to murder his wife because of the religious indoctrination he suffered as a boy on the knees of his father. Like Miss Edith Gee, his "creative fire" has been foiled by a narrowminded tradition that confuses chastity with goodness, but in his case, instead of turning inward and causing harm to himself, he is impelled by his "Father" to go after his unfaithful spouse with a carving knife. As for James Honeyman, as a congenital introvert who was insufficiently socialized in childhood, his misdirected "creative fire" leads him to try to invent a gas of which a "whiff will kill a man" (EA, 225). He succeeds only too well, so that in the end, his gas not only kills a man but multitudes of men, women and children, including himself and his whole family. Behind these cautionary, psychosomatic poems—especially the last two—there may also lurk Auden's suspicion, explicitly voiced in "September 1, 1939," that the social consequences of misdirected creativity may in fact be incalculable, as in the case of Adolf Hitler.

Even after Auden came to believe in the primacy of a social rather than psychological diagnosis of an England where nobody was well, he never lost his belief in the continuing relevance of psychology to that diagnosis. Characteristically, when he met Nancy Spender in 1935, and saw that she was having difficulty coping with her then husband, Bill Coldstream, he suggested that she might find emotional relief in joining the Communist Party (K. Bell, 1). And in the epilogue to *Look, Stranger!* (also dating from 1935),

Auden names Schweitzer, Freud, and Groddeck as leading figures of the age who were motivated by a vision of "the really better World." (Auden, *Look*, 64) All this helps to explain why Auden's later recollection about his psychological use of Marx in the thirties is probably fairly accurate, except for the qualification at the end: "Looking back, it seems to me that the interest in Marx taken by myself and my friends . . . was more psychological than political; we were interested in Marx in the same way that we were interested in Freud, as a technique of unmasking middle-class ideologies, not with the intention of repudiating our ideas, but with the hope of becoming better bourgeois . . ." (quoted in Davison, 29). Or as Cecil Day-Lewis put it at the time with unconscious humor, many young writers "are torn between their political sympathies and their desire to stand up for the unconscious" (Day-Lewis, *Time*, 68). Stephen Spender, too, thought of psychology as a necessary leavening for doctrinaire Communism. In *The Destructive Element* (1935), he suggested that "the Communist writer should read the clinical discoveries of psycho-analysts, and that he should respect, even if he does not accept, the conclusions of Freud and Jung." He then went on to advocate a creative synthesis of Communism and psychoanalysis, concluding that in "the work of W. H. Auden one sees such a synthesis attempted" (Spender, *Destructive*, 255–57).

In two important essays dating from 1935, Auden attempted to clarify his thinking about the relation of the public or social world to the private or psychological one. In the first, "Psychology and Art To-day," he argues generally that "Freudianism cannot be considered apart from other features of the contemporary environment," and in a complex diagram depicting the salient features of the three main periods of history—roughly equivalent to the Marxist division of Feudal, Capitalist, and Proletarian, though Auden significantly avoids using such ideologically loaded terminology—he mixes psychological and Marxist/Leninist concepts. Under "personal forces" in the incipient third period, for instance, he lists "the unconscious directed by reason," but under the heading of "Economic System" he puts down "Planned socialism" (EA, 337–38). In the fifth section of the second essay, "The Good Life"—a section called "Communism and Psychology"—Auden indicates the main links between them: to begin with, both are concerned "with unmasking hidden conflicts;" secondly, both "regard these conflicts as inevitable stages which must be made to negate themselves;" thirdly, Communism takes priority over psychology, Marx over Freud, because hunger precedes sex; and finally, and a little redundantly, probably for emphasis, both provide for the possibility of freedom by "unmasking and making conscious the hidden conflicts." Unlike Communism, however, psychology has allowed itself to become "a quack religion for the idle rich" because it has hitherto failed to recognize that neuroses are really "distorted versions of something which, if you choose to act, you can alter" (EA, 351–52).

In terms of his poetical practice, all of this meant that Auden tended to become a clearer and more accessible poet, that is, more public or socially committed and less private or psychologically oriented. Though, aside from the few explicitly Communist poems dating from the autumn of 1932, he rarely wrote overtly left-wing, propagandistic poems again, he did clearly continue to conceive of his poetry as performing a collective social as well as an individual function. His more overtly propagandistic plays are, of course, another matter. As he argues at the end of "Psychology and Art To-day," "there must always be two kinds of art, escape-art, for man needs escape as he needs food and deep sleep, and parable art, that art which shall teach man to unlearn hatred and learn love. . . ." (EA, 341–42) More specifically, the function of parable art was, as he put it in the introductory essay to his (and John Garrett's) anthology, *The Poet's Tongue* (1935), not to tell people what to do—that is, not to be merely didactic and propagandistic—but to extend "our knowledge of good and evil, perhaps making the necessity for action more urgent and its nature more clear" (EA, 185). Auden liked the phrasing of the last part of this aesthetic pronouncement so well that he re-used it almost immediately in the 1935 birthday poem for his friend Christopher Isherwood ("August for the People"), where the novelist is praised for making "action urgent and its nature clear." (EA, 155)

Parable poetry—in other words, serious, intellectually challenging poetry—had a specific social function. Like the parables that Jesus was fond of using to express his teaching, Auden's parables did not exist in a social, moral or aesthetic vacuum. They were deliberately intended to illustrate what kind of action was appropriate in what kind of social circumstances. This is the formula according to which some of Auden's best-known poems of this period were written, notably "Spain" with its famous/notorious conclusion about "the conscious acceptance of guilt in the necessary murder" (EA, 425). Here indeed the poet is making action—in this case, so it would appear, plain murder—urgent, though its nature is hardly rendered overly clear.

The poet, as Auden argued in the third part of his long "Letter to Lord Byron" (1936), finally had to leave the long self-indulgent party in the ivory tower, which had begun in the nineteenth century with the isolation of the artist from the rest of society, and had not even been seriously interrupted by the Great War. But with the coming of the Depression, the party had turned sour and it would no longer be possible to gaze out of the window, in the company of Baudelaire, at the supposedly uncomprehending workers below. The long weekend was over, and

> To-day, alas, that happy crowded floor
>   Looks very different: many are in tears:
> Some have retired to bed and locked the door;
>   And some swing madly from the chandeliers;
>   Some have passed out entirely in the rears;
> Some have been sick in corners; the sobering few
> Are trying hard to think of something new.
>
>   (EA, 187)

Auden here envisions himself as belonging to this small category of the sobering, though not necessarily altogether sober, few; and he continued to make this claim more or less consistently from about 1932 (or even earlier) until about 1937 or 1938. By the end of the thirties, however, he was beginning to have serious reservations about both the artistic party and the political party, though he hesitated to express those reservations unambiguously in public. Much later, he confessed that the turning point occurred during his brief stint as a would-be Loyalist activist in Spain during the Civil War in the winter of 1937. There, he realized that, whatever his conscious political sympathies might be, his personal feelings were deeply wounded at the sight of the destruction of the churches in Barcelona and the news of the killing of priests. Even sympathetic observers like Franz Borkenau testified to the truth of these atrocities (Borkenau, 71–75). However, it apparently took Auden quite some time before he could acknowledge the full impact of what he had seen. So, rather disingenuously, in a talk given at Shrewsbury School more than a year later (in November 1938), he told his audience that "the churches were not burnt . . . by Communists nor Fascists, but as a work of spontaneous hatred by the people against a wealthy landlord, the Church" (quoted in S[kinner], 715). Still, eventually—somehow, though Auden never really said how— the sight of these atrocities reawakened the latent religious impulse in him (Pike, 41). Here again, as in even his most socially committed poetry, the private psyche got in the way of the public man, forcing him eventually to "choose" between them. Now for him, too, action became urgent and its nature clear. Now he opted for the private person over the public rhetorician, for the inner man over the outer. Not that this choice was ever altogether final or complete.[6]

Nor, to be fair to Auden, was it altogether new. Auden had always possessed a strong anti-rhetorical, anti–"public-man" streak, even at the very beginning of his writing career, as is evident from his choice of poetic models like Edward Thomas, Robert Frost, Laura Riding and especially Thomas Hardy, all of whom, even if they did not exactly follow Verlaine's advice to wring the neck of Eloquence, at any rate had a habit of tweaking her nose.

According to Stephen Spender's semi-fictional persona in *The Temple*, Wilmot and Bradshaw (semi-fictional versions of Auden and Isherwood in the late twenties) "despised everything public, political and journalistic," whereas he himself had a mind that was "vulgar, public, detestable as its targets. He might himself be a public man, making speeches, writing letters to the newspapers, always enraged, always self-righteous" (Spender, *Temple*, 178). Not long after the Second World War, Auden wrote an acquaintance at Harvard, Theodore Spencer, that he "found Yeats' poetry boring and faux because he claims to be naive and isn't. On the other hand the attempt of a poet like Laura Riding to dispense with *all* rhetoric and be absolutely honest, seems to me a false over-simplification in the other direction" (quoted in Mendelson, *Later*, 246). Moreover, even when Auden was, or thought he was, committing his worst rhetorical sins, his diction often succeeded in puncturing the would-be rhetorical windbag, as he does repeatedly in *The Orators* (mostly by means of comic contrast) or even in the great elegy on Yeats, where he uses deliberately colloquial words like "guts" or "silly" to lower the rhetorical temperature. Edward Mendelson even goes so far as to claim that "[w]henever Auden wrote a poem he recognized as grand, emphatic, and false, he immediately followed it with one that was quiet, tentative, and truthful" (*Later*, 78).

Significantly, Auden's lasting suspicions of poetical rhetoric link him closely with the theoretical preoccupations of some the most celebrated Anglo-American critics of his time. His insistence during the later thirties that poetry should express plain *truth*, rather than emotionally satisfying lies, echoes I. A. Richards' influential distinction between the "referential" use of language and the "emotive" one. For, according to Richards, "[a] statement may be used for the sake of the *reference*, true or false, which it causes. That is the *scientific* use of language. But it also may be used for the sake of the effects in emotion and attitude produced by the reference it occasions. This is the *emotive* use of language . . . we may either use the words for the sake of the references they promote, or we may use them for the sake of the attitudes and emotions which ensue" (Richards, 267). Brooks and Warren make a slightly different but equally influential distinction in *Understanding Poetry* (1938), where, following the example of John Crowe Ransom, they equate poetic language with the language of particulars, and scientific language with the language of generalization and abstraction. In their terms, then, what the later Auden seemed to be doing in his poetry was to use referential language that became poetic by virtue of its particularity—not that he actually ever entirely avoided abstractions and generalizations. His penchant for moral allegory simply ran too deep for him to manage that. Auden could never stop being a teacher and preacher, any more than he could stop being a poet. But at least he wanted to be honest, like those scientists in "Ode to Terminus" who "to be truthful, / must remind us to take all they say as a tall story," lest he too become "abhorred in the Heav'ns" as "are all / self-proclaimed poets who, to wow an / audience, utter some resonant lie" (CP, 609).

III

By December 1936, Auden had reached a decision to go to Spain as a soldier in the International Brigade. Shortly before leaving, he wrote E. R. Dodds a letter that sounds suspiciously like a literary testament, but one very different in tone from the one composed jointly with Louis MacNeice and published at the end of *Letters from Iceland* (1936). In this letter, he specifically addresses the issue of the political function of poetry: "I am not one of those who believe that poetry need or even should be directly political, but in a critical period such as ours, I do believe that the poet must have direct knowledge of the major political events." This meant that, as he put it, "academic knowledge is not enough"; a poet had to have experienced in his own person what he wrote about. That is why he needed to go to Spain, not merely as an observer, but as an active participant (quoted in Mendelson, *Early*, 195). At about the same time, he wrote a letter to Klaus and Erika Mann in which he gave them much the same reason, though he phrased it in more activist terms: "I am going to Spain. It isn't enough for us to stand up for our Spanish comrades with words. I want to be with them." Though surprised at this sudden preference for action over words, Klaus and Erika were both pleased by it and, later, when they went to Spain themselves, "in our ears and hearts were beating the rhythms of a poem *Spain* which W. H. Auden had written under the impression of his visit to Spain" (K. Mann, 163).

In the event, Auden never fought in Spain, never even became a stretcher bearer nor drove an ambulance, as was bruited about at the time. Just what he did during his brief stay there has always remained something of a mystery, not least because of Auden's own subsequent mystifications. Not surprisingly, therefore, when he died years later, obituaries in the *Times* and the *Scotsman* (both 1 October 1973) recounted how, as the *Scotsman* put it, he had served "as a stretcher bearer and sanitary worker with the Republican forces." This confusion was probably due to Auden's own uncertainty about what he planned to do (and what he actually did) during his visit to Spain. Just before leaving London on 13 January 1937, he told friends that he was "going to work as an ambulance driver;" and, immediately after arriving in Spain, he told Nancy Johnstone that he hoped to be a stretcher-bearer (Jenkins, "Spain," 88–89). According to Cyril Connolly, however,

Auden mostly played chess while in Spain; and according to Robert Graves, he devoted much of his time to playing Ping-Pong (Sinfield, 202; Graves, *Crowning*, 130).

What he really did, at least in terms of supporting the Loyalist cause, was to make a few propaganda broadcasts on local Valencia radio, which he soon realized served no purpose because most of his listeners understood no English. Two months later, he gave up the struggle and returned to England. Nevertheless, despite his lack of actual experience, he did what he had told Dodds a writer shouldn't do; that is, he wrote about events and people that he had little or no direct, personal knowledge of. He wrote about the war in Spain, though, to his credit, he wrote about it, for the most part, "academically" and oratorically rather than personally. Still, whatever its merits—or demerits—"Spain" is not an authentic poem in the sense that most "war" poems since the Great War have been authentic, that is, written by actual combatants.

The continuing conflict in Auden between his artistic and political consciences is evident, at least in retrospect, in this most remarkable political poem in the Auden corpus. The poem consists of a curious mixture of exhortation, reflection, and dialogue. Without any formal divisions, it nevertheless falls clearly into four separate sections dealing respectively with the past, the present, the future, and then, in a brief coda, with the present again. Specifically, if one includes the stanzas later omitted by Auden in revision, the first part goes up through stanza 5; the second through stanza 14; the third through stanza 19; and the last through stanza 23. All four sections fuse in the final stanza into a kind of eternal present. The past is European history since the consolidation of feudalism and the triumph of capitalism, including the industrial revolution and the age of imperial expansion. It is a kind of summary of Lewis Mumford's *Technics and Civilization*, but very dense and poetic, quite unlike the potted history of the "Commentary" to *In Time of War*, which was written a little later. The future is utopia, that is, a potpourri of hobbies such as breeding terriers; scientific research not only into (the causes of?) "fatigue," but also into the "octaves of radiation," something that would soon be known more ominously as the atom bomb. To this odd assemblage, Auden adds a vaguely Groddeckian "enlarging of consciousness by diet and breathing," supplemented by suburban bicycle rides, and followed by the "rediscovery of romantic love" and/or "the photographing of ravens." Finally, and no doubt most urgently, there is political activity, such as the election of party chairmen by enthusiastic majorities, for, despite utopian conditions, the state of the future, apparently, has not yet withered away entirely. This peculiar catalog of quasi-utopian activity is—and was apparently intended to be—strongly reminiscent of Karl Marx's vision, as expressed in

The German Ideology, of what a future communist society would be like, namely one where people would be able to "hunt in the morning, fish in the afternoon, rear cattle in the evening, criticize after dinner" (Marx and Engels, 22). Unreal or even phony as all this may strike readers living in a very different, "modern" and fast-paced world, Auden apparently took such Marxist utopianism quite seriously. Three years later, in "New Year Letter," he went out of his way to explain why: "Who has ever met a left-wing poet (at least one who has had any success) for whom the real attraction of Communism did not lie in its promise that, under it, the state should wither away for others as it has already withered away for him?" (Auden, *New*, 83). Withering away was something that happened, as it were, branch by individual branch, starting off with individual, left-wing poets like Auden.

"Spain," unlike "A Communist to Others," is not primarily a piece of propaganda, though it obviously contains propagandistic elements, most notably in the portrayal of the future, with its cozy vision of Communist comraderie. But even the present is romanticized; we are told of marvellous metamorphoses in which "moments of tenderness" can "blossom" into ambulances and sandbags, or "hours of friendship . . . flower into," of all things, "a people's army." Even so, the tone of the poem is relatively muted; there are no rantings here against enemies or "splendid" persons, or, for that matter, no mention even of a specific enemy, no smug self-satisfaction in seeing a despised system overthrown. The technique is one of selecting significant but not necessarily dramatic detail, such as the Party member's "flat, ephemeral pamphlet," a kind of detail that, by its confession that ideology and class conflict (and even Civil War) can be dull, makes us sense the existence of a real voice in the poem, and not merely the Voice of the Party. There is also a vaguely symbolic strategy in the poem—never entirely consistent, but effective nevertheless—of identifying Spain with the life force and, even, at moments with the death force, something that almost openly acknowledges in the poem a psychological dimension, and not merely a political one. So, the search for meaning by the poet, the scientist, and the poor fuse into a vast metaphysical prayer to a cosmic, evolutionary, rather than revolutionary Life Force:

>
> Did you not found once the city state of the sponge,
>
> Raise the vast military empires of the shark
> And the tiger, establish the robin's plucky canton?
>   Intervene. O descend as a dove or
> A furious papa or a mild engineer: but descend.

(EA, 211)

The Life Force that replies to their prayer is a voice from within: a voice of individual conscience, not of class or history or party. It certainly is not the voice of the christian dove of peace or a divine Old Testament-like "furious papa," but then, neither is it entirely the voice of a Soviet-style "mild engineer." Rather, it is a weak and ambiguous voice, one that reflects the deepest fears and hopes of those who invoke it:

> What's your proposal? To build the Just City? I will.
> I agree. Or is it the suicide pact, the romantic
>   Death? Very well, I accept, for
> I am your choice, your decision: yes I am Spain.
>
> (EA, 211)

The real problem with this voice is not so much its manner as its matter. The "choice" it offers the political pilgrims journeying to Spain is, in fact, no choice at all. While, as he had done earlier in *The Dog Beneath the Skin*, Auden appears to be offering a choice here—that is, both Spain and the "life" become personified or allegorized choices—the alternatives are, in fact, phony. Only fascists and fools, it is obvious, would be fanatical or stupid enough to choose the "suicide pact" or the "romantic death" over the much more comfy and promising Just City. Not that at least some of the critics haven't fallen for Auden's rhetorical ploy. In one of the standard overviews of modern poetry, C. B. Cox and A. E. Dyson remark, without discernible irony, that "[f]or the last time in twentieth-century English poetry, a poet offers an heroic myth to his readers. Here you may choose, and if we [sic] win, the Just City will arise" (Cox, 97). That Auden was himself so caught up in the political mind-set of the times that he failed to notice that he wasn't offering a real choice between viable alternatives is evident from the letter he wrote Stephen Spender not long after the publication of *Dog Beneath the Skin:* "Actually the moral I tried to draw is always, 'You have the choice. You can make the world or mar it.' Free-will means you can choose either to fear thought or love understanding" (Jenkins, "Eleven," 66). Once again the "choice" offered by Auden here is phony, resembling in this respect not only the false choice in "Spain" but also the disingenuous "choice" presented in what was to become the most famous left-wing pamphlet of the late thirties, *Authors Take Sides On the Spanish War*. There, many of the literary celebrities of the age (on the right as well as on the left) were asked to answer the following loaded question: "Are you for, or against, the legal Government and the People of Republican Spain? Are you for, or against, Franco and Fascism?" (*Authors*, unpaginated: third paragraph) This part of the pamphlet was signed and perhaps even drafted, among others, by Auden and Spender.

Nevertheless, though the choice may have been false, the voice of "Spain" was utterly real. There can be no question of its sincerity, because its ultimate source was not Soviet uplift but, rather, that oddly and mythically Quixotic, strangely Christlike Auden who in the winter of 1937, according to Claud Cockburn, tried to make his way, mounted on a donkey, to the Valencia front (Cockburn, "Conversation," 51).[7] There is no idealization in this poem of the motives of those who join the International Brigade. They include not only the idealists, but also the fatalists and the romantic self-glorifiers. Nor is there, at this point at least, an easy schematization that permits us to conceive of life and history in simple Marxist terms. The Life Force is emphatically not a category in which orthodox Marxists think.[8] (To be sure, George Bernard Shaw did think of history in such terms, but then the Fabians generally, and Shaw in particular, were never orthodox in their socialist convictions.) This is a poem that, as Samuel Hynes has written, "eludes partisan capture." (Hynes, 255) The ambiguities of motive become even more apparent in the stanzas subsequently omitted by Auden, in which occur the transformations of ordinary life into military action:

> Our thoughts have bodies; the menacing shapes of our fever
>
> Are precise and alive, for the fears which made us respond
> To the medicine ad, and the brochure of winter cruises
>   Have become invading battalions;
> And our faces, the institute-face, the chain-store, the ruin
> Are projecting their greed as the firing squad and the bomb.
>
> (EA, 425)

What Auden is returning to here is a much earlier and more complex conception of political action that arises not simply out of external socioeconomic considerations, but also out of internal psychological states, a conception underlying, among other works by Auden, *The Orators*, as well as his later play, the *Ascent of F6*.

But even when Auden is ideologically orthodox, the precision of his language can lead him to stray from the prescribed party line. This is particularly true of the famous/infamous passage concerning "the deliberate increase in the chances of death; / The conscious acceptance of guilt in the necessary murder." Orwell was to censure this passage for having been written by a kind of scoutmaster of the Left who had never seen anyone actually being murdered. Orwell, on the other hand, had just returned from Spain himself, where he had seen people being murdered and not just killed. (Indeed, he had barely escaped being both killed at the front by fascists and murdered in Barcelona by Stalinists.) He therefore thought he knew that real murderers, such as Stalin and Hitler, would never use realistic language, preferring instead euphemisms like "liquidation." Orwell's strictures ring true, and they have served to discredit "Spain" and Auden's politics during the thirties generally; but, persuasive as they are, they are ultimately beside the point, for, although Stalin and Hitler are deservedly seen as incarnations of evil in our time, it is nevertheless probably true to say of them that they too, like Auden, never (or at least "hardly ever") personally murdered anyone, despite being directly and indirectly responsible for the murder of millions. The real point here, I think, does not concern bloody hands but poetry. Neither Stalin nor Hitler were poets. They were politicians who, as Orwell himself demonstrated in another famous and much anthologized essay, use words to mask their motives and meaning rather than reveal them. Hence the euphemisms. A real poet does not deal with euphemisms, even though it might be ideologically expedient for her to do so. That is something Orwell, though not in a literal sense a poet himself, should have realized.

What I have said here ought not to be taken to mean that an ideology based on deliberate and necessary murders is good. As Auden was later to tell Monroe K. Spears,

> I was *not* excusing totalitarian crimes but only trying to say what, surely, every decent person thinks if he finds himself unable to adopt the absolute pacifist position. (1) To kill another human being is always murder and should never be called anything else. (2) In a war, the members of two rival groups try to murder their opponents. (3) *If* there is such a thing as a just war, then murder can be necessary for the sake of justice. (Spears, 157)[9]

The definition of murder put forward by Auden here is, to be sure, not quite the one that "every decent person" would be likely to accept, especially not with respect to his claim that soldiers in a "just" war are committing "murder." To a degree, Auden seems here to want to commit his necessary murders and retain his innocence, too.[10] How unsure he was about the ethics of killing emerges clearly from his comments on the subject in the long essay he wrote at about the same time for Clifton Fadiman's collection *I Believe* (1939): "It is always wrong in an absolute sense to kill, but all killing is not equally bad; it does matter who is killed" (EA, 379) Here again, Auden makes a clear distinction between some killings (murders?) that, if not "necessary" or even "deliberate," are nevertheless less morally reprehensible than others. And even later, in "New Year Letter," he has no qualms about writing about the Spanish War and those who learned there the lesson "Of sanctity in violence" (Auden, *New*, 87). In any event, whatever his misgivings, he later revised the notorious passage to attenuate its bloodthirstiness, partly, no doubt, because he felt the justice and not merely the sting of Orwell's remarks.[11] But the word "murder" stayed in. Murder, for the Auden who was now, once again, becoming more of a Christian and less of a Marxist, was murder whether perpetrated by the Left or by the Right, in a just or an unjust cause.

A year later, returning from another war—in China this time—Auden once again tackled and tried to answer the question as to how justice or necessity might be linked historically to violence, especially in the context of war. "Certainly praise," he insisted, is due to "life as it blossoms," because life has brought forth beauty and happiness for some people, as well as having produced an occasional (unnamed) great man. But life has also brought unhappiness and injury to many people. What is more, "the will of the Unjust / Has never lost its power." Against such an indifferent (or at best disinterested) Life Force, the state can only defend itself by means of "the Fairly-Noble unifying Lie," meaning presumably the necessary lie— perhaps a lie like Ibsens's "life-lie" in *The Wild Duck*—that suffering in the actual here-and-now will be compensated for by bliss in the uncertain future. This, as Auden knew full well, was a lie told by social and religious utopian dreamers alike, including Marx. The voice of History, however, warns us that "[t]he Good place has not been" and that humans are a "race of promise that has never proved its worth." History also tells us that the "quick new West is false" and that the "passive flower-like people" of China are "wrong" (CP, 256). To whose voice, then, should we listen? To the voice of the joyous but quite amoral life force? Or to the voice of a profoundly moral but utterly pessimistic, helpless, and grieving History? To this question the poem gives no final answer, though it is significant that History has the last word.

Although Auden's ambiguous feelings about the war in Spain helped make his poem about it more complex and, from an aesthetic point of view, more satisfying, one can understand why, on a personal level, he came to believe that it was dishonest. After all, at the time that he wrote it, he had already felt, as he later admitted, a powerful antipathy against the fanatical anticlericalism of the Loyalist forces. Not that Auden's left-wing politics were, or had ever been, uncomplicated. As his new "brother-in-law," Klaus Mann, commented when he met Auden in Amsterdam not long after his return from Spain, the latter's enthusiasm for revolutionary politics was "a great deal less naive than the rhetorical sentimentality or the pedantic self-righteousness of most of the other radical, leftist bards." A person of Auden's complex nature would never, in Mann's view, permit himself to be consumed or defined by a single outlook or feeling. Besides, even while he was laying down the political line for the other "comrades," Auden retained the right to hold certain "ironic reservations" for himself. "It was extraordinary," Mann remarks, "to watch Auden's behavior in the circle of his friends and disciples. What a contorted, multi-faceted young master he was!" (Mann, 333; my translation) Just how contorted and multifaceted his ideological gymnastics were at this time may be appreciated from the fact that when, more than a year later, he traveled with Isherwood to China, he still identified himself, or at any rate allowed himself to be identified, as a "leftist writer" while at the same time enjoying the hospitality of the British Amabassador, including the use of his chauffeur-driven limousine (Auden and Isherwood, *Journey*, 171).

Still, even though Auden probably felt uncomfortable about parts of "Spain" while writing it—at least those parts that he excised when he republished it—there is no doubt that he continued to feel strongly about it and about his experiences during the Spanish Civil War in general. Hence his uncharacteristic silence for so many years about what he had seen there and how he had felt about it. It's clear that he did not relish the prospect of becoming a "lost leader," though eventually, and almost inevitably, he did. But even if "Spain" really was, as he later concluded, dishonest, he never considered it a mere "exercise," as Stephen Spender claimed it was in *The Creative Element* (1953), using his habitual dispensation of critical fog to cloud the issue. Writing about Orwell's strictures and Auden's supposedly reprehensible notion of history at the close of "Spain," Spender urges us not to "forget that despite his support of the Spanish Republic his poem is an exercise in a logic of the imagination. *Spain* is really the working out in imaginative terms of the effects of an attitude towards the Spanish War with which he sympathized, but which he treats here as a hypothesis for his poetic logic. The working out of this hypothesis leads him to conclusions which when they were arrived at were as untenable to him as they appear to Orwell" (Spender, *Creative*, 152). Spender himself, however, had put forward much the same argument in almost identical language, but without the excuse of poetry, when he wrote in May 1937 that "[s]ince the war must be won if the revolution is to be retained, there is nothing to do but accept it as a terrible necessity . . ." (Spender, "Heroes," 715). Auden, however, or so it would seem from Spender's subsequent "exercise" in critical acrobatics, was merely thinking out loud poetically when he wrote "Spain." Later on, he went on to publish it as a kind of absentminded afterthought. Hence, if Spender is to be believed, Auden's advocacy of necessary murder was merely a passing hypothesis, not really intended to be taken seriously but belonging, rather, to some special category of speculation called "poetic logic."

IV

"Spain" was soon to suffer the fate of Auden's other political verse. It joined the category of poems that he was ashamed to have written and refused to have reprinted. Two years after the poem was published, Auden underwent a complete revulsion against all overtly ideological poetry. Poetry, as he now maintained in the great elegy on William Butler Yeats, was something that made nothing happen, or, in the somewhat less memorable but no less categorical words uttered by the Counsel for the Defense in Auden's "The Public v. the Late Mr. William Butler Yeats" (1939): "The case for the prosecution rests on the fallacious belief that art ever makes anything happen, whereas the honest truth, gentlemen, is that, if not a poem had been written, not a picture painted nor a bar of music composed, the history of man would be materially unchanged" (EA, 393). To introduce politics into poetry now became, for Auden, the prime literary sin. "Unless you take part in the class struggle," the voice of the low decade's infernal tempter had whispered, "you cannot become a major writer" (EA, 403). A month after he finished the elegy on Yeats, he told Louis MacNeice that he was "no longer in any way a 'fellow-traveller'; since getting off that particular train, he has decided . . . that it was not his job to be a crusader, that this was a thing everyone must decide for himself, but that, in his opinion, most writers falsified their work and themselves when they took a direct part in politics . . ." (quoted in Homberger, 29).

Auden regretted bitterly that he had once yielded to the voice of fashionable political temptation, but his very regret suggests something other and more than just a guilty conscience. It suggests, I think, in its intensity and in its subsequent preoccupation with censoring the offending political passages out of his early poems or with abandoning those poems altogether, a doubt that poetry might after all make something happen—but the wrong thing. Why else make such a fuss? Why else seek so laboriously to obscure and even bury the young poet who had once sought to use poetry as a weapon? If poetry makes nothing happen, then there is no need for regrets and revisions, except for purely poetical regrets and purely poetical revisions. But Auden's revisions were hardly ever just poetical. They were political; and so, too, were the regrets. "All I have is a voice," he told his readers at the end of the low, dishonest decade, "to undo the folded lie." But what he did not tell his readers—perhaps because they were only too aware of it already—was that it was none other than himself who, during the past decade, had lent his own, so very able voice—and hands—to putting in several of the most notable of those supposedly lying folds.[12]

The really big lie, as Auden discovered when he returned from his journey to the war in China, was not so much the one that was told by romantics or journalists (the "folded lie," as John Fuller notes, probably refers to newspapers) (Fuller, *Commentary*, 292). The really big lie is the one told by language itself. Auden now realized that at that very moment so long ago when mankind started to confer names on animals and things, mankind also began unconsciously to use words to replace reality. And, along with the rest of mankind, the poet—not just Yeats, but Auden too, and, for that matter, every other poet, past, present, and future—has repeated Adam's primal sin of turning life into an abstraction of words that

> bred like locusts till they hid the green
> And edges of the world: and he was abject,
> And to his own creation became subject;
> And shook with hate of things he'd never seen,
> And knew of love without love's proper object,
> And was oppressed as he had never been.

(EA, 252)

But if language lied, it lied indiscriminately, on the political left as well as on the political Right. "You were silly like us" Auden told Yeats, and then went on to claim that, paradoxically, only those could be forgiven for committing the sin of language who had sinned *fortiter*, as Yeats himself had done, or Kipling or Paul Claudel, as well as, though he didn't specifically say so, Auden himself. For if language lies, time forgives, because time worships language as it does not worship courage or morality or even physical beauty. It is for this reason that time is prepared to pardon "cowardice, conceit" and even confer honor upon cowards and egomaniacs by virtue of the admittedly "strange excuse" that they had written or used language well. But if this was true, then it was also true that a powerful "lying" poetry written by great poets was truer—or at least more enduring—than the truly true but low-keyed poetry Auden now claimed to be endorsing.

As with Auden's other political poems, there is also a problem in the Yeats elegy as to what specific actions it makes urgent and clear, a problem that is touched on most strikingly in Auden's assertion that poetry makes nothing happen. The two crucial words in this statement are "poetry" and "happen." "Poetry" in this context means all poetry but it also specifically means Yeats's poetry; in other words, it means modernist poetry of the highest order. What about "happen"? Here, Auden seems to mean that Yeats's poetry was unable to affect either the mad course of Irish history or the lamentable state of its climate:

3: POETRY AND POLITICS IN A LOW, DISHONEST DECADE 147

> ... mad Ireland hurt you into poetry.
> Now Ireland has her madness and her weather still,
> For poetry makes nothing happen ...
>
> (EA, 242)

It is obvious that no one can reasonably expect poetry to change the weather. After all, what *is* able to change the weather? The Communist Party, perhaps? Nevertheless, I think it is arguable, without trying to seem paradoxical, that even if Yeats's poetry has not changed the Irish weather, it has changed our response to the Irish weather. No one who has ever read Yeats will ever look upon the actual Lake Isle of Innisfree and not sense the purple glow that he put there; or pay a visit to Coole Park in the summer rain and not see a still October twilight with nine and fifty swans floating down the cold, companionable stream.

As to the course of Irish history, Auden's contention is, at the very least, debatable. Surely the fact that a great poet like Yeats involved himself poetically in the struggle for Irish independence—unorthodox as that involvement may have seemed at times to more conventional revolutionaries—made that struggle worthy and respectable in the eyes of others, not least in the eyes of the English enemy. In this way, Yeats's poetry made something happen, or prevented something from happening, even if there may not be a single actual historical event for which his poems could be adduced as the specific cause, though naturally Yeats himself, great egomaniac and great writer that he was, thought otherwise.

It is significant that Auden chose to write the first of his memorable elegies of the thirties and early forties about Yeats, a writer whom, up to this point, he had virtually ignored, devoting only two lines to him in the "Testament" section of *Letters from Iceland*.[13] As with the other great elegies in the English tradition—including Yeats's own on the Easter Rising or on Major Robert Gregory—this elegy is really more about the mental and emotional state of the author himself than about its ostensible subject. Indeed, it seems clear that Auden is preoccupied with Yeats at this crucial period in his life—in his criticism as well as in his poetry—because he sees in him a mirror image of himself. Yeats too had tried to change the world around him, using his poetry as the means. Late in life, Yeats had even grown convinced of his success, when in "Man and His Echo" he wondered out loud if his play *Cathleen Ni Houlihan* might not have been the immediate cause of the Easter Rising in 1916. For the new Auden, that is, for the Auden who now came to think of the thirties as a low, dishonest decade, such an attitude was silly, but it was no longer silly in isolation; it was "silly like us." Auden too now believed that he had been silly to think that poetry could affect social behavior, either individually or collectively, that it could make anything "happen." Poetry, he now asserted almost defensively, was only a *way* of happening, a "mouth." It no longer mattered what one wrote, but only how one wrote what one wrote.

Privately, however, Auden condemned not only the manner but also the matter of Yeats's verse. In 1947, he told Alan Ansen that he was "surprised there haven't been more attacks on Yeats as a fascist. He's really dangerous without being direct" (Ansen, *Table*, 49). Later the same year, while preparing a talk for an upcoming meeting of the Modern Language Association, he concluded that "the more I read him, the less I like him." Yeats was "a horrible old man" who didn't even have the courage of his own "crazy mythology." Rilke and D. H. Lawrence, on the other hand, did: "I like *really* crazy people like Rilke, yes, and D. H. Lawrence." The final, off-putting touch was that "of course, his people weren't related to the Butlers at all" (Ansen, *Table*, 72). On the other hand, as late as 1962, Auden referred publicly to Yeats as having written "great poetry about the Troubles in Ireland" (*Dyer's*, 81). The opinions, so it would appear, both literary and otherwise, of the private Auden did not always match up neatly with those of the public Auden. As for Yeats himself, despite the reservations he expressed in the Oxford anthology, he thought well enough of Auden's work on the whole. In a letter written in early 1937, Yeats says that he "admire[s] Auden more than I said in the Anthology (his best work has not been published). The young Cambridge [*sic*] poets write out of their intellectual beliefs and that is all wrong" (Hone, 487). Nevertheless, Yeats was not entirely naive about the commitment to Communism on the part of Auden and his friends. "Many of these poets," he wrote in 1936, "have called themselves communists, though I find in their work no trace of the recognized communist philosophy, and the practicing communist rejects them" (Yeats, Introduction, xxxvii).

"I too have tried to be modern," wrote W. B. Yeats in 1936, and this, at least, was a goal for which the young Auden did not censure him (Yeats, Introduction, xxxvi). For the rest, on the surface at least, the early Auden and the late Yeats seem very different, almost diametrically so. One thinks first of the political differences, with the young Auden far to the left, a fashionable fellow traveler; the old Yeats very far to the right, virtually a fascist, or so at least some of his contemporaries, including Auden, believed. Put less polemically, there is a sharp difference in cultural terms between Yeats the nationalist and Irishman (or at least the Anglo-Irishman), who is tied to Irish history, myth and tradition, who is the poet of Thoor Ballylee; and Auden, who is very much the internationalist, the poet who dropped more names even than he did articles, and ran through more ideas than any serious writer after Aldous Huxley, an intellectual/sexual tourist who first discovered Berlin for a literary generation—for the "found" or politically engaged generation that arose after the preceding one had lost itself in Paris; the poet who seemed perpetually on the go—when not in Berlin, then in Belgium, in Iceland, in Portugal, in Spain, in China, or in the United States. The Auden of the thirties is the naughty infant of English literature, playing games with and against the establishment, cocking snooks and pulling faces. The old Yeats can be naughty too, especially when he meets Crazy Jane, but his is a violent, passionate anger. It is, to use one of his favorite words in old age, "cold," intellectual, and almost humorless despite his sometimes professional (Anglo-)Irishness. The late Yeats is a lonely figure, isolated politically and literarily, laughed at for his supposedly loony spiritualism and despised, as well as secretly envied, for his dirty-old-man sexuality. The young Auden, on the other hand, is so integrated with his immediate environment that his existence as a distinct personality sometimes seems questionable, as if there were no Auden but only an Auden group, a MacSpaunday monster, as Roy Campbell called it. The contrast could hardly be more clear-cut: Yeats, very much the traditionalist, the remnant of a bygone age; Auden, the modernist, the harbinger of the new.

Yet the opposition, striking as it is, weakens if viewed from other perspectives. John Bayley—and, to some degree, Richard Ellmann—see both writers as late romantics, agreeing here with Edmund Wilson and C. M. Bowra, who interpret the modernist movement not as a break with, but as a continuation of the romantic movement (Bayley, 142). Auden himself probably shared this view, on the grounds that modernism for him represented a break with an older aristocratic tradition (both social and aesthetic), occurring sometime in the mid-nineteenth century, so that Poe and Baudelaire were to him the first genuinely modern poets because "they were the first poets (with the possible exception of Blake) who, born into the modern age—that is to say, after the mutation of the closed society of tradition and inheritance into the open society of fashion and choice—realized what a decisive change this was" (Baudelaire, Introduction, xi). In making this claim, Auden is, of course, merely putting into historical perspective Eliot's celebrated assertion that Baudelaire was the modernist poet par excellence.

Romanticism is a heritage gladly and explicitly acknowledged by Yeats, but fiercely denied by the young Auden. But what, if not romantic, is Auden's preoccupation with rebellion, with leadership, with mysterious conspiracies and obscure feuds? For the young Auden just as much as for the young Yeats, Blake is a hero and a model, an apparent madman who is really sane, an inveterate enemy of the smug, self-satisfied bourgeoisie. Indeed, *the* enemy looms large both in the work of the young Auden and of the late Yeats, though he is not absent from the early Yeats either, as he is not, for instance, in "September 1913." And although this enemy is in many ways a different one for each poet, the fact that both view their work as a contribution to the struggle against him is a unifying factor.

Both writers are also convinced—Yeats from the very beginning of his writing career and the young Auden until pretty near the end of the thirties, though not thereafter—that poetry does not only exist for its own sake, but that it can and should play an important role in shaping society, that poets are, in the words of another profoundly influential romantic poet, the unacknowledged legislators of mankind. For Louis MacNeice, indeed, it was Yeats who provided the poetic model for his generation rather than T. S. Eiot. Surprising as it may seem to hear Louis MacNeice denying the influence of Eliot on Auden and even asserting that his group of friends was in active revolt against Eliot—a very odd assertion in Auden's case particularly, since Auden admired Eliot immensely and received considerable help from him—nevertheless surprise does eventually yield to at least partial agreement. Eliot, so MacNeice argues, had what he calls an essentially feminine theory of poetry, whereas Yeats and the Auden group, by contrast, had a masculine one. "In England about 1930," he writes, "a school of poets appeared who mark more or less of a reaction against the influence of Eliot." The latter had "maintained that the poet must adapt himself to his world; if his world is difficult and complex, his poetry must be difficult and complex. . . . Poets like Auden and Spender abandoned this feminine conception of poetry and returned to the old arrogant principle—which was Yeats's too—that it is the poet's job to make sense of the world, to simplify it, to put shape on it. The fact that these younger poets proposed to stylize their world in accordance with communist doctrine or psychoanalytical theory (both things repugnant to Yeats) is comparatively irrelevant. Whatever their system was, they stood with Yeats for system against chaos, for a positive art against a passive impressionism" (MacNeice, 191).

MacNeice's choice of the word "system" in connection with the psychopolitics of the Auden group is probably meant to be deliberately suggestive, for it evokes and perhaps invokes Yeats's by then notorious "system," as outlined in his occultist *A Vision* (1925 and 1937). This work and the poetry reflective of it—really, just about all of the later Yeats's poetry—has from the very beginning presented an obstacle to many readers of Yeats, including Auden. As Richard Ellmann observes, "Yeats was a peculiar encumbrance for young poets. Those who went up to Oxford in the late 1920s—Auden, MacNeice, and Spender—were puzzled whether to regard him as a monument or a folly." Even though Auden eventually came to realize that Yeats was neither monumental nor foolish, he never quite lost the feeling that there was something disreputable about Yeats's insistence on establishing personal relations with the spiritual world. The Prosecutor in Auden's essay, "The Public v. the Late Mr. William Butler Yeats"—an essay exactly contemporaneous with Auden's great elegy on Yeats—echoes at least partly Auden's own sentiments when he maintains that in 1900, Yeats "believed in fairies; that was bad enough; but in 1930 we are confronted with the pitiful, the deplorable spectacle of a grown man occupied with the mumbo-jumbo of magic and the nonsense of India." Even in the later and much more favorable essay on "Yeats as an Example" (1948), Auden wonders out loud about how "a man of Yeats's gifts [could] take such nonsense seriously" and dismisses *A Vision* as "Southern Californian" and "essentially lower-middle class."

Auden is voicing here an objection to the later Yeats that has not lost appreciably in validity or relevance in the intervening years, though one could certainly wish for a more temperate and less snobbish statement of it. Nor is there any doubt about Auden's right to make such an objection, only about its appropriateness, for if Yeats's inveterate occultism was Indian nonsense or Southern Californian bad taste, one wonders what to say about Auden's own sometime espousal (among other things) of the odd psychological theories of D. H. Lawrence's *Fantasia of the Unconscious*, or the even odder psychosomatic ones of Georg Groddeck and Homer Lane, not to mention his poetical identification with the "Bwili" (or Malekulan epileptic flying tricksters) of the man whom even Auden later referred to as "looney Layard." Are lines like "Sir, no man's enemy forgiving all, but will his negative inversion" any less mumbo-jumbo than "Turning and turning in the widening gyre, the falcon cannot hear the falconer?" Both assertions are equally based on assumptions about the poet's (and humanity's) relations with God and/or the unconscious self that most supposedly normal people would reject as eccentric and possibly mad. To be sure, Auden's eccentricity or madness seemed more in the intellectual mainstream at the time, especially after he began to subordinate his eclectic psychological ideas to Marxist sociological ones; but Yeats was not entirely alone in his spiritualist mania either. Even Eliot has his divine thunder speak in Sanskrit at the close of "The Waste Land," and Aldous Huxley, after first mocking Indian mysticism in *Jesting Pilate* even more caustically than Auden, was at this time beginning his slow conversion toward such so-called nonsense, a place where Hermann Hesse had already preceded him and where he was to be joined not long thereafter by none other than two of Auden's closest friends, Gerald Heard and Christopher Isherwood.

Though the episode is not generally known, it seems that in fact Auden himself did not prove entirely immune to the Buddhist enchantments of Southern California. Writing to his friend, Mrs. E. R. Dodds, from Laguna

Beach in August 1939, he informed her that, since he had recently adopted a pacifist position, he needed now to "look for a Yogi teacher or someone when I get back to New York. The trouble with the Christians was that they separated the contemplative and the active life." Realizing that his new change of heart (and religious persuasion) might occasion surprise among friends and risibility among enemies, Auden cautioned her not to "tell a *soul* about this as everyone will giggle and think I've gone crazy." Back in New York in November of the same year, he reported that, although he hadn't "started Yoga yet," he had begun "a preparatory course of physical exercises with a German girl; *most* painful, but illuminating" (Bodleian, MS. Eng. lett. c. 464).

How close Auden actually came in the late thirties to expressing an outlook reflective of at least one of the principal Buddhist ideas is apparent in the syntactically challenging second stanza of one of his most celebrated love lyrics, "Lay Your Sleeping Head, My Love" (1937):

> Soul and body have no bounds:
> To lovers as they lie upon
> Her tolerant enchanted slope
> In their ordinary swoon,
> Grave the vision Venus sends
> Of supernatural sympathy,
> Universal love and hope;
> While an abstract insight wakes
> Among the glaciers and the rocks
> The hermit's sensual exstasy.
>
> (EA, 207)

Auden puts forward here, as he did too in the political ballads that he wrote later in the same year—but in this instance wittily rather than grimly—the anti-Christian notion that there is no essential dividing line between physical and spiritual phenomena: "Soul and body have no bounds." Aside from being a fundamental tenet of Buddhism, Auden had of course encountered the idea ten years earlier in Georg Groddeck's work. Now, however, he was so convinced that dualism was wrong that he identified it not only with Plato but also with Rousseau and Hitler, whereas the exponents of monism were his current heroes, Blake, Voltaire, Goethe and Marx (Mendelson, *Later*, 41). The "ordinary swoon" of the lovers on Venus's enchanted slope is an imaginative elaboration of the female anatomical *mons veneris* or "mount of Venus," whereas the hermit's sensual ecstasy alludes not only to Donne's famous poem (based on an analogous conception of spiritual/sensual love) but also to the sensual temptations of St. Anthony. What all this amounts to is that Yeats and his alleged Indian nonsense were not really so distant from Auden and his erotic mountain-climbing as might have appeared at first glance.

Even politically speaking, there are striking resemblances between the early Auden and the late Yeats. Though to the general public eye, Auden and company usually seemed exponents of left-wing or even Communist ideas, to some contemporary observers, including Stephen Spender, it was unclear as to whether some of Auden's work was advocating a Communist revolution or a fascist coup. The ambiguity of the early Auden's politics is perhaps best epitomized by his assertion (in 1935) that the two figures of his time who most successfully combined the inner and the outer life were T. E. Lawrence and Lenin. In this context, it is worth recalling that when T. E. Lawrence died in a fatal motorcycle accident, he was on his way back from the post office after sending a telegram arranging for a personal meeting with Hitler (Aldington, 386). Of course, just because Auden admired T. E. Lawrence does not make Auden into a Fascist or even a proto-Fascist, but what it does make clear is that the lines between fascism and Communism were fluid in the Britain of the early thirties in a way that not only is impossible to conceive today, but which seems incredible that it ever was possible. It was possible, for instance, for John Strachey to be one of the closest political allies of Oswald Mosley while head of the New Party at one moment and his outspoken Communist enemy the next.

On a purely literary level, too, though the young Auden seemed modern and even hypermodern to his first readers, there were obvious and powerful traditional elements in his poetry from the very beginning, including a fondness for intricate metrical and formal experimentation reminiscent of Hardy rather than Eliot. Much of his earliest poetry is also heavily indebted to old English models like "The Seafarer" and "The Battle of Maldon" (one recalls in this connection that Auden studied Old English under Tolkien at Oxford) and to the Old Norse sagas. Auden, in fact, half-seriously thought of himself as descended from Icelandic ancestors, and indeed there is in the Sagas a figure called Authun the Bear.[14] "Paid on Both Sides" takes its title from a line in *Beowulf* and fuses fragments of dream psychology with, among other things, traditional folk mummery plays. So that, while there is nothing equivalent here in terms of scale to Yeats's early use of Irish mythology and legend, there is certainly enough conscious traditionalism in the early Auden, enough of an attempt to link his poetical practice with the very beginnings of English poetry, to suggest a strong methodological and perhaps even ideological link between the two poets.

All this is not to say that early Auden and late Yeats are really more alike than they are different, something I certainly don't wish to claim. But it is to say that Auden and Yeats often respond in very similar ways (structurally at least) to similar problems and situations, and that, as MacNeice recognized, their poetry, during much of the thirties at least, is always mimetic in the sense of representing an effort to make sense of what once was called the real world—the real political and social world around them.

V

Among the best-known poems that Auden wrote during the late 1930s is "Musée des Beaux Arts" (December 1938). Not only has it been frequently anthologized, but it has even put in a kind of cameo appearance in a David Bowie movie. Part of its popularity is no doubt attributable to its treatment of a theme that concerns us all and that was becoming acutely relevant at the end of the low dishonest decade, namely human suffering. The war in Spain was going badly and so was the war in China, from which Auden had only recently returned. The prisons and concentration camps were filling up in Germany and, less avowably, in the Soviet Union; and there was little doubt that another major war was growing increasingly "inevitable" in Europe. But the poem's popularity is due not merely to its thematic universality and relevance; it is also due to its apparent lucidity and its unpretentious

"Landscape with the Fall of Icarus," c. 1560 by Pieter Bruegel. Courtesy of The Royal Museum of Fine Arts, Brussels.

tone. Basically, all the poem seems to be doing is, first, enumerating various, thematically appropriate details from different paintings by unnamed "Old Masters," and then going on to describe in somewhat greater detail a specific painting about the fall of Icarus by the Flemish Old Master Pieter Brueghel. Added to this is some overt editorializing on the part of the speaker, regarding the supposed infallibility of the Old Masters when dealing with the theme of suffering. The essential meaning of the poem appears to lie on the surface, so that it hardly needs further critical elaboration or, at best, only some minor commentary concerning the identity of the various Masters and the paintings that are alluded to in the poem. But here, as so often in Auden's work, appearance belies reality.

First to the poem itself:

About suffering they were never wrong,
The Old Masters: how well they understood
Its human position; how it takes place
While someone else is eating or opening a window or just walking dully along;
How, when the aged are reverently, passionately waiting
For the miraculous birth, there always must be
Children who did not specially want it to happen, skating
On a pond at the edge of the wood:
They never forgot
That even the dreadful martyrdom must run its course
Anyhow in a corner, some untidy spot
Where the dogs go on with their doggy life and the torturer's horse
Scratches its innocent behind on a tree.

In Brueghel's *Icarus*, for instance, how everything turns away
Quite leisurely from the disaster; the ploughman may
Have heard the splash, the forsaken cry,
But for him it was not an important failure; the sun shone
As it had to on the white legs disappearing into the green
Water; and the expensive delicate ship that must have seen
Something amazing, a boy falling out of the sky,
Had somewhere to get to and sailed calmly on.

(EA, 237)

Just how remarkable and even odd this poem really is only becomes apparent when it is examined more closely, and especially when it is viewed in the context of the kind of poetry Auden had been writing about human suffering earlier in the decade, such as, for example, "A Communist to Others" or even "Spain." It is simply "something amazing"—and must have seemed so to at least a few of the poem's first readers—that the same poet who had so recently and violently urged the need for social action and so notoriously identified its Marxist nature, that this same poet should now invite his readers to, as it were, discard their Marxes and Lenins in favor of entering the Museum of Fine Arts. Quite suddenly, and quite inexplicably, it was the old aesthetic masters, not the new political ones, who knew about the cause of suffering. Suffering was no longer conceived of as the result of social injustice, something one could learn about (and also learn how to palliate and perhaps eliminate) by consulting psychiatrists or political philosophers. Now human suffering became something about which a group of pre-modern painters already knew everything there was to be said, and indeed had already "said" it. And what's more, "they were never wrong." *Never*! As if to make sure that we haven't misread the word, Auden (or at least his speaker) repeats it a little later in the poem, when he tells us that the Old Masters also "never forgot" about the invariably unheroic and even sordid context of human suffering.[15]

Auden, to be sure, had not altogether changed his mind about humanity's often unfortunate relation to its social environment. There are still traces of social criticism in the poem and there is unquestionably an ironic treatment of the various responses to Icarus's death. The expensive delicate ship, for example, is almost certainly carrying a cargo of goodies for Capitalists. There is no doubt that if it had been less commercially minded, it could have turned about to rescue (or at least attempt to rescue) Icarus, but it had other, apparently more pressing engagements and so it merely "sailed calmly on." It is the adverb "calmly" that conveys Auden's irony here, implying that nothing of importance has occurred, nothing that did or even should ruffle people's feelings. It's only another boy falling out of the sky—nothing to worry about, in other words, as there might have been if some more valuable cargo had been at stake. The same is true of the other sentient elements of the picture, at least those enumerated by the speaker, namely the ploughman and the sun. Both belong to the "everything" that turns away "quite leisurely" from Icarus's suffering. There is no rush, no feeling of urgency, no discernible need for action. For the ploughman, extraordinary events like young men dropping from the heavens have no significance. His principal concern is rather for ordinary things like ploughing, sowing, and harvesting. As for the sun, though it bears some direct responsibility for Icarus's fall, it too expresses no concern, but continues to behave quite "naturally," not bothering to grow dim or stand still from wonder or grief. Like the ploughman, its response to Icarus's private disaster is calm and leisurely. But Auden's sociopolitical ironies notwithstanding, the unmistakable message of the poem is that suffering is an inescapable part of the human rather than the social condition—an existentialist phenomenon, rather than a Marxist or

Freudian one (and indeed, at about this time Kierkegaard began to replace Marx and Freud as Auden's preferred reading). For what can be done to save Icarus? Should the ploughman call a nautical ambulance—or the Communist Party? Should the little ship transmute into the Battleship Potemkin? Would it make any difference if the horse stopped scratching its behind? Or the children skating?[16]

Odd, too, in view of Auden's attack on Yeats's supposedly "lying" poetry at this time, is the striking resemblance that "Musée des Beaux Arts" bears to one of the latter's poems published earlier that year (1938) in *New Poems*. This is "Lapis Lazuli," the second part of which focuses, like Auden's poem, on a particular work of art that has something to teach humanity about living and dying:

> Two Chinamen, behind them a third,
> Are carved in Lapis Lazuli,
> Over them flies a long-legged bird
> A symbol of longevity;
> The third, doubtless a serving man,
> Carries a musical instrument.
>
> Every discolouration of the stone,
> Every accidental crack or dent
> Seems a water-course or an avalanche,
> Or lofty slope where it still snows
> Though doubtless plum or cherry-branch
> Sweetens the little half-way house
> Those Chinamen climb towards, and I
> Delight to imagine them seated there;
> There, on the mountain and the sky,
> On all the tragic scene they stare.
> One asks for mournful melodies;
> Accomplished fingers begin to play.
> Their eyes mid many wrinkles, their eyes,
> Their ancient, glittering eyes, are gay.

(Yeats, 342)

Like Auden's ploughman and ship, Yeats's Chinese sages take in the whole of the human "tragic scene" from a distance, but they react in a manner that goes beyond even the formers' calm and leisurely response. The scene they are watching from on high, though never specified, would have been immediately recognized by every contemporaneous reader, namely the images of human suffering brought about by the Sino-Japanese War and daily displayed on the front pages of the newspapers. Even so, the wise men aren't just calm; they are *gay*. But their gaiety is not active in any way; it is purely spectatorial and sedentary. Though it includes calmness, it goes beyond mere calmness into something resembling a Buddhist state of bliss. The sages are not merely resigned and/or indifferent, as Auden's ploughmen and ship are; they are delighted, happy. Unlike the "hysterical women" at the beginning of Yeats's poem, these men of precious stone remain motionless, listening to a mournful music that paradoxically delights them. They are utterly undisturbed by the violence that surrounds them—and us. For Yeats, in this instance at least, poetry—he specifically mentions Shakespeare's *Hamlet* elsewhere in the poem—also makes nothing happen, except inwardly.

Like Auden's Old Masters, Yeats's old Chinamen understand the immutable verities of existence, and the futility of attempting to change them. All one can do is to change one's attitude toward those verities, rather like Camus's imagined Sisyphus. Entering the museum in order to gaze at the paintings of the Old Masters, or looking at a precious stone carved into a work of art—these are the (only) things we can and should do; they are the only *actions* to perform if we wish to gain a modicum of calmness, perhaps even gaiety. While it may be regrettable that, as Yeats's speaker tells us, Aeroplane and Zeppelin come out and King Billy—not just William of Orange but also Kaiser Wilhelm II and perhaps even Chancellor Adolf Hitler—begins to pitch bomb-balls, or, as in Auden's poem, human beings fall to their deaths out of the blue sky, these are marginal events of which one takes cognizance only to dismiss them in favor of what truly matters: ploughing the earth, sailing the sea, climbing the mountain of truth. In these two poems, Yeats and Auden are, so it would appear, not so far apart after all.

Aside from the surprising agreement with Yeats, there are some other surprises in "Musée des Beaux Arts." The "miraculous birth," for instance—presumably a reference to Christ's birth—appears to have no direct relevance to the stated theme of human suffering; it is rather an occasion for joy. So one wonders why it is cited here as one of the principal examples of human suffering. John Fuller's answer to this question is that "the allusions to the Nativity create the poem's concealed subject, what it is really *about*," namely, Auden's imminent return to the faith of his childhood (Fuller, *Commentary*, 267). But to read the poem in this primarily autobiographical way is to completely disregard its explicit focus on human *suffering*. So too, the "dreadful martyrdom" is also presumably a reference to Christ, but this time to the crucifixion, as depicted in Brueghel's "Procession to Calvary," and hence, it can have little direct relevance to a specifically *human* suffering, since Christ is divine.[17] That he is also the *son of man* is, of course, true too, but his humanity is de-emphasized by Auden's earlier reference to his *miraculous* birth. Finally, while Icarus was undeniably human, he is not an historical, but a mythological figure, so that the indifferent response of the ploughman and the sailors to his suffering may be excused on the grounds that they may not have recognized the relevance of this particular "disaster" to their own more realistic, if also not altogether real, human lives; and besides, in Ovid, the ploughman, shepherd and fisherman are all convinced that the flying figures of Daedalus and Icarus are gods (Ovid, 188). In any event, both Christ and Icarus are extraordinary figures, whose suffering is so noteworthy that, among other things, it has caught the attention of various Old Masters.[18] Whatever else one may say of it, it belongs to a different realm of suffering from that of the anonymous "comrades" in "A Communist to Others" or the equally anonymous travelers to the Spanish Civil War in "Spain." Christ and Icarus's suffering is a "named" suffering that is linked to them as individuals; it is a suffering that has a moral meaning, as well as, in the case of Christ, an immeasurable religious influence.

As if these problems were not enough, there is a difficulty connected with Auden's conception of "Old Masters." To begin with, as just about all of the commentators on the poem are agreed—it is one of the few things on which they are agreed—only one Old Master is really being referred to here, namely Pieter Brueghel (or, more customarily, Bruegel) the Elder (c. 1525–69). Brueghel was the foremost exponent of the so-called school of Mannerist painting in the Netherlands during the sixteenth century, though his importance was only (re)discovered at the end of the nineteenth century. The best collection of his paintings is housed in the Kunsthistorisches Museum in Vienna, but the paintings being referred to in this poem, including the one about Icarus, are primarily (perhaps even exclusively) located in the Musées Royaux des Beaux-Arts in Brussels. Auden saw them there while living in Brussels in late 1938. At the time he visited the museum, the "Landscape with the Fall of Icarus" (the official name) was apparently hanging in a special alcove together with several other important Brueghel pictures: "The Adoration of the Kings," "The Massacre of the Innocents," and "The Numbering at Bethlehem. " It would therefore seem reasonable to suppose that such details as are not to be found in the Icarus painting may have been drawn from the others (Kinney, 529; Fuller, *Guide*, 121). Here, however, a subsidiary problem arises, namely that none of the Brueghel pictures in Brussels (or anywhere else, for that matter), shows a horse scratching its behind on a tree, or dogs going on with their doggy lives—that is, urinating or defecating if one takes up the implications of the word "untidy" mentioned in the proximity of a tree.[19] Auden, of course, may simply be making up these semi-humorous details in order to sharpen the contrast in his poem, or, alternatively, he may be referring to paintings by other Dutch and Flemish Old Masters. After all, Auden's singling out Brueghel by name in the latter part of the poem does not necessarily imply that the paintings of the Old Masters referred to in the first part are also by Brueghel. On the contrary, the phrase "in Brueghel's *Icarus*, for instance," clearly suggests that the speaker is commenting on a painting by a "typical" Old Master. If this is true, however, then the critics must be wrong in assuming that only Brueghel's pictures are featured in the poem.

Not all critics are convinced that the frame of reference should be limited to those Brueghel pictures housed in the Royal Museum at Brussels. Max Bluestone, for instance, considers the Winterthur version of "The Adoration of the Magi" more pertinent than the one in Brussels, and refers specifically to the Vienna version of "The Massacre of the Innocents" rather than to the one in Brussels (Bluestone, 333). Similarly, P. V. LePage believes that the "Procession to Calvary" (Vienna) is being referred to in the first part of the poem (LePage, 254 n). Still, Brueghel is the only Old Master who is consistently named in connection with the poem. How very odd this is becomes apparent only when one recalls that the epithet "Old Masters" is generally taken to refer to just about all painters from the early Renaissance through the seventeenth century.[20] Taken in this broader and more usual sense, the "Old Masters" customarily depict suffering very differently from the way Brueghel does (or is said to do) in Auden's poem. Certainly, the great Italian and Spanish Renaissance painters, such as Titian or El Greco, depict suffering—Christ's suffering especially, that is, suffering that is emblematic of all other suffering—as very much the center of attention, with a variety of subsidiary figures consumed either by grief or engaged actively in the process of furthering that suffering. There is no sign anywhere in their paintings of dogs or horses that are otherwise occupied, or even of skating children or ploughing ploughmen. This is even true of a painter in the Northern European tradition like Rembrandt, whose celebrated technique of *chiaroscuro* is, in fact, deliberately designed to lead the eye towards the emotional center and away from other, more "irrelevant" aspects of the painting.

Randall Jarrell is one of the very few readers of Auden's poem to have commented on the peculiar way in which the "old masters" are said to depict suffering there. In his poem, "The Old and the New Masters" (1964) Jarrell points out, quite rightly, that

> About suffering, about adoration, the old masters
> Disagree. When someone suffers, no one else eats
> Or walks or opens the window—no one breathes
> As the sufferers watch the sufferer.

(Jarrell, 332)

One of the old masters Jarrell refers to specifically is the Flemish painter, Hugo van der Goes (c. 1435/40–92), whose "Nativity" (usually called *The Portinari Altarpiece* [Myers, II, 536–37]) shows not only angels, Magi, shepherds, saints (and even animals), adoring the newborn Christ, but also anachronistically portrays the person who commissioned the painting, along with his family, as

> kneeling, looking: everything
> That was or will be in the world is fixed
> On its small, helpless, human center.
>
> (Jarrell, 333)

Though Jarrell never mentions Auden by name, the reference to "Musée des Beaux Arts" is umistakable, as is the criticism of the poem's conception of how the old masters depicted suffering. To be sure, Jarrell does concede that "after a while the masters show the crucifixion / In one corner of the canvas," but this occurs primarily because of a reconception on their part of man's place in the universe (and his relation to God) caused by the Copernican revolution. Jarrell does not refer to Brueghel in this connection but rather to the Italian painter Paolo Veronese (1528–88), who was called before the Inquisition in 1573 for including in one of his paintings, as Jarrell notes, some "dogs playing at the feet of Christ." (In the first part of the poem, Jarrell had used Veronese's *St. Sebastian Mourned by St. Irene* to make his case against Auden's supposedly mistaken view of the Old Masters.) In any case, Veronese's work was primarily carried out in the period following Brueghel's death, so that by implication Brueghel's pictures are apparently not to be included in Jarrell's "after a while." As for the "new Masters," in Jarrell's view, they don't even bother to depict Christ at all, or even dogs, whereas the "last master," a practitioner of abstract art, has relegated the planet Earth, in the form of a "bright spot," to a corner of his canvas. In the end, then, not only has suffering disappeared, but so have God and humanity. And so have the masters.[21]

Contrary to the opinion of Jarrell, while Brueghel was not unique among Old Masters (especially of the Flemish School) in relativizing or "contextualizing" human suffering, he is undoubtedly by far the best (and the best known) Old Master to practice this technique. Even the tradition to which he belongs has only a few other noteworthy exponents—with Joachim Patinir and Brueghel's own son, Pieter (called "the Younger"), being two of those few (Roberts, 15)—so that, for all intents and purposes, it was born in the generation preceding his own and died in the following generation. To be sure, Brueghel's importance as a painter of humorous and fantastic pictures continued to be recognized long after his death; and his influence as a landscape painter survives even to this day. But these are aspects of his work that are quite distinct from the one that Auden is isolating in his poem, namely Brueghel's characteristic relegation of events and people usually thought of as "central" to the margins of his pictures, or of making them seem smaller by placing them in the background. For example, in his "Procession to Calvary" (Vienna), it is at first difficult to discover the figure of Christ, so obscured is he by other, larger figures in the foreground. The most extreme example of this technique of decentralization, however, is the Brussels version of the "Landscape with the Fall of Icarus," where in the bottom right hand corner of the picture, Brueghel has placed two legs and part of a hand sticking out of the water. The only actual evidence that these are meant to testify to the fall of Icarus are the title of the picture and a few, tiny, isolated feathers shown drifting slowly down towards the drowning Icarus.

There are actually two nearly identical versions of this painting, one (not the painting Auden saw in Brussels) showing Daedalus flying, with arms and wings outstretched, at the top of the picture, a little to the left of center. In this position he may be visible to the Shepherd, but not to any of the other figures in the foreground of the picture. Daedalus himself seems to be looking down, with an expression of grief, at the disappearing legs of Icarus, but he is making no move to go to his aid. There is also no sun visible in this picture, though a great deal of suffused light appears in the bottom center where the sun is located in the other picture.

Brueghel's picture(s) of Icarus's fall has/have occasioned almost as much controversy among critics of Auden's poem as the poem itself. Christoph Bode's essay, for example, is mainly devoted to explaining why the sun is located on the horizon in the Brussels version of Brueghel's picture, whereas according to Ovid it should be high in the sky. Bode's answer to this apparent paradox is that Brueghel wishes to show, in this way, that Icarus is solely responsible for his "disaster." The sun (or Nature or Providence) is blameless in the matter (Bode, 89). While Bode's theory is not inconsistent with Brueghel's iconographic habits, it does not take into account the fact that the version of the painting in which the sun is invisible nevertheless shows an identical pattern of shadows, suggesting that the missing sun has simply been painted over. (The pattern of shadows in both versions is clearly revealed in the black and white reproductions in Seidel and Marijnissen, [74–75].) Gustav Glück also remarks on the curious position of the sun in the Brussels version of the painting, but proffers no explanation for it. He does, however, refer to the existence of yet a third version of the picture in which neither Icarus nor Daedalus appear (Glück, 44). J. Van Lennep also offers an intricate interpretation based on alchemical lore in which, among other things, the apparently odd position of the sun is in fact a hermetic reference to the alchemist's "philosopher's gold" (Arpino, 92). John Fuller resolves this complex issue simply by proposing that the fact that the sun is setting shows that "it has taken time for Icarus to fall after the melting of his wings" (Fuller, *Commentary*, 267). All of this iconographical speculation, of course, has very little to do with Auden's actual use of Brueghel's paintings in the poem, though there is an understandable interest on the part of Auden's critics in those paintings themselves. So, along with the odd position of the sun, there has been some puzzlement about the head of an apparently dead man lying in the bushes at the extreme left center of the picture. Peter Verdonk speculates that it may be an allusion to Daedalus (Verdonk, 78). Rosa and Welch, who dispute that it is a corpse at all, are unique in identifying a "dead lamb" lying near the left foot of the ploughman (Rosa and Welcher, 141). According to de Tolnay, however, these apparently odd details are explicable by reference to Brueghel's iconographic technique. So, the fact that the ploughman pointedly ignores both the corpse in the bushes and the dying Icarus confirms the old proverb that "no plough stops for a man who is dying." Furthermore, according to de Tolnay, the sword stuck in a purse which the ploughman has left lying on a rock to his left is a "symbol of human folly," illustrating the proverb that "sword and money need intelligent hands," whereas the bag filled with seed not far from the ploughman's left foot (Rosa and Welcher's dead lamb) alludes to the Biblical proverb that a grain of corn cast on rocky ground will not grow. All of this serves, in de Tolnay's view, to illustrate the vanity of Icarus's venture (de Tolnay, 28; my translation).

Just what Auden's conscious intention might have been in categorically identifying the highly unusual practice of a single Old Master with that of all other Old Masters is unclear, though certainly a consequence of that identification is the implication that premodern painting has a relevance to life that modern or contemporary painting does not—a generalization that may also apply by extension to other contemporary arts, like poetry, for example. (This is evidently a conclusion that Jarrell also drew from his reading of the poem.) That Auden was indeed motivated in this way is perhaps to be seen in his decision to focus the latter half of the poem on the suffering of Icarus, rather than continue with that of Christ. Though Icarus himself is not an artist, he undoubtedly belongs to a family of artists. His father, Daedalus is, in fact, the archetype of the artist, as readers of James Joyce can attest. In the second section of *The Orators*, Auden himself had already written a long poem in which the hero is a "high flyer" destined to fall, and one of the possible models for Auden's Airman was, as we have seen, Lauro de Bosis, the Italian poet who had not only written a long poem entitled *Icaro* but had actually died when his plane crashed into the sea. What Auden may be implying, then, is that the relationship of the Old Masters to the new non-masters—or the old traditional art to the new, traditionless art—is like that of Daedalus to his son Icarus. The Old Masters were aware of a larger reality that allowed them to understand life and cope with it more successfully than their modern heirs, whose failure to heed the example of their fathers causes them to take foolish risks and brings about their (artistic) downfall.

It is also possible that Auden may have had in mind Baudelaire's poem, "Les Plaintes d'un Icare" (from *Fleurs du mal*), since the latter has come to be considered archetypal of the artist manqué. The lack of wings is, to be sure, not always or necessarily preferable to their possession, even when misused. In "The Maze" (a poem excerpted from "New Year Letter," written not long after "Musée des Beaux Arts"), Auden presents the human condition as one in which "anthropos apteros" or "wingless man" wanders helplessly lost through the maze of life, perplexed and looking up at the sky, wishing "he were a bird." (CP, 237) An even more likely source is that greatest of "old masters," namely, Shakespeare, whose insistence on expressing the "whole truth" was famously described by Samuel Johnson in his *Preface to Shakespeare* (1765): "Shakespeare's plays are not in the rigorous and critical sense either tragedies or comedies, but compositions of a distinct kind . . . expressing the course of the world, in which the loss of one is the gain of another, in which, *at the same time, the reveller is hasting to his wine, and the mourner is burying his friend* . . ."(Johnson, 15; my italics). How much Auden was aware of Shakespeare's old mastery at roughly this time is apparent from his remark to Theodore Spencer about "The Sea and the Mirror," subtitled "A Commentary on Shakespeare's *The Tempest*," that it was his "Ars Poetica," an attempt to show "in a work of art, the limitations of art" (quoted in Mendelson, 205).

Be this as it may, the aesthetic and ethical principles that Auden (or at least his speaker) is endorsing in "Musée des Beaux Arts" differ considerably from his earlier views on these subjects. They are also based on what appears to be a highly original interpretation of Brueghel's painting and, indeed, of his whole technique of relativization and contextualization. Understandably, critics have been hesitant to conclude that Auden arrived at his novel interpretation of Brueghel unassisted. Maurice Charney, for example, shows that Auden's views on Brueghel's *Icarus* are anticipated by Sir Lewis Namier in *England in the Age of the American Revolution*, in a passage where Namier argues that "the true humor of the tragedy is not so much the pair of naked legs sticking out of the water, as the complete unconcern of all the potential onlookers; not even the fisherman on the shore notices what has happened" (Charney, 130). However, Charney provides no evidence that

Auden had read Namier's book or had any connection whatever with Namier. Namier, to be sure, was not alone in perceiving the unusual significance of Brueghel's work. Closer to Auden's hand would have been Charles de Tolnay's study of *Pierre Bruegel l'Ancien*, published in Brussels in 1935, in which the "Landscape with the Fall of Icarus" is seen as being "of the greatest importance for understanding Bruegel's philosophical thought," since, in it, Brueghel subverts Ovid's text (his source for the Daedalus/Icarus story). He is, as de Tolnay points out, "the first to have shown the ploughman at work, the shepherd leaning on his crook, the fisherman with the rod in his hand. But he does so by turning the text upside down: instead of looking with astonishment at Daedalus and Icarus flying in the heavens like gods [as they are described as doing in Ovid, 188], the indifferent ploughman keeps ploughing, the shepherd turns his back on Icarus, looking unmoved straight ahead into the void, and the fisherman remains absorbed in his fishing; even the partridge [Daedalus's transformed nephew, Talus, whom he had murdered], which in Ovid keeps on beating its wings in order to mock Daedalus eternally, stays immobile on its branch; and even better, the ship in whose proximity the disaster unfolds moves away towards the sun, its sails billowing." After claiming that none of Brueghel's successors understood the point of what he was doing, de Tolnay goes on to say specifically of Icarus: "As if lost in this vast landscape, the fall of the hero remains unnoticed by everyone: a little episode of no importance amid this immovable nature, dominated by the unique magic of the sun. The classical myth loses all its importance alongside this new conception of the cosmos; the picture highlights the subordination of human existence to the eternal laws of nature" (de Tolnay, 27–28; my translation).

It is possible that Auden may have read de Tolnay on Brueghel, given the fact that de Tolnay's book had been published in Brussels only a few years earlier and may even have been available in the museum itself. It is possible—but there is no actual evidence to prove it. (Their shared emphasis on the sun may suggest, however, a debt on Auden's part to de Tolnay, though, of course, the sun plays a major role in Ovid's retelling of the story as well.) Much more likely, however, is the possibility that Auden derived his interpretation from Aldous Huxley's ground-breaking essay on Brueghel in *Along the Road* (1925). Like every other thinking poet of his generation, Auden knew Huxley's work well (especially his fiction) and occasionally refers to it, though not always by name.[22] The striking parallels in thought and even in phrasing suggest that Auden had primarily Huxley's Brueghel essay in mind, especially the section dealing with Brueghel's "Procession to Calvary." Of this picture Huxley says that, of all the pictures he has seen dealing with the subject, "this Calvary of Brueghel's is the most suggestive and, dramatically, the most appalling. For *all other masters* have painted these dreadful scenes from within, so to speak, outwards. For them Christ is the centre, the divine hero of the tragedy; this is the fact from which they start; it affects and transforms all the other facts, justifying, in a sense, the horror of the drama and ranging all that surrounds the central figure in an ordered hierarchy of good and evil. Brueghel, on the other hand, starts from the outside and works inwards. He represents the scene as it would have appeared to any casual spectator on the road to Golgotha on a certain spring morning in the year 33 A.D. Other artists have pretended to be angels, painting the scene with a knowledge of its significance. But Brueghel resolutely remains a *human* onlooker. What he shows is a crowd of people *walking briskly* in holiday joyfulness up the slopes of a hill" (Huxley, 149–50, my italics).

The italicized words in the previous passage show a clear link to Auden's poem, specifically to the idea that the Old Masters were very good at understanding the distinctively "human position" of suffering by showing how it takes place, for example, when others are "just walking dully along." This is precisely the point Huxley is making about Brueghel, with the chief difference being that, in Huxley's description, the others are walking *briskly* rather than *dully* along. Another passage in the essay suggests further similarities, with Huxley arguing that Brueghel's pictures "show him to have been a man profoundly convinced of the reality of evil and of the horrors which this mortal life, not to mention eternity, hold in store for *suffering humanity*. The world is a horrible place; but in spite of this, or precisely because of this, men and women *eat*, drink, dance, Carnival tilts against Lent and triumphs, if only for a moment; *children play* in the streets, people get married in the midst of gross rejoicings" (Huxley, 148–49; my italics). Here again, there are some obvious similarities between Huxley's and Auden's texts, most notably the emphasis in both on a *suffering humanity* that is condemned to suffer alone and unattended, while other adults eat and children play. As Huxley was to maintain in a later essay, "Tragedy and the Whole Truth," pure tragedy (or any pure emotion, for that matter) is incompatible with a consciousness of the whole truth, for pure tragedy is only possible when the surrounding human context is removed (Huxley, "Tragedy," 12–16).

If we accept the idea that Auden is picking up on an interpretation originally put forward by Aldous Huxley in his essay on Brueghel, does this mean that his poem is really nothing more than a versified elaboration of that essay? No, I think not. For one thing, Auden differs radically from Huxley in his conviction that Brueghel's characteristically relativized way of depicting suffering is true of *all* Old Masters. For Huxley, on the other hand, Brueghel is unique. Important, too, is the fact that "Musée des Beaux Arts" is not merely a discursive analysis of Brueghel's paintings but an actual recreation in another aesthetic medium of what those paintings, especially "Landscape with the Fall of Icarus," attempt to do. The degree to which Auden's own poem is "decentered" is hinted at in the way it downplays its complex rhyme scheme, with some of the end rhymes so distanced from each other that they are scarcely noticeable (LePage, 257). Similarly, Auden's title "decenters" the subject of his poem by placing an apparently undue importance on the building (and perhaps also on the institution) where the paintings are kept, just as Brueghel's title, "Landscape with the Fall of Icarus," makes the landscape (actually more of a seascape) seem even more important than the human beings and even implies that they are part of that landscape.[23] In Auden's case, his title may even represent an oblique announcement of his newly discovered preference for art over politics, or of truth over rhetoric. Truth, we are made to realize, is where the Muses are, not the politicians. Or, as Auden put it a year later in the title (drawn from Blake) of his largely autobiographical collection of aphorisms, *The Prolific and the Devourer*, truth is the province of the "prolific" (the artist), not of the "devourer" (the politician). By this time, to be sure, Auden had become something of an Old Master himself, and though he never seriously claimed to be infallible on the subject of human suffering (despite his ingrained habit, especially in conversation, of laying down the law), his poetry never again became subservient to political expediency, either of the Left or of the Right. Like the expensive, delicate ship in Brueghel's painting, his poetry now had other concerns, had somewhere else to get to (specifically, the United States), and sailed calmly on.

4

The American Auden: A Poet Reborn?

"God bless the U.S.A., so large,
So friendly, and so rich."

—"On the Circuit" (1963)

"The object of poetry is not Truth, the
object of poetry is poetry itself."

—Baudelaire

I

W. H. AUDEN BECAME AN AMERICAN CITIZEN IN 1946 AFTER HAVING BEEN A MORE or less permanent resident of New York City since January 1939. His first visit to the United States, however, had taken place half a year earlier, when he had traveled in the company of Christopher Isherwood by train from the West Coast and stayed in New York for a couple of weeks in the summer of 1938. At the time, both were on the last leg of their *Journey to a War*, which had taken them to China for a tour of the Sino-Japanese conflict. A few months later, the two friends were to sign a contract for a travel book about the United States, presumably something along the lines of the exuberant *Letters from Iceland*, which Auden had done, together with Louis MacNeice, in 1936. Unfortunately, nothing came of the idea, though one can perhaps get an inkling of what it would have been like from part 3 of Auden's *New Year Letter*, published in 1940.[1] It was an idea that actually went as far back as 1937, when Auden had thought of doing a travel book on America, not with Isherwood, but with Stephen Spender. America was obviously a place Auden had, for some time, been determined to take a closer look at and write something about, preferably in the company of an old friend (Mendelson, EA, xix–xx). As it turned out, his first years in New York would turn out to be, according Edward Mendelson, "by far the most crucial and decisive period of his adult life . . ." (Mendelson, "Auden," 31).

Auden was almost thirty-two when he came to live in New York; he was also by this time the leading British poet of his generation. Although he had spent parts of the previous decade outside of Britain—in Germany, Belgium, Denmark, Portugal, France and Spain, as well as in Iceland and China—he considered himself, and was rightly considered, very much an English poet, habitually portraying in his work a poetic landscape and referring to places and people that were unmistakably British. Hence, his decision to leave Britain for America was not, and could not have been, a merely private one, even discounting the fact that it coincided with what was widely and rightly seen as the inevitable onset of another world war. But of course, that fact cannot be discounted, so that when the war broke out, he became, in the eyes of many British contemporaries, not merely an American, but also a renegade and a coward. How deep this feeling sometimes ran is apparent in the British novelist Anthony Powell's cruel comment on reading of Auden's death in 1973: "No more Auden. I'm delighted that shit has gone" (quoted in Davenport-Hines, 180).

Just when and why Auden decided to stay in America and become an American citizen is, like so many other important events in his life, a little fuzzy. William Empson, who saw him briefly in New York in mid-1939, thought that Auden's decision to stay in in the United States was primarily political. To him "it seemed plain that he could not have stayed in England to be Churchill's Laureate, since he believed that England was imperialist but America wasn't, whereas I could safely go home and do the minor propaganda jobs which would be required of me, having no such fame" (Empson, "Wartime," 31). Auden's brother John, however, told Evelyn Waugh after the war that Auden had expressed his intention to become an American citizen as early as August 1938, when he was staying in Brussels, but this claim does not altogether jibe with an excerpt that his most recent biographer, Richard Davenport-Hines, provides from a letter by Auden to the same brother, dating from April or May 1939. There, after telling John of the depth of his love for the recently met Chester Kallman, Auden views it as a "snag" that he will now "have to become an American Citizen as I'm not going to risk separation through international crises" (quoted in Davenport-Hines, 176, 188). In mid-June, however, his mind was apparently still not entirely made up, for he wrote an English friend, James Yates, that "I have almost definitely decided now to become an American citizen" (Quoted in Mendelson, *Later*, 52). Auden, in other words, if we are to take him at his word, had not originally planned to become an American when he went to New York for the second time, though of course he may have intended to stay on indefinitely while retaining British citizenship. He changed his mind, apparently, only after meeeting Kallman.

Despite the muddle, one is probably justified in saying that there is no need to doubt the general accuracy and sincerity of Auden's account, since he must have been very much aware of the drastic and nearly tragic complications that, for just such reasons, had recently beset Spender and Isherwood's relations with their respective lovers.[2] It seems fair to conclude, then, that though there were obviously also other, less pressing and less personal reasons, it was primarily Auden's love for an American that persuaded him to become an American himself. A few months later, Auden made his decision public in a lecture at Harvard, and in 1940, he took out citizenship papers.[3]

Initially at least, Auden's residence in the United States should not have been surprising to either his British or his American readers. Like Isherwood, Auden could easily have replied to the English super-patriots who accused him of having run away that he didn't "look at it that way because my whole life was running away from England" (Dunaway, 63). Young as he was, Auden had already established a clear pattern of discovering "new country," to cite the celebrated title of one of the first anthologies to publish his work. In approach and subject matter, too, Auden was an innovator, grafting Eliot and Hopkins to Brecht, Cole Porter, Gertrude Stein, Georg Groddeck, John Layard and Karl and even Groucho Marx. His earliest poems showed him to be a master of what his friend Isherwood called "the Waste Land Game" (Isherwood, *Lions*, 191), and even after he had stopped playing this particular game during the later thirties in favor of other games invented by Rilke and Yeats, Auden invariably was able to provide his audience with the newest and most fashionable poetical product. As he was later to remark in his autobiographical "Profile:"

> His guardian angel
> has always told him
> What and whom to read next.

(CP 582)

Going to the United States, then, was in this sense nothing new; it was—or seemed to be—merely another episode in Auden's by now habitual quest for novelty. Nor was Auden unique among British writers and intellectuals in selecting the United States as the place where the action—and the money—was. Aside from Isherwood, other friends and acquaintances such as Louis MacNeice, Benjamin Britten, Peter Pears, Gerald Heard, and Aldous Huxley had already settled down, or were about to, for the time being at any rate, in New York or Los Angeles. Of all of these, however, only Auden was to identify himself unabashedly as an American.[4]

II

The first reference to Auden as an American poet actually predates his permanent settlement in the United States. Though it's unclear who is ultimately responsible for it, it derives either directly or indirectly from Delmore Schwartz. In the fall of 1938, hoping to drum up favorable reviews and publicity for his forthcoming *In Dreams Begin Responsibilities*, Schwartz asked his publisher, James Laughlin, to send out advance copies to various notables, including Auden. In Auden's case, however, he specified that the book jacket not be sent along, since on it Schwartz was described as "the American Auden" (Atlas, 128). Clearly, at this point Auden was so little an American that Schwartz was worried that he might be surprised (and dismayed) by being confronted with the unexpected existence of an American alter ego.

On a more serious level, Edmund Wilson remarked in 1945 that Auden "in fundamental ways . . . doesn't belong in that London literary world—he's more vigorous and more advanced. With his Birmingham background . . . he is in some ways more like an American. He is really extremely tough—cares nothing about property or money, popularity or social prestige—does everything on his own and alone" (Quoted in Davenport-Hines, 230). Though the idea expressed here of Auden as a kind of working-class fusion of Hemingway and St. Francis gives one pause, it is surely significant that America's leading critic of the period should have begun to claim Auden for America even before the latter had officially turned American himself. Wilson seems actually, however, to have been of two minds regarding the question of Auden's national identity. In a later essay entitled "W. H. Auden in America," (1956) Wilson observes, quite oblivious of his earlier remarks, that Auden has remained "basically English" despite his long residence in America, and that he "is English in his toughness, his richness, his obstinacy, his adventurousness, his eccentricity." He then goes on, again a little inconsistently, to observe that "with Auden the process of Americanization had already begun in England. He had been reading American writers, had tried his hand at American ballads, and had shown, in these and in 'The Dance of Death,' published in 1933, that he had already—in a rather surprising way—got the hang of the American vernacular." Auden, in other words, though fundamentally English, had become Americanized before he became American. Assuming American citizenship, therefore, was merely the logical outward adjustment to his internal development. As for the benefit Auden derived from his new American identity, that was chiefly, in Wilson's view, the achievement of "a mind that feels itself to be at the center of things," a possession not to be despised, since it "is certainly one of the best things an American can hope to have." (Haffenden, 406–7)

To be sure, Wilson's idea of Auden's having been "Americanized" long before coming to America was not really original. It was anticipated by Horace Gregory in his review of Auden's *Double Man*, where we are told that "Mr. Auden's verse is not American, nor is it entirely British . . . It is sensible to admit that whatever 'Americanisms' appeared on the surfaces of Mr. Auden's early poems were those that showed a reading of T. S. Eliot and the acquisition of American phrases and turns of speech that had become fashionable at Oxford and in London during the first half of the nineteen-thirties" (Gregory, 580). As for the idea that American poetry of the 1950s was at the center of the literary universe—and that the center of this center was New York—this idea is developed more fully and convincingly in Robert von Hallberg's *American Poetry and Culture, 1945–1980* (1985).

Another notable critic and poet, Louise Bogan, is less explicit about Auden's status as an American writer in her *Achievement in American Poetry* (1951), but the fact that she discusses Auden at some length in a book devoted exclusively to American poets is noteworthy in itself, as is her linking of Auden with Eliot as poets espousing an orthodox faith that affected the whole "climate of American poetry." Indeed, she goes on to say that "the influence of Auden was for a time not only pervasive but overpowering" (Bogan, 100–101). Auden's influence on American poetry is a subject I want to defer until later, but, for the moment, what should be noted is that it is viewed here as having been, for a certain ill-defined period (the later forties, presumably), as greater than that of any other living poet.

In 1948, Auden was awarded the Pulitzer Prize for Poetry, an award specifically reserved for American poets, and by the end of the decade, Auden had become so widely accepted a fixture on the American poetical scene that he was appointed, together with Conrad Aiken, Louise Bogan, T. S. Eliot, Robert Lowell and Allen Tate, to the Library of Congress Committee that was to award the first Bollingen Prize. Their choice, Ezra Pound, was to cause a sensation and was to place Auden at the very center of American literary politics. By the early fifties, Auden was getting his work published in collections with names like *New Poems by American Poets* (1953, edited by Rolfe Humphries) and, in 1956, Auden himself edited and wrote an introduction for *The Criterion Book of Modern American Verse* (the "Criterion" here has nothing to do with Eliot's journal of the same name, which had ceased publication a decade and a half earlier). Auden's selection began with five poems by Edwin Arlington Robinson and concluded with two by Anthony Hecht.[5]

The most explicit and vociferous proponent of Auden as an American poet, however, is unquestionably Leslie Fiedler. In his *Waiting for the End* (1965), Fiedler proposes that, along with Theodore Roethke, Auden "had come to seem, over the past decade, one of the two most eminent poets producing verse in America." Going on to declare, first in italics, and then in the first person plural, that in the forties, writers of Auden's generation in America as well as Britain were faced with the choice to "*die forever or be totally reborn*," only Auden (so Fiedler) "has been successfully born again; and in his second birth he is an American, an American poet of the Fifties. The work he produced in the early Forties seems to us now, in large part, tentative and uncertain, though, alas, not frankly so; for he had invented a rhetoric to conceal from himself and his readers alike his failure to find, at that point, satisfactory themes and an adequate new voice. But beginning with *Nones* and *The Shield of Achilles*, the second Auden, the American Auden, had entered into full and secure possession of his craft again, rendering in poems like 'In Praise of Limestone,' [composed in 1948] reflections of the Mediterranean landscape in an American eye; in others, like 'The Shield of Achilles,' a view of the eastern European scene out of the deepest American political imagination. . . ." Fiedler's paean to the fifties' American Auden culminates, a little inconsistently, with a description of Auden's Harvard Phi Beta Kappa poem (a poem dating from 1946) as revealing not only "traces of Eliot's satirical style" but also "a sense of the American poet in his endless comic war against the American comic cliché" (Fiedler, 225–26).[6]

More recently, the *Columbia History of American Poetry* (1993) contains a chapter entitled "American Auden," written by Claude J. Summers.[7] While Summers does not refer to Fiedler, he also suggests, though in a more muted post-modernist manner that, in coming to America, Auden underwent something very much like a rebirth. "Auden's embrace of America at that particular moment," Summers writes, referring to the year 1939, "was absolutely necessary for him, both as a person and as an artist. Voluntary exile offered him the scope he needed to complete a project of refashioning himself and his gift that had begun earlier; it allowed him to create an American (or, as he would have described it, a New York) self significantly different from the persona in which his early fame had trapped him" (Summers, 506). Unlike Fiedler, however, Summers views the American Auden as confined primarily to the decade of the forties, for he proceeds to divide the late Auden into "two periods based on his summer residences" in Italy and Austria, following, in this respect, Auden's own implicit lead in *Collected Shorter Poems, 1927–1957* (also adhered to by Edward Mendelson's edition of the *Collected Poems*), by grouping the poems from 1939 to 1947 (actually 1948) into a unit that John Fuller had earlier referred to as poems of the "New York period" (Fuller, *Guide*, 166). Despite this restriction, however, Summers goes on to claim, somewhat ambiguously, that Auden's "later volumes," though not always well received by the critics, "constitute an achievement unique in American poetry" (Summers, 525).

Robert Caserio, on the other hand, focuses entirely on the forties in his 1997 essay on "Auden's New Citizenship." Caserio begins dramatically by asserting that when Auden became an American, he was undergoing a "conversion" equivalent to his roughly simultaneous [re]"conversion" to Christianity. Then, after a reading of *The Age of Anxiety* that emphasizes its rootlessness—only one of the four main characters is, as Caserio points out, a native-born American—and an interpretation of *For the Time Being* that turns Mary into Chester Kallman, Caserio concludes by suggesting that Auden's real motive for assuming American citzenship was to become a temporary lodger in a half-way house—or, more precisely, in a half-way country. But if this is so, then it becomes difficult to understand just how or why we should bother to think of Auden's determination to become American as a "conversion." If anything, it seems rather more like a convenience than a conversion, but then, if we are to believe Caserio, "motives are always what's lacking, or rather what's always cunningly hidden, in Auden's life and in his poetry" (Caserio, 96).

The American Auden, then, has by now become a well established figure, at least as well established as the English Eliot. Both men spent almost exactly half their lives as citizens of the United States and Great Britain; both were at least partly impelled to change their nationality for public reasons of politics and religion, as well as for private ones of family and sexuality. Both nevertheless retained strong residual loyalties to their countries of origin, and both in an important sense transcended their new as well as their old nationalities to become not simply American or British but, in Santayana's phrase, citizens of the world.[8]

III

Auden's American identity is something he felt differently and more or less strongly about at different periods in his life. From the moment he arrived in New York in January 1939, however, he realized that at some basic level being in America would make a major difference and that he also wanted to be thought of as an American—and to think of himself as one. Writing to an English friend, Margaret Gardiner, later that same year, he observed that living in the United States was "the most decisive experience of my life so far." He then went on to explain why that was so: that is, because the experience "has taught me the kind of writer I am, i.e. an introvert who can only develop by obeying his introversion. All Americans are introverts" (Berg, 19 November 1939).

This explanation is, of course, almost as absurd as it sounds, but it does reveal the extraordinary lengths to which Auden was prepared to go in order to prove to others (and to himself) that by going to America he had become a new man—a new American man. Despite this very odd and fortunately shortlived theory about an essentially American introversion, Auden was, in fact (like most Americans), much more of an extrovert than an introvert. He became most ebullient and even aggressive about his Americaness when he first returned to Britain in the uniform of an American Army officer just after the war. There he brashly flaunted his already mildly (and self-consciously?) American-accented English and gave vent to easily resented generalizations regarding the supposed provinciality and cultural inferiority of Britain vis à vis the United States.

The painter Nancy Spender was put off by his "exaggerated American voice." (Bell, 3) According to Humphrey Carpenter, Auden claimed that his newly flattened American *a* was actually a leftover from his Yorkshire childhood (Carpenter, 333). With rather less assurance, G. S. Fraser observes of this same "American short 'a' " that Auden "has adopted it with delight—or reverted to it, since it is standard Northern and North-Midland English." Fraser goes on to conclude that Auden's "voice" is therefore basically identical with that of the New England settlers, a voice to which "the American ear can easily tune in" (Fraser, 56–57). That is not, however, how Raymond Mortimer thought about it. Contrasting Auden and Isherwood's spoken English with that of another exile, Aldous Huxley, he remarked that the latter, unlike the former, "had not even changed his English accent" (Huxley, 137). What is more, Peter Conrad claims that Auden deliberately "set about speaking American English, turning his native language into an awkward acquired idiom, flattening and clipping his vowels and cherishing local usages like 'gotten.' . . . His affectations were intended not to help him pass as an American but to alienate him from his English contemporaries" (Conrad, 216). Though Conrad provides no specific sources for his assertions, there can be no doubt that, even as late as 1972, Auden was still looking down his American nose at the British: "Well, the difficulty about England is the cultural life—it *was* certainly dim and I suspect it still is" (quoted in Newman, 39). Such behavior is, of course, rarely forgotten or forgiven, and a decade later, at Oxford, Auden was to be repaid in kind (or rather unkind), when his candidacy for Professor of Poetry was opposed because, among other things, he was American. After nevertheless being elected, he was then subjected to ridicule in the Christ Church Common Room for the same chauvinistic reasons.[9]

How very American Auden sometimes felt himself to be emerges vividly from the closing lines of his Frostian poem, "A Walk After Dark" (1948):

> But the stars burn on overhead,
> Unconscious of final ends,
> As I walk home to bed,
> Asking what judgment waits
> My person, all my friends,
> And these United States.
>
> [CP, 268]

It should be noted that the concern expressed here, insofar as it is national, is solely for the United States, not for Britain or for any other part of the Western World. It was also in an apparently similar mood that Auden wrote to an English friend in 1939 that "God willing, I never wish to see England again. All I want is when this [war] is over, for all of you to come here" (EA, xx). When the war ended, Auden did nevertheless see England again during a brief stop-over on his way back to the United States from Germany. There he was greeted by Robert Graves's snide remark that "the rat returns to the unsunk ship . . ." (Graves, BBC). It was a view widely shared in England at the time and one that is not wholly dead today.

Not that Auden was by any means naive or uncritical about the country of his adoption. The poems of the forties are set with suspicious frequency in seedy metropolitan bars where alienated people gather to lose themselves in drink. Both "September 1, 1939" and "The Unknown Citizen," written within the first year of his residence in the United States, contain attacks on a consumer society that may provide adequately for external needs ("He was fully sensible to the advantages of the Instalment Plan / And had everything necessary to the Modern Man, / A phonograph, a radio, a car, and a frigidaire") but has no conception of any spiritual dimension ("Was he free? Was he happy? The question is absurd. / Had anything been wrong, we should certainly have heard" [CP, 201]). It is also to this aspect of American life—its superficiality and conformity—that Auden is referring in his "New Year Letter" (the new year is 1940), when he remarks that

> More even than in Europe here
> The choice of patterns is made clear
> Which the machine imposes, what
> Is possible and what is not . . .
>
> (CP, 190)

The machine may also take the form of a jukebox or a radio or even a "Wallomatic" (all machines that appear in *The Age of Anxiety*), blaring forth insipid music or mindless advertising. But primarily, the machine is a cultural or bureaucratic machine whose association with lesser and more obvious mechanical devices is symptomatic of its own essentially mechanical nature and structure. The Babel-like towers of Manhattan that grope the sky in the opening section of "September 1, 1939" are a powerful representation of that larger, more abstract and anti-spiritual social machine and its concomitant "lie of authority," a lie based, as he put it in one of the first major essays he wrote in the United States, "I Believe," on the premise that "[w]e do not see a state, we see a number of individuals" (EA, 373). Ironically, in view of the occasion, Auden is here restating almost verbatim Nietzsche's contemptuous verdict as uttered by his mouthpiece Zarathustra: "State is the name of the coldest of all cold monsters. Coldly it tells lies too; and this lie crawls out of its mouth: 'I, the state, am the people.' This is a lie! It was creators who created peoples and hung a faith and a love over them: thus they served life" (Nietzsche, 160).

Auden may, however, also have been influenced in this view of the United States and specifically of New York by Lewis Mumford's critical view of technology and urbanization. He refers knowledgeably to Mumford in "Letter to Lord Byron" (EA, 175) and he reviewed Mumford's *The Culture of Cities* in October 1938, as well as, a good deal less enthusiastically, *The Condition of Man* in 1944. In a letter to E. R. Dodds, written in early 1940, Auden blames the "Machine Age" for the destruction of tradition and dissolving "the personal nexus of artist and audience" (Bell, "Change," 109). Moreover, although this was a time when Auden was preoccupied with the Utopian question (an almost archetypically American question, one might add) of how to go about building what he called the "Just City," nevertheless the real city that he chiefly inhabited at this time never served as a model for it. On the contrary, considering that very unutopian metropolis from the point of view of a bar stool located in a dive on Fifty-Second Street, the speaker of "September 1, 1939" concludes that it is a place where only through "ironic points of light" can "the just exchange their messages."[10] Loyalty and intelligence, as he observed in another essay written in America in 1939, "are mutually hostile," a profoundly ironic remark to make in the context of the accusations of disloyalty that were then being leveled against him in England (EA, 386).

Irony is also the medium and the message of "Under Which Lyre," the Phi Beta Kappa poem that the newly-minted American citizen Auden wrote for delivery at Harvard in 1946. Here the "Just" are the followers of the god Hermes, a private and playfully ironic deity, worshipped by lonely scholars and undergraduate nonconformists who adhere to the celebrated decalogue with which the poem concludes. Their opponents, on the other hand, are pompous and important public bores, devotees of an Apollo whose "radio Homers all day long / In over-Whitmanated song" (CP, 261). Not that Auden completely endorses the esoteric, introverted and elitist values of an American Hermes over those of an exoteric, extroverted and Democratic American Apollo; the pun in the title should be enough to warn us against doing that (lyre/liar). But there can be no doubt where his preferences lie: for an uppercase Truth and against a merely useful knowledge; and for the private inward self and against empty public posturings. Significantly, the Hermetic Ten Commandments are phrased negatively in such a way as to suggest that in following them we are breaking an unstated but clearly implied positive, Apollonian decalogue, so that when we are told, "Thou shalt not do as the dean pleases, / Thou shalt not write thy doctor's thesis / On education," we realize that this is precisely the kind of thing Apollo's followers do in fact do (CP, 261–62).

In the very different context of Auden's most ambitious poem of the 1940s—actually, the most ambitious poem of his whole literary career, *The Age of Anxiety* (1944–46; 1948)—Auden shows Rosetta (the character who in some ways most closely approximates his own self, given her British origins and her obsession with a fantasy British landscape) thinking to herself ironically about the "public" Christian ethic in ways that echo (or possibly anticipate) the critique of Apollonian America in "Under Which Lyre:"

> Your lie is showing.
> Your creed is creased. But have Christian luck.
> Your Jesus has wept; you may joke now,
> Be spick and span, spell out the bumptious
> Morals on monuments, mind your poise
> And cues, attract Who's-Who,
> Ignore What's-Not. Niceness is all and
> The rest bores.
>
> (CP, 403)

Niceness is all, not readiness, not ripeness. Auden, who by now was officially American as well as once again officially Episcopalian, was by no means unaware of—or unprepared to give voice to—the criticisms that could be leveled against his American nationality and religious values.

Of course, being critical of American society and of American morality is by no means un-American; on the contrary, it is as traditionally American as Mark Twain's Huck Finn and Sinclair Lewis's Babbitt. "Every poet," as Auden remarked, "is at once a representative of his culture and its critic" (*Dyer's*, 352). That is why Auden was concerned that his criticism of America be perceived as coming from an *American*. So, when Alan Ansen was typing up a final copy of *The Age of Anxiety*, he told him that he wanted its language to be "thoroughly American" (Mendelson, *Later*, 264 n). Very American too, I think, are Auden's repeated attempts during the 1940s to write serious, "big" or so-called major poems. To be sure, one of his earliest works, *The Orators*, had been as lengthy as anything in verse that he was to write subsequently, but, whatever *The Orators* is, it is not a successfully integrated poem. *New Year Letter*, on the other hand, as well as *For the Time Being*, *The Sea and the Mirror*, and *The Age of Anxiety* are, while not without their own thematic and technical difficulties, unmistakably integrated poems. They also belong, unfortunately, to that segment of the Auden poetic corpus that has suffered most from critical neglect, in part certainly because they are deeply infused with Auden's newfound religious fervor (still today an unpopular critical commodity) but also because they are so very long and, one must also admit, long-winded. Philip Larkin's response to *The Age of Anxiety*—that he had not been able to finish reading it, nor had he met anyone who had—is not something I agree with, but I can understand where he is coming from (Haffenden, 417). Certainly, as with Samuel Johnson's notorious comment about *Paradise Lost*, one could not wish it, or them, any longer. While this is not the place to enter into an extended commentary on any of these works, it needs to be said that they certainly bear out Robert von Hallberg's observation that "American culture seems automatically to foster poets who deliberately try to be major" (Hallberg, 26). Especially in the last poem of the series, *The Age of Anxiety*, one has the feeling that Auden is consciously attempting to write the "Great American Poem," a work that will fuse Jungian psychology with Kierkegaardian existentialism, join a medieval dream vision in the manner of Langland (and written in Langland's alliterative verse) to an up-to-date social satire, and embed alienated characters within fragments of a traditional love story—all elements of a poetic whole that seems intended to provide a symbolic key for its time. Auden, it would appear, was still intent on playing the Waste Land Game that he had learned so well when he started off as a young Eliotesque poet in the mid-twenties, though by now the rules and significance of the game had changed radically.

In his introduction to *The Criterion Book of Modern American Verse* (1956), Auden suggests a number of ways in which American poetry differs from British poetry. While these suggestions are interesting in and of themselves, they are of even greater interest in determining how (and if) Auden viewed his own work of the forties and fifties as American rather than British.[11] Comparing Longfellow, for example, with Tennyson (a selection of whose poems he had edited in 1944), Auden remarks that the former possesses "a curiosity about the whole of European literature," whereas the latter's interests are relatively narrow and provincial. The same, I think, could and should be said of Auden's own internationalist bent, as compared with, say, the provinciality of Betjeman or Larkin or even Hardy, so that, in this sense, he is certainly very much an American poet. Auden then goes on to compare briefly Tennyson's "Ode on the Death of the Duke of Wellington" with Whitman's "When Lilacs Last in the Dooryard Bloom'd," remarking that the former is unmistakably a poem written to mourn "a great public figure," but that "it would be very hard to guess from the words of Whitman's poem that the man he was talking of was the head of a State; one would naturally think that he was some close personal friend, a private individual" (CB, 10).

Auden himself, of course, was a master of the public elegy—one of the very finest writing in English during the twentieth century. One need only think of his great elegies commemorating Yeats, James, and Freud. But what he says of the relation between Tennyson and Whitman also provides an insight into the relation between these magisterial formal elegies and a poem that is generally not taken into account in discussions of Auden's elegies. The poem is simply and anonymously entitled "Dirge," and it comprises most of the fourth part of *The Age of Anxiety*. As John Fuller was the first to point out, this poem is almost certainly intended as an elegy for President Franklin Delano Roosevelt.[12] Fuller, however, does not explain why it is not identified as such, nor why its tone of evident personal grief should be so mingled with peculiar conceits, such as the one that tells of "reforming the weeds / Into civil cereals" (a reference apparently to New Deal agricultural reform), or quasi-mythical allusions intended to evoke Roosevelt's heroic stature (and his routing of old-style conservatives, as Beowulf had long ago routed the predatory Grendel):

> For he ignored the Nightmares and annexed their ranges,
> Put their clawing Chimaeras in cold storage,
> Berated the Riddle till it roared and fled,
>   Won the Battle of Whispers,
> Stopped the Stupids, stormed into
> The Fumblers' Forts, confined the Sulky
> To their drab ditches and drove the Crashing
>   Bores to their bogs,
>   Their beastly moor.
>
> (CP, 394–95)

It is only after picking up the clue dropped by Auden in his introduction to the *Criterion Book of Modern American Verse* that one realizes what Auden's intention is: namely, to commemorate a great American president in much the same way (but using very different poetic techniques) as an earlier great

American president had been commemorated by another great American poet.

What is, of course, also surprising about "Dirge"—and what perhaps accounts for the fact that it neglects to mention Roosevelt by name—is that it shifts in and out of the serious, the not-so-serious, and even the funny. This is undoubtedly odd for an elegy. But such sudden and jarring shifts in diction and tone are (and were already) characteristic of Auden's poetry, even in formal elegiac contexts. Compare, for instance, the tone of "You were silly, like us," in the elegy for Yeats, or the almost sacrilegious conceit in the same elegy comparing the transformation undergone by Yeats's poems in the minds of his readers with the transubstantiation of the body of Christ in Catholic doctrine ("the words of a dead man / Are modified in the guts of the living" [EA, 242]). What Auden seems to be doing here is introducing a new manner into what he believes to be the overly serious tradition of American poetry. For American poetry, in his view, may have "many tones, a man talking to himself or one intimate friend, a prophet crying in the wilderness, but the easy-going tone of a man talking to a group of his peers is rare; for a 'serious' poet to write light verse is frowned on in America and if, when he is asked why he writes poetry, he replies, as any European poet would, 'For fun,' his audience will be shocked." (CB, 18). Regardless of whether Auden is right or wrong in making this assertion (I myself think he's wrong), it does help to account for the kind of mixed thing he's producing in a poem like "Dirge." As Richard Eberhart was to remark of Auden's mission in America:

> You had come to defend in the American scene
> The idea of something new . . .
>
> (Eberhart, 239)

From Auden's point of view, at least insofar as it relates to light verse, this "something new," however, was really something rather old as well as something characteristically British.

Even though Auden rightly considered himself an expert on light verse and wrote some very good examples of it himself, it is difficult to accept without qualification his assertion that serious American poets were ever denigrated for writing light verse. The most obvious instance of a modern serious poet who also wrote light verse is T. S. Eliot, and Eliot needs to be considered as having been at least partly American. It is true, however, that the poetic tradition that mixes light with serious verse is one that goes back to the Metaphysicals, but here again it is T. S. Eliot, more than any other modern poet, who was responsible for reviving that tradition. In this context it should also be added that if Auden is right about the characteristic tone of

American poetry being that "of a man talking to himself or one intimate friend," then the essentially antirhetorical tone of poems like "In Praise of Limestone" or "The Cave of Making" is something Auden owes to his American experience. This would appear to confirm John Fuller's assertion that such "relaxed conversationalism" was the "chief stylistic influence that America provided" for his work, but it might also indicate that David Perkins is right when he points to "one of the most striking features of Auden's style from almost the start of his career, namely his use of the conversational" (Fuller, *Guide*, 166; Perkins, 161–62). So it would seem that, if Auden was not yet an "American" poet when he began writing seriously in the late twenties, he was certainly predisposed to become one eventually.

Even more interesting and revealing, I think, are Auden's remarks on the radically different natural and social environments facing the British and the American writer. "Until quite recently," Auden writes, "an English writer, like one of any European country, could presuppose two conditions, a nature which was mythologized, humanized, on the whole friendly, and a human society which had become in time, whatever succession of invasions it may have suffered in the past, in race or religion more or less homogeneous and in which most people lived and died in the locality where they were born." The echo here of T. S. Eliot's notorious phrasing in *After Strange Gods* is probably deliberate, especially in view of Auden's comments on Eliot's notion of tradition a few pages later. The point seems to be that Eliot, as an American writing in England, is conscious of the assumptions underlying English writing in a way that few genuinely English writers are. Similarly with Auden vis à vis American literature. Auden's discussion here of the English writer's relation to Nature may also owe something to Aldous Huxley's classic essay, "Wordsworth in the Tropics." Auden alludes to Huxley's essay, though without mentioning it by name, when he remarks in his essay on Robert Frost that "a poet brought up in the tropics cannot have the same vision as poet brought up in Hertfordshire . . ." (*Dyer's*, 345).

The English writer's relation to Nature, in short, is intimate and personal, as is his relation to his society, which of course doesn't necessarily mean that he had to be in favor of or even to like either one. The American writer, on the other hand, was confronted by Nature on an utterly nonhuman and even inhuman scale, a Nature that dwarfed mere human beings and their feeble and transitory social agglomerations. Auden goes on to describe the impression produced by the vast American emptiness as seen from a plane crossing the United States at night. Only then, he says, can anyone "born on the other side of the Atlantic . . . realize that, even if there is no longer an actual frontier, this is still a continent only partially settled and developed, where human activity seems a tiny thing in comparison to the magnitude of the earth . . ." (CB, 11–12).

It is this supposedly characteristically American conception, I think, that helps to explain the otherwise astonishing absence—the utter and complete absence—of depictions of natural landscape in Auden's poems placed in an American setting. So, one of Auden's most celebrated poems of landscape, "In Praise of Limstone," written during Auden's American period, describes a landscape that is distinctly Italian; and the same is true of the quasi-Virgilian series of poems, "Bucolics"(1952/53), where the only specifically American geographical feature, Lake Michigan, is dismissed, along with Lake Baikal in the then Soviet Union, as too big and therefore "estranging" (CP, 430). Auden's practice here is in striking contrast with the poems he wrote during earlier phases of his career. The English Auden, for example (so-called by Edward Mendelson and referring to the poet who wrote between 1927 and 1939), frequently depicts recognizably English or Scottish landscapes, and so, for that matter, does the Italian Auden or the Austrian Auden with respect to the landscapes of those countries. But not so with the American Auden. Whenever the American Auden presents his readers with a recognizably American context it is always a cityscape rather than a landscape. American nature, it appears, is simply too overwhelming to be fitted into verse.

To be sure, Auden's favorite landscapes never did consist, even when they were located in Britain, Italy, or Austria, of straightforward scenes of quasi-Wordsworthian bliss, of places where Nature never had betrayed the heart that loved her. Though undoubtedly humanized, Auden's landscapes are more often humanized by means of (antiquated) machinery rather than more traditional methods of cultivation. And indeed, Italian Nature can also sometimes be as formidable and alien as American, as it is, for example, in "Goodbye to the Mezzogiorno." However, when in "Prologue at Sixty" (1967), Auden gazes fondly at the Austrian countryside and especially at that particular part of it that he now owns and that "after ten years / into my love has looked itself," he goes on to list other names that are affixed to his "numinous map." These include landscapes in England and Iceland but not in the United States. There he enumerates only the urbanities of Middagh Street, Carnegie Hall, and the Con-Ed stacks. Small wonder, then, that towards the close of the poem Auden concludes that he is not really an American at all:

>Who am I now?
>An American? No, a New Yorker,
>Who opens his *Times* at the obit page.

(CP, 623)

As Auden grew older, he also grew less willing to cope with the complexities of American metropolitan existence. Since Kallman was now regularly spending his winters in Athens, Auden was increasingly alone and feeling lonely. Writing to his old friend, E. R. Dodds, in January 1966, he complained of bus and subway strikes, adding on a more personal note: "My kitchen roof leaks. Cockroaches abound! O New York!" (Quoted in Davenport-Hines, 323). Less and less did he agree with Rosetta that "America was the best place on earth to come to if you had to earn your living" and more and more did he wonder out loud with her about why it had "to be so big and empty and noisy and messy" (CP, 346). Like Rosetta too he was becoming obsessed with a nostalgia for the more imagined than remembered ideal England of his childhood, an Edwardian England that he thought had nurtured him and made him happy. It was at this time that he wrote the opening lines of his autobiographical "Profile":

> He thanks God daily
> that he was born and bred
> a British Pharisee.
>
> (CP, 581)

When, on 15 April 1972, he left the United States to take up what he thought would be permanent residence in Oxford, he intended never to return. And he never did. Not that the (re)reborn Pharisee found life in Britain any more congenial than he had in New York. If anything, he was now even more alone. He had become, it seems, too much of an old fogey to live in chaotic New York, and too much of a straightforward American to tolerate the polite backstabbings of an Oxford Common Room. Uncertain where he belonged or really what to do next, he left to spend the summer in Austria. He had less than a year to live.

IV

Aside from being flattered that Auden wanted to think of himself as an American poet—and be thought of as one—what difference does it make to us as Americans (or should it) that Auden was American or English—or Italian or Austrian, for that matter? On some level it seems absurd to insist on the particular national identity of poets and writers in general, though of course the whole tradition of teaching, writing about, and marketing literature in the United States has been to insist absurdly on this point. American literature is and apparently must be taught in courses specifically designated as such, and so too English literature, French literature, Spanish literature, etc. Publisher's catalogs invariably follow the same national and nationalistic categories. Instead of diminishing, the trend in fact seems to be increasing: Anglophone Irish literature and Canadian literature, for example, are more and more coming to be viewed "professionally" as areas so distinct from English or American literature that they require their own national course designators. Indeed, it has come to seem only right and natural that every national or cultural group, especially when thought of as having been previously marginalized, must now be recognized as having its own separate canon of worthy or even great writers.

It is obvious that much of this concern for establishing and maintaining an apparently "natural" link between nationality and literary production has to do with cultural prestige. Great nations must have great cultures; and great cultures must, among other things, have great poetry. It works the other way around as well—no nation without a great culture or great poets can be great. And it follows too from this kind of thinking (or feeling, rather) that the greater the poetry, the greater the cultural prestige that rubs off on fellow nationals. English people, for example, who may have never read a line of Shakespeare can nevertheless confidently look down their noses on members of less fortunate national groups who possess no equivalent literary "giant." Being looked down on in this way, of course, produces feelings of inadequacy and resentment, feelings with which Americans in particular have been long familiar. How deeply (and absurdly) such feelings can rankle may be seen from Herman Melville's indignant reaction to Sydney Smith's silly remark about no American writer being read in the four quarters of the globe. "Believe me, my friends," Melville was consequently moved to prophesy, "that men not very much inferior to Shakespeare are this day being born on the banks of the Ohio. And the day shall come when you shall say, Who reads a book by an Englishman who is modern?" (Cowie, 404).

Nationality in literature, then, whether we like it or not, makes a difference, a fact that Auden seems to have grasped instinctively and very quickly. Remaining an Englishman in America, he realized, would have meant remaining content with the role of sympathetic commentator on the sidelines. He might very well have turned into a species of poetical but more acerbic Alistair Cooke, someone given to making knowledgeable pronouncements on Americans to a primarily British audience (or the other way around). This was clearly a fate that Auden, who from the very beginning of his career had consciously aimed at becoming nothing less than a great poet, was not willing to accept (Carpenter, 54). But if he wished to shape his new world and not merely to observe it, he needed to be part of that world: he needed to become certifiably American. So, on purely pragmatic grounds, if no other, there was an obvious necessity to remake himself, to arrange for a speedy "rebirth." Hence, whether crassly deliberate or not (probably not), Auden did what was required; he promptly immersed himself in American life and letters in a way and to a degree that suggested he had never known anything else. Distancing himself from Isherwood—geographically and otherwise— and establishing a new and intimate connection with Kallman and his circle of friends helped speed the process.

To be sure, as Edward Mendelson remarks of all of Auden's major geographical removals, starting with the one to America, "[e]ach move coincided with fundamental changes in his work and outlook, and brought him to the landscape he thought most suitable to the kind of poetry he wanted to write" (Mendelson, *Later*, xviii). Going to America, in other words, allowed him to write the new kind of poetry that he needed to write—a more discursive, reflective, and above all, more ambitious poetry—one that at the same time was fortunately recognized by many American readers as characteristically "American." Being in America also meant that he could distance himself from himself, that is, from the old British self that had come to be identified in the public mind—for better or worse—with a poetry of psychosocial advocacy. Removed from the immediate scrutiny of London critics, Auden could now use the "isolation" of New York to reshape himself into a new kind of poet. As he put it in a 1940 review of Yeats's *Last Poems*, poets were either "Puritanical" or "Esthetic." The former group tended to "defeat its own purpose by producing drab stuff which is so harsh to the ear and lacking in pattern, that no one can take any pleasure in reading it." Whereas the latter (including Yeats and, by implication, Auden himself up to this time) ignored "the fact that the artist is a human being with a moral responsibility to be honest, humble, and self-critical," thereby leaving "the poet too easily content with ideas which he finds poetically useful and effective. Not bothering to re-examine them, to throw out the false elements and develop the rest further, he is prevented from *reaching his full poetical stature*, and remains playing variations on the old tune which has served him so well in the past" (Auden, "Yeats," 14; my italics). Auden was determined not to remain confined, as Yeats had been, in the "prison of his days." In America he could break free and become another kind of poet altogether. He could be "reborn."

American Auden, generally speaking, spans the period from 1940 to 1972, but he is most particularly or peculiarly American only during the early years of this period, from about 1940 to 1948, before, that is, he began spending his summers in Ischia and Kirchstetten. That the American Auden was unmistakably a different kind of Auden from the Auden of the thirties was something that even British observers eventually came to admit. So, writing in the mid-fifties, Auden's first notable British academic critic, Richard Hoggart, though discerning nothing specifically American about him, calls the period after Auden's move to America his "Second Phase," and argues that the beginning of this new phase coincides roughly with a shift away from Freud and Marx and towards Kierkegaard and Reinhold Niebuhr (Hoggart, 25). Even more clearly and sympathetically, the British poet and critic John Fuller regards Auden's move to America in 1939 as an attempt at renewal and "self-discovery, an environmental act of good faith in respect of his personal quest for truth . . ." (Fuller, *Guide*, 132). Most British critics were less well-disposed, however. Philip Larkin probably represents the prevailing British view most accurately when he pronounced the later or American Auden inferior to the younger or English one. By emigrating to America, Larkin claimed, Auden had damaged his poetry irreparably, for "at one stroke he lost his key subject and emotion—Europe and the fear of war—and abandoned his audience together with their common dialect." Nor was he able to compensate for this loss by establishing a new, genuinely American identity. "If his poetry could once take root again," Larkin opined, "in the life surrounding him rather than in his reading . . . then a new Auden might result, a 'New Yorker' Walt Whitman viewing the American scene through lenses coated with a European irony" (Haffenden, 416, 418).

Not that some Americans did not share Larkin's preference for the early over the later Auden. So, John Berryman praises only the Auden of the early poems, though he claims that his "love for that man has never altered / thro' some of his facile later books" (Berryman, 172). Even an otherwise very sympathetic American critic like David Perkins concludes that Auden's later work, "though it is intelligent, amusing, graceful, and gracious . . . is not very exciting. To the extent that Auden's poetry survives, it will be the poetry of the thirties . . ." (Perkins, 168–69). How deeply—and personally—Auden himself, however, resented the idea that he might have become a worse poet after he left Britain emerges dramatically from a letter he wrote to his old friend and admirer, Naomi Mitchison in April, 1967, after the latter had ventured on some mild criticisms of Auden's later style in her contribution to the 1967 *Shenandoah* commemorative issue: "The reason (artistic) I left England and went to the US was precisely to *stop* me writing poems like *Sept. 1st, 1939*, the most dishonest poem I have ever written. A hang-over from the U.K. It takes time to cure oneself. . . . Surely I am the best judge of what is essential [in his poetry]. At any rate I expect personal friends like you, my dear, to respect my judgement as policy, which is professional judgement, rather than yours. P. S. Believe it or not, I have got better. Try 'Thanksgiving for a Habitat' " (Berg, 1 April 1967).

At first glance, it may seem surprising that Larkin should have chosen

Whitman as the one American poet with whom to compare Auden. For, aside from their homosexuality (unacknowledged on Whitman's part) and their shared preference for metropolitan New York and long poems, Auden and Whitman seem to have had very little in common as artists. Whereas during his American period Auden soon become known for writing apparently loose, reflectively ironic, but quite self-consciously formalist poetry, Whitman had never been celebrated for anything but his quite unironic and very self-consciously antiformalist poetry. While the American Auden tended to look inward and comment obliquely on the social world around him, Whitman, on the other hand, seemed to boom or blast away about democratic vistas in an unabashedly extroverted manner that struck Auden as symptomatic of all that was wrong with American art. But if Auden differed radically from Whitman, then, implicitly at least, this difference seemed to place his status as an American poet in question, at any rate, from a European perspective. For ever since D. H. Lawrence's *Studies in Classic American Literature* (1923), Whitman had become for Europeans incomparably the most American of American poets, if only because there was no one like him anywhere else (until Lawrence, that is). For the rest, it looked as if American writers were virtually indistinguishable from their British or European counterparts. "Where *is* this new bird called the true American?" Lawrence had inquired sardonically. "Show us the homunculus of the new era. Because all that is visible to the naked European eye, in America, is a sort of recreant European" (Lawrence, vii). So far as many non-recreant Europeans (including Larkin, apparently) were concerned, then, only Whitman could provide a credible standard by which the degree of "Americanness" in an American writer might be measured. Poets like Wallace Stevens and T. S. Eliot—not to mention prose writers like Henry James and Sinclair Lewis—could therefore be dismissed as mere Eurocentric homunculi.[13]

This stereotypically exclusive identification of American traits with the Whitmanesque tradition is naturally something that Auden, along with most American poets of his and the immediately following generation, refused to accept (the obvious exception is Allen Ginsberg). American poets were not, in his view, just optimistic, extroverted "over-Whitmanated" songsters; they were also pessimistic, introverted poets like Melville; they were also ironic, deliberately self-deprecating poets like Frost; they were also witty, word-playing poets like Marianne Moore; or form-following, intellectual poets like Stevens—and, for that matter, Auden himself. America was big enough, pace the ghost of Whitman, to embrace a multitude of contradictions and oppositions and nevertheless make the resulting multiplicity very much her own. Not that becoming an American was for Auden ever something merely superficial. Coming to America came to mean a great deal more to him than a simple change of address.

Auden realized very soon that his move to America would inevitably entail his becoming a new kind of poet and that in some deep spiritual sense—that is, not merely relating to his love for Chester Kallman—he had reached the end of a lifelong quest for moral and even religious certainty. This realization is most vividly represented in the poem he wrote about Herman Melville in March 1939 (the same month he met Kallman). While the poem is unquestionably primarily a poem about Melville's life and Melville's discovery of spiritual peace, it seems equally evident that Auden was working out his own problems of identity through the subjective correlative of Melville's career. Since the poem is too long to reproduce in full here, the reader unfamiliar with it will have to be content with a summary and a few excerpts. The poem begins with a description of the return home (to New York, though the city is not named) of the seafarer to his wife and to "an extraordinary mildness." Having survived immense, complicated, and hateful storms in distant corners of the world, he has finally realized that "the truth was simple." This simple truth is simply that "Goodness existed: that was the new knowledge."

Anticipating both "September 1, 1939" and Hannah Arendt's *Eichmann in Jerusalem*, Auden's Melville goes on to reach the further insight that

> Evil is unspectacular and always human,
> And shares our bed and eats at our own table,
> And we are introduced to Goodness every day,
> Even in drawing rooms among a crowd of faults . . .

(CP, 200)

The storm-tossed nightmare of his previous existence is now concluded, and for the first time he perceives clearly something else that his nightmare had distorted, namely that

> Even the punishment was human and a form of love:
> The howling storm had been his father's presence
> And all the time he had been carried on his father's breast.

(CP, 200)

The storm at sea, it turns out, had been merely the externalization of his own psychic disturbance, a punishment inflicted unconsciously by himself on himself. His father—and his Father—had really cared deeply for him and watched over him throughout. Filled with this new and simple knowledge, Melville is finally at peace:

> Reborn, he cried in exaltation and surrender
> "The Godhead is broken like bread. We are the pieces."
>
> (CP, 200)

Having entered into a new existence, he is now able to tap constructively the resources of an inner life that had previously been expended in complex and futile fury. The poem closes as Melville "sat down at his desk and wrote a story" (CP, 200)—perhaps "Billy Budd," as John Fuller suggests (Fuller, *Guide*, 169).[14]

One is tempted to make the identification with Auden complete and say that Auden now sat down at his desk and wrote *New Year Letter*, or *For the Time Being* or even *The Sea and the Mirror*. But he did not. He did, however, sit down and write "Herman Melville." And he did begin to accept a new and simple truth that was both religious and aesthetic. He would return to the faith of his childhood and of his father—and of his Father. And he would henceforth abjure a poetry of mere rhetoric, no matter how effective, in favor of a poetry of truth, though Auden, I am sure, never thought that such a poetry would or could be aesthetically ineffective. Beauty was not truth for this new Auden; truth was truth, and truth was goodness. He was, as he said so simply and yet with such new conviction about Melville, reborn.[15]

Almost prophetically, however, Auden soon realized that his newly confirmed condition of quasi-Virgilian peace and piety would not be greeted with universal approbation by his critics (or even possibly by his friends). In one of the so-called "Shorts" written about a year after "Herman Melville," Auden comments ironically on the links between poetry, altered convictions and the aging poet's fickle audience:

> With what conviction the young man spoke
> When he thought his nonsense rather a joke;
> Now, when he doesn't doubt anymore,
> No one believes the booming old bore.
>
> (CP, 232)

Not that the middle-aged Auden was easily intimidated by the prospect of boredom, either given or received, no more than Goethe himself (the idol of Auden's later, quite unbooming years) had been, or so, at any rate, Auden claimed to believe. Besides, "rebirth" was unmistakably an essential component of the American way of life, as could be seen from a comparison of the European versus the American sense of place. In Europe it was difficult if not impossible for all but the "exceptionally gifted or adventurous," so Auden argued in the introductory essay to *The Criterion Book of Modern*

American Verse, to do anything more than accept life as it was locally lived; at best they could "try to change it by political means" (CB, 14). In the United States, on the other hand, it was easy for quite ordinary people to pull up stakes and move on to somewhere else. The effects of this fundamental difference on both psyche and society were, as Auden recognized, profound.

They were not, however, necessarily altogether positive. American mobility might lead to new places and new selves, but it also could, and presumably often did, lead as well to a new superficiality of human intercourse, as depicted for example in *The Age of Anxiety*. European stability of place and stability of identity, on the other hand, was unfortunately conducive to social stasis and stagnation, but they did possess the redeeming virtue of fostering a sense of permanence in personal relations. American mobility also altered people's conception of time along with their relation to space. "To be able at any time to break with the past," Auden remarks, "to move and keep on moving lessens the significance not only of the past but also of the future which is reduced to the immediate future . . ." (CB, 15). It is perhaps this aspect of time, conceived of as being "different" in the United States, that impelled Auden in 1939 and in the years immediately following to write poems in which time and not, as in earlier poems, place, figures prominently (even in the titles)—a characteristic that Edward Mendelson sees as helping to define Auden's new American sensibility and identity (EA, xx).

Unlike Europeans, for whom—whether conservative, liberal, or radical—future time was a logical and perhaps even to some extent foreseeable consequence of present time, Americans believed the future was essentially "unpredictable." For them, therefore, "no failure is irredeemable, no success a final satisfaction" (CB, 15). And for them, too, given this open and indeterminate view of the future, political action became relatively unimportant if not altogether irrelevant. For this American Auden, who by 1939 had come to the conclusion that literature and politics do not mix well, or as the great elegy on Yeats notoriously put it, "poetry makes nothing happen," it must have been part of the appeal of the United States that literature in general and poetry in particular no longer needed to concern themselves unduly with such matters.

Indeed, the elegy on Yeats, one of the first poems Auden completed in America, provides a specifically American context—even an American map—for his new conception of poetry. Like the Mississippi,

>   it survives
> In the valley of its saying where executives
> Would never want to tamper; flows south
> From ranches of isolation and the busy griefs,

> Raw towns that we believe and die in; it survives,
> A way of happening, a mouth.
>
> (EA, 242)

The poetry that makes nothing happen is specifically an American poetry, for apparently, America is quite different from Yeats's "mad Ireland" (and perhaps also, by implication, mad Europe as a whole), which "hurt" Yeats into poetry. America is a place where poets live out their lives remote from those busy places (like New York?) where executives conduct their business, because the "busyness" of poetry is carried out in isolation, in ranches and raw towns, where it is still possible to believe in something honestly and even die for it, though only in bed. It flows south, rather than east or west, and presumably mouths in the Gulf of Mexico, because in February 1939, when Auden was finishing his poem commemorating the great Irish poet who had died in France the previous month, "nothing" was happening (or about to happen) there, as it was in both Europe and Asia. The American landscape was raw and unfinished, compelling its poets to live alone, but at the same time it was also virginal and "sane."[16]

If, by reading Auden's work in terms of what he himself thought was the primary characteristics of modern American poetry, Auden may be seen to emerge as a characteristically American poet himself, then it also seems fair to conclude that Auden indeed had been "reborn" when, in 1939, he disembarked in New York. That a rebirth had taken place, though not necessarily at that time or quite in those terms, was certainly the conviction of another notable American poet and staunch admirer of Auden's work, James Merrill. Though Merrill only met Auden once in person—and then only very briefly (in Athens in 1965)—he knew a great deal about Auden through his friendship with Chester Kallman (Merrill, *Different*, 230). In Merrill's long, multi-segmented poem, *The Changing Light at Sandover* (1992), Auden puts in several posthumous appearances via the Ouija board, together with Yeats and a miscellany of other figures, both literary and otherwise. Summoned by Merrill a short time after his death, Auden informs him how pleased he is with his "NEW PROLE BODY / And likened Heaven to a NEW MACHINE." He also urges Merrill and his companion David to hurry off immediately to Oxford, where they are to locate and burn a box of presumably compromising papers he had left behind.[17] (Merrill, *Sandover*, 87).

Aside from the unlikelihood of the aged Auden's enthusiasm for proletarians or new machines (both of whom/which he had come to abhor), the whole idea of a reborn, otherworldly Auden participating in a table-rapping seance seems perverse. After all, Auden had famously censured Yeats in 1939 for providing "the pitiful, the deplorable spectacle of a grown man occupied with the mumbo-jumbo of magic and the nonsense of India." And in the spring of 1973, in one of the last poems he was to write, "No, Plato, No," he stated unambiguously that "I can't imagine anything / that I would less like to be / than a disincarnate Spirit" (CP, 669). If, nevertheless, in spite of such explicitly articulated aversion, it was indeed Auden's fate to take part in Merrill's seaside "Seminar," how astonished that disincarnate spirit must have been to learn that in his penultimate incarnation he had been neither British nor American, neither poet nor gay, but a Chinese Court physician named You Li who, before being stabbed to death in 1906, had fathered thirty children (Merrill, 514).[18] That Merrill himself, however, didn't quite believe in this fantastic transmigration of Auden's soul is perhaps evident in the very choice of name for his supposed Chinese predecessor ("You Li[e]").

If Auden's influence on American poetry did not always assume such idiosyncratic or otherworldly forms, that influence was nevertheless, as Louise Bogan once remarked, acknowledged for a few years to be almost supernatural. According to Karl Shapiro's *Essay on Rime* (1945),

> The man whose impress on our rhetoric
> Has for a decade dominated verse
> In London, Sydney and New York is Auden.
>
> (Shapiro, 41)

With this critical judgment Elizabeth Bishop would certainly have agreed. While still at college, as well as subsequently throughout the thirties and forties, she and her poetry-reading-and-writing friends "read him constantly. We hurried to see his latest poem or book, and either wrote as much like him as possible, or tried hard not to." (Bishop, 47) The other poets who supposedly fell most markedly under Auden's dominion were John Berryman—who in "Shirley & Auden" claims that he "recognized Auden at once as a new master"; Berryman's close friend, Delmore Schwartz, as well as, in a few specific poems, Theodore Roethke, Randall Jarrell, [Donoghue, 97, 132, 139], and John Hollander (Perkins, 391). Hollander in fact at one time felt himself to be so overwhelmed by Auden's influence that before publishing his first collection of verse, he "still had to rewrite in proof many lines ... to expunge embarrassingly blatant echoes of his voice" (Hollander, 501). To these poets one might add the names of John Ashbery, Karl Shapiro, Anthony Hecht, Richard Wilbur, and especially Richard Howard (Hamilton, 238). Just what Auden's influence consisted of, however, is rarely made clear for any of these poets, though in the case of Jarrell, as Ian Sansom's recent study makes clear, the influence emanated primarily from the great, so-called "lying" poems of the middle to late 1930s (Sansom, 281). The same is true, according to Robert Richman, of Karl Shapiro, as well as of Elizabeth Bishop who, when Auden died, said that she "admire[d] almost all his poems except the later preachy ones" (Richman, 74; Bishop, 47). In fact, insofar as one can generalize usefully about Auden's influence on American poetry at all, that influence undoubtedly derives more immediately and noticeably from the work of the young or English Auden than it does from the older American one—from the Auden, in other words, who was a notoriously committed social (even socialist) poet, someone who often sought to use poetry as a weapon, who mixed seeming whimsy with riddling obscurity, outrageous didacticism with equally outrageous slapstick, and who simultaneously appealed to an audience that was elitist and popular. These are definitely not characteristic traits of the American Auden, so that we are left with the rather odd and anticlimactic conclusion that the American Auden had relatively little impact on the work of the following generation of American poets. Only the English Auden did. (Given the popularity of the young Auden in the United States, it may therefore not be surprising that his first commercially published collection of poetry, *Poems* (1930), apparently sold more copies in one New York bookstore alone than it did in all of Britain [Bloomfield, 5].)

This is, of course, not altogether true, and it is especially not true in the case of Richard Howard. Several of Howard's poems deal specifically with encounters with Auden—"For Hephaistos," "Again for Hephaistos," and "Audiences"—and they capture perfectly Auden's later voice and manner without in the least turning into pastiche. Alluding unmistakably to the tragic figure of the crippled artist, Hephaistos, in Auden's poem, "The Shield of Achilles," Howard describes Auden in "For Hephaistos" (1966) as an archetypal craftsman who taught a whole generation how to speak truly:

> And yet you taught me, taught us all a way
> To speak our minds, and only now, at last
> Free of you, my old ventriloquist,
> Have I suspected what I have to say
> Without hearing you say it for me first.
>
> (Howard, *Damages*, 64)

The "truth" here is an overt truth about how to bid farewell to dead friends and contemporaries (alternate selves, as it were)—in this instance, Cocteau, Roethke, and MacNeice, who are all referred to in the subtitle of the poem—as well as the more oblique truth about shedding, while yet retaining, past loves and lovers. It also means confronting the present potent poetic and moral influence whom one must thank and acknowledge (as Auden often did himself in the cases of Frost, Yeats, and others), while at the same time liberating oneself from him.

The truth is also, according to Howard's appropriately Audenesque elegy, "Again for Hephaistos" (1974), a very personal truth about being homosexual (hence Hephaistos as cripple), a truth that Auden more than any other poet of our time, "taught" all those, who, like Howard, both read him and knew him personally, to "speak their minds about." That is something they could not have done if they had not read him first or learned from his example. It is for this reason, as the closing lines of the poem put it, that "After you, because of you, / all songs are possible." Only after Auden came to America did it become possible for a "serious" American poet like Howard to publish a "song" like this one with its offhand and quite casual confession about its author being a "cocksucker" (Howard, *Fellow*, 12). In this way the American Auden exercised a powerful influence by just being what he was: a great poet who was also widely known and accepted for being homosexual.

Though in a very few instances—and thoroughly only in the case of Randall Jarrell—critics have attempted to gauge the nature and extent of Auden's influence, what G. T. Wright wrote more than fifteen years ago nevertheless remains true: "The influence of Auden on contemporary American poetry still has to be studied in detail." It also remains true that, as Wright remarks, one of Auden's principal legacies to American poetry has been his unflinching belief in the value of "metrical verse and regular stanzaic forms," a tradition pursued loyally by such eminent American poets as Wilbur, Hecht, Hollander, and Merrill, despite the growing dominance of free verse. So too, in Wright's view, Auden's fondness for shifting tones, for odd vocabulary, and for variable levels of diction helped stem for a time a movement towards neo-romantic exuberance, though subsequently "only a few American poets have found it possible or desirable to mix that easy style with formal verse" (G. Wright, 192). However, Auden's at times convoluted syntax and often complicatedly parodic style—both very apparent in *The Age of Anxiety* but still formidable obstacles in a late poem like "Dame Kind"—may have discouraged potential disciples rather than encouraged them to attempt imitation (Bahlke, 173–74). Though Wright does not make the specific connection, Auden's use of syllabic verse shortly after his arrival in United States in 1939 probably also helped make acceptable a kind of verse hitherto associated almost exclusively with Marianne Moore. Syllabics were a way, as Wright points out, of avoiding the "too pretentious prophetic note" that Auden had come to identify with the heavily accented verse of Yeats and other vatic enemies of an uppercase Truth. (G. Wright, 169)

As for the latest generation of American poets, Auden's work no longer exercises the influence it once did on their predecessors, the generation of

Merrill, Hollander or Howard. Still, here and there echoes of his voice may be discerned among younger admirers, as they are, for example, in Tony Hoagland's "Auden," a poem which acknowledges his personal weaknesses ("*Nicotine, caffeine, amphetamine*—these were three of W. H. Auden's favorite words . . .") but at the same time urges his would-be detractors to recall that as he grew older he not only grew uglier, he also grew wiser. His need for drugs and other stimulants was really a function of his deep concern for humanity:

> He had to stay up sometimes
> three days and nights
>
> to feel a feeling to completion
> watching the whole planet heat up
> and then cool off.
>
> feeling the warehouse of his skull
> creak and groan in its accommodation
> wondering if he could get the whole
>
> thing in . . .
>
> (Hoagland, 26)

To be sure, Auden's influence—large, small, real, or imagined—should in no way affect his status as an American poet. If influence on American poets were to be taken seriously as the primary criterion for poetic standing in the United States, then Shakespeare would be the most American of American poets. Indeed, as Auden believed, one of the defining characteristics of American poets was that they tended not to resemble or influence each other. "To some degree every American poet," Auden argued in *The Criterion Book of American Verse*, "feels that whole responsibility for contemporary poetry has fallen upon his shoulders, that he is a literary aristocracy of one" (CB, 18). The American poet was also, to sum it all up in a once celebrated phrase, the American Adam, fated to be always starting off anew, always reborn.

Nevertheless, though poetic influence should not be taken into account as a primary factor in determining Auden's American identity, it needs to be said that the Auden of the American period certainly exercised an influence on the readership and institutions of American poetry. While Shakespeare undoubtedly had more influence on the development of American poetry, Shakespeare had not selected relatively unknown young poets for the Yale Younger Poets series, as Auden had (including Adrienne Rich, W. S. Merwin, John Ashbery, James Wright, John Hollander, and William Dickey), and then gone on to write introductions for them. Nor did Shakespeare help found (together with Lionel Trilling and Jacques Barzun) the most formidable intellectual book club in the United States, the Readers' Subscription, and then go on to write frequent reviews on poetic and other subjects for its journal, *The Griffin*. Nor, finally, did Shakespeare edit and introduce, as Auden had, a notable and unusual selection of modern American poetry, in which, to be sure, he did not include any of his own poems.

V

And what about the other way around? What about the influence of American poetry on Auden? From the moment his first volume, *Poems* (1930), was published, it was clear to some of his readers and reviewers that Auden's cryptic manner was at times much indebted to the equally mysterious manner of the American poet Laura Riding, a debt deeply resented both by Riding herself and by her then companion, Robert Graves. Auden, however, never openly acknowledged his indebtedness, unless his reference to Graves's having been a "help" may be interpreted more broadly to include Riding as well (CP, 671).[19] Though less noticeable in his early published work, the influence of another, more traditional (but no more tractable) American poet, Robert Frost, was eventually also to be gratefully admitted. In the very late "A Thanksgiving," Auden mentions Frost, along with Thomas Hardy and Edward Thomas, as one of the three poets at whose feet he sat "when I started to verse." That Auden's memory served him well in this respect emerges clearly from Katherine Bucknell's edition of his *Juvenilia*, where several poems show traces of Frost's influence and one, "Damming Stream," is virtually a pastiche (*Juvenilia*, xxxvi, 82–83). And then, of course, there was the so-called Waste Land Game that Auden had learned to play from another distinguished American poet who was also to become his first established promoter and commercial publisher. And, though he nowhere publicly thanks William Carlos Williams, he did tell Monroe K. Spears on 11 May 1963 that "an important influence on my most recent work, beginning with *Homage to Clio* [1955] . . . has been the last poems of W. C. Williams, though I hope the influence is diminished enough not to be obvious." (Berg)

In context, Auden's words of thanks to Frost suggest that his interest in the American poet was of brief duration and of importance only while he was an apprentice poet. That is not, however, an accurate rendering of the complex and enduring relationship between Auden and Frost. It does not, for example, take into consideration the extended introduction to a 1936 selection of Frost's poems, which formed the basis for the essay later published in *A Dyer's Hand* (1962). Nor does it acknowledge that Frost was to become the leading American poetic influence on Auden's own work during the American years. How important the fifties Auden considered Frost to be may be seen from his placing the latter's poem, "The Gift Outright" as the epigraph to his anthology of modern American verse.[20] Frost is also given pride of place by having more of his poems printed in the collection than any other poet.

Part of the reason for Frost's prominence (and T. S. Eliot's absence, something no doubt also partly due to the difficulty and expense of securing reprint rights), is Auden's apparent conviction that Frost was a very *American* poet in a way that other American poets whom he also admired were not, such as Wallace Stevens, Marianne Moore, or T. S. Eliot himself. In the introduction to the *Criterion* anthology, Auden quotes a stanza from Frost's "Come In," remarking on "how American in rhythm as well as in sensibility" it is (CB, 11). Somewhat later, he goes on to observe that "American poetry has many tones, a man talking to himself or one intimate friend, a prophet crying in the wilderness, but the easy-going tone of a man talking to a group of his peers is rare" (CB, 18). This observation echoes, in part almost verbatim, a sentence in Auden's essay on Frost, where "Frost's tone of voice" is decribed as being "even in his dramatic pieces . . . that of a man talking to himself, thinking aloud and hardly aware of an audience" (*Dyer's*, 344). Frost, in other words, was for Auden—from the point of view of "tone" at least—the archetypal modern American poet.

Frost's conception of the function of poetry was also congenial to the American Auden. (Frost, on the other hand, appears to have had little use for Auden—American, English, or otherwise.) In Auden's view, Frost was to be esteemed because he was not an "Ariel-dominated" poet like Yeats, who was allegedly prepared to walk (or flit) over the dead body of truth in order to reach the Neverland of beauty. Frost was firmly ensconced in the camp of the Prosperians; he was a poet who aimed for truth rather than beauty and "knew that they are not identical." Frost, therefore, in Auden's view ran a risk greater than the facile Arielite, who if he failed, could fail in only one way—"his poem may be trivial." The failure of the Prosperian, however, "can be worse than trivial. It can be false . . ." (*Dyer's*, 337–41).

As John Fuller pointed out more than twenty-five years ago, at least one of Auden's mature poems, "Their Lonely Betters" (1950), has a specifically Frostian dimension (Fuller, *Guide*, 224). (Two other poems written at about the same time, "The More Loving One," and "A Permanent Way" are also Frostian in tone and outlook; and a third poem, "Walks," written in 1958, reads almost like a parody of "The Road Not Taken.") More recently, Anthony Hecht has explored this dimension in greater detail, arguing that the final words of "Their Lonely Betters," "promises to keep," serve to signal its kinship with Frost—specifically with the Frost of "Stopping by Woods on a Snowy Evening:"

> As I listened from a beach-chair in the shade
> To all the noises that my garden made,
> It seemed to me only proper that words
> Should be withheld from vegetables and birds.
>
> A robin with no Christian name ran through
> The Robin-Anthem which was all it knew,
> And rustling flowers for some third party waited
> To say which pairs, if any, should get mated.
>
> Not one of them was capable of lying,
> There was not one which knew that it was dying
> Or could have with a rhythm or a rhyme
> Assumed responsibility for time.
>
> Let them leave language to their lonely betters
> Who count some days and long for certain letters;
> We, too, make noises when we laugh or weep:
> Words are for those with promises to keep.
>
> (CP, 444)

Unlike Fuller, who finds the feeling of the poem to be "beautifully and stoically understated," as it presumably might have been in a typical Frost poem, Hecht thinks Auden was mistaken to invite comparison with Frost. For unlike Frost, Auden was supposedly ill-equipped to generalize about the ways of birds and bees. Frost, in Hecht's view, would never have asserted, as Auden does, that birds are incapable of lying. Birds *are* capable of lying. The catbird, for example, or the mockingbird lie, and the name of the cuckoo too is rightly related to that of the cuckold. "Finally," Hecht concludes, "Frost would have known that spousal fidelity is so rare among birds that the exceptions (turtledoves, cardinals, love-birds) are always commented upon. He would therefore not have written a poem in which birds are made at once more ignorant and innocent than humans" (Hecht, 317).

Prospero, it would appear, has failed here. He has produced a false poem. He has failed to recall, that is, if he ever knew to begin with, that some birds are in fact capable of lying, and that most birds are given to promiscuity.

Without wishing in any way to claim poetic infallibility for Auden or to question Hecht's perfect right to find fault with Auden's zoological knowledge, this particular criticism strikes me as oddly beside the point. To begin with, it takes no cognizance of the specifically biblical context of the poem. The speaker, after all, is sitting in a *garden* listening to birdsong and to the rustling of the vegetation, an archetypal situation to which virtually all readers at the time would have responded with recognition. Just in case we miss the cue, however, we are subsequently informed that the robin who is performing his song has no "Christian name." The poem is about a postlapsarian world that has left humanity (ironically?) morally superior ("better") than the rest of creation but has also imposed the condition of loneliness as the price for that superiority. Humanity is now not only superior, it is also separate from all other created beings. And, because it does have a Christian name, it also has a future—of redemption or damnation, as no bird or animal does.

What, however, most obviously distinguishes, as well as separates, humanity from the world of animals and vegetables is language or words. All of creation shares noise, but words are "withheld" from all but the speaker's kind. Noise can effectively communicate emotional information throughout all the orders of nature—"We too make noises when we laugh or weep"— but words are limited to those who have abstract "promises to keep," in other *words*, to a humanity that inhabits a *moral* universe defined by language. Not possessing words but only noise, the animal and vegetable worlds are outside the moral world, which is also the world within time.

From the point of view of the naturalist—that is, the point of view of Hecht or Hecht's version of Frost—it could be added that Auden not only errs here by asserting that birds (and, by implication, all other animals) are incapable of lying, but that he errs in other ways as well. Animals, after all, often do appear to know that they are about to die, and, further, some of them at least also possess a sense of time, since time-recognition is essential to all migratory species. Finally, while birds may not be able to produce rhymes, it seems absurd to deny them a sense of rhythm. The very fact that the robin is shown to be able to perform a "Robin-Anthem" should have alerted Auden to the fact he was contradicting himself here.

One could go even further and note that it is particularly unfortunate that Auden, who prided himself on his knowledge of the natural sciences and tried to keep up with developments in this area by regularly reading the *Scientific American*, should be convicted of such ignorance. Marianne Moore, who knew something about animals (both real and imaginary) esteemed Auden as "a notable instance of the poet whose scientific predilections do not make him less than a poet . . ." (Moore, 86). Or is it really Auden's ignorance? Or only the "ignorance" of the speaker of the poem, who is himself as deeply sunk in the world of language as he is in his "beach-chair in the shade"? Or, more persuasively perhaps, is it not a matter of ignorance at all but really one of *consciousness*? For a robin may produce rhythm in his song and a parrot may even produce rhymes, but are these birds aware of what they are doing? Are they aware in the sense of being self-conscious about it? Not likely. Certainly, naturalists have provided no evidence for such self-consciousness. So too with the catbird who lies or the birds who are "unfaithful." They are also utterly unconscious of the human or moral ("Christian") dimensions of their sounds or actions. They don't know they are lying; they don't know they are being untrue. They also don't know if they are speaking the truth or are being "true." They don't even know that they don't know, because they lack the words and consciousness through which to know. And that is also why they neither belong to the moral category of the "better" nor to the social one of the "lonely," as we do and must.

As for Frost's more accurate and truthful depiction of the animal world, this notion seems hardly confirmed by reference to his poems. In "Stopping by Woods on a Snowy Evening," for example—the poem to which the closing line of Auden's poem seems to allude—the speaker's horse is first described as thinking "it queer / To stop without a farmhouse near," and later the horse asks "if there is some mistake" by shaking his harness bells (Frost, 207). In another poem, "The Oven Bird," the eponymous bird is linguistically even more sophisticated: "He says that leaves are old and that for flowers / Midsummer is to spring as one to ten" (Frost, 116).

What to make of these remarkably articulate animals? Should we say that they might be considered appropriate in Aesop's fables or a Disney cartoon, but not in poems that make a serious claim to zoological truth? Again, I think not, for these animals don't "speak." It is the *speaker* who speaks through them. Frost's humans are as lonely as Auden's, amply provided with extensive psychological desert places of their own. As Hecht himself observes, both poets, different though they may be in many ways, were "deeply preoccupied with loneliness" (Hecht, 316).

In the notes to the first long poem of the American years, "New Year Letter," Auden observes that American literature is essentially "a literature of lonely people" (*New*, 143).[21] In this respect too, Auden, not only as writer but also as human being, was fated to become an American—an *isolato* like Poe or Melville or Dickinson. He was glad to be alone, and to be left alone, during his first years in New York. From the very beginning, the American Auden cherished a privacy the English Auden had ceased to enjoy once he became a celebrity in the early thirties. This loneliness or privacy (or "introversion") was a considerable part of the appeal that his new megalopolitan environment exercised for him. Or so it seemed at first, especially after meeting Kallman, someone he was happy to be "alone with together." And, of course, living in the writer's commune at Middagh Street or among the bustle of students at Swarthmore or in Ann Arbor, Auden's initial loneliness was always a matter of choice. Not that he could not imagine it otherwise, as the alienated people of "The Age of Anxiety" ominously suggest.

Eventually, however, loneliness turned from choice to necessity. A late poem, simply entitled "Loneliness" (August 1971), depicts an Auden who is desperately afraid to be alone, who almost pathetically looks forward to the momentary companionship provided by a promised visit from Kallman. Auden's last years, as described by his biographers Humphrey Carpenter and, more recently and revealingly, Richard Davenport-Hines, depict a man helplessly in search of a former, less lonely self—in America, in England, and in Austria. To cite Frost again, in the end, he seems not to have known "what to make of a diminished thing."

5

The Sage of Kirchstetten: Thinking and Thanking

"Auden was as little American as he was Austrian. But he was a New Yorker and a Kirchstettener."
—Franz Richter (1984)

"Poetry is not magic. In so far as poetry, or any of the other arts, can be said to have an ulterior purpose, it is, by telling the truth, to disenchant amd disintoxicate."
—W. H. Auden (1962)

I

"Auden is in a German period," Robert Craft noted in his diary with evident lack of enthusiasm not long after Auden had left Italy and Ischia for Austria and Kirchstetten, a self-translation from Mediterranean sunlight to provincial fog, from classic wit to Teutonic dullness. Four years later, after listening to Auden spout quotations from Karl Kraus, Craft exasperatedly hoped that "the crest of his Teutonic period must soon be due," but several months thereafter he still found Auden making literary references that were "exclusively German" (Craft, 70). Craft was not alone among Auden's friends to view this newborn Anglo-American Austrian poet with grave reservations. "I would say," is the melancholy assessment of Auden's New York friend Vassily Yanovsky, "that the end of a certain happiness in Wystan's life coincided with his move from the Mediterranean blue of Ischia to the grey place in Austria of which he was so fond and proud" (Yanovsky, 25).

Whatever the merit of these views as literary or metereological criticism, the real point that Auden's friends forgot was that he had always preferred fog to sunlight, that from the very beginning of his career he had perceived and presented himself as a "northerner," a poet who had raided *Beowulf* and the sagas for poetic matter and form, a towheaded Yorkshireman who as a child had loved Hans Christian Andersen's "Snow Queen," and had vacationed in the Pennines and the Orkneys, a wild young man who only half-jestingly referred to himself as descended from Viking ancestors and whose first major journey (or quest, rather) had been to the Berlin of the late twenties.[1] The truth is that, by leaving Italy for Austria, Auden was not entering a German period at all; he had already been in a German, or at least Germanic, period for most of his life, so that the decade or so that he had summered in Italy actually constitutes a deviation rather than the norm. Returning northward, he was returning to himself.

Although later in life Auden liked to claim that in going to Berlin at the age of twenty-one he was going to an "unexplored city," one about which he knew nothing beforehand, Christopher Isherwood remarks pointedly in *Lions and Shadows* on Auden's earlier reading of Christian Morgenstern's poems (Auden, "Going," 53; Isherwood, *Lions*, 214). And one of his best Oxford friends, Gabriel Carritt, remembers Auden lending him copies of plays by Ernst Toller and Bertolt Brecht well before his departure for Germany (Willett, "Auden," 163). Whom ought one believe here? Probably Isherwood and Carritt rather than Auden, since the latter's long-term memory about the details of his youth was notoriously unreliable, as another Oxford friend, Richard Crossman, once had occasion to note (Crossman, 239–40). After first mistakenly denying that he had ever written a poem quoted by Crossman, Auden admitted that he possessed "a marvellous censor that refuses to let me remember, if it's any way back, anything unpleasant." As for Auden's "explorations" in darkest Germany during the late twenties, Stephen Spender quotes Isherwood's reaction on his first visit to the red-light district of St. Pauli in Hamburg, that he had heard much about it from Auden "when he first opened up Hamburg in 1927" (Spender, *Temple*, 182).

In any event, it is clear that it did not take Auden the explorer long to find what he was looking for: not only Brecht and Toller, but also Kaiser, Wedekind and Lampel; not only literature, but also life: the boys and the bars, "Looney" Layard, expressionist films, politics, and the excitements of living at the edge of the precipice at this critical moment in German and world history. All of these discoveries and emotions, together with the enveloping mood of obscure conflict and impending disaster, are present in the poems of this period. Berlin, like the very different Kirchstetten many years later, left an impact on Auden's imagination that makes it difficult if not impossible to understand, and therefore appreciate, what he wrote then and in the period immediately following without taking those experiences into consideration.

In some ways, the German connection became even stronger after Auden left Berlin. As we have seen, Auden's overtly propagandistic poetry and plays, notably *The Dance of Death* and "A Communist to Others," show the influence of Brecht, so that it ought not to be surprising that Brecht's first letter to Auden after meeting him in London in 1935 began by addressing him as "Comrade Auden" (Willett, 165). Nor should Auden's continuing interest in things German be in any way surprising, for to a very considerable degree that interest was, given the political and historical context of the thirties and forties, natural and inevitable. The coming to power in Germany of the Nazis in 1933 focused the eyes of the world on the spectacle of the horrifyingly rapid and complete transformation of that country from one of the freest and most tolerant in Europe to the dark center of tyranny and hatred.

Auden's greatest poetry, however, was not written under the aegis of Brecht's influence, but under that of the Austrians Rilke and Kafka. It is worth pausing briefly here to note that long before Auden had any inkling of his future status as an anglophone Austrian poet, he showed an unmistakable, though apparently unconscious preference for contemporary Austrian over contemporary German writers. Of Kafka, Isherwood writes that "you can trace his influence in the works of Auden," which is probably an exaggeration (Isherwood, "German," 255). With few and relatively unimportant exceptions, it is virtually impossible to detect any specific "traces" of Kafka's influence, though the general mood of struggle against unknown enemies, often disguised as seemingly harmless fellow citizens, is apparent throughout *Poems* (1930) and *The Orators*. So is the theme of the quest that Auden isolates in a 1941 review as "perhaps the best way of approaching his [Kafka's] work," and that is certainly not a bad way to begin looking at Auden's own work either. Still, Kafka's influence here must be qualified by the larger influence of Auden's lifelong love for the fairy tale, as well his long-standing interest in Anglo-Saxon poetry. In both of these, the quest is a predominant structural and thematic element (Auden, "Wandering," 85). Also, though the use of parables, as Samuel Hynes has emphasized, is certainly typically Audenesque, it is even more characteristic of Kafka (Hynes, 14–15). Nor is their use of the parable by any means identical. For the early Auden especially, the parable (outside the plays, that is) tends to be brief and primarily didactic, as in the "Prologue" and "Epilogue" of *The Orators*. The extended or "real" parable is rarely so central to his art or so fully developed as in Kafka. The exception here is "The Sportsmen: A Parable," which is really more of a parody of Kafka than an imitation, what with its oblique praise of the Soviet Union and its disguised critique of the politically uncommitted T. S. Eliot (EA, 369). Here, Kafka becomes more of an allegorical container for Marxist didactic sentiments rather than an integral aesthetic presence.[2]

Auden's debt to Rilke, on the other hand, is both larger and more subtle. Suggestively, the period of Rilke's greatest influence coincides with that of

Yeats, just as the influence of Brecht coincides with that of Eliot. Again, specific "traces" are relatively few, though definitely more numerous than in the case of Kafka. As long ago as 1948, B. J. Morse noted that lines 99 through 126 of "New Year Letter" constitute an almost literal and unacknowledged expansion of the last sonnet in the second part of Rilke's *Sonnets to Orpheus* (CP, 163). Despite this literary theft, however, Auden and Rilke remain, in Morse's view, "irreconcilable opposites . . . in habit of thought and approach," since Auden's poetry is supposedly vitiated by his "intellectualized, problematical politics" in a way that Rilke's is not (Morse, 276). For Peter Demetz, on the other hand, Auden's politics prove no hindrance to Auden's successful imitation of Rilke: "Above all it is the epic element that fascinates Auden in Rilke's *Dinggedichte*: the sustained dry tone of relation which again in the final line contains the possibility of drawing an almost epigrammatical moral." And further: "In the period from 1935 to 1940 Auden seemed virtually to concentrate on training himself in the Rilkean sonnet; in the end he attained such facility in imitating his model that he wasted his perfected technique on every possible object and often degenerated into mechanical Rilkean mannerisms" (Demetz, 25, my translation).[3] More positively, Sigurds Dzenitis has noted that Auden's emphasis during the late thirties on the function of the poet as praiser (as at the close of the Yeats elegy, for example) derives directly from Rilke's concept of *rühmen* or "praise" (Dzenitis, 96). For Monroe K. Spears, on the other hand, Auden's primary debt to Rilke is his habit of "putting unidentified persons, indicated only by pronouns (*he, she, they*), in usually symbolic landscapes, with the sonnet beginning in the middle of an unexplained situation." In this way, Auden manages—when he pulls it off, that is—to produce "a fresh union of abstract and concrete, of generalization about life and particular example." When he fails, however, "the oblique and riddling approach which is a necessary part of the technique leads to nothing but hopeless obscurity." Spears then cites as an example of Auden's successful adaptation of Rilkean technique, the poem, "Control of the Passes," dating from 1928 (!), apparently oblivious to the fact that most critics are convinced that Rilke's influence does not make itself felt until the mid-thirties (Spears, 25–26)[4]

In Volker Klöpsch's view, Auden's relationship to Rilke starts around 1936 and falls into two quite distinct phases. During the first, Auden learned from Rilke the technique of developing original imagery so as to render "concrete" and accessible abstractions that would otherwise have made his poetry abstruse and thin. This is especially true of the sonnet sequence in *Journey to a War*, where Auden uses typically Rilkean "abstract/concrete" similes such as: "He added meaning like a comma" or "They carry terror with them like a purse." (Indeed, in Klöpsch's view, the whole idea of writing a sequence of non-Shakespearean sonnets derives from Rilke.) The influence of Rilke reaches a high point in the sonnet on "Orpheus" (1937), though Auden's most explicit poetic acknowledgment of that influence occurs only in the nineteenth of the *Sonnets from China* (Klöpsch, 86–92, 101):

> When all our apparatus of report
> Confirms the triumph of our enemies,
> Our frontier crossed, our forces in retreat,
> Violence pandemic like a new disease,
>
> And wrong a charmer everywhere invited,
> When generosity gets nothing done,
> Let us remember those who looked deserted:
> To-night in China let me think of one
>
> Who for ten years of drought and silence waited,
> Until in Muzot all his being spoke,
> And everything was given once for all.
>
> Awed, grateful, tired, content to die, completed,
> He went out in the winter night to stroke
> That tower as one pets an animal.
>
> (CP. 156)

The unnamed "one" is, of course, Rilke, who in 1922, during a sustained burst of creativity, completed his *Duino Elegies* at Muzot Castle in Switzerland. That Auden intended his poem as a kind of mini elegy for Rilke is suggested by the parallel between the opening line of this poem and three of the opening lines of the great elegy on Yeats, completed two years later: "The mercury sank in the mouth of the dying day. / What instruments we have agree / The day of his death was a dark cold day" (CP, 197). Significantly, the "humanization" of the instruments, along with the land and cityscape later on in the poem, are all typically Rilkean devices, rather than Yeatsian ones.

The second, largely negative phase of Auden's reception of Rilke's poetry is essentially one of rejection, beginning with the attempt to make Rilke the butt of "cute" jokes like the one about Rilke "whom die Dinge [the things] bless / The Santa Claus of loneliness." While the motives behind this turning away from Rilke are unclear, they may have been due to Auden's increasing commitment to Christianity, something Rilke opposed in later life (Klöpsch,

104). As for Auden's notorious claim that he had to revise the "Sonnets from China" in order to "eliminate all the articles which were a result of his [Rilke's] influence," this statement is, I think, as absurd as it sounds (André, 7). He had already made a similar but more muted claim in *Collected Shorter Poems* to the effect that "in the nineteen-thirties I fell into some very slovenly verbal habits. The definite article is always a headache, but my addiction to German usages became a disease" (CSP, 16). Only a few years earlier, Auden's poetry had supposedly been suffering from a lack rather than a surfeit of articles, something he also ascribed to German influence.[5] But, as Auden himself pointed out in 1939, Rilke's contemporary impact "is not confined to certain technical tricks" (CSP, 16). Hence, it seems fair to conclude that Auden's blaming Rilke for stuffing his poems with articles relates more to his fondness for pulling people's legs than to explaining specific traits of his own poetry. In the 1973 BBC broadcast with Richard Crossman, however, Auden was prepared to acknowledge a more substantial, if no less baleful, debt. Rilke, so he claimed, had tempted him to be "*schöngeistig*, [to write] a sort of poetry with a capital 'p' " (Crossman, 240). Auden does not go on to provide specific examples, but what he may be referring to (especially since in the same context he repeats his habitual attack against Yeats's rhetoric) is his yielding to the sin of preferring beauty to truth. Where might he have committed such sins? Just about anywhere in the poetry from approximately 1936 to approximately 1941, the period of Auden's most beautiful and moving—and perhaps most frequently revised—poems.

Though Auden never mentions it directly, what he learned from Rilke was not simply *Schöngeistigkeit*, but also how to write a kind of gentle, reflective, elegiac poetry, one that celebrates the way the world is, with all its faults, rather than seeks to change it; a poetry that often deals with the life of things, of plants and animals (though Lawrence is important here too), comparing them implicitly or even explicitly with the life of men; a poetry in which human life is expressed "in terms of landscape; a poetry that incorporates the world of art not merely as a decorative aid but as a moral sphere of being" (Auden, "Rilke," 135). Formally, Rilke's influence takes shape not only in Auden's sudden predilection for sonnets but also for the elegy, though the choice of the latter genre may have been as much inspired by Yeats as by Rilke. A poem like "Musée des Beaux Arts" is, as D. J. Enright suggests, a good example of Auden's use of Rilkean subject matter and technique, and many other examples could be drawn from *Journey to a War* (Waidson, 351). But even poems written as late as "In Praise of Limestone" and "Their Lonely Betters" still show signs of Rilke's influence, especially in their characteristically Rilkean preference for mixing tactile with abstract imagery.

Auden's interest in Rilke peaked around 1940. In September of the previous year, he had reviewed the Leishman/Spender translation of the *Duino Elegies*. The review opens with the assertion that "not the least interesting phenomenon of the last four years has been the growing influence of Rilke upon English poetry," and then goes on to speculate that this influence is greater in England and America than in Germany. After considering in some detail Rilke's "most immediate influence . . . upon diction and imagery," he states his conviction that "it is . . . no accident that as the international crisis becomes more and more acute, the poet to whom writers are becoming increasingly drawn should be one who felt that it was pride and presumption to interfere with the lives of others . . . one who occupied himself consistently and exclusively with his own inner life" (Auden, "Rilke," 135). It is Rilke, then, who gives the lie to Yeats by telling us that "poetry makes nothing happen"; and it is Rilke who gives the lie, too, to the younger Auden who had once believed that it did. For this reason, as Auden stated in a later review of Rilke's *Letters* and *Selected Poems*, "one should be grateful for every attempt to make Rilke's poetry better known" (Auden, "Poet," 59)

By 1956, however, Auden had, with apparent regret, come to the conclusion that, while he still thought of Rilke as a "great poet . . . I cannot read him any more." (Auden, *Dyer's*, 51). Towards the end of his life, Auden was to include Rilke in the list of writers whose influence was "bad," though he never felt it was so bad as to be "positively evil," as in the cases of Brecht, Frost, and Yeats (Willett, 174). His reaction against Brecht is to some degree comprehensible as a rejection of the Brecht he had come to identify within himself, though, oddly enough, he kept on translating and adapting Brecht long after recognizing his supposed balefulness; and the same holds true, *mutatis mutandis*, for his rejection of Yeats. But why Frost, whom he praises elsewhere as being more truthful than Yeats, and even than Hardy? (Auden, *Dyer's*, 353). And why Rilke? What could they possibly have done or written to so antagonize him?

In "A Thanksgiving," one of the very last poems he ever wrote (dating, apparently, from May 1973), a poem that names and thanks his literary ancestors and culminates with the name of Goethe, Auden includes (among others) Frost, Brecht, and Yeats as, respectively, poets at whose feet he sat or from whom he received instruction and help. But in this distinguished list he does not name Rilke. Nor, for that matter, does he include Kafka or D. H. Lawrence or T. S. Eliot. The "worst" here, it would appear, have usurped the place of the merely "bad" and even of the "good." This is a peculiar thanksgiving indeed. Inevitably one is left to wonder why.

What is more, one is left to wonder if one is meant to wonder, if such wonderment is not in fact the purpose—or, at any rate, one of the primary purposes—behind Auden's repeated and yet inconsistent acknowledgment, rejection, vilification, and even annihilation of his literary grandfathers and fathers—to wonder if the aged Uncle Wiz is not playing the same game here with his literary posterity that he had so often and effectively played with his literary contemporaneity. Whatever the case and whatever the reasons—fear of harassment by McCarthy has been suggested (Willett, 174–75), as well as a penchant for trying on various psycho-political hats (or heads) (Hoskins, 192–93), to which one might add just plain old snobbery, envy, and/or literary giant-killing—revising his "true ancestors" became almost as much a compulsion with Auden as reformulating the poems of his youth. He was the third son, the lucky one, striking out on a quest that would always have a happy ending. So it seemed to him, only half in jest, but to the listeners of this oft-repeated tale it became increasingly apparent that as the goal of the quest happened to change, so did the presumed father.

II

One senses some of the same sort of quasi-humorous perversity in Auden's choice of Kirchstetten as the place to spend just about all of the springs and summers of his final years. No doubt he knew how many if not most of his friends felt about this choice. As the autobiographical vignettes in "Profile" reveal, there was not much that the aged Auden did not know about how the outside world, including the world of his friends, viewed him. Austria, while self-assertively not or no longer part of Germany—and in spite of having perhaps always represented a more acceptable Italianate Germany, as, for instance, Peter Porter tries to persuade us that Austria did and does—this Austria was nonetheless still too close to being and to having been part of Germany not to represent an affront to the prevalent anti-German sensibilities of the Anglo-Saxon world during the first couple of decades of the postwar period (Porter, 103). Significantly, Auden's elegy for Josef Weinheber, written on the twentieth anniversary of the suicide of an Austrian poet who, had been a Nazi, has been passed over virtually in silence by the critics.[6]

Auden's preference for the German-speaking world, both early and late, was part of a conscious strategy of annoying (and perhaps also of trying to break down) the conventions and prejudices of his surroundings. In the long 1965 *New Yorker* essay-review of Evelyn Waugh's and Leonard Woolf's autobiographies—probably the closest Auden ever came to writing an autobiography himself—he remembers going to Berlin in 1928 as a defiant gesture against the Francophilia of his parents' generation. (Auden, "As," 190) In 1950 or thereabouts, when he wrote the inroduction to the volume of Victorian and Edwardian poetry that he coedited with Norman Holmes Pearson, he went out of his way to blame the French for starting political and moral turmoil that had just culminated five years earlier. "In view of the subsequent history of Germany," he wrote, "it is important to remember that it was France, not Prussia, which declared war in 1870. The initial betrayal of Europe was the *coup d'état* of 1851, and Napoleon III, with his combination of force and appeal to the masses, was, as De Tocqueville realized, a novel and sinister phenomenon, the first dictator of the modern type" (Auden, *Victorian*, xv). Even very late in his career, Auden was convinced that being pro-German meant being anti-French. In a 1963 symposium on the question of Britain's entry into the Common Market, something that Auden strongly supported, he confesses that the word *Europe* conjures up "certain sacred names . . . Lichtenberg, Hölderlin, Nietzsche, Nestroy, Rimbaud, Christian Morgenstern, Valéry, Kafka, Karl Kraus, Rudolf Kassner." He then draws the reader's attention to the fact that in this list "German names predominate," going on to explain that "no Englishman falls in love with Europe as a whole; he falls in love with a particular landscape and language." In Auden's case—and he is prepared to admit that "there are not many of us"—he was one of those eccentrics "who fell in love with the German language" (Auden, "Going," 53). The list, however, suggests that it was as much literature as language that he fell in love with.

    This catalog is reminiscent of a somewhat better-known hypothetical one (Auden loved making lists and catalogs, often autobiographical in nature) that occurs in the opening essay on "Reading" in *The Dyer's Hand* : "If I were to attempt to write down all the names of all the poets and novelists for whose work I am really grateful because I know that if I had not read them my life would be poorer, the list would take up pages. But when I try to think of all the critics for whom I am really grateful, I find myself with a list of thirty-four names. Of these twelve are German and only two French. Does this indicate a conscious bias? It does" (Auden, *Dyer's*, 8). Even in the middle of the war against Germany, Auden wrote Norman Holmes Pearson that "it is a German age, and the chances are, I have a suspicion, that after the war it will continue to be. What other country has produced anything comparable to the cumulative effect of—to name a few—Rilke-Kafka-Berg-Strauss-Barlach-Klee-Husserl-Heidegger-Scheler-Barth-Groddeck-Koehler" (Quoted by Mendelson, *Later*, 419). It is difficult to avoid the impression after reading such passages that Auden was not only conscious of his bias in favor of German writers, but that he exulted in it. Hence, Vassily Yanovsky was probably not exaggerating when he recalled that the late Auden "made a point of disliking the French, denying even their great poetry" (Yanovsky, 15). It is in this context that his moving elegy for his friend Lewis MacNeice, "The Cave of Making," should be read, the poem in which he expresses his longing to become "if possible, / a minor atlantic Goethe."

Auden's fascination with Goethe in later life is probably attributable to his sense that, *mutatis mutandis*, Goethe's life prefigured his own. Certainly, this is the case when he speaks of the young Goethe writing *Werther* for therapeutic reasons, implying that the same holds true of his own early work: "He finds himself obsessed by certain ways of feeling and thinking of which his instinct tells him he must be rid of before he can discover his authentic interests and sympathies, and the only way he can be rid of them forever is by surrendering to them. Once he has done this, he has developed the necessary anti-bodies which will make him immune for the rest of his life. As a rule, the disease is some spiritual malaise of his generation [i.e., left-wing politics in Auden's case]. If so, he may, as Goethe did, find himself in an embarrassing situation" (Auden, *Dyer's*, 18). How closely the late Auden came to be identified with certain aspects of Goethe is apparent from Spender's reaction when he visited Auden in Kirchstetten: "Staying with him in Kirchstetten and finding in our bedroom a copy of his volume *About the House*, consisting of charming poems about each of the rooms in the house, I could not help thinking that anyone who read this without ever having visited Auden in Audenstrasse might suppose it to be about a house like Goethe's in Weimar" (Spender, Preface, 8).

In "The Cave of Making," Auden expresses his admiration for Goethe because Goethe "bears witness" (as Plato also did in his cave) to a Truth he knows full well is not a truth, something "the Francophile / gaggle of pure songsters / are too vain to" do (CP, 522–23). Dull Goethe may be—in fact dull he undoubtedly is—and so presumably is the culture of which he is the chief glory, but he and it respect and acknowledge the outer world, including the outer human world, as the self-directed French and their uncritical admirers, the Francophiles, presumably do not (Auden, *EA*, 150). Beneath Auden's dangerous juggling with national stereotypes here, one can sense the bedrock of the old (and very German) distinction between "culture" and "civilization," the former running very deep and being the product of a felt sense of community, the latter superficial and characteristic of legalistic states as well as legalistic states of mind.[7] So some significant part of Auden's returning northward to Kirchstetten was due his own experience of and love for the German-speaking world and its literature and culture. Then, as he kept repeating almost ad nauseam to visiting interviewers, there was the proximity of a world-class opera and the ready availability of decent wine. What he did not say, but what almost certainly also influenced his decision, was that Kirchstetten was very much off the beaten tourist track, thus virtually eliminating the likelihood of unwelcome visitors; and that, further, from the perspective of the Kirchstetteners themselves, he would be too much of an outsider, socially, linguistically, and sexually speaking, for him to have to worry much about the niceties of village "family" life, as might have been the case had he chosen to settle in an English village instead.

Another important and usually unacknowledged factor was that life in Kirchstetten and in Austria generally (including tickets for the world-class opera) was incredibly cheap in the mid- to- late fifties, and indeed continued to be so until the end of the sixties. Cheap, that is, for someone like Auden whose income was calculated in United States dollars. Though this income was to some extent taxed, Auden received an exemption from the Austrian Value Added Tax at the special intercession of the Austrian Chancellor, Bruno Kreisky. ("Auden in Kirchstetten", 75)[8] In this connection, it should also be noted that Humphrey Carpenter's sums for what Auden paid for his house in Kirchstetten or the supposedly munificent salary he gave his housekeeper, Emma Eiermann, are drastically off and should be reduced by as much as sixty to seventy percent (Carpenter, *Auden*, 387–88). So, instead of paying $12,000 for the house, as Carpenter claims he did (apparently using the 1980 exchange rate), Auden actually paid $4,750 (plus another $1000 for the furniture); and as for "overpaying" Emma Eiermann, something Carpenter quotes Auden as having been happy to do, her monthly stipend amounted to all of $40. This left Auden with a considerable surplus, since by his own calculations the Feltrinelli Prize had been worth over $33,000 (Berg, letter to Hedwig Petzold, 20 June 1957). All of this concern over monetary calculations, of course, should not be taken to mean that Auden was not at times very generous, but it does mean that he also had a sensitive nose for good value. And that is precisely what he got in Kirchstetten.[9]

Going to Kirchstetten, then, was not only a positive gesture; it was also a negative one: not overrun, not expensive, not England, not Italy, not New York. For Auden it meant too, I think, an escape from the person he saw himself turning into. Obscure, provincial, plain Kirchstetten was a place where he could abandon some of the theater of his life, for just as he came to reject theatrical poetry, so he came to reject the theater of life—the theater of the poetry circuit, the theater of the cocktail party, the theater of protest by a younger generation he could neither understand nor tolerate. In Kirchstetten, in other words, he could indulge more easily and less self-consciously the person he now thought he really was: an old fogey who preferred the world of pre-1914 to that of post-1945. As part of that old world,

Kirchstetten was also a place that lived up to its name: the place of the church. Here he could let his religious impulses loose, all the more so perhaps because the church in this place was Catholic and therefore less likely to be censorious of religious self-expression than staid Episcopalians in New York. Besides, there were ample, if rather simple, quasi-Edwardian satisfactions for the ego to be found here as well. In Kirchstetten he was without doubt the very biggest of fish and could, undisturbed and unrivaled, play either the country squire or a kind of autocrat of the cocktail hour combined with demonic mother, an eccentric dragon in slippers.[10]

Visiting Auden in Kirchstetten, accompanying him on his daily rounds, seeing him being greeted respectfully with a "Grüss Gott, Herr Professor!" by the Kirchstetteners, his old friend Margaret Gardiner thought him fully at home in his new/old world (Gardiner, 18). Was this true? To prying interviewers, certainly, he would invariably proclaim his happiness, his domestic bliss in provincial, small-town Austria. Golo Mann, another old friend who visited him there, was also struck by the way Auden had been integrated into the community, especially in religious terms: "[H]e went to Mass and on Corpus Christi marched in the procession, immediately behind the *Bürgermeister*. The village treasured that; and he treasured the village" (G. Mann, 10). Certainly, Kirchstetten seems to have satisfied the late Auden's love for ritual and routine, perhaps even some of his longing for community, though it is clear (and was clear to Auden) that, despite Franz Richter's claim to the contrary, he was not really considered a Kirchstettener by the villagers, as his poetical predecessor Weinheber had been.

Franz Hitzenberger's prediction, made not long after Auden started spending his summers in Kirchstetten, that he would soon be so well known in Austria that he would have to make his trips to Vienna "incognito," never came true—no doubt much to Auden's delight (Hitzenberger, 6). Though the official Austrian literary establishment took appropriate cognizance of his presence, with the Austrian Literary Society arranging for occasional talks and readings, including the last one, given the night before he died, and with the Austrian Government awarding him the highest literary honor in its possession, The Austrian State Prize, still, for the most part, lowercase Austrian literary society—that is, actual writers—tended to ignore his existence. To be sure, so did Auden tend to ignore theirs, for despite the fact that his knowledge of the German (and Austrian) classics was considerable, he knew almost nothing about contemporary Austrian literature. How little he was known to the general Austrian public is apparent from a story Auden's Austro-British friend, Stella Musulin, told me about how a young man who had spent a whole evening in a Vienna café with Auden, later asked her, as she gave him a lift home in her car: "Who *is* Professor Auden?" (see Appendix).

5: THE SAGE OF KIRCHSTETTEN: THINKING AND THANKING   215

As for the Kirchstetteners, initially, at least, they rather comically misundertood the relationship between Auden and Chester Kallman, being convinced that the latter was his personal cook, something that impressed them enormously. Later on, when Auden's homosexual preferences became public knowledge in the infamous episode following the arrest of his young Austrian friend, Hugerl, the Kirchstetteners began to view him in a more negative light and to laugh at him behind his back. Even Pastor Lutskandl was put out by the affair. Auden's squirarchical status was only restored when a TV crew from Austrian Television came out to make a film about his life in Kirchstetten.[11] This caused the whole community to take pride once again in their famous (if also now rather notorious) fellow citizen. Artists, after all, had licence to behave differently from the rest of Austrian humanity. Now, years later, with his former house (or parts of it) turned into a museum, and with the street on which it borders renamed the "Audenstrasse," the locals display his books on their shelves, and on All Hallows' Eve make sure that his grave next to the Town Church is overflowing with flowers.

Kirchstetten, then, may not have been home exactly, but it was as close as he would ever come to home, and probably ever wanted to come. Though remaining "a transplant / from overseas," now "at last" he was "dominant / over three acres and a blooming conurbation of country lives." For such a habitat he was prepared to give thanks:

> what I dared not hope or fight for
> is, in my fifties, mine, a toft-and-croft
> where I needn't ever be at home *to*
>
> *those I am not at home with*, not a cradle,
> a magic Eden without clocks,
> and not a windowless grave, but a place
> I may go both in and out of.
>
> (CP, 520–21)

In another one of his fine Kirchstetten poems, "Whitsunday in Kirchstetten," Auden returns to this theme of the outsider who paradoxically feels at home:

> When Mass is over,
> although obedient to Canterbury,
> I shall be well gruss-gotted, asked to contribute
> to *Caritas*, though a metic come home
> to lunch on my own land: no doubt, if the Allies had not
> conquered the Ost-Mark, if the dollar fell,

> the *Gemütlichkeit* would be less, but when was peace
> or its concomitant smile the worse
> for being undeserved?
>
> (CP, 559)

Auden's choice of the word "metic" here is significant, since it is a word that, in modern times, was put into circulation by the semi-fascist *Action Française*, and so forms a link with the "Ost-Mark," the name that the Nazis used for Austria after annexing it in 1938. "Metic" is nicely translated by the Austrian poet Johannes W. Paul as *Zugereister*, a word which accurately catches the sense of not belonging and yet of somehow not being entirely a stranger. *Zugereister* is not *Ausländer* (foreigner), just as "metic" is not "alien" (Paul, 133). A metic is someone who seems to belong but in fact does not.

In the Kirchstetten poems, Auden often inserts German words or phrases or even quotations (as in the elegy for Weinheber), some of which are not even italicized as being non-English in origin, and virtually none of which is ever translated. What, for example, is the "common" Anglo-American reader to make of the opening half-line of "Whitsunday in Kirchstetten:" "*Komm Schöpfer Geist*"? From the context, he probably realizes that it is sung and has something to do with the Catholic Mass, but just what that something is he is incapable of saying, for unlike Eliot Auden provides no notes. What about *Gemütlichkeit* ? This is one of those evocative German words, like *Sehnsucht* or *Heimat*, which is virtually untranslatable. As for "Ost-Mark," the same reader, unequipped with German, might perhaps guess it to refer to the currency of the sometime German Democratic Republic. And what about the unitalicized (and un-umlauted) "gruss-gotted" (the usual greeting in rural Austria)?

Sometimes Auden makes it even more difficult for his audience by translating a German word literally without any indication that this what he has done. So, for example, near the beginning of "Thanksgiving for a Habitat" Auden makes a parenthetical reference to "our half-strong" who "might hang their jackets / while mending their lethal bicycle chains" (CP, 519). Though it is fairly easy to guess (correctly) that these half-strong are most likely juvenile delinquents, it is difficult to grasp just why Auden calls them by this peculiar name. The answer is very simple and yet not so simple: because the German word for juvenile delinquents is *Halbstarke* or "half-strong."

What is the point of all these unexplained German words and allusions? Part of the point is almost certainly to provide a kind of cultural/linguistic context for the Kirchstetten poems that will make them "feel" like poems

5: THE SAGE OF KIRCHSTETTEN: THINKING AND THANKING 217

coming from Kirchstetten. The person who has written these poems is one who is privately and emotionally steeped in Austrian and Kirchstetten lore. Hence, not only the German words, but also the references to people like Emma Eiermann or Pfarrer Lustkandl who, outside the narrow confines of Kirchstetten, have no public significance at all. The late Auden understood fully as well as the early Auden, though in a very different way, that poetry—if it is to *work*—must be rooted in private and personal experience, that it must make the reader *feel* that such is the case even at the risk of making him pay a heavy price in obscurity for entering that world. For Auden all poetry—as with Tip O'Neill, all politics—was local. Only upon a strong foundation of private identity can a successful public life be built; and as with life, so with poetry.

The public dimension of the Kirchstetten poems is often historical, with references to the relatively distant past when the Turks overran the area or the Bavarians settled it; or to the more recent past when the Nazis ruled Austria, times contrasted to the present when Kirchstetten and neutral Austria generally show a peaceful face and the past is apparently forgotten. Some forty kilometers away, however, the Iron Curtain stood until not so long ago as an ominous reminder of one of the links and divisions of past and present. Auden was fond of taking his visitors to have a not too close look at the barbed wire and the watch towers.

The contrast between past and present is crucial especially to a public understanding of the series of poems Auden privately called his *Hausgedichte* (Fuller, *Commentry*, 484) and first published in *About the House* under the title "Thanksgiving for a Habitat," which is also, a little confusingly, the title of one of the poems in the series. These poems, composed between 1958 and 1964, represent, it is safe to say, the apex of Auden's achievement in Kirchstetten and constitute one of the most unpretentious and yet remarkable poetical sequences of the twentieth century, a sequence that fuses the quiet formal mastery of the veteran craftsman with the loose, almost casual tone of the rural sage; and that mixes references to people and ideas from a great variety of places and times with an intense sense of belonging to a particular locality—to Kirchstetten. Yet, at the same time, there runs through the poems a kind of puzzled ironic good humor that it should be *this* place that has become home to a much-traveled, middle-aged Anglo-American literary intellectual. Addressing Kallman in the last poem of the series, Auden remarks—using a syntactic structure that is almost German—that

>   after twenty-four years
>   we should sit here in Austria

> as cater-cousins, under the glassy look
> of a Naples Bambino,
> the portrayed regards of Strauss and Stravinsky,
> doing British crossword puzzles,
>
> is very odd indeed.
>
> (CP, 538)

As always with Auden, the poems are double in their insistence on the often irreconcilable claims of the private and public, of inner and outer worlds. Here, the opposition also extends to the usually conflicting worlds of nature and man, including the contrast between human time (the clock) and natural time (the seasons)—a contrast formally represented and reconciled by Auden in writing exactly twelve poems: for twelve is both the middle of day and the end of night, and it is also the enumeration into human months of the nonhuman annual rhythm of the seasons. So, for example, the opening poem, "Prologue: The Birth of Architecture," invokes the remote, prehistorical past of the "gallery-grave and the hunt of a wren-king" only to juxtapose it immediately with the "Low Mass and trailer camp" of the present (CP, 518). This apparently vast lapse of time is then translated into a fused human/natural context of the "carbon clock," by which it is at once reduced to a mere "tick." Inevitably, this is not a temporal measure humans can cope with. Natural and human time combine better in the now proffered chronology of its already being "millions of heartbeats ago / back to the Bicycle Age." Here, the public dimension again merges with the private, because the heartbeats belong both to all of us generally as well as to the speaker individually; moreover, for the speaker time begins at this particular point, "before which is no *After* for me to measure, / just a still prehistoric once" (CP, 518).

Without going into every detail, one can follow the same pattern in the second poem, "Thanksgiving for a Habitat," which opens humorously (indeed, humor for Auden is a habitual link between the private and public realms of being) with the conceit of a modern funeral conceived in terms of a prehistoric ritual burial:

> Nobody I know would like to be buried
> with a silver cocktail shaker
> a transistor radio and a strangled
> daily help . . .
>
> (CP, 519)

The third poem, "The Cave of Making," begins with a comparison of Auden's study to Weland's smithy—and the title, of course, evokes both the womb and Plato. The fourth, "Down There," about the cellar, reminds the speaker of prehistoric cave dwellings; the contrasting fifth, "Up There," devoted to the attic, describes it as a place for keeping in clockless storage items out of the personal past (chiefly female), a kind of combination of public eternity and private memory.

The sixth poem, dedicated to Isherwood and focusing on the anal pleasures of the W.C., sees the act performed here as simultaneously disconnected from time (since, unlike sex, all ages of mankind are able to enjoy the "primal pleasures" of a "satisfactory dump") and yet as being the archetype of all aesthetic creativity: an "ur-act of making" (CP, 526–27). The eighth poem, about the bathroom (one needs to remember here that on the continent W.C. and bath are traditionally placed in separate rooms), rehearses in a shower of syllabic verse the history of bathing in the West, from "river-cult in torrid Greece" to Rome and up through the unwashed centuries until John Bull invented the hip-bath (CP, 528). The following poem about the kitchen is set in a context that includes feudal kitchens and prehistoric hearthstones. The tenth poem, on the dining room (a room, by the way, that did not exist as a separate entity in Kirchstetten, but was established, as the need arose, at one end of the living room), evokes feasts of mammoth marrow or Long Pig celebrated "before the last Glaciation," feasts that will continue till Doomsday, "when at God's board / the saints chew pickled Leviathan" (CP, 533). The eleventh (and next to last) poem balances the second with a similar fusion of private and public past: the bedroom is not only the place where we return from named and numbered personages to "naked Adam and Eve," it is also the place where Auden himself made his "infantile entrance into Edwardian England." And Auden's own awakening in Austria is compared to "that joy in beginning / for which our species was created" (CP, 535). The final poem, the twelfth, deals with the living room, the space shared by Auden and Kallman with occasional visitors, friends and strangers; it is the only poem of the series (except for the ninth, the guest room, in which a similar interaction takes place), in which the contrast of past and present plays no significant role. Here it is space rather than time that matters; here, in the poem's closing exhortation, love takes precedence over truth; here the inevitable separation of singular "I" and "Thou" can at least entertain the prospect of a plural "we"; here, private can turn with decorum into public, and vice versa (CP, 537). Fittingly, time past and time future conclude in time present: in the twelfth room.

The point of these continuing and developing temporal and spatial contrasts—or at least one of the main points—is to suggest the rhythmic, repetitive pattern (hence the verse) of man's life in nature, but also his ability, as a conscious human being, to choose within a context of differing patterns and rhythms (hence the variety in the verse forms), a distinction Auden liked to concretize by using the words "behavior" and "deed" (or, with a perhaps ironic echo of Marx, "necessity" and "freedom"), implying that a fully free life can only be lived within freely acknowledged constraints. Also, the house stands for a human construct surrounded by a natural given, a world, both inanimate and animate, from which man is separated and to which he is also joined. House and nature, in combination, constitute "habitat." But habitat is also habit, a personal or private as well as a public condition. It is not only a place but also a state of mind one can go in and out of.

The house, with its various rooms (and their varying functions), also allows for private and public identities within the purely human context: the bathroom at the one extreme and the living room at the other. Finally, the house is also the inner, private man taken as a whole, with the outside of the house as a whole being the public man, much as in Forster's famous analogy in *The Longest Journey* or in his symbolic rendering of the same idea in *Howards End*. It is a microcosm of the "Just City," Auden's quasi-Utopian ideal during his last years. Significantly, in this final sense, Auden remains almost entirely private, just as Forster would have wished him to be.

The twelve poems of "Thanksgiving for a Habitat" constitute nearly half of the total output of what may be called the characteristically Kirchstetten poems, as opposed, that is, to the considerably larger number of poems that were composed in Kirchstetten but have no other significant relation to the place.[12] Almost all of the "real" Kirchstetten poems were written in the decade of the sixties; certainly all of the best ones were. It is as if Auden needed a few years of acculturation before his emotional involvement with Kirchstetten grew sufficiently strong for him to be able to express it in poetry; and also as if, with death perceptibly nearer by the beginning of the seventies, Auden's sense of earthly place was gradually yielding to loneliness and a sense of ending.

Inevitably, as a coherent sequence, "Thanksgiving for a Habitat" is able to render more concentratedly, and therefore more memorably, Auden's sense of "belonging" to his new/old Austrian world than do the other, more isolated expressions of his life there, however powerful they may be individually. Both groups of poems, though in differing measure, share similar preoccupations: the process of aging in a context of personal, historical, natural, and even religious time; the need for a self-conscious cultural, religious, and geographical context to reinforce one's individual sense of identity—and, in the contemporary world, the growing probability that such a context will not long survive; the conviction that aesthetics and ethics must be one; the nature of friendship and spiritual kinship, among intellectual equals (e.g., Louis MacNeice or Josef Weinheber) as well as social unequals (Emma Eiermann or Hugerl); the perspective of the cultural outsider who has become something of an insider; and, most consistently perhaps, the relation of human to nonhuman nature, both animate and inanimate—or what might be called the theme of "man's place in nature."

How "Austrian" are these poems? There is absolutely nothing Kafkaesque about them, and they reveal virtually no trace of Rilke's influence, except possibly in their preoccupation with the relation of the animate to the inanimate world or in the sustained contrast between the brevity of time present and the long flow of time past, with both times contrasted yet again with a timeless eternity. But "Thanksgiving for a Habitat" has none of the self-conscious self-importance, none of the ambitious Great Books quality of, say, the *Duino Elegies*—or *The Age of Anxiety*, for that matter. On the contrary, the tone is deliberately anti-masterpiece, anti-Great Work of Art. It is this aspect of Auden's later verse that appealed particularly to the anti-rhetorical fifties and early sixties; it is this that made the Kirchstetten Auden seem so similar in tone and spirit to another self-imposed, self-consciously sophisticated provincial poet like Larkin, despite the hostility with which the latter publicly treated him. Aside from the obvious Austrian context and subject matter, then, these poems are chiefly Austrian in that they resemble most the Kirchstetten poems of Josef Weinheber, whose collection *Kammermusik* ["Chamber Music"] anticipates, in some ways, the overarching analogy of Auden's sequence, the analogy between humanly ordered external space (the house, the rooms) and humanly created internal space (love, friendship, cultural tradition). To be sure, in this connection it should be noted that Weinheber's later poetry, like Auden's, also derives significantly from Horace, strongly endorsing the latter's preference for the honest country over the sophisticated city, solid craftsmanship over slick showiness, actual living speech over stilted poetic diction.

But was it necessary for Auden to have written "Austrian" poetry in order to qualify as an "Austrian" poet? Not really, I think. Auden's most valuable contribution to Austrian literature and to the Austrian cultural scene generally was his continued presence over a long period in an Austria that, by virtue of its exposed and marginal postwar geographical position at the edge of the Soviet Block as well as its sometime intimate association with Nazi Germany, had turned into a provincial backwater and cultural pariah during the immediate postwar period. To some admittedly small, but nevertheless significant, degree, Auden's presence in Austria and his use of an identifiable Austrian context in the Kirchstetten poems helped restore Austria to international respectability. It was very much a part of the cultural bridge-building between the English-speaking and the German-speaking worlds that was so much a part of Auden's life from the moment he left Oxford and went to Berlin. The Austrian State Prize, which Auden received not long after moving to Kirchstetten, was an honor that he had long and richly deserved.

III

Auden unquestionably came closest to being Austrian on the final day of his life, 28 September 1973. He spent the evening before his death reading from his poetry to a largely German-speaking audience in the elegant Palais Palffy in the heart of Vienna, just opposite the Imperial Palace and around the corner from the Opera. The reading, sponsored by the Austrian Literary Society, was to mark the publication of the first collection of Auden's poems in German translation—in fact, the first translated collection of his work to appear at all. It was a great and moving occasion, and at its close, Auden received a standing ovation. A few hours later, he lay dead a few streets away in the Hotel Altburgenhof, having suffered cardiac arrest apparently while asleep. He had gone out quietly as he had wished and hoped, but also in triumph, fittingly an Austrian triumph.

Very Austrian, too, was his burial in Kirchstetten, jointly conducted by representatives of the Anglican and Catholic Churches, with the cortège accompanied by the pagan strains of Wagner's "Siegfried's Funeral March." There he rests now, occupying a prominent place in the little yard surrounding the church, the only major English-language poet to be interred in a German-speaking country. That too is somehow fitting: the Austrian earth has received its honored guest.

While Auden is undeniably Austrian now, there remains nevertheless a good deal of dispute (not to say anguish) about the supposedly inadequate reception he was given by Austrian literary circles during the period of his residence above ground in Kirchstetten. Stella Musulin especially, who knew the Austrian Auden well and to whom Auden dedicated "Stark Bewölkt," has leveled strong charges of neglect. "Did young people go to see him," she inquired caustically in 1977, "in order to learn from this inspired teacher, who knew more about the form and technique of poetry in every culture and epoch than anyone else in our time? Did older poets go to visit him, who 'shared [his] love of the word' in order to utter 'over a golden Kremser many a long language on syntax, commas, and versification?' Those meetings did not take place—or not in the way that Auden would have liked, and, viewed from this perspective, his years in Austria consist of a chain of missed opportunities" (Musulin, "Zwei," 12, my translation). This charge is echoed in the program of the "W. H. Auden in Austria" exhibition held in the spring of 1978 in the Lower Austrian city of Wiener Neustadt, an exhibition sponsored by the Cultural Office of that city, by the International W. H. Auden Society, and by the Cultural Forum of the Province of Lower Austria. In one of the introductory statements published in the exhibition program, Dr. Franz Slawik, head of the Cultural Forum, alludes to Musulin's essay, and ruefully agrees that the Austrian literary world and Auden's world never really managed to intersect, hoping nevertheless that there might yet be a successful posthumous coming together on the occasion of this exhibition. "It is one of the seeming paradoxes of the spirit," writes Slawik, "that there should be places to make up for missed meetings, even if only posthumously" (Slawik, [2], my translation).

The review of this exhibition, published in Vienna's (and Austria's) leading daily newspaper, *Die Presse*, also engages in some prominent chest-beating. Beneath the accompanying unflattering photograph of a turtlenecked, open-mouthed, bewrinkled and bedraggled Auden about to inhale a cigarette (and looking a little like a neglected turtle himself), there is the following rubric: "The Anglo-American poet W. H. Auden lived pretty much unnoticed in Lower Austria. Now there is an official attempt to remember him." The opening paragraph is heavily ironic: "Though Auden received regular visits from a few faithful friends, nevertheless the public agencies responsible for poets took little account of this metic during his lifetime, probably mindful of the principle that true greatness will reveal itself unassisted sooner or later anyway. By that time of course the true greats are, alas, mostly dead."[13]

One wonders whether all this guilt is really justified. Auden was undoubtedly, as we have seen, interested in the Austrian literary world, but his preference was, though in a sense different from Slawik's, for posthumous encounters rather than live ones. Rilke, Kafka, Kraus, Weinheber, even Brecht (who held Austrian citizenship for most of his postwar years) were regular if not always friendly or well-received spiritual visitors in Kirchstetten. That none or almost none of the younger generation of Austrian writers bothered to look up Auden is naturally unfortunate, but not really unusual in the context of Auden's minimal contact with the younger generation of British or American writers. Those younger Anglophone authors whom he did meet and liked, such as John Fuller or Andrew Motion, he met either through his habitual participation in the Poetry International Festival or through his "at homes" in a coffee shop during his tenure as Professor of Poetry at Oxford. For the rest his relations with the contemporary English-speaking literary world, both physical and spiritual, were confined to his own or to the immediately preceding generation. Significantly, the very curious *A Certain World*, a commonplace book (consisting, that is, of excerpts from his

reading) which in his foreword Auden claims to be "a sort of autobiography
... a map of my world" (but with no Freud, no Groddeck, no Eliot, no Marx
on this map), in this work there are only six passages by authors born in the
1920s, two born in the 1930s, and one in the 1940s. Among all these the
only two well-known names are those of Michael Hamburger and Andrei
Voznesensky. This bears out, in his own person at least, Auden's claim that
"a poet over thirty may still be a voracious reader, but it is unlikely that
much of what he reads is modern poetry" (*Dyer's*, 9). In fact, the only books
of poems by poets of younger generations that he reviewed after the onset of
middle age were Philip Larkin's, Geoffrey Hill's, and Chester Kallman's.
What is more, to the absence of contemporary poetry, one has to add the
absence of contemporary fiction (a single exception: Muriel Spark), the absence of contemporary drama, and the absence of contemporary criticism.
The Auden of the 1920s and even 1930s who impressed everyone whom he
met as being absolutely up-to-date, did keep on being up-to-date, but only
with the writers of the 1920s and the 1930s, though an honorable exception
should be made for his service on the editorial board of the Yale Series of
Younger Poets from 1947 to 1958. Perhaps this apparently deliberate restriction of his interest to the past or to his own coevals is a function of what he
recognized as his besetting fault, the failure to grow up, a permanently adolescent egotism.

In any event, it is apparent that the Austrians need not take their neglect
of Auden during his lifetime too much to heart; and besides, they have made
up for it amply since. In addition to the collection that appeared just before
his death, *Gedichte/Poems* (1973), there is a further collection, published
exactly ten years later, bearing the name *Poems/Kirchstettner Gedichte:
1958–1973*.[14] Like the previous collection, it is bilingual, but it differs in
seeking to present a full translation of the poems of a coherent period—those
written in Kirchstetten after 1958—and translated by a single person, Johannes W. Paul. The older collection, on the other hand, is something of a
mixed bag, with some of the translations having been published earlier in
the equivalent of little magazines (mostly in Germany), though the majority
of the translations was specially commissioned. Nevertheless, according to
the brief afterword by Wolfgang Kraus, the selection of the poems was made
in "close collaboration" between Auden and the translators, and the German
texts were also checked and authorized by Auden himself (Auden, *Gedichte*,
220). (More on this point later.) Paul's translations, of course, lack any such
authorization, though they may enjoy a kind of posthumous blessing, since
according to the introduction by Peter Müller and Karlheinz Roschitz, just
before his death, Auden was considering a thoroughly revised complete edi-

tion of the poems written in Kirchstetten and was hoping that this work would then be rendered into German by a single translator (Paul, 7).

It is difficult to estimate just how carefully Auden checked the translations in the 1973 collection. It is a little easier to speculate about whether Auden possessed the requisite linguistic and other means to do so. The mid-to-late Auden, as anyone who has even looked cursorily at his literary production must realize, was very much interested in the translation process, both theoretically and practically. The value of poetic translation is something he certainly ranked very highly. Reviewing an edition of Pound's translations in 1953, he claimed that whenever English poetry seemed to have come to an impasse (as it did in the early years of this century), "it was always translation that came to the rescue" (Auden, "Translation," 75).

How good was Auden's German? His spoken German was heavily accented, ungrammatical but intelligible, definitely good enough to use for effective communication in most ordinary situations. Jon Bradshaw, who visited him in 1971 for *The Observer*, claimed that "his German is excellent" but added a little snidely that "his English is roughly inflected" (Bradshaw, 36). Cornelia Jacobsen, who interviewed him in 1965 in Berlin while he was staying there on a Ford Foundation Grant, also judged Auden's spoken German to be very good, but could not say the same for his knowledge of contemporary German literature (Jacobsen, 20). Another German interviewer, Horst Bienek, claimed that Auden spoke "a somewhat cumbersome but nevertheless lovable German. As soon as you grow accustomed to his melody [intonation], you can easily follow what he is saying; indeed, his phrasing is characterized by a charm that goes with the personality of a man of experience, a great writer" (Berg, Bienek, 9 September 1965). Golo Mann, however, provides him with his most impressive testimonial when he observes that Auden "grasped every nuance of the language," being able to understand fully, for example, the Viennese dialect jokes of Qualtinger's famous cabaret impersonation of Herr Karl (G. Mann, 9). Auden himself was more modest. Writing to James Stern in October 1959 about translating Brecht, he tells him that his "practice is to read the original first for its meaning (my German is much better now) and then put the original out of my head and re-create" (Willett, 172).

Auden's parenthetical comment, of course, is chiefly concerned with written German, not spoken. It also suggests, given the fact that Auden had spent only two summers in Austria when he wrote it, that his reading and speaking knowledge of German probably got better in succeeding years. Hence, though the German quotations in his poems are not always grammatically faultless—they sometimes possess, as Johannes W. Paul puts it diplomatically, those "small, so very charming mistakes that a foreigner makes"—

Auden nevertheless had a more than sufficient command of the language to be able to evaluate translations of his own work into it.

Did he really do so, as Kraus claims? Perhaps he did, for on an earlier occasion when he was confronted with poor translations of his work into German, he had tried to do something about it. Writing to Elisabeth Mayer in October 1962, he told her about a German translation of "Caliban to the Audience" read by a professional actor in the prestigious Burgtheater, along with some other translations of unspecified poems: "The actor from the Burgtheater read about ten pages of the Caliban magnificently—you know how difficult it is. The other translations—O dear—I had never looked at them carefully before. I managed to correct some of the worst howlers, but I don't understand why people attempt translating poetry—it earns them no money—who obviously are incapable" (Berg). Despite this cautionary experience, there is some evidence to suggest that Auden did not bother to check these translations "carefully" beforehand either. For example, in the translation of "In Praise of Limestone" by Herta Staub (done, apparently, specifically for the collection), the lines "And not to be pacified by a clever line / Or a good lay . . ." (CP, 414) are translated as "Und auch nicht zu befriedigen mit klugen Grenzen/ Oder genussreichem Lager . . ." (Auden, *Gedichte*, 79), which re-translated into English reads "And not to be pacified either by clever frontiers / Or a pleasurable place of rest. . . ." The remainder of the translation is actually pretty good, despite these very striking howlers. It is possible, of course, that Auden, as he was skimming the translation, simply failed to notice anything amiss: possible but unlikely. In a 1970 interview with Roy Perrott—not an excessively long time before he got to look at the German translation of "In Praise of Limestone"—he remarked, referring most likely to the same passage: "And—ha!—there was that French version which turned my line 'a good lay' into 'un bon poème' " (Perrott, 25). Having been thus alerted to a translator's potential unawareness of colloquial meanings of the word "lay," as well as to potential insensitivity to rapidly shifting levels of diction (one of Auden's favorite poetic techniques), he would presumably have turned to these lines above all if he been going over the poems with any care.

Though just about all of the German/Austrian versions of Auden's poems in this collection are competent, the best ones are those by the Austrians or Austrians-in-exile Erich Fried, Ernst Jandl, and Hilde Spiel. Jandl's versions of "Roman Wall Blues" and "As I Walked Out One Evening" are especially good, even if in the former poem he fails to find a German equivalent for the eye/sky rhyme in the final couplet, and in the latter loses Auden's ballad meter (in the fifth stanza) and uses imaginatively inferior images: for example, "Vaguely life leaks away" becomes "Wird das Leben in Nebel verstreut" or, literally, "life is strewn into fog" (Auden, *Gedichte*, 25, 27). His translation of the Yeats elegy (alas, the revised version) is extraordinarily fine, with only one doubtful spot: the "executives" of section 2 of the poem become *die Exekutive* or the "police" (Auden, *Gedichte*, 37). Erich Fried's version of "The Managers" is also virtually a complete success, with only a slight loss of humor when he turns Auden's wonderfully whimsical "umbrella of cherubs" into a plain old *Ehrengeleit* or "guard of honor" (Auden, *Gedichte*, 53). Hilde Spiel's translation of "Goodbye to the Mezzogiorno" is very fine, but she blunders comically in "Under Sirius" when she renders "Or the wind of the Comforter's wing" (referring to Death) as *Oder deine Bettdecke so heftig schwinge*, that is, "Or your bedding swing so violently" (Auden, *Gedichte*, 57).

Translations, of course, are never perfect, especially poetic translations. As a translator of poetry himself, Auden knew that very well, and whether or not he ever became aware of some of the weaknesses of the 1973 German versions of his poems, he nevertheless had good reason to be grateful for their overall strengths and for their occasional remarkable successes. The same must be said of Johannes W. Paul's more recent translations, limited entirely to the poems written after 1957—in other words, to the so-called Kirchstetten poems. Not all of these poems, of course, have close or even remote connections to Kirchstetten or even to Austria generally, but the assumption underlying the title is that they were all written in Kirchstetten. This assumption is almost certainly mistaken, but it does contain a suggestive and important truth. Namely, to judge by the (admittedly speculative and often incomplete) dates given by Edward Mendelson in the *Collected Poems*, most of Auden's poetical composition does in fact seem to have taken place during his stays in Kirchstetten. For Auden New York, then, meant chiefly prose; Kirchstetten, poetry.

Without entirely sharing their sentiments, one can understand the Austrians' desire to focus on that part of Auden's work that, however tenuously, can be associated with his life in Austria. Hence, it should not be surprising to discover Auden's *Poems 1958–1973* becoming identical with Auden's *Kirchstettner Gedichte 1958–1973*, or that even the earlier *Poems/Gedichte* should be heavily biased in favor of the post-1957 Auden. There is, after all, also the *English Auden* (1927–1939), consisting of poems by a poet whose permanent departure for the United States at the end of the thirties meant, as we have seen, for numerous British critics the beginning of the end of a promising poetical career. And there is, as I have tried to show in an earlier chapter of this book, a self-conceived (and sometimes also self-deceived) American Auden. Literary chauvinism, it should hardly need repeating, is no monopoly of Austrian translators and Austrian cultural ministries.

In his interesting afterword to his translation of the Kirchstetten poems, Johannes W. Paul sees the main difficulty in bringing Auden's work successfully across into German as consisting in an inescapable choice between rendering his form or his substance. Convinced that the one must be sacrificed to the other, Paul very consciously has chosen to sacrifice substance to form, justifying his choice with the claim that the previous translators had already chosen the other alternative (Paul, 356–57). Whatever one may think of Paul's reasoning, the lines he draws are at least very clear.

Too clear, in fact. For if he were merely interested in rendering the form, he could just as well have left the poems in the English original or have filled in the various forms with a content of appropriate, meaningless sounds. This is obviously not what he has done. Though he does not say so, what he actually means, then, is that whenever he perceives a conflict between the meaning of a poem and its formal qualities, he has altered the meaning, if in doing so he can manage to preserve the formal qualities. A careful examination of Paul's versions shows that there are relatively few such conflicts, and that on the whole, he has been quite successful in translating both form and content. Which is not to say that occasionally there are not problems with the content plain and simple, but these are problems, generally speaking, that do not arise out of implacable conflicts with form.

Put bluntly, the problem sometimes seems to arise, as in the earlier set of translations, from a failure to understand the poetry. Paul's translation of the last two lines of the opening stanza of "The Sabbath," for example, is simply wrong. Instead of having the "most fastidious nostril among" the animals notice that "that fellow" (man) is no longer there, Paul has that fellow with the most fastidious nose seem suddenly to have vanished (Paul, 23). There is a similar, though more comic, misunderstanding in his version of "Thanksgiving for a Habitat." Where Auden tells us that

> city planners are mistaken: a pen
> for a rational animal
> is no fitting habitat for Adam's
> sovereign clone. . . .

(CP, 520)

Paul translates "pen" as *Feder*, meaning "pen" as writing instrument rather than as a structure for keeping animals in confinement (Paul, 47). And in "The Cave of Making" the "Hindu integers" (or arithmetical numbers), which alone speak truthfully to stomachs, become Hindu ascetics ("Hinduasketen") who alone speak successfully to stomachs (Paul, 53).

Sometimes the problem derives from not recognizing a literary allusion:

thus the translation of the academic graffito about Rider Haggard loses its point by failing to hint that "SHE" is a character in Haggard's fiction (Paul, 33). Even where Paul has apparently conformed to the supposed necessity for choosing form over content, the effect is more like letting out air from a balloon rather than admiring the formal beauties of what is left of the balloon. Auden's clerihew about Bridges runs as follows:

> Said Robert Bridges,
> When badly bitten by midges:
> "They're only doing their duty
> As a testament to my beauty."
>
> (CP, 511)

Paul translates this into:

> Sprach Robert Brücken
> arg zerstochen von Mücken:
> 'Sie ziehen deshalb ihre Runden,
> um meine Schönheit zu bekunden.'
>
> (Paul, 31)

Granted, there are very few Austrians who would know who Robert Bridges is or that he was once famous for having written a long poem called *The Testament of Beauty*; but is such ignorance sufficient cause for creating a meaningless figure named Robert Brücken (a word signifying "bridges" in German) simply in order to find a rhyme word for *Mücken* (midges), or to delete all the literary (and academic!) flavor of the poem by making Brücken into a merely crude egotist? For someone named Oskar Wild such narcissism might have made sense, but not for an utter nonentity like Robert Brücken. In Paul's translation, not only the content but also the whole humorous point of the enterprise has been sacrificed to a rigid insistence on form. That this need not always be the case, however, is borne out in several triumphantly successful translations like the clerihew on Thomas Acquinas, which is easily as good as Auden's original (Paul, 29).

In the end, perhaps, the main conclusion to be drawn from this transformation of Anglo-American Auden into Austrian Auden is that inevitably there will and must be changes and adjustments as Auden shifts (and is shifted) from one national/cultural identity to another. Auden understood the truth and necessity of this process very well. He describes it happening almost prophetically in one of the most famous and powerful poems he ever wrote, "In Memory of W. B. Yeats:"

> Now he is scattered among a hundred cities
> And wholly given over to unfamiliar affections;
> To find his happiness in another kind of wood
> And be punished under a foreign code of conscience.
> The words of a dead man
> Are modified in the guts of living.
>
> (EA, 242)

Like Yeats, Auden has now become his admirers, including his Austrian admirers, and the words of this great dead poet will continue to be modified in the guts (and, one hopes, also in the minds) of the living in Austria and everywhere else.

Appendix: Auden in Austria: Two Interviews

I. Mr. Peter Müller, president of the Austrian Auden Society. The meeting took place on Tuesday, 13 March 1990, from 10 A.M. to about 11:30 A.M., in the Press Bureau of the Office of National Monuments, located in the Schweizerhof of the Imperial Palace in Vienna.

P. M. is easy-going and self-confident, about forty-five, of medium height, sporting a brown beard, cut short, and ditto hair. He is dressed in a fairly informal manner, though not so much as to offend the conservative antiquarians whom he no doubt usually has to deal with in his capacity as director of the Press Bureau of the Austrian Office of National Monuments. There is an air of the artist about him; hence, it's not surprising to learn that he writes himself, though apparently not "creatively." At the moment, he's doing a coffee-table book on the Empress Elizabeth's travels, for which he's found some new/old pictures. Obviously, he's pretty active, able, and respected. Various calls came in while we talked, which he kindly put off. Also once an odd, overfed, overalled man came in, and P. M. had him look at a book with photos (as above, I think), for duplication.

He told me that he first met Auden on the train to Kirchstetten, where he himself lived then—or perhaps only in the environs. Auden was alone in the train compartment, surrounded by papers, some of which were also strewn on the floor. They gradually drifted into conversation—P. M. was only in *Mittelschule* then (about the equivalent of 9th grade), but he had heard of Auden already, and had even read something of his. Auden invited him to come by for a visit, and he did. Thereafter he returned often, though he assured me he was never amatorily involved. He observed wryly how previous interviewers had hedged about trying to find out this bit of spicy information. Auden was very schoolmasterly in his attitude towards him, telling him he must get to know or read this or that book; P. M. remembers especially Auden's urging him to find out about Wittgenstein, which he was later grateful for. He had long discussions with him about the Austrian poet Joseph Weinheber, whom P. M. feels Auden took to largely because of his fellow feeling for Kirchstetten. Auden felt strongly and genuinely moved by the villagers' respect for him as well as for the place of honor that he had in village and church activities and ceremonies. He always occupied the honorific *Or*-

gelsitz (organ seat) in the top, back part of the church during services. From this lofty abode of honor, Auden would habitually bellow forth the songs during Mass, mostly off-key. Once, a replacement came for Pfarrer Lustkandl and, hearing Auden's very vocal accompaniment, turned around in amazement to look at whoever was making all the noise. P. M. added that he was familiar with local church gossip because he had formerly been an altar boy to Pfarrer Lustkandl, the village priest whom Auden mentions in one of his Kirchstetten poems.

Auden actually was much more nervous when he had to give the annual dinner for the village dignitaries than he ever was for any world-famous visitor. P. M. observed that Stella Musulin has written amusingly about this aspect of Auden's life in Kirchstetten. Without his strong emotional ties to the village, Auden might very well have left Austria when he got into tax difficulties with the Austrian Government, difficulties from which then Chancellor Kreisky only partly rescued him. He was certainly tempted to leave, so P. M. remembers Auden telling him. Speaking of money matters, P. M. remarked that Auden tended to be something of a tightwad, especially with little things like cigarettes. But he did incur big expenses with Kallman and the latter's numerous pals and parasites.

When Auden first came to Kirchstetten, the locals thought he came with his own cook, that is, Chester Kallman. At that time, the house was surrounded by a great deal of land, all of which was later parceled up and sold by Kallman, though a plot was given to the church. P. M. and the Austrian *Auden Gesellschaft* (Auden Society), he says, have been instrumental in saving the house, which since 1988 has enjoyed special status as a national monument. At the moment, the Lower Austrian Provincial Museum is paying for the repairs to the roof next to what used to be Auden's study, and this part of the building will be kept separate from the rest of the house as the actual Auden museum. There, Auden's inventoried belongings will be on exhibit. The remaining rooms are in the hands of Frau Strobl's son, who had wanted to sell the whole house at first but changed his mind when he met a woman who liked the place, and they decided to remodel it. Otherwise, the Auden Society would have bought it with contributions amounting to 1,500,000 Austrian shillings (about $150,000 in 1990).

The conversation then returned to the locals' mistaking Chester Kallman for Auden's cook. They were very much impressed by Auden's bringing along his own servant and thought Auden must obviously be an aristocrat. Later on, there was much disillusionment and consternation when they discovered through the notorious Hugerl scandal that Auden was homosexual. Thereafter, they viewed him askance and even laughed at him behind his back, though the upper crust of the village pretended nothing was amiss.

Pfarrer Lustkandl, however, was in fact rather taken aback. All this blew over, however, when an Austrian TV crew came out from Vienna not long thereafter to make a film of Auden's life in Kirchstetten. The whole community suddenly became immensely proud of their fellow citizen Auden, so that his sexual sins were forgiven. He was an artist, after all, and artists were known to sometimes behave oddly. Nowadays Auden's books are bought by locals and displayed on their bookshelves, though they can scarcely read a word of English. On All Hallows' Eve, his grave is overflowing with flowers. Last year, the Auden Society could hardly find room for their annual wreath. The Austrian Auden Society, by the way, apparently consists of no more than two members: P. M. and Karlheinz Roschitz, his coeditor. There is no need for more members, P. M. says, since he already has too many other things to do.

Auden was an absolutely terrible driver. Towards the end of his life, he had his housekeeper, Frau Strobl, get her license so that she could drive him places. His daily round in Kirchstetten followed a strict routine. He always went alternately to one of the three *Gasthäuser* "inns" in the village, so as to be fair to all of them. He often went to the opera in Vienna, though he rarely drove. When he did drive, it was only with Kallman. He got his tickets for the opera through the office in the *Opernpassage*. He would write to them with instructions and then pick the tickets up himself. He had no telephone, so he was always writing lots of letters, but mostly they were one-liners. The only "real" correspondence, he thinks, was with Stella Musulin, who also kept an eye on his house while he was away. She was the person he trusted most.

P. M. told me that sometime around 1970 he arranged for Auden to give a talk in Neulenkbach, a small town near Kirchstetten, in connection with a meeting of contemporary Austrian poets of which he himself was the organizer. Auden agreed but then asked for a fee of $1000, which, so P. M. told him, was several times the amount he had budgeted for the whole meeting. Auden then thought this over and said that he wanted a fee of 1000 schillings, at that time about $50. So Auden could be generous, but in his own typically eccentric way. P. M.'s impression is that Auden spent, or rather wasted, a great deal of money on Chester Kallman and his hangers-on, and that this contributed to his constant worries about money.

Auden had little contact with the Austrian literary scene, though he would have liked to have had more. When P. M. brought Austrian poets by to meet and talk with him, however, Auden would often turn uncharacteristically shy. Auden's German was actually quite good, easily intelligible once you got used to it; he could and often did carry on long conversations on complicated subjects without ever seeming to tire. Kallman's knowledge of German, on the other hand, was rudimentary.

II. Meeting with Stella Musulin at Schloss Friedau in Ober Grafendorf, Lower Austria (about 10km southwest of the city of Sankt Pölten. 28 March 1990. 4–6 P.M.) The meeting was facilitated by Peter Müller, though Brigitte Reiffenstein, Librarian of the English Institute at the University of Vienna, also suggested that I should try to interview her.

S. M. is about seventy-five, frail though still alert. She speaks slowly, and thinks about what she is going to say beforehand. This is not necessarily something caused by age or illness, although it is evident that she suffers from Parkinson's disease. We spoke in English—S. M. is British—but her German is fluent and virtually without accent, as I know from talking to her on the telephone. She is cared for by a young woman, perhaps Rumanian, who also speaks some English. She told us that she also has a Rumanian refugee doctor living on the premises, who looks after her. She lives alone in a set of rooms off to one side of the house, though her nephews and their families also live in other parts of the buildings. We (my wife, Evelyn, a native Austrian, also came along) were invited for tea at 4 P.M., arriving slightly late because we had difficulty finding a place at which to buy flowers on the outskirts of Sankt Pölten. It was a lovely spring day, with leftover wetness from the morning rains. Schloss Friedau is an architecturally undistinguished edifice that dates, from the looks of it, for the most part from the early nineteenth century, about 1830, I'd say. There are some older buildings to the side of it, which are the only ones that are inhabited; these were originally the servants' quarters and stables, etc. Off to one side is the *Orangerie*, probably dating from the eighteenth century; it too looks disused and in a sad state of disrepair. The lived-in parts have been fixed up and modernized to varying degrees and the surrounding grounds are at least kept mowed, though that's about all. In the park there are a few old trees, some with limbs lopped, standing around looking lost.

The buildings are visible from the highway passing by in front, just as you reach the turnoff for Ober Grafendorf. The situation was probably pleasant in former times, though now some new residential buildings of an average sort partly obscure the view and wholly damage the impression of the place. Here and there one catches glimpses of oddments of discolored statuary as one drives in under the branches of the trees lining the boulevard. Altogether, the numerous buildings seem to have been placed in arbitrary relations to each other. According to S. M., the Schloss itself was last inhabited in 1955 (or shortly before), by the Russian occupiers; they had used it since the end of the war, or rather abused it. S. M. told of her mother-in-law going out to the commanding Russian officer, offering him as much timber as he wanted, if only he and his men would refrain from breaking off beams and other supporting structural elements for use as firewood. The Schloss itself is now the property of the Lower Austrian Provincial Government. Nothing seems to have been done to it or for it, except for the bricking up of an occasional window. The structure is probably sound, however.

We conversed in English, as being the language most appropriate to talking about Auden. I asked her about how she got to know Auden. Through the daughter of Hofmannsthal, she said, who knew him (how, was not mentioned). She wrote him and went over for tea. Later—perhaps a few days later—Auden called her and asked for her help in giving a tea party for some of the Kirchstetten locals, including Pfarrer Lustkandl and a schoolmistress. All went well. This was sometime in the early 1960s. Thereafter, they soon became close friends; she would often stop by to see Auden on her way to Vienna or on the way back. She lived mainly in Vienna then. Often she would only stop for a cup of tea, or to return some books that Auden had lent her, or to bring him something or other from Vienna that he couldn't get locally. She also has various Auden clippings and correspondence with Auden, mostly written from New York but also from Berlin, when Auden was there on a fellowship in 1964. She offered to let me look at these at some future date.

I asked her about her published remarks about the supposed neglect of Auden by Austrian writers, and I also asked where exactly she had originally published those remarks. She said that the "official" Austrian literary establishment had done right by him, namely the *Österreichische Gesellschaft für Literatur* (Austrian Society for Literature), which had regularly arranged and paid for talks and readings. He was also awarded the *Staatspreis*, the most prestigious Austrian literary prize. But the Austrian writers themselves had not, on the whole, responded with equal enthusiasm. S. M. knew Thomas Bernhard personally, and had once asked him if he would like to meet Auden. Bernhard had told her, no, he wouldn't. She mentioned various other examples. The only real success he had with a contemporary Austrian literary figure was his meeting with Friedrich Heer, then in charge of the artistic management of the Burgtheater. Auden got on famously with him. I asked about Auden's knowledge of contemporary Austrian literature. According to S. M., his knowledge was minimal, possibly nonexistent, though he possessed a very considerable familiarity with the German classics. He also had a strong interest in seeing them well translated. At one point he planned, together with S. M., on approaching the Ford Foundation with a proposal to look over the existing translations of the German classics in order to see whether they were still usable; those that weren't would then be translated anew by well-known Anglo-American literary figures. Nothing came of the idea, however, beyond a list of names on the back of an envelope.

How much was Auden's work or status known to people in his immediate surroundings? Mostly, not at all. S. M. told a story about Auden's being taken to the hospital in Sankt Pölten after his car accident and she calling to find out how he was. She was told that there was no one there by the name of Auden and no one knew of any famous poet being treated there. [It occurred to me later that Auden might have been registered under "Wystan," since the Austrian hospital staff might not have been sufficiently familiar with English usage to be able to distinguish between first and last names. But that, too, would of course testify to local unawareness of Auden's fame.] S. M. also recounted an anecdote about a young man who spent a whole evening at Auden's table in a Vienna café and to whom she then gave a lift home. In the car he then asked her: "Who *is* Professor Auden?"

Did this situation seem to bother Auden in any way? Not at all, so S. M. replied. The only thing Auden really minded was pretense. Mostly Auden would try to be kind to people and not seek to overawe them. When her teenage son, for example, asked him one day what the point of poetry was, he humbly tried to explain. She does not feel that Auden was lonely while living in Kirchstetten. When they met they mostly *blödelten* "kidded around"; they never commented on his poetry except to say that she liked it when Auden would send her a poem, as happened when he sent her the Weinheber elegy from Berlin.

When I mentioned Golo Mann's comment that Auden "understood every nuance" of German, she agreed, though she added that he made many mistakes in grammar and pronunciation in conversation. With people who understood English, he would sometimes speak English while they replied in German, as he did with Heer, for example. He did very little reading of Austrian papers or even German papers, and in that sense, wasn't really living in the German-speaking world.

During the last years of his life, he was badly shaken by tax problems. Auden was misadvised by his accountant and lawyer about his tax liability as an Austrian resident. He then had to spend "all his savings" in order to pay the taxes that were due, the total of which was, however, halved at the intercession of Kreisky (to something like 500,000 shillings or close to $25,000). This is an episode she is writing about in her piece for *Auden Studies 2*; there she quotes from or transcribes a letter Auden wrote to the tax authorities, a letter she found in his house after his death and after other papers had been removed. Apparently, the tax people had claimed that Auden was liable because he had been inspired by the Austrian landscape to write his poetry.

S. M., so it turns out, has actually published very little about Auden, chiefly an essay—perhaps a shortened version of her 50-minute Austrian radio talk, delivered during winter 75/76—published in *Der Morgen*. She also spoke publicly about Auden in English to PEN in London on 26 June 1976, and a couple of days later, repeated the same talk in German to the Austrian Institute in London. During the eighties, she was commissioned by the Niederösterreichische Verlag (Lower Austrian Provincial Publishers) to write a piece on Auden for some unnamed bilingual publication, which she did. However, due to lack of funds, this never appeared, athough she was paid for her contribution.

Notes

1. For an account of Larchfield Academy in Auden's day (including its then impoverished state), see Smith, "Loyalty," 61.
2. Contrasting his approach to writing with the "realistic" one of Christopher Isherwood, Auden in 1935 referred to himself as a "parabolic writer" (Jenkins, "Eleven," 64).
3. Auden makes the same point in his 1966 interview with Stanley Kunitz (Kunitz, 95).
4. Auden's public censure of Spender was subsequently published in the *Kenyon Review*, 26, 1 (winter 1964), 190–91; 204–8.
5. In "Squares and Oblongs" (1948), Auden repudiates what he had said earlier (and would say again later) about the didactic and therapeutic functions of poetry.

Chapter 1: Crossing Frontiers

1. According to Walter Allen, Isherwood's early fiction, except for the *Berlin Stories*, may be thought of "as equivalents in fiction of Auden's early verse" (Allen, 234).
2. For surveys of the thriller fiction of the period, see Richard Usborne, *Clubland Heroes* (1953); Patrick Howarth, *Play Up and Play the Game* (1973); and LeRoy Panek, *The Special Branch: The British Spy Novel, 1890–1980* (1981). The classic general treatment of this type of fiction is George Orwell's "Boys' Weeklies" (1939).
3. Sidney Poger suggests that the armbands may serve the purpose of setting off "political and racial identities; the Nazis wore armbands to set them off from the general public, and they would soon require the Jews to wear yellow armbands to identify themselves." This suggestion fails to take into account that Communists also wore armbands, and that their purpose was not so much to distinguish themselves from other people as to assert their group solidarity and to prevent mistaken identification during street brawls and other political situations. As for the armbands worn by Jews during the Nazi regime, at the time Auden wrote his revised stage directions, this was still several years in the future and therefore has no direct relevance to *Paid on Both Sides* (Poger, 25).
4. There are, to be sure, other possible meanings and derivations of these names. So, near the beginning of Anthony Collett's *The Changing Face of England* (one of the young Auden's favorite books), it is said of the sandbank called the Nore that "it is simply the estuarine antitype of Noar Hill, near Selborne, and other Nores or *Nowers* elsewhere" (Collett, 6, my italics). As for "Shaw," it is derived from an Old English word signifying a small copse or wood.
5. The fact that Red Shaw is killed while in the process of "begetting" (and while also

apparently still "unforgetting") is clearly relevant here. Anne's final remark to John before he is shot resonates in this context: "But what has become of the dead? They forget" (EA, 15).

6. Weighing the pros and cons of the theory that a naturally heterosexual Auden had been made and kept homosexual first by Isherwood and later by Chester Kallman, Stephen Spender concludes that this theory is probably wrong. To be sure, he points out that "it was Christopher who persuaded him to break off the engagement" with Sheilah Richardson, but he later minimizes the importance of that act, by recounting Auden's conviction that "he regarded changing his sexual disposition as a matter of will—something which he would be able to make himself do—a self-imposed cure—of which he was capable" (Spender, *Journals*, 366).

7. For a description of Auden's 1929 Journal, see Luke, 103.

8. Though it seems obvious that Auden's preoccupation with frontiers and spies at this time bears an immediate relation to his life in Berlin, Stephen Spender argues instead that the "images of barriers, impassable frontiers, broken bridges" in his early poems "seem to express his feeling of personal isolation, but in impersonal guise" (*DNB*, 24).

9. Katherine Bucknell, in her thoughtful analysis of the poem, does not identify Layard with this particular friend but rather with the solitary, weeping figure whom the speaker encounters at the outset of the poem. Her reason for doing so is an entry in Auden's 1929 Journal in which he refers to seeing Layard looking "awful, like an embryo chicken" after visiting him in the hospital. Layard was at this time recovering from his suicide attempt. Bucknell does not, however, consider the possibility that Auden may have used the image in the poem before, rather than after, applying it to Layard (Bucknell, 196). Nor does she recognize the importance of the Berlin background to an understanding of the poem.

10. Writing to Spender in the spring of 1940, Auden told him that "my dominant faculties are intellect and intuition, my weak ones feeling and sensation. This means I have to approach life via the former; I must have knowledge and a great deal of it before I can feel anything" (Jenkins, "Eleven," 72).

11. These lines could serve as an epigraph to *Paid on Both Sides*, and were probably written at about the same time Auden was composing the lullaby/elegy recited by Joan in the play.

12. Stephen Spender knew Curtius well enough to recommend his friend, William Plomer, to his attention in May 1930 (Alexander, 167).

13. The "dragon's day" may allude, as Joost Daalder points out, to Yeats's "Now days are dragon-ridden" from one of the poems about the Irish Time of Troubles, "Nineteen Hundred and Nineteen." Auden may have intended to suggest that a more widespread civil conflict, or rather revolution, was in the offing (Daalder, 334).

14. He does, however, refer to Auden playing "his old boyhood game of spies and counterspies" in the uncollected poem, "Interview," which Auden published in 1933 (Beach, *Making*, 116).

15. Beach's idea of obsessive images may owe something to Delmore Schwartz's 1939 essay about the "Two Audens," one of whom was "the clever guy, the Noel Coward of literary Marxism," and the other, "a kind of Sybil who utters telltale symbols in a psychoanalytic trance." Auden as Sybil was fascinated by "a romantic set of symbols, which continually recur and which are used at very important moments of the poem." These symbols consist primarily of islands, mountains, frontiers, water, birds, and stones (Schwartz, "Two," 34–38).

16. In this respect, Auden's spies differ markedly from most of the thriller fiction of the period where the enemy is usually portrayed as a foreigner.

17. Despite its high spirits, *The Dance of Death* was definitely not what the old Auden claimed it had been, namely a "nihilist leg-pull" (Miller, 82).

18. A similar passage is preserved in a later manuscript version of the play, reproduced in the textual notes provided by Edward Mendelson (*Plays*, 540–41).

19. The old Auden, however, no longer approved of the high spirits (and political outlook) that the young Auden had expressed in *The Dance of Death*. In 1957, he wrote on the title page of his friend A. H. Campbell's copy: "This is rubbish" (Campbell, in conversation with the author, 1 January 1974).

20. How the idea of becoming a "unit" in a civilian army would have been understood by Auden and Isherwood's audience is clarified by Arthur Koestler's account of the difference that belonging to the Communist Party made to his life. Unlike other intellectuals with whom he worked in Berlin in the early thirties, "only two of us were members of the C. P.—[Alfred] Kantorowicz, who was a free-lance contributor to several Ullstein papers and myself; and we were the only ones who punctually attended the meetings of the caucus, who took the matter seriously and knew what we were about. *We were disciplined members of a civilian army* acting under instructions; the others were free agents, divided and confused, as intellectuals always are in matters of practical action . . ." (Koestler, *Invisible*, 46, my italics).

21. Here, Francis receives treatment at the hands of a madwoman reminiscent of the youth's unpleasant "welcome" home provided by the lunatic giantess (Britain) in the "Prologue" to *The Orators*.

22. However, the idea that human psychology could be represented effectively in quasi-allegorical ways also struck other thirties intellectuals like C. S. Lewis, who persuasively elaborates this perception for medieval texts in *The Allegory of Love* (1936).

23. Eliot Weinberger, "James Jesus Angleton 1917–1987," in *Outside Stories, 1987–91* (New York: New Directions, 1992), 51–52.

24. At least since Joseph Warren Beach's *The Making of the Auden Canon* (1956), Auden's revisions, excisions, and omissions have been the subject of heated discussion. Auden himself claimed that he had undertaken to revise his poems for aesthetic reasons only, and for many years this view was strongly endorsed by his friends, especially Stephen Spender. In 1978, however, Spender explicitly admitted that "Auden's rejection of his Thirties' past is shown most specifically in his censoring his work which contains Marxist ideology . . ." (Spender, *Thirties*, 234). Though always outwardly deferential, Spender's relationship with Auden was not without its inner tensions. So, what he says in his introductory discussion of the changes he made (or declined to make) when he collected his own poems in 1955, has a clear but unavowed bearing on Auden's very different practice in his *Collected Poetry* ten years earlier. At that time, Auden had notoriously not only ordered his poems alphabetically instead of chronologically, but had ruthlessly omitted and/or revised all or parts of some of his best-known poems. Spender, on the other hand, claimed that in collecting his poems, his aim was "to make as many improvements as possible, without 'cheating.' The awareness of the danger of 'cheating' implies a consciousness of obligations: obligations to the reader, and, more important, obligations to remain true to the felt experiences from which the poems, when they were first written, arose." Spender also implies, though he does not say so, that Auden "cheated" by not meeting similar obligations to his readers, including the obligation, in Spender's words, to adhere to "the order in which the poems were written . . . and not to alter drastically those poems which are, I think, fairly well known: poems which, partly just because I feel they are known, seem to have passed out of my hands beyond recall" (Spender, *Collected*, xv–xvi).

Chapter 2: The Group

1. Day-Lewis wrote similar stuff in more public contexts, as he does in "The Magnetic Mountain:"

> Wystan, Rex, all of you that have not fled,
> This is our world, this is where we have grown
> Together in flesh and live . . .
>
> (Day-Lewis, *Collected*, 27)

By the mid- to late-Thirties, however, Day-Lewis seems to have drifted out of core "group" membership. Cyril Connolly, for example, who claimed to have known the "whole group" mentions only Auden, Spender, Isherwood, and MacNeice (Sinfield, 202).

2. Cyril Connolly claims that, aside from the Auden group, there were also "other important groups—Evelyn Waugh, Elizabeth Bowen, the Powells, Henry Green, William Plomer, the Lehmanns, John and Penelope Betjeman, the international left-wing writers round *New Writing*, the poets round Geoffrey Grigson's *New Verse*. There was also the outsider George Orwell . . ." (Sinfield, 203).

3. In this connection, it is worth noting that Roberts was vice-president of the University Socialist Society while at Cambridge in the mid-twenties, and that, after graduating, he joined the Communist Party, only to be expelled after a few months for "deviationism" (Roberts, *Collected*, 21).

4. Auden published a favorable review of Caudwell's book in *New Verse*, 25 (1937), 20–22.

5. Spender, however, does recall that already at Oxford Auden, when pressed, would identify his political allegiance as "socialist" (Spender, *Thirties*, 16).

6. As Münzenberg's former lover and companion, Babette Gross, points out, "Münzenberg has been called the inventor of the 'fellow travellers,' those auxiliary troops of Communism which remain invaluable to the present day and which are recruited largely from the ranks of the intellectuals. Without being party members, they display active sympathy for Communism and give it moral support in public. Münzenberg did not invent them, they existed from the start. His achievement was to mobilize them on a scale hitherto unknown and to put them in the service of the Communists" (Gross, 216).

7. For a discussion of the "group" aspects of the Cambridge Spies, see Andrew Sinclair's *The Red and the Blue* (34–41).

8. Just how closely it follows certain features of Icelandic literature only became clear when Auden began working with Peter Salus on a translation of the *Edda* in 1966. Salus then discovered that the "Airman's Alphabet" is derived directly from the *Edda* or, more likely, from the translation of it made by Bruce Dickens that Auden had used while he was an undergraduate at Oxford. In that copy, Salus found penciled markings in Auden's hand referring to various runic poems as well as to the Old High German *Lay of Hildebrand* and the Old English *Deor*. On the back leaf there was "written what appears to be the first draft of the 'Airman's Alphabet' " (Salus, 145).

9. In the 1970s, Rickword remembered Auden's politics in the 1930s as being serious, sincere, and confused: "He was a bit left then, wasn't he? He went out to Spain, too, to give him his due. I think he was serious. He was very aware of the decadence of bourgeois society. He didn't really know what the alternative was, and neither did Spender or any of his friends" (Lucas, 7).

10. In the early summer of 1933, a concerned Spender wrote Auden about the ambiguous relation of *The Orators* to fascism, and Auden told him that he "entirely agree[d] with you about my tendency to National Socialism, and its dangers" (Jenkins, "Eleven," 62). Spender himself was to come under scrutiny for suspected Fascist sympathies in T. C. Worsley's semi-fictional account, *Fellow Travellers*. Speaking about Martin Murray's novels (i.e., Stephen Spender's poetry), Lady Nellie (probably Naomi Mitchison) says that they are thought to be

"crypto-Fascist. I don't think that's quite fair. But I see what they mean. It's that atavistic Liberalism, and will he ever get out of it?" (Worsley, 43). Worsley went to Spain with Spender early in 1937, and later that year he collaborated with Auden on a Marxizing pamphlet, *Education: To-Day—and Tomorrow* (1939), a title that distinctly evokes the refrain in "Spain."

11. There was also a precedent for D'Annunzio's aerial exploits, namely the 800,000 leaflets dropped on 10 July 1908 by Marinetti and his futurist cohorts from the clock tower in Venice, denouncing the "past-loving" inclinations of Venice's inhabitants and visitors.

12. Auden's admiration for T. E. Lawrence was, apparently, returned in full measure. According to Robert Graves, Lawrence spoke to Liddell Hart with "near-awe" of Auden's poetry (Graves, *T. E. Lawrence*, 160).

13. There is a remote possibility Auden may have known of Knebworth through Layard's connections with Homer Lane's disciples and admirers, of whom the Earl of Lytton was one.

14. Wyndham Lewis returned the compliment, at least as far as Auden was concerned: "I like what he does. He is all ice and woodenfaced acrobatics" (W. Lewis, *Blasting*, 304).

15. Stephen Spender, in conversation with the author, April 1975.

16. Auden may also be drawing on C. G. Jung's "On the Psychology of the Trickster Figure" here. In that work, Jung argues that the trickster figure is "so unconscious of himself that his body is not a unity, and his two hands fight each other" (Radin, 203).

17. According to Richard Aldington, T. E. Lawrence told Liddell Hart that "the Fascists had been after him, and he had replied that he would not help them to power, but if they gained it, he would agree to become 'dictator' of the press for a fortnight" (Aldington, 386).

18. My 1977 *PMLA* essay first pointed out the link between Layard's anthropological work and Auden's *The Orators*, a link that I uncovered by following up the published hints provided by Isherwood and Spender.

19. Given Auden's overt use of Dante's *Inferno* as one of the "schemes" for *The Orators*, it seems likely that he wanted his readers to bear in mind Dante's sympathetic comments about the "sodomite" Brunetto Latini (Dante, 193).

20. Stephen Spender seems to be alluding to this passage in *The Orators* when, in *The Temple*, he has Simon Wilmot (W. H. Auden) tell Paul Schoner (Stephen Spender) that he and his longtime lover are "only happy 10,000 feet above the earth. . . . You're both Heaven Reachers. That is why you are so tall. You want to get away from your balls" (Spender, *Temple*, 8). It is perhaps significant in this context that the first poem Spender prints in his *Collected Poems, 128–1985* is called "Icarus" and describes an "Airman" who is

> The aristocrat superb of all instinct.
> With death close-linked
> Had paced the enormous cloud, almost had won
> War on the sun;
> Till now, like Icarus mid-ocean-drowned,
> Hands, wings, are found.
>
> (Spender, *Collected, Poems*, 17)

Chapter 3: Poetry and Politics in a Low, Dishonest Decade

1. He did, however, reprint the poem again in 1938 in a Left Book Club anthology, for which he also wrote an introduction. There he claimed that "the primary function of poetry, as of all the arts, is to make us more aware of ourselves and the world around us" (Auden, Introduction, 9). In 1964 he allowed Skelton to republish the poem in an anthology of thirties

verse, despite his conviction, also expressed in 1964, that "[t]he most painful of all experiences to a poet is to find that a poem of his which he knows to be a forgery has pleased the public and got into the anthologies. For all he knows or cares, the poem may be quite good, but that is not the point; *he* should not have written it" (Auden, *Dyer's*, 18).

2. Auden may have had in mind here the so-called "Bolshie Chorus" sung to the tune of "Keep the Home Fires Burning," which was taught to pupils at the I.L.P. Training and Discussion School in the twenties:

> Wage the class war strict-ly
> Put the job through quick-ly
> Hang the rich on lamp-post high
> But don't hang me.
> Stick to Marx my heart-y
> *Damn* the Labour Part-y
> Keep the hell-fires burning bright
> For the bourg-eoi-sie.

(Paton, 285)

3. How liable even hard-nosed realists like George Orwell were to "romanticizing" the worker is evident from his description of the Italian volunteer at the beginning of *Homage to Catalonia*.

4. Edward Mendelson is surely mistaken when he argues that the speaker is "a Communist telling Auden what he needs to learn" (Mendelson, *Early*, 143). After all, whatever else Auden may have been at this time, he was not one of the working-class "comrades" pouring "from office, shop and factory" to the "roar of the sirens." Yet it is specifically this group whom the speaker is addressing at the beginning of the poem.

5. Liberalism continued to function as a bogey for Auden even long after his abandonment of Marxist social analysis. In a 1944 review of Lewis Mumford's *Condition of Man*, Auden argued that, while liberalism might be able to unmask "the vices of the Old Order," it was helpless against a New Order whose values were deliberately antiliberal. "What," Auden inquired ironically, "is little Bo-Peep, whose liberal Super-Ego, as Mr. Mumford would call it, is shocked by carniverous habits, to do when her very own sheep start behaving like wolves?" (Auden, "In," 595–96). A few years earlier, in 1939, he had stated quite unambiguously that "Liberal Democracy has failed, and failed completely" (*Prose*, 463).

6. It should be remembered that, to some degree, Auden had always opposed the confusion of rhetoric and poetry. *The Orators* shows how conscious he was of the dangers of rhetoric even in his early poetry. In the preface to the first of the two "group" anthologies, *New Signatures*, Michael Roberts says of the poem, "Sir, no man's enemy . . . ," that, "by the use of half-rhymes," Auden manages to avoid "the heroics, the emotional overstatement, which might so easily have destroyed the sincerity" of this sonnet.

7. Unfortunately, this story, as Claude Guillot points out, is almost certainly a Cockburnian canard (Guillot, 98).

8. There is, however, an analogue in Cecil Day-Lewis's notion, as elaborated in his essay on "Writers and Morals," of the life force impelling the writer to assume a Communist position (Glicksberg, 317).

9. Spears omits Auden's concluding barb at Orwell: "It is rather comic that Orwell should have failed to see this since, at the time, he was himself a combatant, busy trying to murder [sic] Franco's soldiers" (Berg, 11 May 1963). In his 1971 review of Orwell's *Collected Essays*, Auden concluded that Orwell was astonishingly fair to other writers, with the notable exception of "the poets, including myself, who began to publish in the thirties." Auden re-

jects the notion that he was ever much of a political poet, for "aside from a few plays, very little of the poetry I wrote in that decade was overtly political: basically I have always thought of myself as a comic poet" (Auden, "Orwell," 87).

10. Similarly, as George Mills Harper points out, Stephen Spender did not hesitate in 1937 to advocate "deliberate violence" or the use of "ruthless force from which a new and juster order might emerge" (Harper, 70–71). Cyril Connolly, reviewing the poem in June 1937, felt no qualms at quoting the "necessary murder" stanza and finding it "very fine" (Connolly, "To-day," 926).

11. Edward Mendelson claims categorically that none of the changes Auden subsequently made in the poem "has anything to do with Orwell's objections"; instead, in his view "their purpose is to rid the poem of all traces of determined History" (Mendelson, *Early*, 320, 323). In *W. H. Auden: A Commentary*, John Fuller argues, however, that Auden made his revisions "in response to the *Adelphi* article," in which Orwell had already made much the same criticism of "Spain" as he did later in "Inside the Whale" (Fuller, *Commentary*, 286).

12. Auden occasionally, along with some of his friends—notably Stephen Spender—maintained that his revisions were aesthetically rather than politically motivated (Kunitz, 102). Still, as is clear from his admission in 1966, the changes he made to "Spain" were due to what he thought was its "dishonesty" rather than any supposedly artistic demerits: "A dishonest poem is one which expresses, no matter how well [i.e., from an aesthetic point of view], feelings or beliefs which its author never felt or entertained" (Auden, CSP, 15). Auden addresses the problem of the writer changing while his readers remain unchanged when, speaking of Goethe, he says that "[w]hat he wrote in order to exorcise certain feelings is enthusiastically welcomed by his contemporaries because it expresses just what they feel but, unlike him, they are perfectly happy to feel in this way; for the moment they regard him as their spokesman. Time passes. Having gotten the poison out of his system, the writer turns to his true interests which are not, and never were, those of his early admirers, who now pursue him with cries of 'Traitor!' " (Auden, *Dyer's*, 18–19).

13. As Edward T. Callan points out, Cecil Day-Lewis had introduced Auden to Yeats's late poetry while both were still at Oxford in the late twenties. However, aside from a few undergraduate imitations, according to Callan, Yeats exercised no real impact on Auden's thinking and writing until the late thirties. (Callan, "Auden," 298–99). According to Stephen Spender, however, the publication of *The Tower* in 1928 influenced Auden deeply, as, for example, in "I Chose This Lean Country" in *Poems* (1928). (Spender, "Influence," 34) F. R. Leavis also claims that several of the early published poems of Auden show Yeats's influence, and Howard Nemerov hears frequent but unspecified echoes of Yeats in Auden's poetry. (Leavis, 324; Nemerov, 131)

14. Also, as Auden no doubt knew, there is in *Egil's Saga* a skaldic poet named Auðun who "had been skald to Halfdan the Black, the father of Harald the King" (Eddison, 11). During his second visit to Iceland, Auden "half-jokingly" told the Icelandic writer, Sigurður A. Magnusson, that he was descended from "one of the original settlers of North Iceland, Auðun Bjarnason, the grandson of an English earl" (Magnusson, 176n).

15. It is odd that Auden never revised "Musée des Beaux Arts" to remove the "lie" of the opening line, as he so notoriously did with other poems written at approximately the same time, notably "In Memory of W. B. Yeats" and "September 1, 1939." Was it because he didn't think this particular "lie" was political in nature? Or was it because, unlike other lies, this one suited his new politics?

16. Rather predictably, Terry Eagleton complains that Auden here views suffering "not as especially symptomatic of such a social condition, but as an inevitable 'human position' . . ." (Eagleton, 180).

17. Max Bluestone argues that while Auden has Christ's crucifixion in mind when he refers to the "dreadful martyrdom," the specific reference is actually to Brueghel's painting, "The Massacre of the Innocents" (Bluestone, 333). If, however, my suggestion is correct that Auden is following Huxley's lead in this poem, then it seems more reasonable to suppose that Auden is primarily alluding to Brueghel's "Procession to Calvary." P. V. LePage, who does not consider Huxley in his discussion of the poem, also thinks "Procession to Calvary" a more likely model for Auden than "The Massacre of the Innocents." Of the latter painting, he says that "it does not portray a 'dreadful martyrdom;' it portrays a dreadful massacre" (LePage, 254 n).

18. According to Christoph Bode, Auden has misunderstood the moral significance of Brueghel's depiction of Icarus's fall. For Brueghel, Bode maintains, Icarus was a fool who got what was coming to him, whereas for Auden, Icarus is an emblem of human suffering. If, however, Auden "misunderstood" Brueghel's painting, he is in good company, including such commentators as Aldous Huxley, Lewis Namier and Charles de Tolnay (Bode 88–89).

19. There are, however, several dogs in the "Massacre of the Innocents," a copy of which is in Royal Museum in Brussels. According to P. V. LePage, the "Procession to Calvary" contains most of the elements mentioned in the first part of Auden's poem, including "a horse scratching its behind, an untidy spot with a great clutter of people, a corner for Calvary, dogs, a man chasing his hat, someone walking dully along, children playing, the family of Christ reverently, passionately waiting" (LePage, 254 n). After a careful search of the painting, however, I have been unable to discover any horse in it that is scratching its behind on a tree, nor are any of the dogs shown going about their doggy business in the sense apparently intended by Auden. Also, though Christ's family appears to be waiting reverently, they are hardly "passionately" awaiting Christ's death, nor are all of them "aged," for that matter. In this last respect, Auden's description fits "The Adoration of the Magi" better than it does "Procession to Calvary," since in the former, various old people are depicted as reverently and passionately awaiting their turn to see the Christ Child.

20. Auden may have known Frank Rutter's book, *The Old Masters* (1926), which surveys Italian, Flemish, Dutch, German, and Spanish painters from Cimabue to Rembrandt. Like Auden, Rutter also emphasizes "the human and historical interest of old pictures" and claims that "the emotional and intellectual history of Europe is writ large for those who will, in the works of the Old Masters" (Rutter, 16, 18).

21. Dannie Abse takes Jarrell's logic a step further in his poem, "Brueghel in Naples," by arguing that the painter—and, by implication, the poet—pay(s) heed to the "aesthetics of disaster" rather than to the disaster itself. William Carlos Williams, on the other hand, emphasizes in "Landscape with the Fall of Icarus" the burgeoning "pageantry" of springtime and the "sweating in the sun" that environs Icarus as he drowns "quite unnoticed" (Williams, *Pictures*, 4).

22. In the 1939 essay, "I Believe," Auden mentions Huxley's novel *Brave New World* (EA, 375), and in "Making, Knowing and Judging" Auden quotes a selection from Aldous Huxley's *Texts and Pretexts* (*Dyer*'s, 45). After reading Huxley's novel, *Eyeless in Gaza*, in 1936, Stephen Spender wrote Christopher Isherwood that he hoped "Wystan doesn't fall for it" (Spender, *Letters*, 120). That there was no great danger of this happening is evident from Auden's remark about Huxley's *After Many a Summer* (1939): "Huxley's new novel about Hearst is *awful*" (Quoted in Bell, "Change," 112). Huxley, on the other hand, thought well enough of Auden to consider collaborating with him (and Isherwood) on a dramatic version of Lawrence's *Lady Chatterley's Lover*; and it was chiefly due to Huxley's intervention that Stravinsky asked Auden to write the libretto for *The Rake's Progress* (Huxley, *Letters*, 456, 636).

23. The opening chapter of Eugene Fromentin's *Masters of Past Time*, entitled "The Gallery at Brussels," points out that it is "above all a Flemish Gallery" (Fromentin, 7). This fact may help account for Auden's insistence in the poem that all "Old Masters" depict suffering in the way that Brueghel does, an assertion that holds true only to the extent that genre painting was more of a tradition in Flanders and the Netherlands than elsewhere.

Chapter 4: The American Auden

1. Not long after his arrival, Auden told the *New York Times* that he was planning to write a book about America and was looking for a job in a private school so as to gather the requisite experience for it. Though the job soon materialized, the book didn't (Carpenter, 254). The two friends did manage, however, to compose a scenario for a film that was to be called *The Life of an American*. And, together with another friend, Benjamin Britten, Auden coauthored the opera *Paul Bunyan*, which is still occasionally performed. Critics of the first production found that "the American story showed too many English traces of tone and content" and that the character of Paul Bunyan himself was reminiscent of an "idealized schoolmaster" (*Libretti*, xvii–xix).

2. Isherwood's lover Heinz was forced to return to Nazi Germany (Isherwood, *Christopher*, 276–87); and Spender's lover, "Jimmy Younger," was nearly shot as a deserter in the Spanish Civil War (Spender, *World*, 128 ff).

3. Richard Davenport-Hines misunderstands U.S. citizenship regulations when he implies that Auden deliberately retained British citizenship until 1946. According to naturalization laws then in force in the United States, applicants for citizenship needed, among other things, to prove continuous residence in the United States for five years prior to qualifying for citizenship.

4. Isherwood also eventually became an American citizen but he never stressed his "Americanness" in the way that Auden did, perhaps because of his commitment to pacifism and to what at the time must have seemed a very atypically American Buddhism. One needs to recall in this connection also that Auden never became as much a member of a "British Enclave" in New York as Isherwood, initially at least, did in Los Angeles. Auden's attachment to Kallman immediately provided him with a new circle of American friends and acquaintances, as did his stints of teaching at the University of Michigan and Swarthmore College. Moreover, Auden was lucky in choosing to come to the United States when he did, for despite their prevailing isolationism, the late thirties were a period when Americans were largely pro-British, no doubt partly because of the common fear of the Fascist threat in Europe and of Japanese aggression in the Pacific. Symbolic of this sense of shared identity, for example, is the fact that two of the principal "Southerners" in that most American of cinematic epics, *Gone with the Wind*, were in fact British: Vivien Leigh and Leslie Howard. Other British movie stars of the time who passed as Americans include Elizabeth Taylor, Erroll Flynn, and Cary Grant.

5. That Auden chose Robinson to begin his anthology with is significant in light of Isherwood's remark that Robinson was the subject of one of Auden's first "crazes" as a beginning poet; another was Emily Dickinson. According to Isherwood, both "left plenty of temporary damage but few lasting traces" (Isherwood, *Exhumations*, 22).

6. In a more muted fashion and restricting himself to the decade of the Forties, Frederick McDowell anticipates Fiedler when he remarks that "[t]he keeping alive of the poetic impulse may have been the result of a transplantation to a new environment in the early 1940's. In

America Auden renewed the powers which had been exhausted in the England of the 1930's . . ." (McDowell, 254–55).

7. There is also a chapter on "The American Auden" in G. T. Wright's book on Auden (127–34), but it does not deal with the ways in which Auden's poetry may be usefully thought of as "American." Peter Conrad's chapter on "Theological America: W. H. Auden in New York" asserts that Auden came to America, not to be an American but to be an "alien," someone lacking a national "identity" (Conrad, 194–235).

8. The comparison of American Auden with English Eliot was one that often occurred to contemporaries. So, in 1967, Robert Lowell remarked that "last winter, John Crowe Ransom said to me that we had made an even exchange, when we lost Eliot to England, and later gained Auden. Both poets have been kind to the lands of their exile, and brought gifts the natives could never have conceived of" (Lowell, 41).

9. According to Peter Conrad, during this first postwar visit to Britain, Auden "caused universal offense by complaining how cold English houses were and ridiculing the penury of a rationed existence. Most outrageously of all, he contended that London hadn't been seriously damaged by bombing." As for his failed stay at his Oxford college in 1972, "he scandalized the sanctimonious diners at High Table in Christ Church by asking when they started masturbating or whether they peed in their bathroom sinks" (Conrad, 215).

10. Even as late as 1951, Auden returned, in "Fleet Visit," to this theme of American superficiality, when he implicitly contrasted the American sailors, whose interest is limited to comic books and baseball, with the Greeks who once disembarked on the shores of Troy. Significantly, however, in this poem, the machines—the American ships lying offshore in the "vehement blue"—are now viewed positively, as "structures" which are "humane," both in terms of their abstract beauty and by virtue of the protection they provide for Greeks and Americans alike (CP, 420–21).

11. That Auden was very much taken by the views expressed in this essay may be seen from the fact that he published and republished them in five different places: first in 1955 in the *Anchor Review* under the title, "The Anglo-American Difference," later republished under the same name in Lewis Leary's *American Literary Essays* (1960). Then again in 1956 as the introduction to both the *Faber Book of Modern American Verse* and the *Criterion Book of Modern American Verse*. Its most familiar locus, however, is *The Dyer's Hand* (1962), where it appears under the rubric of "American Poetry."

Reviewing the *Criterion* anthology for the *Sewanee Review* in 1957, Reed Whittemore was put off by what he thought was Auden's brushing aside actual poets and poems in favor of misguided thesis mongering about what really constituted the Americanness of American poetry (Whittemore, 146, 151).

12. While reading parts of the poem out loud to each other shortly after its publication in 1947, Allen Ginsberg remarked to John Hollander that "Dirge" must be about Roosevelt (Hollander, 508). Edward Mendelson, however, claims that the poem has nothing whatever to do with Roosevelt, being solely "a parody and refutation of Jungian mythographies of the kind popularized by Joseph Campbell" (*Later*, 252).

13. See my discussion of the role of Whitman in European conceptions of American cultural identity in Firchow, "Americanness," 62–63.

14. While "Billy Budd" clearly fits the argument of the poem, insofar as it describes the daily conflict of good and evil (Billy and Claggart), it does not really fit the poem's implied chronology of Melville's life. On the face of it, if "Billy Budd" is in fact being referred to here, then, returning from his travels, it took Melville nearly fifty years to sit down at his desk to write "Billy Budd." Bearing this lengthy delay in mind, it would seem more logical for a

novel like *Typee* (1846) to be the "story" that Melville sat down to write. Nevertheless, virtually all Melville critics unhesitatingly accept the identification with "Billy Budd."

15. Alfred Corn points out that Auden's second arrival in the United States coincided with his entering into his thirty-third year, so that "the Christological associations certainly [were] not lost on him as he adjusted to new circumstances" (Corn, 236). Here again the theme of rebirth is struck.

16. To be sure, as Lawrence Lipking points out, Auden "was not at home in raw towns," but it may be that Auden, who had just arrived from Europe, thought of New York as a "raw town" (Lipking, 157). Edward Callan provides an elaborate Jungian reading of this passage in which "south" represents goodness and "north" evil (Callan, 151). Given Auden's traditional fondness for northern places (e.g., Iceland), this seems unlikely.

17. It's unclear whether Merrill was aware that Auden had left behind in Oxford the journal he kept during the latter part of his stay in Berlin in 1929. According to Auden's friend, David Luke, who found the journal in the former's Oxford apartment a few days after his death, much of it is "intimately autobiographical" (Luke, 103).

18. In the "Letter to Lord Byron" Auden, to be sure, did establish—and publish—a correspondence with a dead poet, though he gives no indication of ever having received a reply.

19. Nor does Katherine Bucknell acknowledge it in her recent edition of Auden's *Juvenilia*, though she shows in some detail how pervasive it was for the young Auden in her 1987 Columbia dissertation (188–89, 240). Auden himself shows an awareness of her existence, if not of her work, in the fourth ode of *The Orators*, when he refers to "Robert and Laura spooning in Spain" (EA, 105).

20. Auden echoes Frost's poem in the closing lines of "Vespers" (1954): "For without a cement of blood (it must be human, it must be innocent) no secular wall will safely stand."

21. In a 1940 interview with Benjamin Appel, Auden also remarks that "American literature is one extraordinary literature of lonely people" (Apel, 5).

Chapter 5: The Sage of Kirchstetten

1. Peter Conrad uses climate to contrast Auden and Isherwood's respective places of residence in the United States: "Auden remained in New York, while Isherwood traveled west to California. The city's grim regularity suited Auden the moralist and mock-theologian, who detested the solar optimism of California. . . . Auden's preferred landscapes were mountainous and rainy, Isherwood's glaringly sunny and sandy." Conrad even goes so far as to asssert that "Auden's New York was a man-made version of the Alps" (Conrad, 222).

2. Auden apparently never read Kafka in German. In an unpublished letter to Margaret Church, dating from late 1941, he remarks that "the influence of Kafka is almost entirely due to Edwin Muir's brilliant translations."

3. Volker Klöpsch faults M. K. Spears for supposedly inventing the genre of the "Rilkean sonnet," since, as Walter Mönch pointed out in 1954, "none of the Orpheus sonnets is a sonnet in the classical sense." It seems pretty clear, however, that if anyone (other than Rilke, that is) is to blame for the concept of the "Rilkean sonnet," it is Demetz rather than Spears. Besides, as Spears explicitly notes, "the Rilkean sonnet" is a "sonnet or the recognizable equivalent (often highly irregular in form)" (Spears, 25).

4. Without actually claiming influence, Stephen Spender sees several distinct parallels between "The Journal of an Airman" and Rilke's novel, *Malte Laurids Brigge* (Spender, *Destructive*, 264–67).

5. According to Vilas Sarang, the highest percentage of definite articles in Auden's poetry actually occurs in his volume, *Look, Stranger!* (1936), which predates the period when he fell under Rilke's influence. Sarang suggests (but without actually claiming) that Auden's above-average use of the definite article at this time may relate to his reliance on Freudian and Marxist thought. Certainly, it indicates an abstract, dogmatic outlook that is, in fact, characteristic of this phase in Auden's work. As for the absence of the definite article in Auden's early poetry, Sarang has noted that the poem "Doom is Dark" is 160 words long and has no definite articles in it at all, whereas the second part of "1929" has only one definite article in its 378 words. Presumably, this is linked to what other critics have called the "pidgin English" aspect of Auden's early poetry (Sarang, 78–79, 83). According to David Trotter, the proportion of definite articles in Auden's poetry declined dramatically when he left Europe in 1939 (and, along with it, his hitherto primary subject, namely politics) for America and supposed apoliticism. What's more, he supposedly revised his earlier work with an eye towards "erasing wherever possible the definite articles" (Trotter, 134).

6. Auden was not only unaware of the link between Kirchstetten and Weinheber when he bought his house there, but apparently had not even heard of Weinheber's existence. After a year's stay, however, the latter's works found an "honored" place on Auden's shelves (Hitzenberger, 5–6).

7. Well-known expressions of this distinction occur in Oswald Spengler's *Untergang des Abendlandes* and Thomas Mann's *Betrachtungen eines Unpolitischen*.

8. See also Auden's letter to the the Austrian tax authorities, along with Stella Musulin's essay on Auden's life in Kirchstetten (Musulin, "Auden," 207–34).

9. At the time Auden bought the property, the exchange rate was 25 Austrian schillings for $1 U.S.

10. Though Auden was fond of the people who worked for him and always tried to ensure their welfare, he evidently retained a deeply feudal sense of his position in Kirchstetten. So, writing to his nephew Giles in December 1957, he told him that his cat had "transferred his affections to Frau Eiermann who is one of our peasants" (Bodleian, MS. Eng. let. c. 590).

11. The film was made in a series called "Das Österreichische Porträt" ("Austrian Portraits") in 1967 (Seitz, 411).

12. These are, in the order printed and with the dates given in CP: "Et in Arcadia Ego" (1964); "Ascension Day, 1964" (1964); "Whitsunday in Kirchstetten" (1962); "Three Posthumous Poems" (1964–67); "Josef Weinheber" (1965); "Elegy" (1968); "Lines to Walter Birk" (1970); "Prologue at Sixty" (1967); "Stark Bewölkt" (1971); "Talking to Dogs" (1970); "Talking to Mice" (1971); and "Talking to Myself" (1971).

13. David Axmann, "Heimatrecht und Einkehr in Kirchstetten," *Die Presse* (12 April 1978), 14. My translation.

14. There is also a less comprehensive selection, based largely on the first, entitled *Anrufung Ariels*.

Bibliography

The following abbreviations have been used in the text to refer to collections of Auden's manuscripts: Berg = Berg Collection of English and American Literature, The New York Public Library, Astor, Lenox and Tilden Foundations; Bodleian = Bodleian Library, The University of Oxford (UK); and HRC = Harry Ransom Humanities Research Center, The University of Texas at Austin. Abbreviations referring to Auden's published work are: CP = *Collected Poetry*. New York: Random, 1945; CSP = *Collected Shorter Poems, 1927–1957.* London: Faber & Faber, 1966; CB = *The Criterion Book of Modern American Verse.* New York: Criterion Books, 1956; EA = *The English Auden: Poems, Essays, and Dramatic Writings.* Edited by Edward Mendelson. London: Faber & Faber, 1977.

Aldington, Richard. *Lawrence of Arabia.* London: Collins, 1955.

Alighieri, Dante. *Inferno.* Translated by John D. Sinclair. New York: Oxford University Press, 1977.

Allen, Walter. *Tradition and Dream: The English and American Novel from the Twenties to Our Time.* London: Phoenix, 1964.

André, Michael. "A Talk with W. H. Auden." *Unmuzzled Ox,* I (summer 1972): 5–12.

Ansen, Alan. "From the *Table Talk* of W. H. Auden." *Ontario Review* 30 (spring–summer 1989): 7–18.

———. *The Table Talk of W. H. Auden.* Edited by Nicholas Jenkins. Princeton: Ontario Review Press, 1990.

Appel, Benjamin. "The Exiled Writers." *The Saturday Review of Literature* 22 (19 October 1940): 5.

Arendt, Hannah. "Remembering Wystan H. Auden." In *W. H. Auden: A Tribute.* Edited by Stephen Spender. London: Weidenfeld & Nicholson, 1975.

Arpino, Giovanni and Piero Bianconi. *La Obra Pictórica de Brueghel.* Translated by Francisco J. Alcántara. Barcelona: Planeta, 1988.

Atlas, James. *Delmore Schwartz: The Life of an American Poet.* New York: Farrar, Straus, Giroux, 1977.

"Auden in Kirchstetten." *South Atlantic Quarterly* 75 (winter 1976), 8–19.

Auden, W. H. *Anrufung Ariels: Ausgewählte Gedichte.* Translated by Erich Fried. München/Zürich: Piper, 1987.

———."As It Seemed to Us." *The New Yorker* 41 (3 April 1965): 159–92.

———. *Collected Poetry.* New York: Random, 1945. [Abbreviated CP]

———. *Collected Shorter Poems, 1927–1957.* London: Faber & Faber, 1966. [Abbreviated CSP]

———, ed. *The Criterion Book of Modern American Verse*. New York: Criterion Books, 1956. [Abbreviated CB]

———. *The Dyer's Hand*. New York: Vintage, 1968. [Abbreviated as DH]

———. *The Enchaféd Flood, or the Romantic Iconography of the Sea*. London: Faber & Faber, 1951.

———. *The English Auden: Poems, Essays, and Dramatic Writings*. Edited by Edward Mendelson. London: Faber & Faber, 1977. [Abbreviated EA]

———. *Gedichte/Poems*. Wien: Europa Verlag, 1973.

———. "Going into Europe." *Encounter* 20 (January 1963): 53–64.

———. "The Group Movement and the Middle Classes." In *Oxford and the Groups*. Oxford: Blackwell, 1934.

———. "In Poor Shape." *Sewanee Review* 52 (autumn 1944): 593–97.

———. Introduction to *Poems of Freedom*. Edited by John Mulgan. Left Book Club Edition. London: Gollancz, 1938.

———. *Juvenilia: Poems, 1922–1928*. Edited by Katherine Bucknell. Princeton: Princeton University Press, 1993.

———. *Look Stranger!* London: Faber & Faber, 1935.

———. *Letters from Iceland*. London: Faber & Faber, 1937.

———. *New Year Letter*. London: Faber & Faber, 1946.

———. "An Open Letter to Knut Hamsun." *Common Sense* 9 (August 1940): 22–23.

———. *The Orators*. London: Faber & Faber, 1966.

———. "Orwell, *Collected Essays, Journalism, and Letters*." *The Spectator* (16 January 1971): 86–7.

———. *Poems/Kirchstettner Gedichte: 1958–1973*. Translated by Johannes W. Paul. St. Pölten/Wien: Niederösterreichisches Pressehaus, 1983.

———. "Poet in Wartime." *The New Republic* 103 (8 July 1940): 59–60.

———. *The Prolific and the Devourer*. Hopewell, N. J.: Ecco Press, 1981.

———. *Prose*. Volume I: 1926–1938. Edited by Edward Mendelson. Princeton: Princeton University Press, 1996.

———. "Rilke in English." *The New Republic* 100 (6 September 1939): 135–36.

———. "A Saint-Simon for Our Time." *New York Review of Books* 31 (August 1972): 4–6.

———. "T. E. Lawrence." *Now and Then* 47 (spring 1934): 30, 33. Reprinted in *Then and Now*. London: Jonathan Cape, 1935.

———. "Translation and Tradition." *Encounter* I (December 1953): 75–76, 78.

———. "The Wandering Jew." *The New Republic* 104 (10 February 1941): 185–86.

———. "Yeats: Master of Diction." *Saturday Review of Literature* 22 (8 June 1940): 14.

——— and Christopher Isherwood. *Journey to a War*. New York: Paragon House, 1990.

——— and Christopher Isherwood. *Plays and Other Dramatic Writings, 1928–1938*. Edited by Edward Mendelson. Princeton: Princeton University Press, [1988].

——— and Chester Kallman, *Libretti*. Edited by Edward Mendelson. London: Faber & Faber, 1993.

——— and N. H. Pearson, eds. *Victorian and Edwardian Poets: Tennyson to Yeats*. Harmondsworth: Penguin, 1978.

Authors Take Sides on the Spanish War. London: Left Review, 1937.

Axmann, David. "Heimatrecht und Einkehr in Kirchstetten." *Die Presse* (12 April 1978): 14

Bahlke, George W. *The Later Auden.* New Brunswick: Rutgers University Press, 1970.

———. "Lawrence and Auden: The Pilgrim and the Citizen." In *D. H. Lawrence's Literary Inheritors,* ed. Keith Cushmans and Dennis Jackson. New York: St. Martin's Press, 1991.

Barzun, Jacques. "Meditations on the Literature of Spying." *The American Scholar* 34 (spring 1965): 167–78.

Bassett, R. *Nineteen Thirty One, Political Crisis.* London: Macmillan, 1958.

Bateson, F. W. "Auden's Last Poems." *Essays in Criticism,* 25 (July 1975): 383–90.

Baudelaire, Charles. *Intimate Journals.* Translated by Christopher Isherwood. Introduction by W. H. Auden. London: Methuen, 1949.

Bayley, John. *The Romantic Survival: A Study in Poetic Evolution.* London: Constable, 1957.

Bazeley, E. T. *Homer Lane amid the Little Commonwealth.* New York: Schocken, 1969.

Beach, Joseph Warren. *The Making of the Auden Canon.* Minneapolis: University of Minnesota Press, 1957.

———. *Obsessive Images: Symbolism in the Poetry of the 1930's and 1940's.* Edited by William Van O'Connor. Minneapolis: University of Minnesota Press, 1960.

Bell, Julian. "The Proletariat and Poetry: An Open Letter to C. Day Lewis." In *Essays, Poems and Letters.* Edited by Quentin Bell. London: Hogarth, 1938.

Bell, Kathleen. "Nancy Spender's Recollections of Wystan Auden." *W. H. Auden Society Newsletter* 10–11 (September 1993): 1–3.

Bell, Kathleen, ed. "A Change of Heart: Six Letters from Auden to Professor and Mrs. E. R. Dodds at the Beginnning of World War II." In *W. H. Auden: 'The Map of All My Youth.'* Edited by Katherine Bucknell and Nicholas Jenkins. Oxford: Oxford University Press, 1990.

Benda, Julian. *The Treason of the Intellectuals.* Translated by Richard Aldington. New York: Morrow, 1928.

Bentley, Eric. *The Brecht Memoir.* London: Carcanet, 1989.

Berg Collection of the New York Public Library.

Bergonzi, Bernard. *The Myth of Modernism and Twentieth Century Literature.* New York: St. Martin's Press, 1986.

Berryman, John. *Collected Poems, 1937–1971.* Edited by Charles Thornbury. New York: Farrar, Straus, Giroux, 1989.

Bishop, Elizabeth. "A Brief Reminiscence and a Brief Tribute." *Harvard Advocate* 108: 47–48.

Blair, John G. *The Poetic Art of W. H. Auden.* Princeton: Princeton University Press, 1965.

Bleuler, E[ugen]. *Lehrbuch der Psychiatrie.* 5. Auflage. Berlin: Springer, 1930.

Bleuler, Eugen. *Textbook of Psychiatry.* Translated by A. A. Brill. New York: Macmillan, 1924. (1916)

Bluestone, Max. "The Iconographic Sources of Auden's 'Musée des Beaux Arts.'" *Modern Language Notes* 76 (April 1961): 331–36.

Blythe, Ronald, *The Age of Illusion: England in the Twenties and Thirties, 1919–1940.* London: Hamish Hamilton, 1963.

Bloomfield, B. C. and Edward Mendelson. *W. H. Auden: A Bibliography, 1924–1969*. Second edition. Charlottesville: University Press of Virginia, 1972.

Bode, Christoph. "Audens leidender Icarus: ein symptomatisches Missverständnis." *Germanisch-Romanische Monatsschrift* 33 (1983): 81–93.

Bogan, Louise. *Achievement in American Poetry, 1900–1950*. Chicago: Henry Regnery Company, 1951.

Borkenau, Franz. *The Spanish Cockpit*. London: Faber & Faber, 1937.

Boyle, Andrew. *The Climate of Treason*. London: Coronet, 1980.

Bradshaw, Jon. "W. H. Auden and His Graffiti," *The Observer Magazine* (7 November 1971): 35–45.

Brecht, Bertolt. *Poems*. Edited by John Willett and Ralph Manheim. London: Eyre Methuen, 1979.

———. "Der Flug der Lindberghs (Radiolehrstück für Knaben und Mädchen)." Berlin: Gustav Kiepenheuer Verlag, 1930.

Bucknell, Katherine C. "W. H. Auden: The Growth of a Poet's Mind (1922–1933)." Ph.D. diss., Columbia University, 1987.

Buell, Frederick. *W. H. Auden as a Social Poet*. Ithaca: Cornell University Press, 1973.

Bunting, Basil. "English Poetry Today." *Poetry* (Chicago), 39 (February 1932), 264–71.

Burton, P. H. "Difficult Poetry." *The Listener* 63 (5 May 1960): 787–88.

Callan, Edward. *Auden: A Carnival of Intellect*. New York: Oxford University Press, 1983.

———. "Auden and W. B. Yeats: From Singing Master to Ogre." *Commonweal* 104 (13 May 1977): 298–303.

Carpenter, Humphrey. *W. H. Auden: A Biography*. Boston: Houghton Mifflin, 1981.

———. *The Brideshead Generation: Evelyn Waugh and His Friends*. London: Weidenfeld & Nicolson, 1989.

———. "The Making of the Auden Biography." In *W. H. Auden, 1907–1973. Ergebnisse eines Symposions*. Edited by Michael O'Sullivan. Vienna: Niederösterreichische Gesellschaft für Kunst und Kultur, 1988.

Carritt, Gabriel. "A Friend of the Family." In *W. H. Auden: A Tribute*. Edited by Stephen Spender. London: Weidenfeld & Nicholson, 1975.

Carter, Ronald, ed. *Thirties Poets: 'The Auden Group.'* London: Macmillan, 1984.

Caserio, Robert L. "Auden's New Citzenship." *Raritan* 17 (fall 1997): 90–103.

Caudwell, Christopher. *Illusion and Reality: A Study of the Sources of Poetry*. 1937 Reprint. New York: International Publishers, 1963.

Charney, Maurice. "Sir Louis Namier and Auden's 'Musée des Beaux Arts.' " 39 (January 1960): 129–31.

Charques, R. D. *Contemporary Literature and Society*. London: Martin Secker, [1933].

Churchill, R. C. "The Age of T. S. Eliot." In George Sampson, *The Concise Cambridge History of English Literature*. Second Edition. Cambridge: University Press, 1965.

Cockburn, Claud. *I, Claud. . . .* Harmondsworth: Penguin, 1967.

———. "A Conversation with Claud Cockburn." *The Review*. 11–12 (1964): 51–53.

Collett, Anthony. *The Changing Face of England*. London: Nisbet & Co., 1927. (1926)

Connolly, Cyril. *Enemies of Promise*. London: Routledge, 1938.

———. "To-day the Struggle." *New Statesman*, 13 (5 June 1937): 926, 928.

Conrad, Peter. *Imagining America*. New York: Oxford University Press, 1980.

Constantine, David. "The German Auden: Six Early Poems—Translated by David Constantine." In *W. H. Auden: The Map of All My Youth*. Edited by Katherine Bucknell and Nicholas Jenkins. Oxford: Oxford University Press, 1990.

Corn, Alfred. " 'For the Time Being:' A Relocation of the Poet." In *'In Solitude, for Company': W. H. Auden after 1940*. Auden Studies 3. Edited by Katherine Bucknell and Nicholas Jenkins. Oxford: Clarendon Press, 1996.

Cox, C. B. and A. E. Dyson, *Modern Poetry: Studies in Practical Criticism*. London: Edward Arnold, 1963.

Cowie, Alexander. *The Rise of the American Novel*. New York: American Book Company, 1948.

Craft, Robert. *Chronicle of a Friendship, 1948–1971*. New York: Knopf, 1972.

Crossman, Richard. "Remembering and Forgetting—W. H. Auden Talks to Richard Crossman about Poetry." *The Listener* 89 (2 February 1973): 238–40.

Cunningham, Valentine. *British Writers of the Thirties*. Oxford: Oxford University Press, 1988.

Daalder, Joost. "Yeats and Auden: Some Verbal Parallels." *Notes and Queries* 20 (September 1973): 334–36.

Daiches, David. *Poetry and the Modern World*. Chicago: University of Chicago Press, 1940.

Davenport-Hines, Richard. *Auden*. London: Heinemann, 1985.

David, Hugh. *Stephen Spender: A Portrait with Background*. London: Heinemann, 1992.

Davison, Dennis. *W. H. Auden*. London: Evans, 1970.

Day-Lewis, Cecil. *The Buried Day*. London: Chatto & Windus, 1960.

———. *Collected Poems, 1929–1936*. London: Hogarth Press, 1948.

———. *A Hope for Poetry*. Oxford: Blackwell, 1944.

———. "In Me Two Worlds." *New Oxford Outlook* 1, 2 (Nov. 1933): 187.

———. *A Time to Dance*. New York: Random House, 1936.

Demetz, Peter. "Englische Spiegelungen R. M. Rilkes." *Orbis Litterarum* 11 (1956): 18–30.

deTolnay, Charles. *Pierre Bruegel l'Ancien*. Texte. Brussels: Nouvelle Société d'Éditions, 1935.

Dictionary of National Biography, 1971–80. Oxford: Oxford University Press, 1986. [Abbreviated *DNB*]

Donoghue, Denis, ed. *Seven American Poets from MacLeish to Nemerov*. Minneapolis: University of Minnesota Press, 1974.

Duchêne, François. *The Case of the Helmeted Airman: A Study of W. H. Auden's Poetry*. London: Chatto & Windus, 1972.

Dunaway, David King. *Aldous Huxley Recollected: An Oral History*. New York: Carroll & Graf, 1995.

Dzenitis, Sigurds. *Die Rezeption deutscher Literatur in England durch Wystan Hugh Auden, Stephen Spender und Christopher Isherwood*. Hamburg: Hartmut Lüdtke Verlag, 1972.

Eagleton, Terry. *Exiles and Emigrés: Studies in Modern Literature*. New York: Schocken, 1970.

Eberhart, Richard. *Collected Poems, 1930–1986*. New York: Oxford University Press, 1988.

Eddison, E. R., trans. *Egil's Saga*. New York: Greenwood Press, 1968. (1930)

Eliot, T. S. "Preface" to *Anabasis: A Poem* by St.-Jean Perse. With a translation into English by T. S. Eliot. New York: Harcourt, Brace & Co., 1938. (1930)

———. *Selected Prose*, edited by Frank Kermode. New York: Harcourt Brace Jovanovich, 1975.

Ellmann, Richard. *Yeats: The Man and the Masks*. New York: Macmillan, 1948.

Empson, William. *Collected Poems*. New York: Harcourt, Brace & Co., [1956].

———. "Wartime Recollections." *Harvard Advocate*, 108 (1974): 31.

———. "Early Auden." *The Review* 5 (Feb. 1963): 32–34.

———. *Empson in Granta, 1927–29*. Tunbridge Wells: Foundling Press, n.d.

Fiedler, Leslie. *Waiting for the End: The American Literary Scene from Hemingway to Baldwin*. London: Jonathan Cape, 1965.

Finney, Brian. *Christopher Isherwood: A Critical Biography*. New York: Oxford University Press, 1979.

Firchow, Peter. *The Death of the German Cousin: Variations on a Literary Stereotype, 1890–1920*. Lewisburg: Bucknell University Press, 1986.

———. "The Americanness of the American Short Story." *Journal of the Short Story in English* 10 (spring 1988): 45–66.

FitzGibbon, Constantine. *The Life of Dylan Thomas*. Boston: Little, Brown & Co., 1965.

Ford, Hugh D. *A Poet's War: British Poets and the Spanish Civil War*. Philadelphia: University of Pennsylvania Press, 1965.

Foxall, Edgar. "The Politics of W. H. Auden." *The Bookman*, 85 (1934): 474–75.

Fraser, G. S. "Auden: The Composite Giant." *Shenandoah*, 15 (summer 1964): 46–59.

———. "The Young Prophet." *The New Statesman*, 51 (28 Jan. 1956): 102–3.

Freud, Sigmund. *A General Selection from the Works*. Edited by John Rickman. Garden City, New York: Doubleday, 1957.

Friedrich, Hugo. *Die Struktur der modernen Lyrik von Baudelaire bis zur Gegenwart*. Hamburg: Rowohlt, 1956.

Friedrich, Otto. *Before the Deluge: A Portrait of Berlin in the 1920's*. New York: Harper & Row, 1972.

Fromentin, Eugene. *The Masters of Past Time: Criticism on the Old Flemish and Dutch Painters*. London: J. M. Dent & Sons, 1913.

Frost, Robert. *Collected Poems, Prose, & Plays*. New York: Library of America, 1995.

Fucci, Franco. *Ali contro Mussolini: I raid aerei antifascisti degli anni trenta*. Milan: Mursia, 1978.

Fuller, John. "Early Auden: An Allegory of Love." *The Review* 11–12 (1964): 83–90.

———. *A Reader's Guide to W. H. Auden*. London: Thames & Hudson, 1970.

———. *W. H. Auden: A Commentary*. Princeton: Princeton University Press, 1998.

Furbank, P. N. *E. M. Forster: A Life*. San Diego: Harcourt, Brace & Co., 1981.

Fussell, Paul. *Abroad: British Literary Travelling Between the Wars*. Oxford: Oxford University Press, 1980.

Gardiner, Margaret. "Auden: A Memoir." *The New Review* 3 (July 1976): 9–19.

Glicksberg, Charles I. "Poetry and Marxism: Three English Poets Take Their Stand." *University of Toronto Quarterly* 6 (April 1937): 309–25.

Glück, Gustav, ed. *Das Grosse Bruegel-Werk.* Vienna: Anton Schroll, 1951.

Graves, Robert. www.bbc.co.uk./history/programmes, centurions, auden

———. *The Crowning Privilege.* London: Cassell & Co., 1955.

———. *T. E. Lawrence to His Biographer.* New York: Doubleday, Doran & Co., 1938.

Graves, Robert and Alan Hodge. *The Long Week End: A Social History of Great Britain, 1918–1939.* New York: Macmillan, 1941.

Green, Martin. *Children of the Sun: A Narrative of "Decadence" in England After 1918.* N.p.: Wideview, 1980. (1976)

Greene, Grahame, ed. *The Old School.* London: Jonathan Cape, 1934.

Gregory, Horace. "Review of *The Double Man.*" *The Sewanee Review* 52 (October–December, 1944): 580.

Grigson, Geoffrey. "Education in the Twenties," *New Verse* 29 (March 1938): 19.

———. "Mr. Spender's Book of Criticism." *New Verse* 15 (June 1935): 15–17.

———. "Notes on Contemporary Poetry." *Bookman* 82 (1932): 287–89.

Groddeck, Georg. *Das Buch vom Es.* München: Kindler Verlag, [1923]

———. *Psychoanalytische Schriften zur Psychosomatik.* Edited by Günter Clauser. Wiesbaden: Limes, 1966.

Gross, Babette. *Willi Münzenberg: A Political Biography.* Translated by Marian Jackson. East Lansing: Michigan State University Press, 1974.

Guillot, Claude. "W. H. Auden et la guerre d'Espagne." *Annales de l'Université de Toulouse-Le Mirail* 13 (1976): 95–111.

H. M. "Poetry of the Left." *Poetry* 48 (July 1936): 212–21.

Haffenden, John, ed. *W. H. Auden: The Critical Heritage.* London: Routledge & Kegan Paul, 1983.

Hahnloser-Ingold, Margrit. *Das englische Theater und Bert Brecht.* Bern: Francke Verlag, 1970.

Hallberg, Robert von. *American Poetry and Culture, 1945–1980.* Cambridge: Harvard University Press, 1985.

Hamilton, Gerald. *The Way It Was With Me.* London: Leslie Fravin, 1969.

Hamilton, Ian, ed. *The Oxford Companion to Twentieth Century Poetry.* Oxford: Oxford University Press, 1996.

Hampshire, Stuart. *Modern Writers.* London: Chatto & Windus, 1969.

Handley-Taylor, Geoffrey and Timothy d'Arch Smith. *C. Day Lewis, The Poet Laureate: A Bibliography.* Chicago: St. James Press, 1968.

Harper, George Mills. " 'Necessary Murder:' The Auden Circle and the Spanish Civil War." In *On Modern Poetry.* Edited by Vereen Bell and Laurence Lerner. Nashville: Vanderbilt University Press, 1988.

Häusermann, H. W. "Left-Wing Poetry: A Note." *English Studies* 21 (1939): 203–13.

Hecht, Anthony. *The Hidden Law: The Poetry of W. H. Auden.* Cambridge: Harvard University Press, 1993.

Hecht, Ben. *A Child of the Century.* New York: Simon & Schuster, 1954.

Henderson, Philip. *The Poet and Society.* London: Secker & Warburg, 1939.

———. *Literature and a Changing Civilization.* London: Lane, 1935.

Hitzenberger, Franz. "Amerikas bedeutendster Lyriker trat Weinhebers Nachfolge an." *Neues Österreich* (19 October 1958): 5–6.

Hoagland, Tony. *Donkey Gospel.* St. Paul: Graywolf Press, 1998.

Hoggart, Richard. *W. H. Auden. Writers and Their Work* 93. London: Longmans, 1957.

———. *Auden. An Introductory Essay.* London: Chatto & Windus, 1951.

Hollander, John. "W. H. Auden." *Yale Review* 77 (summer 1988): 501–11.

Holthusen, Hans Egon. "W. H. Auden 75 Jahre" *Neue Deutsche Hefte* 29 (1982): 212–17.

Homberger, Eric. *The Art of the Real: Poetry in England and America Since 1939.* London: Dent, 1977.

Hone, Joseph. *W. B. Yeats, 1865–1939.* New York: Macmillan, 1943.

Hope, Francis. "The Thirties." In *The Modern Poet. Essays from "The Review."* Edited by Ian Hamilton. London: MacDonald, 1968.

Hoskins, Katherine Bail. *Today the Struggle: Literature and Politics in England During the Spanish Civil War.* Austin: University of Texas Press, 1978.

Howard, Richard. *The Damages.* Middletown: Wesleyan University Press, 1967.

———. *Fellow Feelings.* New York: Atheneum, 1976.

Howarth, Herbert. *Notes on Some Figures Behind T. S. Eliot.* London: Chatto & Windus, 1965.

Huxley, Aldous. *Along the Road.* London: Chatto & Windus, 1948. (1925)

———. *Letters.* Edited by Grover Smith. London: Chatto & Windus, 1969.

———. *Music at Night.* London: Chatto & Windus, 1960. (1931)

Huxley, Julian, ed. *Aldous Huxley, 1894–1963: A Memorial Volume.* London: Chatto & Windus, 1965.

Hynes, Samuel. *The Auden Generation: Literature and Politics in England During the Spanish Civil War.* New York: Viking, 1977.

———. "The Voice of Exile: Auden in 1940" *Sewanee Review* 90 (winter 1982): 31–52.

Isherwood, Christopher. *The Berlin Stories.* New York: New Directions, 1963.

———. *Christopher and His Kind.* New York: Farrar, Straus, Giroux, 1977.

———. *The Condor and the Cows.* London: Methuen, 1949.

———. *Exhumations.* London: Methuen, 1966.

———."German Literature in England." *The New Republic* 98 (5 April 1939): 254–55.

———. "The Group Theatre." *The Cambridge Review* 59 (19 November 1937): 104.

———. *Kathleen and Frank.* New York: Simon & Schuster, 1971.

———. *Lions and Shadows: An Education in the Twenties.* New York: Pegasus, 1969.

———."Some Notes on Auden's Early Poetry." *New Verse* 26–27 (Nov. 1937): 4–5.

Jacks, L. P. "Groups and Their Ways." *New Oxford Outlook*, 1, 2 (Nov. 1933): 155–60.

Jacobsen, Cornelia. "Ein halbes Jahr zu Gast in Berlin." *Die Zeit* 20 (23 April 1965): 22.

Jarfe, Günter. *Der Junge Auden: Dichterische Verfahrensweisen und ihre Bedeutung in W. H. Audens Frühwerk.* Heidelberg: Carl Winter Verlag, 1985.

Jarrell, Randall. *The Complete Poems.* New York: Farrar, Starus & Giroux, 1969.

———. "Freud to Paul: The Stages of Auden's Ideology." *Partisan Review* 12 (1945): 437–57.

Jenkins, Nicholas. "Auden and Spain." In *W. H. Auden: The Map of All My Youth.* Edited by Katherine Bucknell and Nicholas Jenkins. Oxford: Oxford University Press, 1990.

———, ed. "Eleven Letters from W. H. Auden to Stephen Spender." In *W. H. Auden: The Map of All My Youth.* Edited by Katherine Bucknell and Nicholas Jenkins. Oxford: Oxford University Press, 1990.

Johnson, Samuel. *Johnson on Shakespeare.* Edited by Walter Raleigh. London: Oxford University Press, 1957.

Kinney, Arthur F. "Auden, Bruegel, and 'Musée des Beaux Arts.'" *College English* 24 (March 1963): 529–31.

Klöpsch, Volker. "Die Versuchung des Orpheus. Der Einfluss Rilkes auf das lyrische Werk von W. H. Auden." *Fu Jen Studies* 16 (1983): 77–109.

Koch, Stephen. *Double Lives: Spies and Writers in the Soviet War of Ideas Against the West.* New York: Free Press, 1984.

Koestler, Arthur. *The Invisible Writing.* Garden City, N.Y.: Doubleday, 1969.

Kracauer, Siegfried. *From Caligari to Hitler: A Psychological History of the German Film.* Princeton: Princeton University Press, 1947.

Kunitz, Stanley. "Auden on Poetry." *The Atlantic* 218 (August 1966): 94–102.

Lampel, Peter Martin. *Revolte im Erziehungsheim.* Berlin: Kiepenheuer, 1929.

Lane, Homer. *Talks to Parents and Teachers, Insight into the Problems of Childhood.* New York: Hermitage, 1949.

Larkin, Philip. *Required Writing: Miscellaneous Pieces 1955–1982* London: Faber, 1983.

Lawrence, D. H. *Apocalypse.* London: Heinemann, 1972. (1930)

———. *Fantasia of the Unconscious & Psychoanalysis and the Unconscious.* London: Heinemann, 1971. (1923)

———. *Studies in Classic American Literature.* New York: Viking Press, 1969.

Layard, John. "Atchin Twenty Years Ago." *Geographical Journal* 88 (October 1936): 342–51.

———. "Degree-Taking Rites in South West Bay, Malekula." *Journal of the Royal Anthropological Institute* 58 (1928): 139–223.

———. "Malekula: Flying Tricksters, Ghosts, Gods, and Epileptics," *Journal of the Royal Anthropological Institute* 50 (1930): 501–24.

———. *The Lady of the Hare* . London: Faber & Faber, 1944.

———. "The Malekulan Journey of the Dead." In *Spiritual Disciplines, Papers from the Eranos Yearbooks.* Edited by Joseph Campbell. New York: Pantheon Books, 1960.

———. "Maze-Dances and the Ritual of the Labyrinth in Malekula." *Folk-Lore* 47 (June 1936): 125–70.

———. "Shamanism: An Analysis Based on Comparison with the Flying Tricksters of Malekula." *Journal of the Royal Anthropological Institute* 50, (1930): 525–50.

———. "Some Impressions." In *Britain and Germany.* Edited by Rolf Gardiner and Heinz Rocholl. London: Williams & Norgate, 1929.

———. *The Stone Men of Malekula.* London: Chatto & Windus, 1942.

[Layard, John] *Spiritual Discipline, Papers from the Eranos Yearbooks.* Edited by Joseph Campbell. New York: Pantheon Books, 1960.

Leavis, F. R. "Mr. Auden's Talent." *Scrutiny* 5 (December 1936): 323–27.

———. *New Bearings in English Poetry.* London: Chatto & Windus, 1961.

Lehmann, John. *In My Own Time.* Boston: Little, 1969.

———. *The Noise of History.* London: Hogarth, 1934.

LePage, P. V. "Rhyme in Auden's 'Musée des Beaux Arts.'" *The Yearbook of English Studies* 3 (1973): 253–58.

Lewis, Wyndham. *Blasting and Bombardiering.* London: Eyre & Spottiswoode, 1937.

———. *Hitler.* London: Chatto & Windus, 1931.

Lipking, Lawrence. *The Life of the Poet: Beginning and Ending Poetic Careers.* Chicago: University of Chicago Press, 1981.

Lowell, Robert. "Five." *Shenandoah* 18 (winter 1967): 45–47.

Lucas, John. "An Interview with Edgell Rickword." In *The 1930's: A Challenge to Orthodoxy.* Edited by John Lucas. Hassocks: Harvester, 1978.

Ludendorff, General Erich von. *The Coming War.* London: Faber & Faber, 1931.

Luke, David. "Gerhart Meyer and the Vision of Eros: A Note on Auden's 1929 Journal." In *W. H. Auden: 'The Language of Learning and the Language of Love.'* Auden Studies 2. Edited by Katherine Bucknell and Nicholas Jenkins. Oxford: Clarendon Press, 1994.

Lytton, Earl of. *Anthony.* London: Peter Davies, 1935.

———. *New Treasure, A Study of the Psychology of Love.* London: Allen & Unwin, 1934.

MacNeice, Louis. *Modern Poetry.* Oxford: Clarendon, 1968.

———. *The Poetry of W. B. Yeats.* London: Oxford, 1941.

———. *The Strings Are False.* London: Faber & Faber, 1965.

———. *Varieties of Parable.* Cambridge: Cambridge University Press, 1965.

Magnusson, Sigurthur A. *Northern Sphinx: Iceland and the Icelanders from the Settlement to the Present.* London: C. Hurst & Co., 1977.

Mann, Golo. "W. H. Auden: A Memoir."*Encounter* 42 (January 1974): 7–11.

Mann, Klaus. *Der Wendepunkt. Ein Lebensbericht.* Frankfurt: Fischer, 1963.

——— and Erika Mann. *Escape to Life.* Boston: Houghton Mifflin, 1939.

Marx, Karl and Friedrich Engels. *The German Ideology*, Parts I & III. Edited by R. Pascal. New York: International Publishers, 1947.

Mason, Eudo C. *Rilke's Apotheosis.* Oxford: Blackwell, 1938.

Masters, Anthony. *Literary Agents: The Novelist as Spy.* Oxford: Blackwell, 1987.

Maxwell, D. E. S. *Poets of the Thirties.* London: Routledge & Kegan Paul, 1969.

McDowell, Frederick, " 'The Situation in Our Time:' Auden in His American Phase." In *Aspects of American Poetry.* Edited by R. M. Ludwig. Columbus: Ohio State University Press, 1962.

Melchiori, Giorgio. *The Tightrope Walkers.* London: Routledge & Kegan Paul, 1956.

Mendelson, Edward. "An Auden Letter About *The Orators*: A Correction." *Colby Library Quarterly* 14, 2 (June 1978): 103.

———. "Auden in New York: 1939–1941." *Adam* 39 (1973–74): 27–33.

———. "The Coherence of Auden's *The Orators.*" *ELH* 35 (March 1968): 114–33.

———. *Early Auden.* New York: Viking Press, 1981.

———. "Editing Auden." *New Statesman* 92 (17 Dec. 1976): 376–78.

———. *Later Auden.* Farrar, Straus & Giroux, 1999.

———. Preface to W. H. Auden, *Selected Poems*. Edited by Edward Mendelson. New York: Vintage, 1979.

———. "The Two Audens and the Claims of History." In *Representing Modernist Texts: Editing as Interpretation*. Edited by George Bernstein. Ann Arbor: University of Michigan Press, c. 1991.

Merrill, James. *A Different Person: A Memoir*. New York: Knopf, 1993.

———. *The Changing Light at Sandover*. New York: Knopf, 1992.

Millard, G. C. "Poetry Nonetheless: Early Auden." *Contemporary Review* 225 (Nov. 1974): 268–72.

Miller, Charles H. *Auden: An American Friendship*. New York: Scribner's, 1983.

Mirsky, Dmitri. *The Intelligentsia of Great Britain*. Translated by Alec Brown. New York: Covici-Friede, 1935.

Mitchell, Breon. "W. H. Auden and Christopher Isherwood: The 'German Influence.'" *Oxford German Studies* I. Edited by T. J. Reed. Oxford: Clarendon Press, 1966.

Mitgang, Herbert. *Dangerous Dossiers*. New York: Donald Fine, 1988.

Moore, Marianne. *Predilections*. New York: Viking, 1955.

Morse, B. J. "Rainer Maria Rilke and English Literature." *German Life & Letters* I (April 1948): 215–28.

———. "Contemporary English Poets and Rilke." *German Life & Letters* 1 (July 1948): 272–85.

Mortimer, John. *Clinging to the Wreckage: A Part of Life*. New Haven: Ticknor & Fields, 1982.

Muir, Edwin. "Books of the Quarter." *The Criterion*. 17 (Oct. 1937): 148–54.

———. *The Present Age from 1914*. New York: McBride, 1940.

———. Review of "Spain." *The Criterion* 17 (October 1937): 148.

Mulgan, John. *Poems of Freedom*. London: Gollancz, 1938.

Murdoch, Iris. *The Sovereignty of Good*. New York: Schocken, 1971.

Muste, John M. *Say That We Saw Spain Die: Literary Consequences of the Spanish Civil War*. Seattle: University of Washington Press, 1966.

Musulin, Stella. "Auden in Kirchstetten." In *'In Solitude, for Company': W. H. Auden after 1940*. Auden Studies 3. Edited by Katherine Bucknell and Nicholas Jenkins. Oxford: Clarendon Press, 1996.

———. "Die zwei Welten des W. H. Auden." *Morgen* 1 (1977): 12.

Myers, Bernard S, ed. *McGraw-Hill Dictionary of Art*. New York: McGraw-Hill, 1969.

Nemerov, Howard. "A Word from the Devil's Advocate." *Parnassus* 4 (fall/winter, 1975): 131–36.

Neruda, Pablo. *Peace for Twilights to Come!* Bombay: People's Publishing House, 1950.

New Verse 26–27 (November 1937). "Auden Double Number."

Newman, Michael. "W. H. Auden." *The Paris Review* 57 (spring 1974): 32–69.

Nicolson, Harold. *Public Faces*. New York: Popular Library, 1960. (1932)

Nietzsche, Friedrich. *The Portable Nietzsche*. New York: Viking, 1954.

Origo, Iris. *A Need to Testify*. San Diego: Harcourt Brace Jovanovich, 1984.

Orwell, George. *A Collection of Essays*. Garden City: Doubleday, 1954.

Osborne, E. A. *In Letters of Red*. London: Michael Joseph, 1938.

O'Sullivan, Michael, ed. *W. H. Auden, 1907–1973. Catalogue of an Exhibition*. Vienna: Niederösterreichische Gesellschaft für Kunst und Kultur, 1984.

———. *W. H. Auden, 1907–1973. Ergebnisse eines Symposions*. Vienna: Niederösterreichische Gesellschaft für Kunst und Kultur, 1988.

Ovid. *Metamorphoses*. Translated by Rolfe Humphries. Bloomington: Indiana University Press, 1967.

Paton, John. *Left Turn!* London: Secker & Warburg, 1936.

Paul, Johannes W., trans. *Poems/Kirchstettner Gedichte: 1958–1973*. St. Pölten/Wien: Niederösterreichisches Pressehaus, 1983.

Perkins, David. *A History of Modern Poetry: Modernism and After*. Cambridge: Harvard University Press, 1987.

Perrott, Roy. "Auden." *The Observer* (28 June 1970): 25.

Perse, St.-Jean. *Anabasis, A Poem*. Translated by T. S. Eliot. New York: Harcourt, 1938.

Pike, James A., ed. *Modern Canterbury Pilgrims*. London: Mowbray, 1956.

Plato. *The Dialogues*. New York: Bantam Books, 1986.

Poger, Sidney. "Berlin and the Two Versions of W. H. Auden's 'Paid on Both Sides.' " *Ariel* 17 (April 1986): 17–30.

Porter, Peter. "The Achievement of Auden." *Sydney Studies in English* 4 (1978–79): 73–113.

Press, John. *The Chequer'd Shade: Reflections on Obscurity in Poetry*. London: Oxford University Press, 1958.

Quennell, Peter. *Baudelaire and the Symbolists*. London: Chatto & Windus, 1926.

Radin, Paul. *The Trickster: A Study of American Indian Mythology*. Commentary by Karl Kerényi and C. G. Jung. New York: Greenwood Press, 1969.

Rees, Goronwy. "Mr. Eliot and Some Others." *New Oxford Outlook* (1934): 243–47.

Replogle, Justin. *Auden's Poetry*. Seattle: University of Washington Press, 1969.

———. "The Auden Group." *Wisconsin Studies in Contemporary Literature* 15 (summer 1964): 133–50.

———. "Auden's Marxism." *PMLA* 80 (December 1965): 584–95.

Rhodes, Anthony. *The Poet as Superman*. London: Weidenfeld & Nicolson, 1959.

Richards, I. A. *Principles of Literary Criticism*. New York: Harcourt Brace, 1938.

Richman, Robert. "The Trials of a Poet." *The New Criterion* 6 (April 1988): 74–81.

Richter, Franz. "W. H. Auden—der Christ." In *W. H. Auden, 1907–1973. Ergebnisse eines Symposions*. Vienna: Niederösterreichische Gesellschaft für Kunst und Kultur, 1988.

———. *Kein Pardon für Genies: 12 Charakterbilder*. St. Pölten-Wien: Verlag Niederösterreichisches Pressehaus, 1982.

Rickword, Edgell. "Auden and Politics." *New Verse*, 26—27 (Nov. 1937): 21–22.

———. *Collected Poems*. London: Bodley Head, 1967.

Riddel, Joseph N. *C. Day Lewis*. New York: Twayne, 1971.

Rilke, Rainer Maria. *Duino Elegies*. Translated by J. B. Leishman and Stephen Spender. New York: Norton, 1939.

Rivers, W. H. R. *Conflict and Dream*. New York: Harcourt, 1923.

———. "Descent and Ceremonia in Amrim." *Journal of the Royal Anthropological Institute* 45 (1915): 229–33.

———. "The Percy Selden Trust Expedition to Melanesia." *The History of Melanesia Society.* 2 vols. Cambridge: Cambridge University Press, 1914.

———. *Medicine, Magic and Religion.* New York: Harcourt, 1914.

———. *Psychology and Ethnology.* London: Kegan Paul, 1926.

———. *Psychology and Politics.* New York: Harcourt, 1923.

———. *Social Organization.* New York: Knopf, 1924.

Roberts, Keith. *Bruegel.* Oxford: Phaidon, 1971.

Roberts, Michael. *Collected Poems.* Edited by Janet Roberts. London: Faber & Faber, 1958.

———. *Critique of Poetry.* London: Jonathan Cape, 1934.

———. Preface to *New Country.* London: Hogarth, 1933.

———. Preface to *New Signatures.* London: Hogarth, 1935. (1932)

———. ed. *The Faber Book of Modern Verse.* London: Faber & Faber, 1936.

Rodway, Allan. *A Preface to Auden.* London: Longman, 1984.

Rosa, Joyce and Jeanne Welcher. "Visions of Icarus: Ovid's, Bruegel's and Auden's." *Bucknell Review* 30 (1986): 131–43.

Rowan, Richard W. *Spy and Counter-Spy: The Development of Modern Espionage.* London: Hamilton, 1929.

Rowse, A. L. *Politics and the Younger Generation.* London: Faber & Faber, 1931.

Rutter, Frank. *Old Masters.* New York: George H. Doran Company, [1926].

Salus, Peter H. "Englishing the *Edda.*" In *Comparative Criticism: A Yearbook.* Cambridge: Cambridge University Press, 1979.

Samuels, Stuart. "English Intellectuals and Politics in the 1930's." In *On Intellectuals: Theoretical Studies.* Edited by Philip Rieff. Garden City, N.Y.: Doubleday, 1969.

Sansom, Ian. " 'Flouting Papa:' Randall Jarrell and W. H. Auden." In *In Solitude, for Company: W. H. Auden after 1940.* Auden Studies 3. Edited by Katherine Bucknell and Nicholas Jenkins. Oxford: Clarendon Press, 1996.

Sarang, Vilas. "Articles in the Poetry of W. H. Auden." *Language and Style* 7 (spring 1972): 77–90.

Savage, D. S. *The Personal Principle, Studies in Modern Poetry.* Port Washington: Kennikat, 1969. (1944)

Scarfe, Francis. *Auden and After: The Liberation of Poetry, 1930–41.* London: Routledge, 1942.

———. *W. H. Auden.* Monaco: Lyrebird,1949.

Schwartz, Delmore. "The Two Audens." *Kenyon Review*, 1 (winter 1939): 34–45.

Seaman, L. C. B. *Life in Britain between the Wars.* London: B. T. Batsford, 1970.

Seidel, Max and R. H. Marijnissen. *Bruegel.* New York: G. P. Putnam's Sons, 1971.

Seitz, Maria. "Wystan Hugh Auden in Kirchstetten." In *Geschichte von Böheimkirchen. Ein Heimatbuch zur Jahrtausendfeier, 985–1985.* Edited by Wolfgang Häusler. Böheimkirchen: Marktgemeinde Böheimkirchen / NÖ Pressehaus, [1985].

Sellers, W. H. "New Light on Auden's *The Orators.*"*PMLA* 82 (October 1967): 455–64.

Shapiro, Karl. *Essay in Rime.* New York: Random House, 1945.

Sinclair, Andrew. *The Red and the Blue: Cambridge Treason and Intelligence*. Boston: Little, Brown & Co., 1986.

Sinfield, Alan, ed. *English Poetry*. London: Sussex Publications, 1976.

Sitwell, Edith. *Aspects of Modern Poetry*. London: Duckworth, 1934.

Skelton, Robin, ed. *Poetry of the Thirties*. Harmondsworth: Penguin, 1964.

Skidelsky, Robert. *Interests and Obsessions*. London: Macmillan, 1993.

———. *Oswald Mosley*. New York: Holt, 1975.

S[kinner], A. N. "Spain." In W. H. Auden, *Prose*. Edited by Edward Mendelson. Princeton: Princeton University Press, 1996.

Slawik, Franz, ed. *W. H. Auden in Österreich*. Wiener Neustadt: Niederösterreiches Kulturforum, 1978.

Smith, Elton Edward, *The Angry Young Men of the Thirties*. Carbondale: Southern Illinois Press, 1975.

Smith, Stan. "Loyalty and Interest: Auden, Modernism, and the Politics of Pedagogy." *Textual Practice* 4 (spring 1990): 54–72.

Southworth, James G. "Wystan Hugh Auden," *Sewanee Review* 46 (April–June 1938): 188–205.

———. *Sowing the Spring: Studies in British Poets from Hopkins to MacNeice*. Oxford: Blackwell, 1940.

Sparrow, John. *Sense and Poetry*. New Haven: Yale University Press, 1934.

Spears, Monroe K. *The Poetry of W. H. Auden*. New York: Oxford University Press, 1963.

Spender, J. A. *The Public Life*, vol. I. London: Cassell, 1925.

Spender, Stephen. "W. H. Auden and His Poetry." *Atlantic* 192 (July 1953): 74–79.

———. "Auden, Wystan Hugh." *Dictionary of National Biography, 1971–1980*. Oxford: Oxford University Press, 1986.

———. *Collected Poems, 1928–1985*. New York: Random, 1986.

——— and Donald Hall, eds. *The Concise Encyclopedia of English and American Poets and Potery*. New York: Hawthorn, 1963.

———. *The Creative Element*. London: Hamish Hamilton, 1953.

———. *The Destructive Element*. Philadelphia: Albert Saiper, 1953.

———. "Der Einfluss Rilkes auf die englische Dichtung." Translated by Erich Fried. *Neue Auslese* 10 (October 1946): 21–25.

———. *European Witness*. New York: Reynal & Hitchcock, 1946.

———. "Heroes in Spain." *New Statesman* 13 (1 May 1937): 714–15.

———. "The Influence of Yeats on Later English Poets." *Tri-Quarterly* 4 (fall 1965): 82–89.

———. "Instead of Death," *Oxford Poetry*, 11 (April 2000), 20–28.

———. *Letters to Christopher*. Edited by Lee Bartlett. Santa Barbara: Black Sparrow Press, 1980.

———."Oxford to Communism." *New Verse* 26–27 (Nov. 1937): 9–10.

——— and John Lehmann, eds. *Poems for Spain*. London: Hogarth, 1939.

———. Preface to *W. H. Auden: Catalogue of an Exhibition*. Edited by Michael O'Sullivan. Vienna: Niederösterreichische Gesellschaft für Kunst und Kultur, 1984.

———. "Rainer Maria Rilke: An Appreciation," *London Mercury* 38 (August 1938): 328–32.

———. *The Temple*. London: Faber & Faber, 1988.

———. *The Thirties and After*. New York: Random House, 1978.

———. *Vienna*. London: Faber & Faber, 1934.

———. "W. H. Auden as I First Knew Him." In *W. H. Auden, 1907–1973. Ergebnisse eines Symposions*. Vienna: Niederösterreichische Gesellschaft für Kunst und Kultur, 1988.

———. *World Within World*. London: Hamish Hamilton, 1964.

———. *World Within World*. New York: St. Martin's Press, 1994.

———. *The Year of the Young Rebels*. London: Weidenfeld & Nicolson, 1969.

Stead, C. K. "Auden's 'Spain.'" *London Magazine* 7 (March 1968): 41–54.

Stephan, Alexander. *Im Visier des FBI: Deutsche Exilschriftsteller in den Akten amerikanischer Geheindienste*. Stuttgart: Metzlar, 1995.

Stonier, G. W. "Review of *The Orators*." *New Statesman* 51 (9 June 1956): 657.

Strachey, John. *The Strangled Cry*. London: Bodley Head, 1962.

———. *The Theory and Practice of Socialism*. New York: Random, 1936.

Strong, Beret. *The Poetic Avant-Garde: The Groups of Borges, Auden, and Breton*. Evanston: Northwestern University Press, 1997.

Summers, Claude J. "American Auden." In *The Columbia History of American Poetry*. Edited by Jay Parini and Brett C. Miller. New York: Columbia University Press, 1993.

Symons, Julian. *The Thirties*. London: Cresset, 1960.

——— et al. "'A Communist to Others:' A Symposium." In *W. H. Auden: The Map of All My Youth*. Auden Studies 1. Edited by Katherine Bucknell and Nicholas Jenkins. Oxford: Clarendon Press, 1990.

"The Thirties: A Special Number." *The Review*. 11–12 (1964).

Thomas, Dylan. *The Poems*. Edited by Daniel Jones. London: Dent, 1971.

Thomas, Hugh. *The Spanish Civil War*. London: Eyre & Spottiswoode, 1961.

Tiddy, R. J. E. *The Mummer's Play*. Oxford: Clarendon, 1923.

Toller, Ernst. *No More Peace!* Translated by Edward Crankshaw. Lyrics Adapted by W. H. Auden. Music by Herbert Murrill. London: Lane, 1937.

Toynbee, Philip. "Five Young Writers Who Changed My World," *Observer* (20 June 1976): 17–19.

———. *Friends Apart*. London: MacGibbon & Kee, 1954.

———. "The World of W. H. Auden." *Observer* (May 2, 1971).

Trotter, David. *The Making of the Reader: Language and Subjectivity in Modern American, English and Irish Poetry*. New York: St. Martin's Press, 1984.

Turville-Petre, F[rancis]. "Excavations in the Mugharet El-Kebarah." *Journal of the Royal Anthropological Institute* 32 (July–Dec. 1932): 271–76.

———. *Researches in Prehistoric Galilee, 1925–26*. London: Council of the British School of Archaeology in Jerusalem, 1927.

Upward, Edward. *In the Thirties*. London: Heinemann, 1962.

———. *The Railway Accident and Other Stories*. London: Heinemann, 1969.

———. "Remembering the Earlier Auden." *Adam* 39 (1973–74): 17–21.

Verdonk, Peter. " 'We have Art in Order That We May Not Perish from Truth:' The Universe of Discourse in Auden's 'Musée des Beaux Arts.' "*Dutch Quarterly* 17 (1987): 77–96.

Wagner, Geoffrey. *Wyndham Lewis.* London: Routledge & Kegan Paul, 1957.

Waidson, H. M. "Auden and German Literature." *Modern Language Review* 70 (April 1975): 347–65.

Wall, Bernard. "W. H. Auden and Spanish Civilization," *Colosseum* III (Sept. 1937): 142–49.

Watson, George. *Politics and Literature in Modern Britain.* Totowa: Rowman & Littlefield, 1977.

Waugh, Evelyn. *The Letters.* Edited by Mark Amory. Harmondsworth: Penguin, 1982. (1980)

Weinberger, Eliot. "James Jesus Angleton 1917–1987." In *Outside Stories, 1987–91.* New York: New Directions, 1992.

Weisstein, Ulrich, ed. *Expressionism as an International Literary Phenomenon.* Paris: Didier, 1973.

Whistler, Laurence. "A Note on the New Auden." *The Poetry Review* 28 (January–February 1937): 7–13.

Whitehead, John. "The Auden Gravy Train." New Review 3 (Nov. 1976): 60–62.

Whittemore, Reed. "Auden on Americans." *Sewanee Review* 65 (1957): 146–51.

Wickes, George. "An Interview with Chrtistopher Isherwood." *Shenandoah* 16 (spring 1965): 23–52.

Willett, John. "Auden and Brecht." In *Transformations in Modern Drama.* Edited by Ian Donaldson. Atlantic Highlands: Humanities Press, 1983.

Williams, Norman. "Private References in *The Dog Beneath the Skin.*" *W. H. Auden Society Newsletter* 10–11 (September 1993): 1–3.

Williams, William Carlos. *Pictures from Brueghel II.* New York: New Direction, 1962.

Wills, William D. *Homer Lane.* London: Allen & Unwin, 1964.

———. "The Influence of Homer Lane." *Hibbert Journal* 64 (Oct. 1965–July 1966): 25–28.

Willson, Robert F., Jr. "The Person in the Poem: Irony in Auden's 'Musée des Beaux Arts.' " *Studies in Contemporary Satire* 3 (1976): 1–8.

Wilson, Edmund. "W. H. Auden in America." *New Statesman* 51 (June 9, 1956): 658–59.

———. *The Shores of Light, A Literary Chronicle.* London: W. H. Allen, 1952.

———. *The Triple Thinkers.* London: John Lehmann, 1952.

Wollaston, A. F. R. "An Expedition to Dutch New Guinea." *The Geographical Journal* 43 (March 1914): 248–73.

Wood, Neal. *Communism and British Intellectuals.* New York: Columbia University Press, 1959.

Woods, Gregory. *Articulate Flesh: Male Homo-Eroticism and Modern Poetry.* New Haven: Yale, 1987.

Woolf, Virginia. "The Leaning Tower." In *The Moment and Other Essays.* London: Hogarth, 1947.

Worsley, T. C. *Fellow Travellers: A Memoir of the Thirties.* London: London Magazine Editions, 1971.

Wright, David. *Roy Campbell.* London; Longmans, 1961.

Wright, G. T. *W. H. Auden.* Revised Edition. Boston: Twayne Publishers, 1981.

Wright, Peter. *Spy Catcher.* New York: Viking, 1987.

Yanovsky, V. S. "W. H. Auden." *Antaeus* 19 (autumn 1975): 107–35.

Yeats, William Butler, Introduction to the *Oxford Book of Modern Verse, 1892–1935.* New York: Oxford University Press, 1936.

———. *Letters on Poetry from W. B. Yeats to Dorothy Wellesley.* London: Oxford University Press, 1964.

———. *The Poems.* Edited by Daniel Albright. London: Everyman, 1994.

Index

About the House, 217
Acton, Harold, 77
Age of Anxiety, The, 13, 176, 178–79, 191, 195, 202
Aldington, Richard, 153
Alleanza Nazionale, 97
Ambler, Eric, 66
André, Michael, 208
Angleton, J. J., 68
Ansen, Alan, 46, 148, 178
"As I Walked Out One Evening," 132
"As It Seemed to Us," 85, 210–11
Ascent of F6, The, 99, 103, 141
Ashbery, John, 193
Atlas, James, 171
Auden group, 12; defined, 70–75; ideological premises of, 82–83; literary "gang" fantasies of, 90; sexual aspect to, 89; Waugh generation and, 75–79
Auden, John (brother): Auden's correspondence with, 169
Auden, W[ystan] H[ugh] (1907–73): "The American Auden," 173–74; American and British poetry, his comparison of, 179–80; American culture, his judgments on, 176; American landscape, his appraisal of, 183; American poetry, his influence on, 13, 193–98; Austrian State Prize (1958), 214, 222; BBC broadcast (1973), 208; becomes American citizen (1946), 168; Berlin boy friends, 48, 50; Berlin journal (1928–29), 47; Bildungsroman, life as a, 20–21; Cecil Beaton's photograph of, 11; Communist sympathies, extent of, 32, 85, 129, 130; death in Kirchstetten (1973), 222; emigration to the United States (1939), 21, 35–36; engagement with Sheilah Richardson broken, 46, 54; family background of, 20; Feltrinelli Prize (1957), 20; Freud lecture (1971), 57; German translations of his poems, 225–29; 33; homosexuality, 12, 46–47, 49, 69, 80, 116, 195, 215; identifying the "enemy," 41, 52, 54–55, 58, 103; in Brussels (1938), 159; in China (1938), 143; in Gutensberg, Germany (1929), 50; in Rügen, Germany (1931), 47; in Spain (1937), 135, 137; influence of American poetry on, 197; influence of Berlin on, 48; influence of Goethe on, 212; influence of Kafka on, 205; influence of Old English works on, 153; influence of Rilke on, 205–9; influence of Robert Frost on, 197–200; influence of thriller fiction on early works of, 39–40; job with U.S. Strategic Bombing Survey (1945), 68; King's Gold Medal for Poetry (1937), 35; Kirchstetten, decision to move to, 203, 213; Kirchstetten poems, historic dimension in, 217; Kirchstetten poems, use of German in, 216; leaves the United States (1972), 184; love for Chester Kallman, 169, 189, 215; marriage to Erika Mann, 67; memorial in Westminster Abbey, 22; nationality and literature, 185; obscurantism in early poetry of, 23–29; parable art defined, 134; poetical rhetoric, his suspicion of, 88, 135, 136, 243 n. 6; poetry defined, 22, 25, 30; political function of poetry defined, 134, 137, 242 n. 1; posthumous fame in Austria, 222–25; Professor of Poetry at Oxford (1956), 20; public and private worlds, his judgments of, 90, 133, 135; public poet, his transition to, 31; Pulitzer Prize for Poetry (1948), 172; religion and beliefs, 10, 20–21, 32, 45, 55, 71, 76, 143, 152, 158, 178–79, 190, 207, 214; talk at Shrewsbury School (1938),

135; teaching positions, 19. WORKS: See under specific titles.
"August for the People," 39, 134
Authors Take Sides on the Spanish War, 140

Bahlke, George W., 99, 195
Barzun, Jacques, 65, 197
Baudelaire, Charles, 23, 134, 149; *Intimate Journals*, 98–99; "Les Plaintes d'un Icare," 164
Bayley, John, 149
Bazeley, E. T., 108
Beach, Joseph Warren, 11, 30, 53, 54
Beaton, Cecil, 76; photograph of Auden, 11
Bell, Julian, 81, 85, 87, 104, 125; censure of Auden and friends, 122
Bell, Kathleen, 132
Berlin, Isaiah, 73, 89
Berryman, John, 187, 193
Betjeman, Sir John, 79
Bienek, Horst, 225
Bishop, Elizabeth, 193, 194
Blake, William, 89, 152
Bleuler, Eugen, 49
Bloomsbury Group, 125
Bluestone, Max, 160; 245 n. 17
Blunt, Anthony, 66
Bode, Christoph, 162; 245 n. 18
Bogan, Louise, 172, 193
Borkenau, Franz, 135
Bowen, Elizabeth: *Death of the Heart*, 65
Bowra, C. M., 73, 149
Boyle, Andrew, 66–67
Bradshaw, Jon, 225
Brecht, Bertolt, 34, 66, 204, 209; "Flug der Lindberghs," 98
Brueghel, Pieter the Elder: "Adoration of the Kings" (Brussels), 159; "Adoration of the Magi" (Winterthur), 160; "Landscape with the Fall of Icarus" (Brussels), 154 *reproduction*; "Massacre of the Innocents" (Brussels), 159; "Massacre of the Innocents" (Vienna), 160; "Numbering at Bethlehem" (Brussels), 159; "Procession to Calvary" (Vienna), 158, 160, 162
Brueghel, Pieter the Younger, 161
Bucknell, Katherine, 45–46, 47
"Bucolics," 183

Bullough, Geoffrey, 27–28
Bunting, Basil, 47
Burgess, Guy, 67, 79
Burnham, James, 81–82
Burrow, Trigant, 46, 49, 115
Burton, P. H., 28

Cambridge Spies, 66, 89
Campbell, Roy, 84
Campbell-Bannerman, Sir Henry, 88
Carpenter, Humphrey, 45, 46, 67, 68, 75–77, 79, 130, 175, 185, 202, 213
Carritt, Gabriel, 73, 204
Carter, Ronald, 122, 130
Caserio, Robert, 174
Caudwell, Christopher, 82
"Cave of Making," 182, 212
Certain World, A, 223
Charney, Maurice, 164
Charques, R. D., 33
Chase, The, 45
Churchill, R. C., 129
Churchill, Randolph, 79
Claudel, Paul, 146
Cockburn, Claud, 65, 141
Coghill, Neville, 33, 73; Auden's correspondence with, 29
Communist Manifesto, The (Marx and Engels), 129
"Communist to Others, A," 12, 32, 120, 139, 204; comedy and Communism linked, 121; liberal intellectual in, 124–27; religion in, 124; speaker's relation to proletariat, 122–24; speaker's relation to the poet, 127
Connolly, Cyril, 24, 132, 137
Conrad, Peter, 175 n. 7, 247 n. 9, 247
"Control of the Passes," 206
Cowley, Malcolm, 81
Cox, C. B., 140
Craft, Robert, 203
Criterion, The, 47
Criterion Book of Modern American Verse, The (edited by Auden), 13, 172, 179–80, 190, 196, 198
Crossman, Richard, 73, 86, 204, 208
Cunningham, Valentine, 128, 130
Curtius, Ernst, 51

Daiches, David, 24
"Dame Kind," 195
Damming Stream, 197
Dance of Death, The, 48, 51, 59–62, 103, 112, 121, 126, 204
D'Annunzio, Gabriele, 96–98
Dante Alighieri, 92
Davenport-Hines, Richard, 46–47, 169, 202
David, Hugh, 47
Day-Lewis, Cecil, 19, 55–56, 64, 71, 73, 74, 81, 85, 122, 129; *The Buried Day*, 71; *A Hope for Poetry*, 72, 104, 131; "Magnetic Mountain," 34; "On the Twentieth Anniversary of Soviet Power," 35; *Oxford Poetry 1927*, preface to (with Auden), 25; *A Time to Dance*, 133
De Bosis, Lauro, 97, 163
de Tolnay, Charles, 163; *Pierre Bruegel l'Ancien*, 165
Deighton, Len, 66
Demetz, Peter, 206
"Dirge," 180
Dodds, E. R.: Auden's correspondence with, 137, 177, 184
Dodds, Mrs. E. R.: Auden's correspondence with, 151
Dog Beneath the Skin, The, 10, 39, 41, 48, 55, 103, 127, 140; two endings to, 62–64
Donne, John, 152
Doone, Rupert, 59
Double Man, The, 32
Driberg, Tom, 66
Duchêne, François, 32, 47
Dunaway, David King, 170
Dyer's Hand, The, 19, 69, 148, 178, 182, 198, 209, 211, 212, 22, 244 n. 12
Dyson, A. E., 140
Dzenitis, Sigurds, 206

Eagleton, Terry, 244 n. 16
Eberhart, Richard, 181
Ehrenburg, Ilya, 86
Eliot, T. S., 25, 47, 78, 91, 149–50, 181, 188, 209; *After Strange Gods*, 182; Preface to *Anabasis* (St.-Jean Perse), 29; *The Rock*, 130; "The Use of Poetry and the Use of Criticism," 29; *The Waste Land*, 23, 113, 151

Ellmann, Richard, 68, 149–150
Empson, William, 82, 169
"Enemies of the Bishop, The," 39
Enright, D. J., 208

Fairlie, G. T. ("Sapper"), 40
Fiedler, Leslie, 172–73
Firchow, Peter, 247 n. 13
FitzGibbon, Constantine, 72
"Fleet Visit," 247 n. 10
Fleming, Ian, 66
For the Time Being, 179
Foxall, Edgar: "The Politics of W. H. Auden," 89
Fraser, G. S., 32, 96, 175
Freud, Sigmund, 21, 46, 49, 108, 115, 133, 157
Fried, Erich, 226; translation of "The Managers," 227
Friedrich, Hugo, 23
Fromentin, Eugene, 246 n. 3
Frost, Robert, 135, 188, 197, 209; "Come In," 198; "The Gift Outright," 198
Fuller, John, 21, 40, 43, 57, 92, 130, 146, 158, 163, 173, 180, 187, 190, 198, 217

Gaitskell, Hugh, 73
Gardiner, Margaret, 214; Auden's correspondence with, 174
Garrett, John, 134
German Ideology (Marx and Engels), 139
Gils Blas (Alain René Le Sage), 65
Ginsberg, Allen, 188
Gladstone, William, 88
Glück, Gustav, 162
Goering, Hermann, 98
Goethe, J. W. von, 152, 190, 209
"Going into Europe," 204
"Good Life, The," 133
"Good-Bye to the Mezzogiorno," 20, 183
Goodman, Richard, 73, 81
Graves, Robert, 138, 176
Green, Martin, 73, 78–79
Greene, Graham, 66, 75; *The Old School*, 100
Gregory, Horace, 172
Griffin, The (journal for Readers' Subscription book club), 197
Grigson, Geoffrey, 74, 82, 104

Groddeck, Georg, 90, 109–10, 112, 133, 151, 152
Groote, Kurt, 48, 121
Gross, Babette, 86
"Group Movement and the Middle Classes, The," 81, 103
Group Theatre, 59, 63
"Guilty Vicarage, The," 40

H[arriet] M[onroe], 131
Haffenden, John, 171
Hallberg, Robert von, 172, 179
Hamburger, Michael, 224
Hamilton, Gerald, 65, 66, 67, 97
Hampshire, Stuart, 92
"Happy New Year, A," 99, 101
Hardy, Thomas, 135, 197
Häusermann, H. W., 86
Heard, Gerald, 151
Hecht, Anthony, 193, 199
Henderson, Philip, 96
Heppenstall, Rayner, 70
"Herman Melville," 189–90
Hesse, Hermann, 151
Hill, Geoffrey, 224
Hitler, Adolf, 132, 152
Hitzenberger, Franz, 214, 249 n. 6
Hoagland, Tony, 196
Hoggart, Richard, 39, 187
Hollander, John, 193
Homage to Clio, 197
Hone, Joseph, 148
Hope, Francis, 85, 94
Hoskins, Katherine Bail, 210
Howard, Brian, 77
Howard, Richard, 193; "Again for Hephaistos," 194; "Audiences," 194; *Fellow Feelings*, 195; "For Hephaistos," 194
Huxley, Aldous, 148; Along the Road, 165–66; *Jesting Pilate*, 151 "Tragedy and the Whole Truth," 166; "Wordsworth in the Tropics," 182
Hynes, Samuel, 75–79, 141, 205

"I Believe" (Auden's essay in Fadiman's collection *I Believe*), 142, 177, 245 n. 22
"I Have a Handsome Profile," 124
Ibsen, Henrik: *The Wild Duck*, 143

"In Memory of W. B. Yeats," 13, 22, 145, 147, 191
"In Praise of Limestone," 182, 183, 208
In Time of War, 10, 138
Isherwood, Christopher, 31, 38, 52, 66, 71, 73, 74, 86, 134, 151; *All the Conspirators*, 64, 80, 94; *The Ascent of F6* (with Auden), 99, 103, 141; *The Berlin Stories*, 85; *Christopher and His Kind*, 86; *The Dog Beneath the Skin* (with Auden), 39, 41, 48, 55, 62–64, 103, 127, 140; *Down There on a Visit*, 118; "The Enemies of the Bishop" (with Auden), 39; *Exhumations*, 52, 66, 246; "German Literature in England," 205; *Journey to a War* (with Auden), 144, 168, 206, 208; *Kathleen and Frank*, 118; *Lions and Shadows*, 23, 49, 65, 74, 90, 106–7, 109, 113, 170, 204; *The Memorial*, 110; *Mr. Norris Changes Trains*, 37–38, 65; "Some Notes on Auden's Early Poetry," 51, 95, 105, 106, 109; "The Youth Movement in the New Germany," 101

Jacobsen, Cornelia, 225
James, Henry, 65, 188
"James Honeyman," 132
Jandl, Ernst, 226
Jarfe, Günter, 129
Jarrell, Randall, 89, 163, 193; "The Old and the New Masters," 160
Jenkins, Nicholas, 137, 140
Journey to a War, 144, 168, 206, 208
Joyce, James, 163

Kafka, Franz, 205
Kahn, Derek, 73
Kallman, Chester, 224
Keynes, John Maynard, 78
Kierkegaard, Søren, 157
Kinney, Arthur F., 159
Kipling, Rudyard, 146
Klöpsch, Volker, 206
Knebworth, Viscount (Anthony Lytton), 102
Koch, Stephen, 89
Koestler, Arthur, 59, 85, 240 n. 20
Kraus, Karl, 203
Kraus, Wolfgang, 224

Lane, Homer, 45, 55–56, 63, 64, 89, 90, 105, 108–13, 151
Larkin, Philip, 179, 187, 224
Laughlin, James, 171
Lawrence, D. H., 21, 31, 89, 98–99, 104, 107, 148, 208–9; *Fantasia of the Unconscious*, 151; *Studies in Classic American Literature*, 188
Lawrence, T. E., 91, 99, 153
"Lay Your Sleeping Head, My Love," 152
Layard, John, 12, 43, 45, 46, 49, 56, 105, 108–10, 113
Leavis, F. R., 71, 78, 121
LeCarré, John, 66
Lehmann, John, 81; *In My Own Time*, 84; "Looking Within," 64
Lenin, V. I., 130, 153
Lennep, J. Van, 162
LePage, P. V., 160, 167, 245 n. 17
"Letter to a Wound," 114
"Letter to Lord Byron," 34, 106, 134, 177
Letters from Iceland, 72, 74, 99, 104, 137, 147, 168
Lewis, C. S., *The Allegory of Love*, 240 n. 22
Lewis, Sinclair, 188
Lewis, Wyndham, 104
Lindbergh, Charles, 98
"Loneliness," 202
Look, Stranger!, 67, 120, 132
Lowell, Robert, 247 n. 8
Ludendorff, Erich, 98, 99
Luke, David, 101, 239 n. 7, 248 n. 17
Lytton, Earl of: *Anthony*, 102

Mackenzie, Compton, 66
Maclean, Donald, 67
MacNeice, Louis, 30, 66, 73–74, 84, 88, 122, 130, 145, 150; *Letters from Iceland* (with Auden), 72, 74, 99, 104, 137, 147, 168; "The Strings are False," 85; *Varieties of Parable*, 26
Madge, Charles, 81
Mann, Erika, 67
Mann, Golo, 67, 214, 225
Mann, Klaus, 67, 143
Mann, Klaus and Erika: Auden's correspondence with, 137
Mann, Thomas, 67

Marx, Karl, 58, 62, 80, 127, 133, 138, 143, 152, 157; as character in *The Dance of Death*, 59
Marxism, 21, 35
Masters, Anthony, 66
Maugham, W. Somerset, 66
Maxwell, D. E. S., 92, 100, 129
Mayer, Elisabeth: Auden's correspondence with, 226
"Maze, The," 164
McNeile, H. C. ("Sapper"), 40
Medley, Robert, 59
Melville, Herman, 185, 188
Mendelson, Edward, 26–27, 97, 99, 136, 168, 186, 191, 247 n. 12
Merrill, James: *The Changing Light at Sandover*, 192; *A Different Person*, 192
Meyer, Gerhart, 48
Milton, John, 92
Mirsky, Dmitri, 105
"Miss Gee," 132
Mitchison, Naomi, 25; Auden's correspondence with, 91, 92, 187
Mitgang, Herbert, 67
Montaigne, Michel Eyquem de, 32
Moore, G. E., 125
Moore, Marianne, 188, 195, 200
"More Loving One, The," 198
Morgenstern, Christian, 204
Morse, B. J., 206
Mortimer, John, 27
Mortimer, Raymond, 175
Mosley, Sir Oswald, 100–102, 153
Muggeridge, Malcolm, 66
Muir, Edwin, 23
Müller, Peter, 224; Firchow's interview with, 231
Mumford, Lewis, 138, 177
Münzenberg, Willi, 86
"Musée des Beaux Arts," 13, 154, 208; Auden's conception of "Old Masters" in, 159–66; figure of Icarus in, 159; resemblance to Yeats's "Lapis Lazuli," 157
Musulin, Stella, 213–14, 222; Firchow's interview with, 234

Namier, Sir Lewis, 164
Neill, A. S., 109

Neruda, Pablo, 122
New Country, 74, 81, 84, 120
New Signatures, 72, 74, 77, 78, 84
New Verse, 74
New Writing, 71
"New Year Letter," 139, 142, 168, 179, 201, 206
Newman, Sidney, 73
Nicolson, Harold, 100–101; *Public Faces*, 101–2
Nietzsche, Friedrich, 177
"1929," 48–53
"No, Plato, No," 193
Nones, 173

"O What Is That Sound," 57
"Ode to Terminus," 137
"Open Letter to Knut Hamsun," 97
Orators, The, 12, 21–22, 25, 26, 41, 52, 55, 56, 136, 141, 179; Airman's conversion, 118–19; Airman's epiphany, 56–57; Auden on structure and meaning of, 91; Auden's self-criticism of, 93; begun at Rügen (1931), 47; Fascist elements in, 95–103; genre of, 92; influence of Layard and Lane on, 105–16; influence of Norse sagas on, 95, 117, 241 n. 8; influence of thriller fiction on, 39–40; political dimension to, 87; role of homosexuality in, 54; uncle-to-nephew relationship in, 117
Origo, Iris, 97
"Orpheus," 207
Orwell, George, 33, 78, 141; *Burmese Days*, 65; *Down and Out in Paris and London*, 65; "Inside the Whale," 34–35, 71; *Nineteen Eighty-Four*, 102
Oxford Outlook, 73
Oxford Poetry, 73
Oxford Poetry 1927, Auden's preface to, 25

"Paid on Both Sides," 12, 47, 48, 50–52, 54, 59–60, 80, 90, 153; influence of Old Norse epics on, 39; revision of, 42; weight of past on present, 43–45
Patinir, Jachim de, 161
Paul, Johannes W., 216, 224–25, 227–28
Pearson, Norman Holmes, 67–68; Auden's correspondence with, 211
Perkins, David, 182, 187

"Permanent Way, A," 198
Perrott, Roy: Auden's interview with, 226
"Petition," 56, 105
Pike, James, 135
Plato, 88, 152
"Platonic Bow, The," 69
Plumb, Charles, 84
"Poem xxii," 89
"Poet in Wartime," 209
Poet's Tongue, The, 134
Porter, Peter, 210
Pound, Ezra, 23, 172
Powell, Anthony, 169
"Profile," 170, 184, 210
Prolific and the Devourer, The, 86, 90, 167
"Prologue at Sixty," 183
"Psychology and Art Today," 59, 62, 133
"Public v. the Late Mr. William Butler Yeats, The," 145, 151
Pudney, John, Auden's correspondence with, 80, 121

Ransom, John Crowe, 136
Rees, Goronwy, 131
Rembrandt van Rijn, 160
Replogle, Justin, 71, 86
Rhodes, Anthony, 96
Richards, I. A., 125, 136
Richman, Robert, 194
Richter, Franz, 214
Rickword, Edgell, 96
Riding, Laura, 135, 197
Rilke, Rainer Maria, 148, 205; *Dinggedichte*, 206; *Duino Elegies*, 207, 209; *Sonnets to Orpheus*, 206
Roberts, Keith, 161
Roberts, Michael, 81, 84, 94
Robson, W. W., 25, 92
Roethke, Theodore, 193
Rosa, Joyce, 163
Roschitz, Karlheinz, 224
Rousseau, Jean-Jacques, 109, 152
Rowan, Richard, 40
Rowse, A. L., 105
Russell, Bertrand, 125
Rutter, Frank, 245.n. 20

"Saint-Simon for Our Time, A," 48
Sansom, Ian, 193

Scarfe, Francis, 89, 99–100
Schwartz, Delmore, 171, 193
Schweitzer, Albert, 133
"Sea and the Mirror, The," 164, 179
Seaman, L. C. B., 102
"Secret Agent," 39
Sellers, W. H., 99
"September 1, 1939," 132, 176–77
Shapiro, Karl, 193
Shaw, George Bernard, 141
"Shield of Achilles, The," 173, 194
Sinclair, Andrew, 66
Sitwell, Edith, 24, 26
Skelton, Robin, 121
Skidelsky, Robert, 102
Slawik, Franz, 223
Smith, Stan, 25
Smith, Sydney, 185
Sonnets from China, 207
Southworth, J. G., 116
"Spain," 12, 32, 134, 138–39, 145
Spark, Muriel, 224
Sparrow, John, 92
Spears, Monroe K., 26, 53, 92–94, 99, 110, 117, 119, 142
Spencer, Theodore: Auden's correspondence with, 136, 164
Spender, J. A., 87–88
Spender, Nancy, 132, 175
Spender, Stephen, 19, 66, 71, 73, 74, 79, 83, 85, 87, 117, 122, 129, 204, 212; Auden's correspondence with, 28, 42, 140, 239 n. 10, 241 n. 10; "Auden and His Poetry," 31, 74; "Auden, Wystan Hugh," *Dictionary of National Biography, 1971–1980*, 53, 239 n. 8; *The Creative Element*, 144; *The Destructive Element*, 82, 86, 96, 104–6, 133; *Heroes in Spain*, 144; "Instead of Death," 119; "Oxford to Communism," 89, 131; *The Temple*, 136; *Vienna*, 64; "W. H. Auden As I First Knew Him," 86; *World Within World*, 73–75, 85, 130, 246 n. 2; *The Year of the Young Rebels*, 85
Spiel, Hilde, 226; translation of "Good-Bye to the Mezzogiorno," 227; translation of "Under Sirius," 227
"Squares and Oblongs," 238 n. 5
Staub, Herta: translation of "In Praise of Limestone," 226

Stephan, Alexander, 67
Stern, James: Auden's correspondence with, 225
Stevens, Wallace, 188
Strachey, John, 100, 153
Strong, Beret, 71, 80
Summers, Claude, 173
Symons, Julian, 78, 129; *The Thirties*, 71, 95

"T. E. Lawrence," 110
Taylor, A. J. P., 73
"Thanksgiving, A," 197, 209
"Thanksgiving for a Habitat," 13, 215–27
"Their Lonely Betters," 198, 199–234, 208
Thomas, Dylan, 23, 72; "Letter to My Aunt," 94
Thomas, Edward, 135, 197
"Three Companions, The," 56–57
Tolkien, J. R. R., 153
Toller, Ernst, 204
Toynbee, Philip, 27
"Translation and Tradition," 225
Trilling, Lionel, 197
Trotter, David, 98
Twentieth Century, 120
Twentieth Century Verse, 71

"Under Which Lyre," 68, 177
Understanding Poetry (Brooks and Warren), 136
"Unknown Citizen, The," 176
Upward, Edward, 73, 74

van der Goes, Hugo, "Nativity" (Portinari Altarpiece), 161
Verdonk, Peter, 163
Verlaine, Paul, 135
Veronese, Paolo, 161
"Vespers," 248 n. 20
"Victor," 132
Voltaire (François-Marie Arouet), 152
Voznesensky, Andrei, 224

Waidson, H. M., 208
"Walk After Dark, A," 175–76
"Walks," 198
Wallace, Edgar: *The Four Just Men*, 40
"Wandering Jew, The," 205
Warner, Rex, 73–74

Waugh, Evelyn, 75–77, 79
Weinberger, Eliot, 68
Weinheber, Josef: Auden's elegy for, 210
Welcher, Jeanne, 163
Whistler, Laurence, 24
Whitman, Walt and Auden: compared, 188
"Whitsunday in Kirchstetten," 215
Whittemore, Reed, 68, 247 n. 11
Willett, John, 209, 210
Williams, William Carlos, 197, 245 n. 21
Wills, W. D., 108–9
Wilson, Edmund, 149, 171
Wittgenstein, Ludwig, 125
Wollaston, A. F. R., 113
Wood, Neal, 85

Woolf, Leonard, 125
Woolf, Virginia: "Leaning Tower," 35–36
Wright, G. T., 11, 195, 247 n. 7
Wright, Peter, 66

Yanovsky, Vassily, 203, 211–12
Yates, James: Auden's correspondence with, 169
"Yeats, Master of Diction," 186
Yeats, William Butler, 147, 195, 209; Auden's judgments of, 148; contrasted with Auden, 149–50; "Lapis Lazuli," 157; *Last Poems*, Auden's review of, 186; *Oxford Book of Modern Verse, 1892–1935*, introduction to, 23, 148; "September 1913," 150; *A Vision*, 150